Exchange in Ancient Greece

Exchange in Ancient Greece

Sitta von Reden

Duckworth

Paperback edition 2003
First published in 1995 by
Gerald Duckworth & Co. Ltd.
61 Frith Street, London W1D 3JL
Tel: 020 7434 4242
Fax: 020 7434 4420
inquiries@duckworth-publishers.co.uk
www.ducknet.co.uk

© 1995, 2003 by Sitta von Reden

All rights reserved. No part of this publication
may be reproduced, stored in a retrieval system, or
transmitted, in any form or by any means, electronic,
mechanical, photocopying, recording or otherwise,
without the prior permission of the publisher.

A catalogue record for this book is available
from the British Library

ISBN 0 7156 3179 9

Typeset by Ray Davies
Printed and bound in Great Britain by
Biddles Ltd, *www.biddles.co.uk*

Contents

Preface to the paperback edition, 2002 — vii
List of illustrations — xi
Introduction — 1

Part I: Exchange and Value in Epic

1. The Scope of Gift Exchange — 13
2. Ownership and Transfer — 45
3. *Kleos* and Commerce in the *Odyssey* — 58

Part II: Exchange in the Athenian *Polis*

4. The Politics of Exchange — 79
5. Market Exchange and Private Profit — 105
6. Trade, Power and Tyranny in Classical Athens — 127
7. Violence and Corruption: Commerce in Tragedy — 147

Part III: The Politics of Money

8. Embedded Money Economy — 171
9. Money in Gymnasium and Palaestra — 195

Conclusion: Rethinking Economics — 217
Bibliography — 222
Additional bibliography, 2002 — 238
Index — 240

Preface to the Paperback Edition

The 1990s saw a profusion of scholarship on gift exchange, reciprocity and money, only the beginnings of which could be taken into consideration in the first edition of this book.[1] The complexities of the ideological pairing of gift exchange and commerce are now much better understood. A discussion of recent trends in the anthropological debate concerning gift exchange can be found in Wagner-Hasel (2000), who also unravels the history of scholarship leading up to Marcel Mauss' influential *Essay sur le don* [1922]. Mauss, she argues, did no more than draw together strands of diverse intellectual debates in law, economics, sociology and anthropology in which the tribal gift served as a counter-image to Western forms of property transfer, acquisitiveness and individualism. In particular, Mauss construed an idealised vision of gift exchange which romanticised collectivism and the totality of tribal social cohesion.[2] Against this background, it has become clear that the opposition between gift exchange and commerce, which has proved as compelling in ancient as in modern times, implies much more than the development of exchange practices.

Richard Seaford (1994) offered an elaborate argument about the close connection between reciprocity and ritual as well as their transformation in the archaic and classical Greek periods, which could be considered only briefly in the first edition of this book (p. 6). He argues that reciprocity was a norm of action before the emergence of the polis, being superseded by the formal, legal and institutionalised procedures of the city state which also transformed the nature of ritual. Reciprocal gift exchange and blood revenge in the pre-political world were replaced in the polis by commodity exchange and law courts regulated by formal rules of equivalence and justice. In contrast to my argument in Chapters 6 and 7, he suggests that images of gift exchange in the classical period demonstrated to civic communities the very difference between contemporary and past realities. In Athenian tragedy, gifts were usually a cue for misinterpretation, serving as symbols of instability and threat to the political rituals of the polis.[3]

An impression of the pervasiveness of the norm of reciprocity and its breadth of application in Greek thought and practice can be gained from the papers given at the Exeter conference in 1993, now published in Gill, Postlethwaite & Seaford (1998).[4] A central theme during this conference was the question of the norms associated with gift exchange on the one hand and commerce on the other, as well as the place of altruism. Is there evidence of the valorisation of altruism in Homeric gift exchange, or should we rather speak of solidarity? This question, which remained controversial during the conference (see Postlethwaite *vs* Gill in the volume), shows how difficult it is to abandon our own conceptual framework when approaching ancient gift exchange through commerce. Hans van Wees' introductory chapter helped to relate discussions among classical scholars to the wider anthropological debate on reciprocity and gift exchange (van Wees 1998).

From a very different vantage point, but nevertheless relevant to the themes of this book, is Lynette Mitchell's *Greeks Bearing Gifts* (1997). Looking at the politics of gift exchange in the late 5th and 4th centuries BC, she was able to show in much greater depth than I had been able to in Chapter 4 the importance of gift giving in interstate relationships of the classical period and the tensions this caused within the democratic Athenian polis.

The role of money in the matrix between gift exchange and commerce has become a crucial question. Recent discussions were stimulated by an unusually close co-operation between historians, literary critics and numismatists.[5] An important problem is the relationship between money and coinage, and the relative impact each had on the transformation of exchange, politics and thought in the Greek polis. Kim (2001) argued that coinage was no more than a convenience in the ongoing process of monetary development. It was predicated on an already established ability to weigh minute quantities of precious metal precisely to a weight standard, many of which were introduced by political governments in the Mediterranean during the archaic period.[6] Thus state authority which, I suggested in Chapter 8, was the crucial condition for, and re-enforcement of public coinage, must be regarded as already underlying monetary exchange before coinage existed. Seaford (1998) therefore takes bullion as the most fundamental monetary development in the archaic world, leading to important conceptual changes. Uncoined precious metal was the first money proper, the major characteristic of which he sees as a 'universal equivalent used as a medium of exchange' (1998: 222). It introduced the idea of total exchangeability, which on the one hand created new social anxieties, but on the other gave rise to new ways of imagining exchange, and the exchanges which constituted, in the eyes of some Presocratic philosophers, the universe.[7] Although I am not fully convinced that bullion was a 'universal equivalent' in the archaic world, nor that money ever is, Seaford's definition of money and its consequences offered opportunities for further debate and, together with Kim's numismatic comments, clarified distinctions within monetary development that may not have been entirely clear in my Chapters 8 and 9.

Kurke (1995; 1999) related a particular system of meaning to the emergence of archaic Greek coinage. The phenomenon of coinage was unprecedented in that it combined the use of precious metal as a medium of exchange with the use of signs as tokens of value. Uncoined precious metal, especially gold, had been associated by the aristocracy with essence, purity, a particular mythical past, and an aristocratic claim to power. Coinage in this world-view was merely functional, a false value, a deceptive signifier, and the currency of new civic elites. It had emerged within the polis, was used by civic governments, and was thus associated within an anti-polis tradition with all that was wrong with civic equality. Kurke offers fascinating readings of late archaic texts,[8] and has been able to relate negative attitudes to money specifically to coinage and the historical context in which it emerged, but she has been criticised for overstating aristocratic resistance to coinage.[9] I have attempted to show (von Reden 1997) that it is very difficult to identify coinage as a clear marker of class or social division in the Greek polis, though it is possible to regard it, with Kurke, as a threat to a traditional aristocratic hierarchy negotiated by gift exchange premised on a 'complete identification of self and status with the precious metals possessed and controlled' (1999: 47). I am, however, inclined to maintain the argument, developed in Chapter 9, that coinage is ambivalently represented in art and texts, and thereby reveals a double standard of its social evaluation, depending on who used it, and especially how it was used.[10]

The particular association of civic power with money in Thucydides – and here we can identify quite confidently *chrêmata* with coined money[11] – has been brought out excellently by Lisa Kallet-Marx.[12] Since Themistocles had persuaded the Athenians to use the silver resources from Laurium for the construction of a fleet that had vanquished the Persians, money had come to represent a particular kind of power. Private wealth had been essential for hoplite warfare, but the need of public monetary funds for naval power was a particular Athenian phenomenon. Monetary wealth generally, but Athenian coinage in particular, were therefore symbolically linked with democracy, naval power and a new secular rationalism. Thucydides demonstrated in effect that the rise and fall of naval empires depended in effect on monetary flow, and not on *hubris* (pride) or fate, nor upon the gods or moral forces governed and manipulated by them (1993: 205).

There has, then, emerged a certain consensus that ancient money, and certainly coinage, developed within a much wider, and culturally more specific context than the model of disembedded exchange suggests.[13] Moreover, it has now become reasonably agreed that a universal model of gift exchange and reciprocity cannot be used as an historical antecedent or anthropological counter-model to an equally universal model of developed market exchange. Yet while this has been acknowledged by at least some ancient historians,[14] it has motivated them very little, in turn, to rethink their approaches to ancient market economics.[15] What we are still lacking is a model of ancient market exchange which can account for, on the one hand, the rapid expansion of markets for the circulation of goods, money and services from the archaic period onwards (Osborne 1996 b), and on the other the continuing perception that market exchange violated the rules of self-sufficiency and reciprocity embodied in a civic moral code (Möller forthcoming). This is all the more deplorable as not only among researchers of Third World capitalism it has become commonplace to consider the historical genesis of markets together with other factors transforming the modern world.[16] The aim of this book, therefore, to encourage research on ancient market economics and its cultural and ideological context, is still open for further discussion and development.

Notes

1. The research for the book was undertaken as part of my doctoral thesis submitted in March 1992. The manuscript for its publication was completed in 1993, and some later bibliography was included while the book was in press.

2. Wagner-Hasel (2000): 27-59.

3. See also Seaford (1998).

4. See also Schofield (1998), inspired by this conference.

5. See esp. Howgego (1995); Kim (2001); and the collaborative volume edited by Meadows and Shipton (2002).

6. See also Howgego (1995): 1-23; Kroll (1998); Kurke (1999): 11 f., and my own attempt of delineating the gradual transition from weighed bullion to coin denominations in penalty clauses of late archaic Greek laws, von Reden (1997). For the amount of weight standards current in archaic Greece, Osborne (1996 a): 253-5.

7. The argument was set out in Seaford (1994): 220-32, and is now developed in greater depth in Seaford (forthcoming).

8. Now also Kurke (2002).

9. Seaford (2002); von Reden (2002): 167 f; and my review in *CPh* 96 (2001): 433-37.

10. I have developed this further in von Reden (2001). The discussion of Chapter 9 can now be read in conjunction with Davidson (1997) who from a very different perspective considers images of commercial exchange in relation to male and female prostitution; see also Kurke (1999): ch. 5.

11. See, most recently, Figueira (1998) and Wartenberg (1995) for the power of Athenian coinage in the Mediterranean during the second half of the 5th century, which may even have led to some form of economic integration of the region during that period; cf. Möller (forthcoming).

12. Kallet-Marx (1993) (1994), and (1998).

13. For the notion of 'disembedded' economics and the place of it in the debate on the nature of the ancient economy, see p. 2 below; and Cartledge (2002): 14 f.

14. See Morris (1994), and, more reluctantly, Davies (1998).

15. See the predominant perspective of the papers included in Scheidel and von Reden (2002), with the laudable exception of Cartledge (2002), esp. 14 f and 29 f.

16. See for example the essays collected in Hefner (1998); and Ray and Sayers (1999).

Illustrations

I am grateful to Mrs M. Kraay, Professor J. Boardman and the museums listed below for giving permission to reproduce illustrations. Special thanks go to Sue Grice, Department of Classics and Archaeology, University of Bristol, for producing line drawings of the maps and of several vase paintings.

Maps

(on pp. 112 and 113)

Athens: the *agora* and environs (after American School of Classical Studies at Athens, *The Athenian Agora*, 1976).
Athens: the *agora* at the end of the 5th century (after Camp, *The Athenian Agora*, 1986).

Plates

(between pp. 180 and 181)

1. a. 7th-century chalcedony scarab. Istanbul 6015 (Boardman, *Archaic Greek Gems*, 1968, no. 517).
   b. Black-figure kylix attributed to the Amasis Painter. New York, Metropolitan Museum of Art 1989.281.62.
   c. 6th-century stater from Cyzicus. London, British Museum 265049.
   d. Athenian 2dr, c. 560-545.
   e. Athenian 2dr, c. 530.
   f. Athenian 4dr, c. 530-520.
   g. Athenian 4dr, c. 520-510.
   Oxford, Ashmolean Museum (Kraay, *Archaic and Classical Greek Coins*, 1976, nos.163, 172, 173, 177).
2. Red-figure kylix. Rome, Villa Giulia 12 B 16 fr (Gerhard, *Auserlesene Vasenbilder*, 1858, vol. IV, fig. 278).
3. a-b. Red-figure krater. New Haven, Yale University 1933.175 (after Koch-Harnack, *Knabenliebe und Tiergeschenke*, 1983, fig. 5).
   c. Red-figure kylix. Bochum, University S 507.
   d. Red-figure kylix. New York, Metropolitan Museum of Art, Rogers Fund 52.11.4.

e. Red-figure kylix. Würzburg, Martin von Wagner Museum L 488.
4 a. Red-figure kylix. Berlin, Staatliche Museen, Antikensammlung F 2292.
  b. Red-figure kylix. Gotha, Museum Ahv. 48.
  c-d. Red-figure pelike. Hessische Hausstiftung, Schloss Fasanerie FAS AV 41, Bildarchiv Museum.
5. Red-figure kylix. Ohio, Toledo Museum of Art 1972.55.
6 a-b. Red-figure kylix. Paris, Louvre G 142 (photo R.M.N).
  c. Red-figure kylix. Munich, private collection (after Keuls, *The Reign of the Phallus*, 1985, fig. 162).
7 a. Red-figure kylix. Vienna, Kunsthistorisches Museum IV 2150.
  b. Red-figure pelike. Syracuse, Museo Archeologico Nazionale 20065.
  c-d. Red-figure alabastron. Berlin, Staatliche Museen, Antikensammlung F 2254.
8 a. Red-figure pelike. Copenhagen, Nationalmuseet CHR VIII 320.
  b. Red-figure kylix. Baltimore, Robinson Collection (after Scheibler, *Griechische Töpferkunst*, 1983, fig. 118).
  c-d. Red-figure kylix. Paris, Louvre CA 1852 (photo R.M.N.).

Introduction

In the late 1st century BC the Greek geographer Strabo, discussing the origins of the wealth of Arabia, wrote as follows:

> The part of Arabia that produces the spices is small and it is from this small territory that the country got the name of 'Blest', because such merchandise is rare in our part of the world and costly. Today, to be sure, the Arabs are well to do and even rich (*euporousi kai ploutousi*), because their trade (*emporia*) is extensive and abundant, but it is not likely to have been so in Homer's time. So far as the mere spices are concerned, a merchant (*emporos*) or camel-driver might attain to some sort of wealth (*euporia*) by trafficking in them, whereas Menelaus needed booty or presents from kings or dynasts who did not only have something to give, but had also the good-will to make him presents because of his distinction and fame.
> (Strab. *Geog.* 1.2.32)

Strabo's argument is one of the most striking examples of trade being compared to gift exchange. For Strabo, gift exchange was the ancient predecessor of long-distance trade, although the people who engaged in it, their motivations, and conditions of exchange were very different. If a country had something to offer that another needed, and that it was willing to give, it could have grown rich by the mechanism of royal gift exchange. Whether or not Strabo had a clear idea of how the wealth of states could be increased through foreign exchange, the comparison of Homeric gift exchange with contemporary trade needed no further justification. In contrast to our own perception, they were related activities.

This book starts from the supposition that the differentiation of economic from social forms of exchange was the result of a long historical and intellectual process in which both Enlightenment thought and the intellectual debates of the 19th and early 20th centuries played an important part.[1] This historical process and related intellectual debates were not just the result of the expansion of markets, trade and money, but a much more complex cultural development in which the individual was conceptually and morally redefined in relation to the collective. The transformation of ideologies and practices of exchange in ancient Greece, which is part of a shared European history and informed modern theoretical debates on gift exchange, may, I hope, contribute to a better understanding of our contemporary differentiation of economic from social forms of exchange.

Although I have chosen a well-defined subject of economic history, I have adopted a different approach. Economic historians and historians of economic ideas usually start from a key issue in economic theory, such as forms of production, labour, distribution, markets, money use, etc., and then explore this problem synchronically or diachronically in historical perspective. Such approaches have the advantage of operating in a well-established intellectual environment in which questions and methods of answering them are more or less clearly staked out. Yet since the economy has come to refer to a largely secular sphere of practice in which individuals are believed to act rationally in their own interest, the profoundly moral, philosophical and metaphysical problems which accompanied the development of markets, money and foreign trade tend to be regarded as irrelevant for economic analysis. It has been emphasised before – most famously by Moses Finley – that the ancient economy was regulated by religious, moral and political concerns.[2] Yet this has led to the rather deprecatory perspective that the ancients had no economy, or could not act in any economically rational way. Only gradually have historians begun to argue that economies which are guided by particular social and moral ideas can nevertheless be efficient, and are no less worthy to be called economies.[3] Political, moral and metaphysical problems are closely bound up with economic activities, and only if these are studied in conjunction can an understanding of economics in historical perspective be achieved.[4]

Although I wish to challenge fundamentally the methodology and intellectual framework of economic histories, the attempt is not new. Karl Polanyi was probably most influential in offering a new mode of analysis for pre-capitalist economies.[5] First, he differentiated three forms of economies, dominated by either 'reciprocity', 'redistribution' or 'market exchange'. Then he argued that in societies marked by reciprocity and redistribution, the economy was 'embedded' in social norms or political administration and thus could not be studied separately from them. Only societies marked by anonymous market exchange, regulated by the supply-and-demand mechanism, had a 'disembedded economy' which could be analysed and understood in its own terms. The notion of embedded economies has proved tremendously helpful for describing economics in pre-industrial and non-western contexts.[6] Yet Polanyi's model still emerged as an economist's perspective, for it concentrated on reciprocity and redistribution only as far as they were the historical and or non-Western counterparts of modern market relationships. Although he acknowledged the fundamental difference of market and pre-market economies, there was no room in his model for the analysis of cultural factors that have become irrelevant in market economics. Moreover, in posing 'reciprocity' or 'redistribution' as channels of exchange in all economies not dominated by market exchange, he failed to appreciate the degree to which there are many different cultural forms of reciprocity or redistribution. Not only pre-industrial economies as such, but reciprocity and redistribution themselves can be regarded as 'embedded' in culturally specific exchange ideologies. My disagreement with Polanyi is therefore fundamental. If reciprocity is considered as a culturally independent form of exchange adopted by certain types of society, the transformation from reciprocity to market exchange becomes a step in a universal evolutionary development. If, by contrast, both reciprocity and market exchange are regarded as ideologies which appear in many societies in different forms, the transformation of gift exchange based on social relationships and trade based on the anonymous market principle, can be envisioned as – at least partly – an ideological process in which political and social boundaries shift under a shifting perception of in-groups and out-groups.[7]

Marshal Sahlins' approach, which is based on Polanyi's but takes it a step further, is therefore more helpful. Sahlins poses a scale of reciprocities based on different degrees of social distance.[8] All forms of exchange are reciprocal. But the looser the bonds between exchanging partners become, the less generously or voluntarily equivalence is calculated. Thus not only the pure gift, for which no return is asked, but also theft and plunder, where people give without consent, are forms of reciprocity. Sahlins, again, constructs a tripartite scheme in which 'generalised reciprocity' forms the most generous extreme. For example, members of a kinship group, friends or neighbours who are socially close give gifts for no, or no immediate, return. 'Balanced reciprocity' is the norm underlying market exchange or trade, where people standing in no binding prior relationship meet in a peaceful or legally regulated place or sphere. Here immediate exchange of equivalent values is appropriate and expected. 'Negative reciprocity' is the mode of exchange between enemies or foreigners not tied by any moral or legal framework. As in theft, plunder and barter, anything goes.[9] Sahlins' model is crucial for understanding the transformation from 'social' to 'economic' exchange as a gradual process that goes along with the transformation of ideologies about who must be regarded as friend, enemy, or 'neutral'. We can begin to see how norms of exchange are determined and understood by the definition of social and political boundaries.[10] Yet Sahlins' model still needs a further dimension which helps to explain why these changing boundaries are so fundamentally bound up with moral and metaphysical re-definitions of individual and collective. Here we must turn to the work of Jonathan Parry and Maurice Bloch.

Bloch and Parry suggest that many societies distinguish between two related but separate 'transactional orders'.[11] The production of crops, the birth of offspring, the inheritance of property, marriage, political service, charity, foreign guest-friendship, trade and market exchange, but also murder, adultery, theft and barter can all be regarded as transactions which in one way or another might call for a return. Yet some of these 'exchanges' are related to the reproduction of the 'long-term' social or supra-individual order, while others are thought to belong to a 'short-term' order marked by the care for personal benefit and self-interest. All societies leave some room for individual concerns, and so, if an exchange is agreed to belong to the short-term order, any self-interest is permitted and socially accepted. But if there is disagreement about the question to which order an exchange is related, or if an individual transgresses the rules appropriate for each transactional order, this person may be charged with immoral or selfish behaviour. So for example, production, consumption and exchange may be regarded as part of the short-term order and thus, as the classical economic school suggests, self-interest is normal and permissible. But they can also be regarded as part of a long-term supra-individual order, guarded by the gods and aimed at the reproduction of human society collectively, and thus not open to individual exploitation. Moral conflicts over selfishness and acquisitiveness thus do not arise, according to Bloch and Parry, because of a universal dismissal of self-interest and profit orientation, but because of culturally specific conflicts over the meaning of transactions and their assignation to particular long-term or short-term orders.

Yet the perception of the boundary between transactional orders is not only open to debate but changes under changing social and political circumstances. As the geographical and social horizons of communities change or expand, the boundary between the two transactional orders are threatened. Members of the same community, or class, may disagree and struggle over the norms of reciprocity that individuals apply to their range of exchanges. In classical Athens, as we shall see, both the *oikos* (household) and the *polis* (city-state) could be regarded as part of the long-term order under divine control, aiming at social reproduction and collective survival. But they could also be described in the negative, as mistakenly short-term human constructs, regulated by human laws and private need. The model of transactional orders and the permeable boundary between a short-term and long-term order can thus help to explain culturally specific debates over appropriate forms of reciprocity, as distinguished by Sahlins.

The analysis of exchange developed in the following chapters has emerged not only from discussions in economic anthropology, but also from current research on the nature of the ancient *polis*. Since Fustel de Coulange's *La Cité Antique*, the role of the *polis* in the development of economy, society and thought has been emphasised. Yet this interdependence has been viewed differently by different scholars, and for present purposes it is important to see the shift in focus. Three directions may be distinguished. First, the sociological approach represented by Max Weber and Johannes Hasebroek; secondly, the socio-political approach suggested by Moses Finley and, with a different emphasis, Éduard Will; and thirdly, the cultural approach influenced by Jean-Pierre Vernant and Pierre Vidal-Naquet.

For Max Weber, the main question was whether urbanisation in the ancient world had had the same effects as in medieval Europe. His answer was negative because, he argued, the Greek city did not integrate industrial production and trade in the same way as the medieval city. The ancient city was a political association of warriors in which the urban centre was a centre of political reproduction and consumption, and not of economic production and commerce. Hasebroek developed this argument by asking whether the Greek *polis* ran a state economy. In other words, did the government of the city develop a national economy aiming at the increase of the 'wealth of the nation' as commended by the mercantilist doctrine? His answer, too, was negative, because the political dividing line between citizen-farmers and non-citizen manufacturers, traders and retailers prevented trade from becoming a concern of the citizen body.[12] For Weber and Hasebroek, the *polis* referred to an urban centre, and the economy to the macro-economy of trade, commerce and investment.

Finley and Will developed a socio-political approach which started from the nature of the ancient city-state, rather than a sociological model of cities. When Will, commenting on Hasebroek, argued that the ancient economy could only be analysed in the framework of the *polis*, he had neither only a state economy nor only trade and industry in mind.[13] Any economic activity in the ancient *polis* was linked to the institutional and ideological conditions of the political community. Will argued that the Aristotelian juxtaposition of *oikonomia* (household management) and *chrêmatistikê* (dealing with goods and money), which had been the point of departure for Hasebroek's argument, did not juxtapose simply wealth creation with agriculture and agriculture with commerce, but opposed two political statuses: autarky, freedom and citizenship on the one hand and dependence, slavery and lack of belonging on the other. Economic issues were bound up with political values. For example, the contrast between wealth and poverty corresponded to those between political competence and weakness, freedom and slavery, or *aretê* (virtue) and *kakia* (badness). In many special analyses Will demonstrated that the economic aspect of activities which we regard as economic remained secondary. Land was a symbol of citizenship and of the continuity of an *oikos* despite representing also agricultural labour, rural subsistence, etc. Money not only represented private exchange and trade but also political justice and public generosity. *Misthos* (remuneration) was the word for 'wage' but also for the gifts of honour distributed for services benefiting the community.[14] For Will the *polis* was above all a category of thought which provided the framework for the moral evaluation of economic and political activities.

Finley, more than Will, adhered to the boundaries that formal economic theory has defined for its subject. The *polis* was not a category of thought but a set of institutions which predetermined activities and their evaluation. While Will insisted on the ambivalence of concepts, referring partly to economic and partly to political, religious and social spheres, Finley relegated the economy to the activities of outsiders.[15] His argument was therefore mainly negative. Greek society was based on status rather than class, that is, on political rather than economic ranking. This implied that the Greek citizen had no motivation for acting rationally in economic terms, because positions of power were negotiated independently of economic success.[16] The overriding importance of citizen status, based typically on land ownership, perpetuated a subsistence economy and prevented the development of market-oriented production. It sustained a categorical distinction between agrarian production and market exchange, the former being the duty of a citizen and the latter the business of outsiders.[17] The free alienation of land and labour, moreover, was constrained by dependence on landownership and citizen status on the one hand, and the availability of slave and non-citizen labour on the other.[18] In this sense the *polis* prevented the development of a political economy and economic analysis in the modern sense.

Although Finley's outstanding contribution to the methodological debate on the ancient economy is unquestioned, he underestimated the relevance of exchange within the politics and society of the *polis*.[19] More fundamentally, his complete elimination of the ideological negotiations about the meaning of the institutions he analysed – such as slavery, landownership, citizenship and credit – neglects an important aspect of these institutions. Forensic oratory and comedy show that such questions as who deserved to belong to the citizen body, who used his inherited land properly, what were morally acceptable forms of credit, and even who was a 'slave', could never unequivocally be answered.

Vernant emphasised the role of the *polis* for the development of ancient thought and political culture. The emergence of formal political institutions which distributed power according to wealth and achievement rather than birth and divine gift led to the perception of a political order that could be discussed separately from the divine or natural order. Human behaviour and politics could now be evaluated independently of religious issues.[20] For Vernant the *polis* was a precondition for the emergence of so-called positivist thought which is characterised not only by its secular mode of argument but also by new definitions of problems. Not only did the laws of nature become an object of enquiry but also questions of justice, the calculation of value and the meaning of time, space and language. Vernant's research has been highly influential among historians and critics. Geoffrey Lloyd, for example, argues that the development of the *polis* was the background for the development from myth to science.[21] Paul Cartledge describes how Herodotus, writing within the same intellectual environment, represents the transition from myth into history.[22] And Simon Goldhill suggests that the development of the classical *polis* led to the challenge of traditional notions of the gods, justice and the meaning of power in society. It created fundamental tensions between private and public interests expressed in Athenian tragedy in terms of a conflict between *oikos* and *polis*, kinship and civic loyalties.[23] Most recently, Richard Seaford has related the emergence of contractual relationships, the calculation of equivalence in monetary units and the emergence of coinage to this intellectual development.[24] The changes that took place in the late archaic and classical *polis* stand for the transformation of an entire world view. As I shall argue in Part II of this book, they relate to the redefinition of transactional orders and therefore to tensions within the ideology of exchange.

Leslie Kurke's research on the victory odes of Pindar exemplifies how this particular process of transformation may be described.[25] In archaic Greece, she argues, human relationships, as well as the relationship between humans and gods, were perceived as exchange. Gift exchange, hospitality to strangers, and gifts accompanying marriage and funeral rites were not only material transactions but statements concerned with the symbolic construction of society.[26] A gift was 'symbolic capital', meaning that the treasure of an *oikos*, where gifts were stored, was identical with its power and fame. Epinician poetry was composed at a time when many moral principles were challenged. Aristocratic values were confronted with a new civic ideology, the primacy of the *oikos* was upset by that of the *polis*, and the introduction of coinage questioned the meaning of wealth embodied in aristocratic possessions.[27] The occasion at which choral poetry was performed was equally ambivalent. Aristocratic traditions were exposed to civic evaluation. Athletic victory, which in the rhetoric of praise was compared to mythical heroism, was celebrated in front of a civic community. Yet the heroisation of individuals was arguably a positive value in these communities. As a result, conflicting types of social exchange clashed and merged, making epinician poetry a testimony to the implicit conflicts of the late archaic city state.[28]

This is particularly apparent in the commercial imagery of Pindar's poetry, Kurke continues. Ancient and modern scholars alike have persistently wondered about the meaning of the commercial metaphors in Pindar.[29] Thus Pindar describes his own poetry as Phoenician merchandise, and the muse of choral poetry as a wage worker, or even prostitute, and he frequently comments on the fact that his poetic work is paid labour.[30] The older philological tradition interpreted these statements as Pindar's personal response to the changed social and economic conditions under which choral poetry was produced. The poet was no longer a participant in a group of peers, as the composers of sympotic lyric had been, but a paid labourer.[31] With a new generation of Pindaric criticism the public and political significance of the poems has come into focus. As Woodbury comments, 'the recommendation of a generous salary to the poet was not meant as an admonition of the patron, nor a device of self seeking, but the general glorification of magnificence.'[32]

Kurke has developed this argument and set it in the perspective of representations of exchange. She shows how the entire spectrum of social exchange which was at stake in the public celebration of athletic victory is cast into images of gift exchange, reciprocity and hospitality. These images were the expressions of a mentality that was typical of Pindar and some of the audience he addressed.[33] Yet the aristocratic world had changed under the influence of trade and a monetary economy. Pindar therefore sets images of trade and commerce in contrast to the traditional imagery of social exchange marked by the offer of *xenia* (hospitality), *dôra* (gifts), *hedna* (brideprice, dowry) and *apoina* (gifts of recompense). Rather than dramatising the conflict between two spheres of exchange, he assimilates them. The beginning of *Isthmian* 2, where Pindar compares the liberal Muse of old with the working girl (*ergatis*) of his days, is a critical reflection upon the effects of the money economy; but in the course of the poem that economy is appropriated for the symbolic economy of the nobility, and expenditure becomes a sign of aristocratic power and prestige.[34]

Kurke, operating with Polanyi's terminology, refers to the traditional sphere of exchange as an 'embedded economy' and juxtaposes it with the 'disembedded economy' of trade and commerce. Moreover, she regards gift exchange as a form of exchange exclusive to aristocratic intercourse and does not consider that much trade and commerce was undertaken by aristocrats in the early archaic period. Concentrating on choral poetry alone, she suggests that Pindar's reconciliation of traditional and new forms of exchange was a reaction to a lack of confidence aristocrats felt in trade and money. All this will be questioned in the course of this book. Nevertheless, Kurke's work demonstrates impressively how the conflicts between different modes of exchange, between different transactional orders, between the power of aristocratic *oikoi* and the *polis*, between heroism and citizenship and between cooperative and competitive values interrelated and conditioned each other. Gift exchange was not simply a proto-economic form of exchange, nor a remote mythical image, but a concept that gave meaning to power, heroic achievement, social solidarity, marriage and religious celebrations. The transformation of that world view caused by the transformation of the political environment meant that gift exchange had lost its object in the political sphere. New forms of exchange were associated with new political values. In that sense, the history of exchange is linked to the history of the *polis*.

In Part I of this book I lay out the range of meanings of gift exchange in heroic poetry, and how these are related to the reality of its audience. Epic crosses the boundary between the human and the divine world so that gift exchange merges into hero cult at the level of social reality.[35] Yet already in Homer there are indications that the boundaries of transactional orders were negotiable. This presents itself in the *Odyssey* where evaluation of Odysseus' exchange behaviour depends on the status he adopts. As a hero, singing of his heroic glory, he receives gifts that he will never return; as a human being, telling about his life and his *oikos* at home, he gathers the means of survival in the context of reciprocal guest-friendship, while as a roaming stranger, telling fictitious stories, he strives for profit.

Different concerns lie behind the texts of classical Athens (Part II). Gifts belonged to a supra-individual order of exchange and referred to the prosperity of the community, not to private wealth. If an individual misinterpreted a gift, and appropriated it for the satisfaction of his private desires, the benefit turned into a profit, the recipient into a merchant or hireling, and the exchange into bad commerce. The boundary between the long-term, or supra-individual, order and a short-term order of human exchange was highly controversial, however, since different views could be adopted as to whether the *polis* belonged to the divine or the human order, or both.

The political and moral implications of the introduction and use of coinage are considered in Part III. Rather than adopt an economic approach, according to which money is related to the emergence of markets and the expansion of trade, I shall ask to what extent coinage was used for social and political purposes, and whether it referred to an economic sphere of exchange alone. The transgression of boundaries is again explored in the final chapter, where I shall engage in the current discussion of the meaning of courtship scenes on vase-paintings, and ask if the representation of money pouches refers to economic payment alone or whether it could function as a symbol of a special gift as well.

In ancient Greece the question of what constituted the long-term and short-term human order led to the discussion of economic matters in a rich social, moral and political context, rather than within a limited analytical framework that disregarded the symbolic and political aspects of economic activity. If this book helps to set the discussion in these richer terms, it will have achieved its aim.

Notes

1. Wagner-Hasel (2000) draws attention to the intellectual tradition of the 19th and early 20th centuries only. See, however, the grander theoretical narratives within which this development has been described, such as Weber [1922] (1972), Polanyi (1944); Foucault (1970), and Bourdieu (1977).

2. Finley [1973] (1985); Finley (1970); Polanyi (1957 a); see, by contrast, Lowry (1987) who emphasises the intellectual continuities between ancient and modern economic thought.

3. Most notably Millett (1991 a) and (1991 b); see now also Morris (1994), although rather critical of Millett. Historians of the Roman economy tend to adhere more strictly to the range of questions of economic history; see now my survey of recent literature on ancient money and its uses in von Reden (2002).

4. See for example Kopytoff (1986); Elwert (1987); Hill (1986); and with a special focus on money Crump (1980); and Bloch and Parry (1989), Introduction.

5. His model is stated most clearly in Polanyi et al. (1957), pp. 1 ff. and Polanyi (1957 b). On Polanyi see also Garlan (1973); Humphreys (1978): 31-75; Figueira (1984); Godelier (1986), pp. 179-207; Jongman (1988), pp. 28-42; Nippel (1990), pp. 124-151, and the short but helpful summary in Austin & Vidal-Naquet (1977), pp. 7-11, and now also Möller (2000). For the substantivist-formalist debate, see esp. Hodges (1987), pp. 1-55, Davies (1973) and Cartledge (2002).

6. See most recently Möller (2000).

7. For reciprocity as an ideological norm rather than a culturally independent institution, see Gouldner (1960); I have developed and discussed this further in von Reden (1998)

8. Sahlins (1972), pp. 196-204. Sahlins uses the term of 'kinship distance' as he concentrates on societies where kinship relations are the most typical socially close relationships. For the Greek polis where civic, friendship and neighbourhood ties were morally more at issue than kinship ties, the term social distance seems more appropriate. See Millett (1991 a).

9. Sahlins (1972), pp. 101-204. Note that barter is taken as a form of negative reciprocity, rather than as a precursor of trade and market exchange where balanced reciprocity is the norm; for further discussion of the place of barter in the development of exchange see Humphreys (1985); and Davies (1992), pp. 24 f.

10. Thus Millett (1991 a); less persuasively, Donlan (1981-2).

11. Bloch and Parry (1989), pp. 24; see now also Kurke (1999), pp. 6, 14 f., and Kurke (2002). The perception of life as a series of exchanges has also been discussed by Schieffelin (1980); Strathern (1988), esp. pp. 1-31; and Davies (1992). Arguably, in ancient Greece exchange did not play the same all-encompassing role as observed in contemporary societies of the western Pacific.

12. Austin and Vidal-Naquet (1977), pp. 5-7; Finley (1981), pp. 3-21.

13. Will (1954 b), pp. 14-16.

14. Will (1955 a), 1975 a), (1975 b), cf. (1972), esp. pp. 676 ff.

15. Finley (1970), esp. pp. 24 f.

16. Finley (1985), pp. 48-50, 183-191.

17. Ibid. Criticism of the Finleyan orthodoxy is becoming increasingly frequent. See esp. Osborne (1991) for a case study with important conceptual implications.

18. On land see (1952), (1981 a), (1975); on labour (1968), (1981 c, e, f).

19. At the empirical level this is now largely compensated for by Millett (1991 a and b) who adopts a Finleyan perspective but takes it an important step further.

20. Vernant (1965 c), pp. 390 ff.

21. Lloyd (1979), esp. pp. 246-264.

22. Cartledge (1995), pp. 18-35.

23. Goldhill (1986), esp. pp. 138 ff. See also Vernant and Vidal-Naquet (1981), pp. 1-5, Segal (1981), and Winkler and Zeitlin (1990), passim.

24. Seaford (1994), esp. pp. 215 ff.

25. Kurke (1991).

26. Ibid., pp. 62-83; 108-133.

27. Ibid. pp. 36-38.

28. See also her discussion of the conflicts between hero and polis in Kurke (1993).

29. For a summary of the discussion see Woodbury (1968), pp. 527.

30. See esp. *Pyth.* 11. 37-48; 2. 63-71; *Isth.* 2.1-14.

31. Along these lines Bowra (1964), pp. 125, 353 ff.; Gzella (1971); Svenbro (1976), pp. 162-193; Gentili (1988), pp. 161 ff., 172. I have discussed the problem in further detail in von Reden (1995).

32. Woodbury (1968), p. 540; cf. Pavese (1966).

33. Kurke (1991), pp. 86-107.

34. Ibid., pp. 240-256; esp. 249.

35. Coldstream (1977).

Part I

EXCHANGE AND VALUE IN EPIC

1

The Scope of Gift Exchange

History in epic

The historical significance of gift exchange in Homeric epic needs no introduction. Finley in his now classic study demonstrated that it was a central concern of heroic exchange: 'There was scarcely a limit to the situations in which gift-giving was operative. More precisely, the word "gift" was a cover-all for a great variety of actions and transactions which later became differentiated and acquired their own appellations. There were payments for services rendered, desired or anticipated; what we would call fees, rewards, prizes, and sometimes bribes.'[1] Since Finley, these observations have been extended and qualified. Donlan analysed in great detail the way in which politics were conducted with gifts, and the kind of political system they were part of. He also tried to find evidence for 'spheres of exchange' which are typical of gift exchange systems.[2] Herman focussed specifically on the meaning of guest-gifts, while Morris surveyed the evidence of marriage transfers.[3] Hooker has warned us not to take the comparison between Homer and historical gift exchange systems too far. Compared with the immense moral force and frequency with which gifts are exchanged in working gift-exchange systems, or even other heroic poetry, in Homer it is nothing but a 'polite custom'.[4]

Despite the invaluable contribution made to social history by Finley and his followers, their historical approach has prevented them from recognising the metaphysical dimension of gift exchange in epic. Gift exchange in the *Iliad* and the *Odyssey* is more than a social or political ritual. Page Dubois, discussing modes of description in epic narrative, rightly remarks that 'precious objects ... gifts of the gods, products of human art, uphold a continuity with the past that defines the hero in relation to his ancestors. As gifts exchanged between gods and men, precious objects serve to bind the divine and human world together. As gifts exchanged between men, these objects represent the obligations men assume in relation to one another in a community. As objects passed from father to son, they provide continuity between generations.'[5] Dubois' observations mark an important shift in the interpretation of Homeric gift exchange. Its historical significance must be sought in being an image of order and other fundamental

metaphysical concerns. From the description of social continuity, attention is drawn to a transactional order which lies beyond social exchange and ties humans to gods and ancestors.[6]

We should agree with Hooker that the typical rules of gift exchange are too often neglected or transgressed in the epics for it to be regarded as a faithful representation of an operating social system. This, however, does not imply that no importance was attached to it, or that it was nothing but a 'polite custom'. One direction in Homeric criticism suggests that the epics are related to an increased activity at Mycenaean graves in the Late Geometric period. The profusion of epic song which resulted in the monumental work of Homer might have its origin in an intensification of hero cult and ancestor worship associated with the graves of the Bronze Age.[7] The Hesiodic tradition of the myth of the 'Five Ages of Man' suggests, furthermore, that early in the 7th century there was a belief in a generation of heroes, immediately before the age of mortal man, which was associated with the wars at Thebes and Troy. Some of these heroes had become immortal and now lived in the 'Islands of the Blest' deserving cultic observance and veneration.[8]

Homeric epic can thus be located in both myth and cult. Yet it is not simply a religious text. Hero cult merges into a political ritual when heroic descent functions as the justification of power for an elite.[9] The epic claim that gifts bestow honour on, and create peace between, heroes, gods and man can be read as the claim that gifts at graves create peace between ancestors and the living and are therefore essential for the stability and continuity of society. We should consider in this context that in archaic Greece grave offerings were constructed as gifts to the dead. As Morris has argued, they can be regarded as a form of 'conspicuous destruction' on the occasion of death rituals. They were given as part of a social competition, marked hierarchy symbolically, and probably implied the hope of a return.[10]

But the question how to use epic as a source for history remains unsolved. Finley tried to disentangle mythical narrative and historical background. He claimed that the epics are historical documents only when they convey a picture which is coherent, or which makes sense to an historian. For him it was a powerful argument that 'gift-giving in the Homeric epics is consistent, I might even say absolutely consistent, with the analysis made by Mauss ... If the practice ... does not reflect a society, but an "heroic ideal" we are driven to the conclusion that by a remarkable intuition, Homer was a predecessor of Marcel Mauss ... .'[11] Similarly, Donlan writes that 'if the examination of reciprocal exchanges ... reveals consistent and coherent patterns, the question of the validity of Homer as an "historical" source will be partially answered'.[12] Literary criticism, by contrast, has offered new readings which change the nature of the epics as a document. They suggest that contradictions in epic descriptions, which from Finley's point of view must be regarded as of little use to the historian, are part of their essential meaning.[13] We must therefore shift our attention from the coherent aspects to the contradictions of gift exchange.

Even if we move our consideration of the importance of gift exchange from a social to a cultic context we still have to ask what society identified itself with heroic poetry. It is generally agreed that the epics were composed for an audience who belonged to more than one local tradition. It is also agreed that heroic poetry in general is a genre in which a particular self-conscious and self-aggrandising class depicts its own ideals; its content is a social elite's normative and ideological story of its own past, and thus of itself.[14] More controversial is the question whether the Homeric poems can offer evidence about the values of a single society and, if so, which historical society this may be. If we assume that the text as we have it is the more or less final version of stories orally composed and transmitted over many generations, we must agree with Snodgrass that the poems contain an arbitrary amalgam of several value systems and conventions.[15] If, however, we follow Parry and Lord in assuming that orally composed and transmitted literature presents a special way of interacting with the past, we must go a step further.[16] Oral poetry, they argue, does not simply carry older material down to later periods, thus confusing traditions which never existed together at any one place, but consciously comments on the past. The past assumes a different role for the audience of oral literature than for the readership of written literature. Since it provides the formulaic and narrative framework in which new problems are expressed, the memory of the past frames the ideology of the present.[17] If Morris calls allusions to bygone institutions, values and culture a strategy of creating 'epic distance', he underestimates the interdependence of past and present which is indispensable for the meaning of epic. Oral epic appropriated the past to give meaning to the present.[18]

It can no longer be at issue, then, whether the poems were produced against a background of one or of several historical periods. More appropriate is the question to what extent the latest audience was able to engage in the images and institutions of the older material.[19] A number of critical studies have suggested that the *Iliad* and the *Odyssey* are critical discussions of their own material.[20] The poems are thematically linked, provide comments on one another and challenge the assumptions contained in formulae and older descriptions. When trying to understand the meaning of gifts, their exchange and mode of evaluation, we must direct our attention to the questions which the text itself asks about gift exchange.

Historical 'evidence' is thus obscured by the mode of composition of the *Iliad* and *Odyssey*. Collecting isolated pieces of evidence and relating them to each other in search of a consistent whole fails to take into account the conditions in which the document was created. As Dubois suggests, the exchange of precious objects gives meaning to a wide spectrum of exchanges including those which link the world of the ancestors and of the gods with the living. Since, however, the epics do not offer unequivocal views on the meaning of life and death, or the communication between humans, gods and ancestors, the metaphysics of gift giving remain similarly undecided. For example, one of the major questions of both the *Iliad* and the *Odyssey* is whether honour and possessions in life have more value than fame after death; Achilles confronts himself with the question whether it is worth exchanging one for the other, and whether gifts can recompense one either for lost honour in life, or for loss of life. Since the hierarchy of these values remains ultimately an unsolved problem, the question whether gifts should be accepted as recompense remains open.

Ambivalent meanings of, and attitudes to, gift exchange do not have their origin only in the ambivalence of metaphysical assumptions. One of the difficulties in interpreting the epics is that they contain different models of political hierarchy. Who is the best of the Achaeans? Is Achilles' refusal to accept Agamemnon's political superiority justified? Are Achilles' martial qualities superior to Odysseus' tricks and plans that aim at survival?[21] Behind the representation of the competition of individual qualities lies the more general question of how to justify power in social and metaphysical terms. In the course of epic composition the answer to this question changed. Each audience had its own Achilles, Hector or Agamemnon. Agamemnon, for example, was at first a Mycenaean king and then the leader of a fragmented political community; and his power was judged again in a new light in the 8th century. For *basileia* (kingship) in the early archaic period had little to do with monarchical kingship.[22] As a result, the wrath of Achilles and his rejection of the royal gifts acquired new political dimensions in the course of epic composition.

It is now commonly assumed that by the 8th century social and political transformations had changed communal life throughout Greece.[23] A system of independent *oikoi* (households), headed by *basileis* with quasi-monarchical power, was gradually superseded by a system which integrated *oikoi* at a higher level of political organisation. The *oikos* remained the dominant social and ethical unit, but the *polis* made its appearance in rudimentary outlines.[24] It is disputed, however, whether these developments left any traces in the epics.[25] Finley argued that there were no traces of the *polis* in either poem. Urban architecture, like city walls, harbours and *agorai*, should not be confused with *polis* institutions. While the former were clearly mentioned in the epics, the latter were absent. Finley did not dispute that *polis* institutions were developing during the 8th century, but the absence of any trace of them in the epics was for him an argument that the epics were essentially composed in the Dark Age.[26] Morris, by contrast, argued that the *agora* in the *Iliad* and the *Odyssey* functions not just as a locality but as a place of assembly with some institutionalised powers. Moreover a certain degree of political organisation was contained in allusions to the administration of justice. In some instances justice is the decision of a *basileus* made in the presence of an

1. The Scope of Gift Exchange

audience, or a group of elders.[27] Seaford supports this view by drawing attention to references to communal ritual, patriotism and a sense of belonging to a *polis*.[28] However, all references are ambivalent evidence if taken in isolation, and we must adopt a new approach that takes into consideration the circumstances of epic composition.

One such attempt has been made by Stephen Scully. To understand the meaning of the *polis* in epic he sets out to trace 'both a process of transmission and an evolution'. The historical city of Homer's day merged with the remembered city of myth; contemporary conditions and inherited formulae conflated Mycenaean and Ionian features.[29] For the Mycenaeans the term *polis* referred to the (often walled) citadel of the king, but by the 8th century the same term had come to refer to the entire community, enclosed by the city wall. While the contrast of Troy (the citadel) and Scheria (resembling in some ways 8th-century *poleis*) has often been regarded by scholars as reflecting a historical shift in the meaning of cities in Homer, both represented a mixture of old and new: the 8th-century urban revolution in Ionia provided a model for the Homeric vision of the *polis*; yet it revitalised old traditions, making it possible to weave the episodes of the Trojan war into the paradigmatic story of Achilles, Hector and the fate of a town. This anachronistic link inevitably raised questions of urban definition, urban enclosure and *polis*-oriented ritual.[30]

Both Scully's approach and his theme provide the background for the following analysis. First, I shall assume that the values and problems addressed in the epics are derived from a poetic interaction of the 8th century with past generations. Secondly, I assume that new problems of social interaction emerged under the influence of the *polis* and that they influenced the normative statements of the epics. Thirdly, the unsettled nature of power and political exchange was part of the exchange between poet and audience who experienced a community in transition. This unsettled situation raised new questions about the meaning of life, fame, property and the *oikos*. Fourthly, I shall take the final version of the poems as containing not a random amalgam of representations of exchange, but a conscious conflation of different meanings of exchange. It has been argued that gift exchange is a system-stabilising mechanism in societies which are controlled by ritual rather than political institutions and laws.[31] When power comes to be controlled by political institutions and a constitution, gifts become less relevant. They then become symbols of friendship, solidarity and peace, particularly in areas which are not controlled by the laws of the state. Homeric epic raises the question whether gift exchange has social, political or metaphysical meaning, or all at once.[32]

We may start, then, from the proposition that the epics have made use of the changing meaning of gift exchange in the course of their literary development. Gift exchange as a social practice was part of many episodes at an early stage of epic composition. Its rules became 'fossilised' in formulae or epithets when the ritual itself lost its immediate social meaning in the life of later audiences. Subsequent generations of poets endowed it instead with a meaning that was associated with the exchange between human beings and their metaphysical environment, symbolising continuity, prosperity and justice. Therefore the epics can be explored at three levels. First, they attest a number of rules and meanings which were at first attached to gift exchange as a social practice; secondly, they contain some veiled criticism and mockery of these rules; and thirdly, they are evidence of how gift exchange was transformed into a moral concept at the time of the incipient city state.

The gift as recompense

Anthropologists have described the gift as an item of exchange which is defined by a specific mode of exchange. Typical of this mode of exchange is the delay between the original gift and its return so that the indebtedness of the recipient is the immediate return for the gift. Related to the type of transaction of the gift is thus a type of dependence which does not necessarily submit the recipient to the donor but creates a social obligation. This obligation being an important result of gift giving, the value of a gift is often regarded as 'symbolic', 'qualitative' or 'subjective', in contrast to the functional, quantitative and objective value of commodities.[33] The essence of gift value, if contrasted with commodity value, is that it can be recognised only in a social context: only if it means something to others does it have a value for the recipient. Its possession satisfies a personal 'need' or 'demand' only in so far as it satisfies a demand for social recognition and honour. Its transaction creates a profit only in so far as it obliges the recipient to the donor. There is no concept of property attached to a gift; its possession is transitory and creates no rights of subjects over objects.[34]

In accordance with this model gifts in Homer are desired and given because they create and sustain social relations between people. In the language of heroes, they attach honour to warriors and create hierarchy and obligation in the warrior community. Old Phoenix beseeches Achilles to rejoin battle before the gifts are withdrawn:

> ... No, with gifts promised
> go forth. The Achaeans will honour you as they would an immortal.
> But if without gifts you go into the fighting where men perish,
> your honour (*timê*) will no longer be as great, though you drive back the
> battle.[35]

Timê (honour) is the thing of greatest value to a hero in life. Another kind of honour, *kleos* (glory), is the reward of valour after death. *Kleos* is the way in which a hero of old is remembered, it is the fame that spreads

1. The Scope of Gift Exchange

through song, his grave and the valuable objects that carry his name. Both *timê* and *kleos* are descriptions from outside rather than something defined by internal qualities.[36]

When honour is damaged, attempts are made to restore it by the offer of gifts. Agamemnon, who has violated Achilles' honour by taking Briseis, tries to restore it by giving gifts equivalent to Achillies' value as a warrior:

> I was mad, I myself will not deny it. Worth many
> fighters is that [one] man whom Zeus in his heart loves, as now
> he has honoured this man and beaten down the Achaean people.
> But since I was mad, in the persuasion of my heart's evil,
> I am willing to make all good, and give back gifts (*apoina*) in abundance.
> Before you all I will count off my gifts (*dôra*) in their splendour.[37]

The gifts of recompense are similar to, and indeed compared with, the recompense which a supplicant offers in order to escape death, or which a relative accepts from the murderer of his kin in order to restore social peace. Thus Ajax reproaches Achilles for not accepting the recompense of Agamemnon, calling him:

> Pitiless. While a man takes from his brother's slayer
> the bloodprice (*poinê*), or a price for a child who was killed, and the guilty
> one, when he has largely repaid, stays still in the country,
> and the injured man's heart is curbed, and his pride, and his anger
> when he has taken the price …[38]

The *Iliad* thus alludes to exchange rituals in which the value of persons was defined by, and exchanged for, the value of gifts. Such exchanges seem to have been associated with justice understood in terms of a peaceful exchange in which the social and physical life of a human being was assessed by surrogate values. The evaluation of humans in terms of gifts and the perception of obligations as an indispensable aspect of human life were thus immediately related.

Yet it is more important that both this mode of evaluation and social bonding are rejected by the main hero of the *Iliad*. The obligation to accept, and the obligations arising from these gifts are social norms which Achilles transgresses. He refuses, first, to accept the gifts of recompense offered by Agamemnon which would restore his honour in life and, secondly, to accept death in battle which would give him honour after life. This double refusal allows the text to introduce scenes of persuasion which compare the offers of the gods with those of men. The crucial question for Achilles being what recompense is sufficient for the prospective loss of life, he comes to the conclusion that the gifts of a king are not enough.

Exposed to the choice between the mortal life of a human being and the immortal life of a hero, he realises that they are incompatible:

> I carry two sorts of destiny towards the day of my death. Either,
> if I stay here and fight beside the city of the Trojans,
> my return home is lost (*ôleto ... nostos*), but my glory shall be everlasting;
> but if I return home to the beloved land of my fathers,
> the excellence of my glory is lost (*ôleto ... kleos esthlon*), but there will be a long life
> left for me, and my end in death will not come quickly.[39]

As Lynn-George has argued, this passage is marked by its emphasis on inevitable loss. The alternatives share a common element stressed by the repetition of *ôleto* (it is lost), which begs the question of what compensation there can be in this situation of inescapable loss.[40] The gifts of Agamemnon, which include a daughter for marriage and glorious prizes from the spoils of Troy, are clearly insufficient. Many times Achilles states his refusal to accept the gifts of the king, but once in particular he compares them to the value of life:

> I will not marry a daughter of Atreus' son, Agamemnon,
> not if she challenged Aphrodite the golden for loveliness
> ...
> For if the gods will keep me alive, and I win homeward,
> Peleus himself will presently arrange a wife for me.
> There are many Achaian girls in the land of Hellas and Phthia,
> daughters of great men who hold strong places in guard. And of these
> any one that I please I might make my beloved wife.
> And the great desire in my heart drives me rather in that place
> to take a wedded wife in marriage, the bride of my fancy,
> to enjoy with her the possessions won by aged Peleus. For not
> worth the value of my life are all the possessions they fable
> were won for Ilion, that strong-founded citadel, in the old days
> when there was peace ...
>   ... Of possessions
> cattle and fat sheep are things to be had for the lifting
> and tripods can be won, and the tawny high heads of horses,
> but a man's life cannot come back again, it cannot be lifted
> nor captured again by force, once it has crossed the teeth's barrier.[41]

Whereas the gifts from the king can in no way be equal to the value of life (9. 385), the unspecified amount of divine gifts is more adequate for such an equation. When Athene tries to prevent Achilles from taking Agamemnon's life in revenge for the loss of Briseis she promises to give 'gifts three times over'. The offer has important implications for Achilles since, if he refrains from killing Agamemnon, the events will unfold as destined by the gods, which means the loss of his own life:

> Come then, do not take your sword in your hand, keep clear of fighting [Agamemnon],
> though indeed with words you may abuse him, and it will be that way.
> And this also will I tell you and it will be a thing accomplished.

1. The Scope of Gift Exchange

> Some day three times over such shining gifts shall be given you by reason of this outrage. Hold your hand then, and obey us.[42]

The recompense which the goddess promises, and which Achilles accepts, is different from that of Agamemnon in that it is undetermined in size and timing. Agamemnon meticulously specifies an inventory of gifts, and promises them partly at once (*autika*, 277) and partly after the sack of Troy.[43] This specificity in timing is reinforced by the speech of Phoenix who, trying to persuade Achilles to reconcile himself with Agamemnon, tells the story of Meleager. Meleager had too long refused to fight, and when finally his wife persuaded him to rejoin the battle, his people would no longer give him the gifts they once had offered.[44] The contrasting representation of the timing of the recompense not merely betrays the distinction between human and divine gifts but also stresses a difference between two orders of exchange. Agamemnon seeks to persuade Achilles, unsuccessfully, with a recompense which originates in the short-term order of human society and which includes, apart from his own possessions, honour bestowed by the other Achaeans (9. 302). Athene's gifts, by contrast, refer to the timeless order of metaphysical justice in which recompense awaits man with 'indefinite certainty' (Lynn-George): neither immediately nor of a specified value.

The gap that lies between Achilles' obedience to the gods and disobedience to Agamemnon is caused by the fact that their recompense refers to different orders marked by a different time scale. *Timê* to be gained and granted by mortals whose life is terminated at the moment of death on the one hand, and *kleos* controlled by the gods and gained by heroes living beyond their lifetime on the other, refer to two different modes of existence in a different time perspective. As long as the two kinds of evaluation do not exclude one another, heroism is unproblematic and military valour is motivated by the prospect of honour bestowed both by humans and by the gods. Sarpedon, for example, exhorts Glaucus to fight because it will both secure his honoured place in society and grant him worship as a hero ('as if we were immortals' (9. 312)).[45] Yet as Achilles has lost the prize of valour, he has lost the faith in human society in which recompense is supposed to be granted for risking one's life before life is lost. He thus oscillates between two extremes, the sub-human status of isolating himself from society and fighting no battles and the heroic (or supra-human) willingness to join battle without any hope of survival. Human gifts no longer have meaning for him since they belong to an order of exchange from which he has dissociated himself.

The alternative to which Achilles exposes himself can be regarded either as foolish or as an attempt to solve an insoluble problem. For the two orders of exchange which Achilles separates are linked despite their different time scale.[46] The conflict of Achilles dramatises the problem of how to act when the exchanges within society and those beyond are not in harmony.

The text itself intimates that the gifts of the gods and the gifts in society come together. It represents Achilles' social isolation as an unfeasible attempt to escape social injustice; he carries the marks of social death in life and anticipates the physical death which he suffers when he returns to the fighting.[47] By refusing to fulfil the obligations he has to the Achaeans and to fight for their victory, he also neglects his obligations towards the gods. The value of his honour assessed in a social context and the value of his life assessed in a metaphysical context cannot be separated even though Achilles would like to do so. The loss of honour in the society of Achaeans is at once linked with the loss of divine favours. In his anger at the withdrawal of his prize Achilles prays to his mother:

> Since, my mother, you bore me to be a man with a short life,
> therefore Zeus of the loud thunder on Olympus should grant me
> honour at least. But now he has given me not a little.
> Now the son of Atreus, powerful Agamemnon,
> has dishonoured me, since he has taken away my prize and keeps it.[48]

The form in which the prayer is cast comprises two complaints at once. The double function of a prize (*geras*) as a sign both of honour in life and of heroic *kleos* after death makes it impossible to tell whether Achilles is protesting against the injustice he suffers in the human or in the divine order. Lynn-George considers only the latter: 'The hero's prayer protests against a loss which defies the heroic structure of exchange: a short life for lasting honour and glory. In his sudden state of loss he claims immortal honour – in the first instance the honour bestowed by the lord of the immortals, Zeus.'[49] Yet it seems that the main problem for Achilles is that honour granted by the lord of the mortals and that granted by the lord of the immortals are interdependent. Although he marks his independence of human society by refusing Agamemnon's gifts he has to accept them in the end because only in this way can he win the rewards promised by the gods in the long term.

This problem runs through the poem and creates a certain inconsistency in Achilles' behaviour. On the one hand he claims that he will never let Agamemnon have his way, even 'if he gave me gifts as many as sand or dust' (9. 385), and on the other he accepts the gifts when taking revenge for the death of Patroclus.[50] Yet this is only seemingly inconsistent since Achilles in fact subverts the gesture of reconciliation. He refuses to share a meal with Agamemnon and he manipulates the meaning of the very gift which would have sealed the reconciliation.[51] Achilles is thus made to accept the recompense of the king in order to restore his social position while not accepting it as a sufficient recompense for his impending loss of life. It seems that the poem tries to make a distinction between a political and a metaphysical order of exchange and yet at the same time represents this distinction as dangerous and destructive.

1. The Scope of Gift Exchange

The choice which Achilles makes leaves no doubt about his moral stance: whereas divine gifts compensate for the loss of life in the timeless span of heroic existence, in the short period of mortal life gifts cannot substitute for the value of a person. As a warrior he chooses revenge, the exchange of body for body. Talking to his divine mother he makes the equation explicit. He re-enters the battle to take Hector's life for that of Patroclus and he will lose his own in return. This is an equal exchange since his life is equal to that of Patroclus, for the loss of which he himself feels responsible. Having neglected a relationship of obligation, which was also a relationship of debt,[52] his own life must be sacrificed. By avenging the life of Patroclus he also avenges many other Achaeans' lives, which again is no unequal exchange as his life was regarded as worth that of many other Achaeans (9. 114.):

> My mother, all these things the Olympian brought to accomplishment.
> But what pleasure is this to me, since my dear companion has perished.
> Patroclus, whom I honoured beyond all other companions,
> equal to my own life (*ison emê kephalê*) ...
> ...
> Now since I am not going back to the beloved land of my fathers,
> since I was no light of safety to Patroclus, nor to my other
> companions, who in their numbers went down before glorious Hector,
> but sit here beside my ships, a useless weight on the good land,
> ... I wish that strife would vanish away from among gods and mortals.
> ...
> Now I shall go, to overtake that killer of a dear life,
> Hector; then I will accept my own death at whatever
> time Zeus wishes to bring it about, and the other immortals.[53]

It may seem contradictory that later Achilles accepts a ransom from Priam for the body of Hector, thereby accepting the exchange of a human body for human gifts after all. Yet on closer inspection the ransom is not taken in order to create peace and end the cycle of blood revenge but is an exploit of which Patroclus receives a share. Talking to the dead warrior in a dream Achilles justifies his behaviour:

> Be not angry with me, Patroclus, if you discover,
> though you be in the house of Hades, that I gave back great Hector
> to his beloved father, for the ransom he gave me was not unworthy.
> I will give you your share of the spoils as much as is fitting.[54]

By offering Patroclus a share of the ransom he also converts the human recompense into a cult offering to a dead man. He thus again represents the idea that gifts bestow honour, and substitute for the loss of life, only in a metaphysical order.[55] Hector's body is worth many gifts to his father, but for Achilles it is the body, not the gifts, which compensates for the loss of Patroclus.

The three main heroes of the Homeric epics, Achilles, Hector and Odysseus, approach heroism – that is, immortal fame and cultic observance – in three different ways. For Hector *kleos* means dying for his wife, his kin, the king and the other Trojans; for Achilles too it can be achieved only through death in battle. But unlike Hector's, Achilles' position implies a conflict: he has to choose between death in a foreign land for the sake of his companions and life in the *oikos* of his family and kin.[56] For a while he refuses to die for his fellow warriors and their commander. Only in the person of Patroclus does his split obligation towards warrior society and towards the members of his *oikos* merge. As Sinos has argued in some detail, Patroclus represents both a companion in arms and a friend in peace at home.[57]

The contrast between Hector and Achilles dramatises different meanings of city and community: Achilles rejects battle because he rejects the community for which he must fight while Hector is drawn into battle by a community which is more complex than the Achaean camp. For Achilles community means submission to a military commander who has violated his honour and to military companions who honour a king who dishonours him.[58] For Hector, by contrast, the city refers to immortal relationships, a wife, a son and the inheritance of an *oikos*, which symbolise the generational link between past and future.[59] His death for the community implies as much a death in exchange for immortality as Achilles' death for Patroclus.

Odysseus in the *Odyssey* triumphs over both these heroes of the *Iliad* in gaining *kleos* by staying alive. While Achilles' return would have meant the loss of *kleos*, and Hector needs no return, Odysseus suggests that returning home can result in *kleos*.[60] In the complex constellation of heroic achievement gifts assume different meaning and therefore different kinds of value. In all cases they belong to the order of exchange in which immortal *kleos* is gained. Yet as this order shifts its place from the battlefield to the *oikos* the value which gifts embody shifts accordingly. Since for Achilles *kleos* can be gained only by sacrificing his life in obedience to the gods, the gifts which he accepts as recompense must belong to the order to which he sacrifices his life. Hector, by contrast, sacrifices his life to the city and family, and so the values for which his body can rightfully be exchanged are the gifts of the treasures belonging to Troy. For Odysseus, *kleos* lies in his return home. This relates the value of gifts directly to the life in the *oikos*. They no longer represent a recompense for life lost but give value to a life regained.

The consequences of the *Odysseyan* concept of gift value are discussed in a later chapter. At this point we can come to the preliminary conclusion that in the *Iliad* the gift symbolises the immortality of heroes. It bridged the gap between life and death. It created the image of a continuous exchange of life for immortality in a supra-individual order and asserted the continuity of society beyond the span of an individual life.

Manipulation of gift exchange

Achilles' acceptance of Agamemnon's gifts of recompense remains a superficial act. He continues to stay apart as a 'fasting individual in a feasting community' (Lynn-George). Formally, though, he takes the gifts as if to prove that he accepts the terms of reconciliation and the established social hierarchy. He acknowledges the pre-eminence of Agamemnon's position outwardly by accepting the king's power to give and take as he pleases:

> Son of Atreus, most lordly and king of men, Agamemnon,
> the gifts are yours to give if you wish, and as it is proper,
> or to keep for yourself ...[61]

The reconciliation is also staged as an act to be seen by the other Achaeans. The gifts are brought out so that 'all the Achaeans can see them before their eyes' and witness the ritual of reconciliation.[62] Although Achilles formally submits to Agamemnon's power for the others to see, re-integration is far from accomplished. He refuses a common meal and a common sacrifice, which would affirm his submission to Agamemnon but is inappropriate for the time while he grieves for unrevenged Patroclus. Thus the submission to Agamemnon implied in the acceptance of the gifts remains secondary to the exchange of body for body enacted in the revenge.

The theme of reconciliation is continued at the end of the *Iliad* when Achilles and the Achaeans celebrate the funeral games in honour of Patroclus. Again the transaction of precious objects, in this case prizes, plays an important part in the ritual but is surprisingly open to manipulation. If we adopt Redfield's view that funerary games are a ritual re-enactment of the reciprocities of combat, in so far as mourners and competitors exchange toil for prizes,[63] the roles of Achilles and Agamemnon are for once reversed. Agamemnon fights and Achilles distributes shares of honour. But when the turn of joining the games and winning a prize comes to the king, Achilles decides that the prize shall be bestowed on the king without competition:

> Son of Atreus, for we know how much you surpass all others,
> by how much you are greatest of strength among the spear-throwers,
> therefore take this prize and keep it and go back to your hollow
> ships ...[64]

Redfield suggests that the gesture indicates political prudence: 'If the king should be defeated the result would be a social anomaly. It is best not to put the matter to the test of competition.'[65] Yet considering that Achilles is only outwardly reconciled to Agamemnon a better explanation is at hand. In an act of apparent generosity Achilles subverts the reciprocities of the games, thereby symbolically subverting the reciprocities of heroic society. Achilles' gesture recalls the ambivalent gesture of Agamemnon earlier in the *Iliad*. Shrouded in the language of recompense, Agamemnon's gifts had aimed at, and were understood by Achilles as, the affirmation of his supremacy. Now it is Achilles' turn to shift the meaning of gifts. While a prize won in battle symbolises the status of its recipient, a gift received for nothing subordinates the recipient to the donor.[66] Converting the prize of the games into a pure gift Achilles tacitly adopts a dominant position. He explicitly accepts but implicitly rejects Agamemnon's supremacy.

We may leave the story of Achilles at this point and look at another episode which shows a similar transformation of gift exchange from a ritual into an image of reciprocity, or if the text so demands, of negative reciprocity. The exchange between Glaucus and Diomedes in book 6 of the *Iliad* is another example of how the epics at the same time invoke the power and manipulate the rules of gift exchange.[67] Yet whereas with Achilles' gift to Agamemnon the manipulation lies in the tacit shift of meaning from prize to gift, in this case it is the overt discrepancy of the language accompanying the exchange and the symbolic language of the exchange itself.

The outward course of the exchange seems to follow the proper custom of the ritual of guest-friendship (*xenia*).[68] Diomedes recognises Glaucus as the son of his father's *xenos*. The bond is affirmed, hands are shaken, vows of friendship are renewed, and finally gifts are exchanged. Yet the values of the gifts are not equivalent. Glaucus, 'stripped of his wits', exchanges gold for bronze, armour worth a hundred oxen for that worth only nine.[69] The episode has puzzled commentators since antiquity.[70] Yet if one allows for the possibility that the author of the *Iliad* used the image of gift exchange as an image of order, rather than as a social norm, the episode can be interpreted more fully. The exchange between Glaucus and Diomedes is consciously constructed as a public display:

> But let us exchange our armour, so that these others may know
> how we claim to be guests and friends from the days of our fathers.[71]

The emphasis on the visibility of the exchange is an introduction to its subsequent subversion. All the Greek and Trojan warriors see how Glaucus accepts bronze for gold while Diomedes carries off the greater value. As Odysseus in the *Odyssey* does time and again, so Diomedes changes a gift into an exploit.[72] Humiliation could not be more complete. Instead of being heroically defeated in battle, the Trojan is defeated in a ritual between *xenoi*. While the words accompanying the exchange affirm friendship, the exchange of the objects itself affirms enmity.

Rituals of *xenia* and reconciliation were traditionally performed by the exchange of words *and* gifts.[73] This made such rituals an ideal medium for the discussion of the discrepancy between speech and action. A climax of cunning was reached when the language of friendship or reconciliation was turned into the opposite by the second, outwardly affirmative, statement of the gifts.

An example from the *Odyssey* may be added. Penelope showing herself in the company of the suitors challenges them to a contest of gift-giving. The Achaeans bring out their gifts to cunning Penelope. Odysseus, however, watching the scenario in disguise, rejoices:

[as] she extracted their gifts from them and charmed their hearts
with soothing speeches, but her mind devised other things.[74]

Penelope turns the gifts into exploits, thus transforming her position from one of inferiority into one of superiority.

Gift exchange appears in epic narrative as a social ritual; yet the obligations arising from gifts can be secondary to other obligations. The norms of gift exchange are thus open to transgression without destroying the people involved. In the following sections I shall show that the decline of the obligatory force of gifts went along with a decline of those aspects of the gift which, according to Mauss, create unbreachable obligations between donors and recipients. Mauss argued that a gift must be returned because it embodies the donor. Since the donor is part of the gift it cannot be kept without keeping a part of the donor.[75] In the gift persons and things merge. Property is equal to properties, or to a collection of detachable attributes of the person. Giving property, or attributes of oneself, binds the donor's person to the recipient's and *vice versa*. This generates a number of further consequences: giving a gift is an act of recognition (honour); it symbolises that the donor recognises who the other is the moment he receives the gift and in the future.[76] The gift therefore acts not only as an object that creates social obligation but also as a means of recognition, social classification and a sign to be remembered.

There are parallels to these aspects of the gift in Homer. Gifts act as signs, they are tokens of recognition, and they are similar to physical properties of the heroes. Yet there are moments when gifts fail to bring about recognition, or when the token of recognition is not a gift. Again we must note that the power of gifts in the epic text is ambivalent. As in the preceding sections, I shall first outline the pattern and then show how it was questioned.

The gift as a sign

The word that comes closest in epic to our term 'sign' is *sêma*. And it is frequently a *sêma* by which a hero is identified, either in life or after death. Like the word 'sign', *sêma* is both a mark carried by a person (or animal) and a sign to be understood by others. The moon-shaped mark on a horse's head and Odysseus' scar are first of all visible marks.[77] There are, however, other examples of *sêmata* which have meaning only for the one who understands them. For example, when lots are cast to determine which of the Achaeans should fight Hector, Ajax puts his *sêma* on the lot like all the other warriors; but at the moment when he wins the lot his *sêma* becomes the divine sign that he is the right person for the fight.[78]

The double function of *sêma* as a mark of a person and as a sign given by, and to, others is necessary for the creation of a hero's identity. As Nagy has shown, *sêmata* are necessary for recognition (*anagnôrisis*). The scar of disguised Odysseus is not simply his mark but a *sêma* for his old nurse and his herdsmen that he is their master.[79] Also the *sêmata* received by Bellerophon from king Proitus when sent into exile are signs by which he is recognised. Bellerophon, having slept with Proitus' wife, is sent into exile with 'murderous signs (*sêmata lugra*) inscribed on a folding tablet'.[80] Although the signs of Bellerophon are given to him on tablets rather than as marks on his body they have the same function as Odysseus' scar: they become the means of a self-disclosure which is necessary to bring about the appropriate alliance (even though this is bad for Bellerophon). They lead to the guest's identification and make him receive the treatment he deserves.[81] A *sêma* attached to a hero is never an absolute sign but needs a mind (*noös*) which is able to recognise the system of signs in which it has meaning.[82] While Eumaeus recognises the scar as the sign that Odysseus has returned, the suitors fail to recognise the many signs which indicate this. When Odysseus begins to kill one of them, 'the fools still did not notice (*ouk enoêsan*) that already the bonds of destruction were fastened on them all'.[83]

A *sêma* is often not simply a mark or drawing but a physical object. So the tombstone is typically referred to as *sêma*. Like other signs, it identifies the dead and serves as a mark for future generations to be seen and understood. The tombstone as a sign seems to have been regarded as a concrete transaction from the past to the present and to the future. There is an interesting association of *sêma* meaning 'tombstone' and *sêma* meaning 'sign' or 'hint' in *Il.* 23. 326 ff. Nestor gives his son a hint (*sêma*) how to win the chariot race during the funeral games of Patroclus. He advises him to pay attention to the tombstone (*sêma*) which serves as the turning point of the course and to take it in a particular way. The *sêma* of a 'mortal who died long ago' (331) is the *sêma* of the father (who is the famous horseman) to his son how to gain honour as a horseman in the games in honour of the newly-dead Patroclus (326). The repetition of *sêma* in different meanings within five lines links the transaction of the father to his son with that of the tombstone to the participants of the funeral games. Or, as Sinos puts it, 'the latent function of the *sêma* (tomb) thus becomes overt: the "hint" becomes the tomb. Likewise, the "tomb" becomes a "hint" of a Dead Man's presence.'[84] If we accept that the presence of the long-dead hero is connected with the newly-dead hero Patroclus in so far as the latter enacts the eternal scheme of *kleos* which the former already embodies, the prizes distributed at his funerary games have a similar function to that of

1. The Scope of Gift Exchange

the tombstone of the long-dead hero.[85] They are the first objects, followed by tombstone and song, preserving the memory of the newly-dead.[86] In the last book of the *Odyssey* Agamemnon describes the funeral of Achilles:

> And then we, the sacred army of Argive spearmen, heaped
> a great and excellent funeral mound up over [Achilles' bones]
> on a strand jutting forward on the broad Hellespont,
> so that it might be seen far over the ocean by men,
> both those who are born now and those who shall be hereafter.
> And your mother asked the gods for beautiful prizes
> and set them up for a contest amid the best of the Achaeans.
> Already you have been present at the burial of many men,
> of warriors; when, because a king has passed away,
> the young men gird themselves and prepare for the prizes.
> But you would have marvelled in your heart most to see those,
> the beautiful prizes that the goddess set up for you,
> Thetis of the silver foot. You were very dear to the gods.
> So you did not lose your name even when you died, Achilles.
> There should be noble renown (*kleos*) for you always among men.[87]

The emphasis on the divine prizes in this, notably epic, memorialisation of Achilles' funeral suggests that the function of prizes, objects of cult, the tombstone of a warrior and epic song were similar. They all transmitted the memory of a dead hero from one generation to the next. The cross-cutting of gifts given in epic narrative, tombstones present to the eyes of the audience of epic and works of art as objects of cult is intimated in the episode of Patroclus' death. While the battle goes on, Achilles' horses, the gifts of the gods, fossilise into a grave stele, contrasting in their eternity and stillness the mortality and movement of the fighting warriors around them:

> ... So they fought on, and the iron tumult
> went up into the brazen sky through the barren bright air.
> But the horses of Aiakides standing apart from the battle
> wept, as they had done since they heard how their charioteer
> had fallen in the dust at the hands of murderous Hector.
> ...
> They were unwilling to go back to the wide passage of Helle
> and the ships, or back into the fighting after the Achaeans,
> but still as stands a grave monument which is set over
> the mounded tomb of a dead man or lady, they stood there
> holding motionless in its place the fair-wrought chariot.
> ...
> As he watched the mourning horses the son of Kronos pitied them,
> and stirred his head and spoke to his own spirit: 'Poor wretches,
> why then did we ever give you to the lord Peleus,
> a mortal man, and you yourselves are immortal and ageless?'[88]

Against this background the particular relationship between gifts and signs in Homeric epic becomes more clear. In book 10 of the *Iliad* Odysseus receives a helmet for his expedition to the Trojan camp:

> And Meriones gave Odysseus a bow and a quiver
> and a sword; and he too put over his head a helmet
> fashioned of leather; on the inside the cap was cross-strung firmly
> with thongs of leather, and on the outer side the white teeth
> of a tusk-shining boar were close sewn one after another
> with craftsmanship and skill; and felt was set in the centre.
> Autolycus, breaking into the close-built house, had stolen it
> from Amyntor, the son of Ormenos, out of Eleon,
> and gave it to Cytherian Amphidamas, at Scandeia;
> Amphidamas gave it in turn to Molus, a gift of guest-friendship,
> and Molos gave it to his son Meriones to carry.
> But at this time it was worn to cover the head of Odysseus.[89]

Both Meriones and Autolycus appear in important functions again in the *Odyssey*. Autolycus is called here Odysseus' grandfather.[90] He was injured when he went on a boar hunt with him which left the scar on his body.[91] Then Odysseus, for whom trickery, thievishness and deceptive story-telling bring about return and *kleos* in the *Odyssey*, inherited these essential qualities from Autolycus who is himself said to have 'excelled all men in thievishness and false oaths'.[92] Finally he received his name from him:

> Then Autolycus answered her, and addressed her:
> My son-in-law and daughter, give him the name, I say.
> I myself come here as one who has been enraged (*odussamenos*) at many
> men and women, throughout the much-nourishing earth,
> and let him be named Man of Wrath: Odysseus. For my part,
> when he reaches his prime, and comes to the great house
> of his mother, to Parnassus where I have my possessions,
> I shall give him some from them and send him back in joy.[93]

Meriones, too, is associated with essential aspects of Odysseus' identity.[94] First, he represents someone who is brave in ambush warfare, for which Odysseus is famous since the Doloneia and which he applies metaphorically throughout the *Odyssey*.[95] Secondly, he stands out as a bowman, beating Teucer at the funeral games of Patroclus in the archery contest.[96] Thirdly, in the so-called 'Cretan lies' Odysseus tells of a number of personal links with Idomeneus which might have been derived from mythical traditions about the relationship between Meriones and Idomeneus:[97] in one story he has killed Idomeneus' son, in another he has been forced by Idomeneus to go to Troy, and in a third he is the younger brother of Idomeneus.[98] All these aspects suggest that the gift of the boar's-tusk helmet is a ritual transaction which invests Odysseus with essential qualities handed down from his ancestors.

Schadewaldt argued thirty years ago that the items which a hero wore

1. The Scope of Gift Exchange

or carried represented his identity and status. A king without his regalia was not a king; a warrior without proper armour was not a warrior, and Odysseus arriving naked at the island of Scheria was not the hero who had captured Troy.[99] This proposition can be extended. Precious objects and clothes were symbols of status because the hero had received them as a gift. Gifts were items of exchange which served to describe a hero among his contemporaries and to later generations. They created both his social status in the narrative of epic and his heroic status among the audience who worshipped and recognised their heroes by the objects of hero cult. One example of an immortal gift passed down from generation to generation is the boar's-tusk helmet. Another gift, this time passed down from the gods to a mortal, is the shield of Achilles. As a work of art it describes, and is an immortal sign of, its owner.[100]

Achilles' shield and its images are an elaborated version of the shields which carried the *sêmata* of a warrior, as can be learnt from late geometric vase painting.[101] The function of the shield is to protect Achilles. When Aeneas and Achilles test the strength of their spears, it exhibits supernatural qualities as it withstands the impact of the spear beyond expectation.[102] Yet its significance goes beyond its outstanding qualities, which after all do not ultimately protect Achilles against death. The shield is a recompense on various levels. On the one hand, it compensates for the lost armour which Achilles had given to Patroclus and Hector had taken when he had killed him. On the other hand, it compensates temporarily for Achilles' vulnerability as it protects him against Hector's attack. Most importantly, however, it serves as a surrogate for his mortal life. It is an immortal work of art made by an immortal and it had symbolised immortality before. For Hephaestus first gave it to Thetis as a sign of gratitude for his life as an immortal which she had restored (18. 408). Being a gift in return for immortality, it then becomes the visual sign of the immortality of the mortal warrior. As Lynn-George writes, 'in its very failure to preserve life the shield signals survival, less for the bearer than as an object which beyond death will, like the tomb, constitute some wonder for the future beholder'.[103]

The drawings on the shield show two cities, one at war, its warriors lying in ambush, and one at peace. Both images represent a world that Achilles abandons in order to attain the glory which epic has designed for him. The moment he decides to rejoin the battle he gives up the return home and the peaceful social world. And the fight in which he kills Hector is an open battle rather than an attack launched from an ambush.[104] His shield is thus the inverse description of his *kleos* as hero, or of 'a social world he cannot take part in'.[105] It identifies Achilles by representing what he has lost at the moment of his death.

In the *Odyssey* there are many objects, especially clothes, which are given as gifts and act as signs of recognition. There is an intimate link between the identification of Odysseus, the garment he puts on and the person who gives him this garment. As Odysseus' identities are manifold the garments he wears are equally varied. Each person with whom he interacts on his return clothes him in a way which not only is useful for him but creates a relationship between him and the donor.[106] When Calypso desires to keep Odysseus away from the world of mortals she gives him the clothes of immortals.[107] The moment he re-enters the world of mortals these clothes weigh heavily, and he replaces them with a veil. This veil is discarded as soon as he touches the shore of Scheria.[108] Having arrived there, Nausicaa, hoping for a husband, clothes him in a garment out of her trousseau. Her mother Arete, in turn, recognises these clothes and, knowing that Odysseus will not become her son-in-law, gives him another set for his return to Ithaca.[109] Circe aims at making Odysseus unmanly while he is naked but when she realises her lack of success she gives him mantle and tunic so that he can depart to the underworld.[110] Athene provides a protective disguise for Odysseus when she gives him clothes that invest him with changing identities. Not only do the gifts of Athene, who is herself best at deceiving, deceive others about Odysseus' true identity, but the deceptive disguise makes Odysseus a deceiver.[111]

Finally, gifts of recognition are part of the description of people to others. Odysseus in disguise describes Odysseus to Penelope. He mentions a gold brooch and tunic which made 'many women look with wonder upon him'. Penelope identifies these as the gifts she herself gave to her husband. When she hears of them from the stranger she 'recognised (*anagnousêi*) as sure ones the signs (*sêmata*) Odysseus [in disguise] gave her'.[112] It is not only significant that Penelope recognises Odysseus by the description of things she once gave to him, but also that these gifts signified to other women that Odysseus was a desirable husband. The gifts endowed Odysseus with the general status of being a good husband, as well as identifying him as the husband of Penelope.[113] This episode gives a full account of the function of gifts as signs: they were objects attached to a person serving as tokens to be recognised both by others as signs of a social role, and by the donor himself as signs of his personal relationship to the recipient.

Gifts and recognition

Often in the *Odyssey* gifts remain unrecognised or fail to create a proper relationship between donor and recipient. These instances can be interpreted as both a decline in the social meaning of gift exchange and its transformation into a more abstract image of exchange between different worlds. The problem of recognition is central and a matter of poetic exploration in the epic text. Furthermore, if the motif of recognising Odysseus stands for the recognition of the cultic role of a hero, the theme obtained a metaphysical dimension for the audience. The recognition scenes are then dramatisations not only of a warrior's return home but also of the recovery of political status and attainment of divine glory. This turns the story of the *Odyssey* into a normative statement about human life, political authority, marriage and life in an *oikos*.[114] The failure of gifts to fulfil their function as tokens of recognition in an interpersonal sense can therefore also be interpreted politically as a failure of gifts to signify status and authority.[115]

Odysseus' wanderings and return bring about a number of situations that require recognition. Yet instead of striving for recognition as king, as hero or as Odysseus, he strives first of all for recognition as *xenos*.[116] Arriving at foreign places, he reveals aspects of himself in the form of stories of his heroic past, or simply by giving his name. In return he asks for gifts and hospitality. Giving credentials and receiving gifts are complementary conditions for the creation of alliances.[117] The fact that valuable objects are given in return for signs of identity, such as a name and a biography, suggests that gifts, names, and stories have a somewhat comparable value in epic.[118] Gifts in their capacity as signs reciprocate the signs of language. This form of reciprocity is expressed in the *Odyssey* above all in episodes which describe the *failure* of creating alliance on the basis of such an exchange.

The impossibility of an alliance between civilised man and the uncivilised world is the essence of the story of the Cyclops. The attempt to communicate with the non-human creature in terms of the human custom of guest-friendship results in a series of perverted exchanges.[119] Although Odysseus never recognises the Cyclops as a human being, he recognises his island as a suitable place for civilised men: '[ships] would have worked to make the island well settled for them, as it is not really bad, and would bear all things in season.'[120] This induces him to approach the Cyclops *as if* he were a human being, which can be taken as a literary strategy of representing norms as they are misunderstood. Odysseus first gives his credentials but not his name:

> We declare we are the men of Agamemnon, son of Atreus,
> the *kleos* of whom is now the greatest under heaven.
> So great a city did he sack, and he destroyed many
> people. And so we have arrived here and come up to your knees
> to see if you provide some guest gift (*xenion*) or otherwise
> give a gift (*dôtinan*), such as is the custom among guest-friends.
> Mighty one, revere the gods. We are your suppliants.[121]

The Cyclops cannot understand the signs of the civilised world, which makes Odysseus respond with a gift and a name which *both* fail to function as signs between guest-friends. The wine he offers to the Cyclops as a guest-gift is called a libation (*loibê*, 9. 349) which signifies the relationship between humans and gods, not between guest-friends. Odysseus' name '*outis*' (nobody), which signifies nothing, destroys communication and alliance altogether. The proper exchange of signs is distorted further by the Cyclops who mistakes Odysseus' gift of human wine as ambrosia which only gods drink (9. 359). In return, Odysseus blinds the Cyclops so as to make recognition (that is, the identification of visual signs) even physically impossible. Interestingly enough, the moment the Cyclops is blinded he recognises Odysseus and utters a curse which is rendered in the same verses as the prophecy made later in the poem by the seer Teiresias, the very person who sees divine signs:

> Grant that the city-sacker Odysseus not go homeward,
> the son of Laertes whose home is in Ithaca.
> But if it is his fate to see his dear ones and arrive
> at his well-established home and his fatherland,
> may he come late and ill, having lost all his companions,
> on someone else's ship, and find troubles at home.[122]

The link which the text itself creates between the Cyclops' curse and the seer's vision confirms that the episode of the Cyclops serves to express the importance of the exchange of signs as a basis for human alliances. The seer embodied to the extreme the ability to read signs and to recognise (*noein, gignôskein*) what they mean.[123]

Another kind of incomplete alliance is formed between Odysseus and the Phaeacians. The Phaeacians represent an abnormal community inasmuch as they are located between two worlds. They live at the intersection of the world of Odysseus' tales and the world to which he returns; and their main function in the poem is to ship Odysseus from one to the other.[124] The two meanings of the island for Odysseus' return are expressed by the ambivalence of his self-representation and, conversely, the kind of recognition he receives from the Phaeacians. They recognise him bit by bit as he offers them parts of his story, yet only after they have mistaken him as a potential husband (Nausicaa) or a trader (Euryalus). Their alliance with him is in the end more successful than that of the Cyclops, but the peaceful members of this society of non-warriors never identify Odysseus as more than a competitor in games.[125] Their inability to exchange on equal terms with Odysseus is paralleled by a discrepancy in their needs. The idea of *xenia* is based on the principle that the present guest will be the future host, yet the Phaeacians do not need a network of guest-friends. They live far off where they do not have to fear that enemies will arrive and attack them, and their voyaging does not require foreign guest-friends since their swift ships can make the longest trip in a single day.[126] While Odysseus needs clothes and hospitality, the Phaeacians need a husband for their king's daughter, a role which Odysseus cannot fill.

Odysseus arrives at the island naked and nameless.[127] When he asks for a rag to wear, Nausicaa gives him a mantle and a tunic out of her trousseau, thereby receiving him into the role of potential husband. Despite the woman's hospitality, and despite his new clothes, Odysseus remains bare of an adequate status. Thus the people in Scheria do not even see him while he walks through their town. It is only in the royal palace,

1. The Scope of Gift Exchange 35

when Alkinous and Arete are alone with Odysseus, that Arete sees the garments which she herself has made. Promptly she inquires who he is. Odysseus still gives only a fragmentary description of himself at this stage, leaving it open whether he is married, whether he is a warrior, and where his *oikos* is. This partial self-disclosure prompts Alkinous to offer him two mutually exclusive gifts: either his daughter in marriage together with a dowry, or an escort home together with guest-gifts. Odysseus has two potential statuses in the eyes of Alkinous, both being considered in terms of the gifts they require. In the course of his stay in Scheria, Odysseus reveals more of himself. He joins the Phaeacians in their feasting, receiving a mantle, a tunic and a talent of gold from each of them. Furthermore, being offended by Euryalus and challenged to a contest by this untypically bellicose Phaeacian, he receives a sword as recompense when Euryalus realises that he was wrong. From the person who has misinterpreted him most at first Odysseus thus gains the most adequate recognition. Finally, Odysseus receives a golden libation cup from Alkinous 'so that he will remember me all his days when he pours in his hall to Zeus and the other gods'.[128] This gift, too, acknowledges Odysseus' status properly as it acknowledges that he will depart and never return to his hosts. The amount of self-revelation Odysseus gives to the Phaeacians thus correlates precisely with the kind of gifts he receives. This surfaces most clearly in a further passage. When Odysseus has gone half way through his stories Alkinous asks him to stay longer and tell more, which will make him 'complete' his gift in return (*pasan dôtinên telesô*).[129] This remark implies that the gifts which Odysseus will take from the Phaeacians are predetermined (and known by the audience of the epics) as well as the fact that he will finish his stories and return home. Yet the gifts are released only gradually. At each stage the gifts he receives reciprocate his self-disclosure, thereby gradually creating his status among the Phaeacians and his heroic status among the audience. The particular problem of the episode among the Phaeacians is the discrepancy between Odysseus' Phaeacian and his personal identity, or the discrepancy between social identity abroad and at home. The Phaeacians can only bestow the former on Odysseus. The poem expresses an uneasy attitude to this problem as it 'reveals the limitations, in this case alarming limitations, to the equation of social and personal identity'.[130]

In Ithaca recognition is more complicated but eventually more successful. As with the Cyclops and among the Phaeacians, Odysseus' re-integration is initiated through the channels of hospitality, guest-friendship and grooming. Since the revelation of Odysseus' identity is more dangerous here than among the Phaeacians, its concealment is more radical. Odysseus is not simply naked but puts on a disguise.[131] In the course of his return, he gradually proceeds towards his recognition as king and master of the household. Each of his hosts offers him a mantle and a tunic which belong to Odysseus' household, if he will provide them with some news about Odysseus. Each thus promises to replace the disguise with Odysseus' own clothes. As Murnaghan observes, the importance attached to the gift of mantle and tunic is not a realistic detail but a literary strategy to dramatise recognition and return. The offer brings to the fore the material function of a gift as a reward with its symbolic meaning as a token of social recognition.[132]

A number of scenes of recognition are based on the assumption that a gift is a sign. Odysseus in disguise tells the swineherd Eumaeus that he knows about Odysseus as he has seen his guest-gifts: 'possessions of bronze and gold and of heavily-wrought iron.'[133] Similarly, as we noted above, Odysseus proves to Penelope that he has seen her husband by describing the brooch which she had given to him.[134] Also, the bow with which Odysseus kills the suitors is a gift from a guest-friend. This gift, too, is a sign which is meant to be recognised by others, although the suitors fail to do so.[135]

It is most important, however, that often the tokens by which Odysseus is recognised are not gifts in a proper sense. To prove to his father that he is his son, Odysseus points out 'gifts' which he had received from him as a boy: 13 pear trees, 10 apple trees, 40 fig trees and 50 vine rows.[136] The fruit trees of an *oikos* are very different from the gifts we know from the *Iliad*: they have never circulated, they are not the work of a craftsman and they are not everlasting. In the *Iliad* trees are invoked as an image of human mortality and the rhythmical recurrence of birth and death generation after generation.[137] Penelope too does not trust in any outward sign of identity. She identifies Odysseus only when he shows her the bed he has made for their marriage. The bed, again, lacks the essential characteristics of a gift: it is fixed to the *oikos*, it is not a conspicuous sign which can be seen by others, it is made by Odysseus himself rather than by a craftsman, and it is made from the wood of the olive, which decays like other organic substances, rather than from an everlasting material.[138] The private relationship between husband and wife is recognised by an object symbolising marriage, mortality and the *oikos*. Also, Telemachus does not recognise his father by the identification of a gift. He simply acknowledges his father when he is told. Goldhill suggests that this is because there are no tokens of identity to be recognised between father and son; the relationship is one of simple acceptance.[139] Euryclea and the herdsmen identify Odysseus by his scar. Again, this is not a gift but a sign inseparably linked to Odysseus' mortal body. His body will decay after his death and is the most typical indication of a human being.[140] It seems that Homer uses ideas associated with gift exchange in hero cult but dismisses gifts as tokens of recognition between living members of *oikos* and *polis*. If the return of Odysseus stands metaphorically for the acceptance of the human condition, as Vidal-Naquet has most convincingly argued, the exclusion of gifts as tokens of recognition in the world to which Odysseus returns convey a clear meaning.[141] Gifts were relegated to the cultic sphere of hero worship and heroic exchange in epic, while in the world of mortals only agrarian

1. The Scope of Gift Exchange

wealth, marriage and procreation could guarantee continuity of life after death, honour and status.[142]

Notes

1. Finley (1978), pp. 61-70, quote p. 66.
2. Donlan (1981), (1981-2); see also Qviller (1981).
3. Herman (1987), see also Murnaghan (1987); Morris (1986).
4. Hooker (1989), esp. p. 90.
5. Dubois (1982), p. 11; see also Lynn-George (1988) and Murnaghan (1987), pp. 91-117, which will be discussed in more detail in the course of this chapter.
6. In the Homeric *Hymns* offerings from men and gods, and between gods themselves, are typically described as gifts (*dôra*) or shares (*gerea*); cf. II. 311, 365 ff. (to Demeter from mankind); 327 (to Demeter from the gods themselves); III. (*Pyth. Ap.*), 190 ff., 270 ff., IV. 127 ff. (from Hermes to the other gods); IV. 291, 442 f., 470 (gifts from Zeus to Hermes); 527 ff. (from Apollo to Hermes); 549 (from mankind to Apollo); 574 (Hades takes no gifts); VI. 246 ff. (treasure stores of the gifts of gods which contain gold, silver, splendid garments and ambrosia); cf. Coldstream (1983) and Hägg (1987) for archaeological evidence.
7. See esp. Nagy (1979), cf. Nagy (1983 b), and Sinos (1980) with Snodgrass (1971), pp. 192 f., 397 f., Coldstream (1977), pp. 346 ff.
8. Hes. *W&D* 157-173; cf. *Aeth.* frgm. 1 (Kinkel). [Clem. Alex. *Strom.* vii. 2. 19.]; cf. Sinos (1980), pp. 18-20.
9. Sinos (1980), pp. 9 f.; cf. Sherratt (1990), pp. 815 f.
10. Morris (1986 a), (1989); see also Coldstream (1983) and Hägg (1987).
11. Finley (1978), p. 145.
12. Donlan (1981-2), p. 137.
13. Homeric criticism has for long been divided as to whether to read the epics as dramatisation of moral conflicts and inconsistencies, or to explain away, as far as possible, contradictions and tensions. Among the studies taken into consideration for the present analysis see esp. Long (1970) and Rowe (1983) against Adkins (1960) and (1971), or Taplin (1980), p. 13 against Finley and Kirk in general. The new criticism exemplified in the works of Nagy (1979), Clay (1983), Edwards (1985), Pucci (1987), Lynn-George (1988), and Goldhill (1991), however, goes a step further in that they regard conflict and contradiction as the consequence of the intertextual debates which are generic to epic poetry.
14. Sherratt (1990), pp. 815 ff.; Hooker (1989), pp. 88 ff.; Morris (1986 b), pp. 124 ff.
15. Snodgrass (1974) against Finley (1978) [1954]. The written version of the epics was probably still changing in later periods, and we should not be too confident that what we read as the *Iliad* and the *Odyssey* were the only versions circulating. Yet a relatively finite stage of composition was most probably reached not later than the 8th century. The latest state of affairs is summarised by Manning (1992).
16. Parry (1971), Lord (1991), pp. 15-37; cf. Kirk (1989), esp. pp. 1-10; and Nagy (1979), pp. 1 ff. For a critical statement see esp. Griffin (1980), pp. 2 f.
17. This becomes particularly clear if one considers the importance of hero cult in the 9th century. See again Coldstream (1977), pp. 341-366; Snodgrass (1971), pp. 389-399; cf. Nagy (1983), pp. 190-191.
18. Morris (1986 b).
19. The older controversy between Finley (1978) and Snodgrass (1974) has now

been taken a step further by the contributions of Morris (1986 b) and Sherratt (1990). Both emphasise that the epics give an historical picture of the ideas of a specific audience. The epics represent rather accurately the unsociological self-definition of warrior elites (Morris (1986 b), pp. 120-129; Sherratt (1990), pp. 815-817). Yet while Morris assumes that the epics reflect the views of an 8th-century audience alone, Sherratt suggests that they contain the ideologies of more than one historical period (Morris (1986) pp. 92 ff.; Sherratt (1990), pp. 817 ff.).

20. See esp. Nagy (1979), Sinos (1980), Clay (1983), Edwards (1985), Pucci (1987), Scully (1990).

21. The rival claims to being 'best' among the Homeric heroes have been discussed frequently. A competition between Achilles and Odysseus is alluded to in the first song of Demodocus (*Od.* 8. 72-82), for which see Nagy (1979), pp. 13-66 and Edwards (1985); the rivalry between Agamemnon and Achilles has been discussed frequently in Homeric criticism and is perhaps most explicit in *Il.* 1. 149-169; Hector's excellence in contrast to that of Achilles is the theme of Redfield (1975).

22. As both Gschnitzer (1965) and Drews (1983), pp. 98 ff. suggest, the term *basileus* no longer referred to a monarchical king by the time of the Dark Age (cf. Morris (1986), p. 99); in times of the early *polis*, political leaders were still referred to as *basileis* but, as we learn from Hesiod, their injustice and abuse of power gave rise to serious criticism. For *basileia* in the early *polis* see Luce (1978), Millett (1984).

23. Coldstream (1977), Snodgrass (1971), (1980).

24. Thomas (1966 a and b), Luce (1978), Morris (1987), pp. 171-210, and for the early 7th century Millett (1984), pp. 103 ff. While Luce and Thomas propose that this was a result of social conflict between the aristocracy and a new social class, Millett and Morris see it rather as a transformation of the distribution of power within a traditional elite.

25. Finley (1978), Adkins (1972 b) and Luce (1978) deny this; against them Morris (1986 b), Scully (1990) and Sherratt (1990), to name only a few participants in a long debate.

26. Finley (1978), pp. 34, 48, 155-157.

27. Morris (1986 b), pp. 102-104 with *Il.* 2. 205 ff., 9. 98 f., 18. 497-508, 23. 485 ff.; *Od.* 3. 244 f., group of elders: *Il.* 1. 237-39, 11. 807; 16. 387; *Od.* 12. 439 f.

28. Seaford (1994), p. 2. For communal ritual see *Il.* 6. 269-311; *Od.* 3. 5-67, 20. 276-278. For patriotism see *Il.* 12. 240-246; cf. 15. 494-497, 16. 830. For a sense of belonging, see above all the references to cities and countries as an element of self-description, cf. *Od.* 15. 404-414, and for the stereotyped enquiry to incoming foreigners where he comes from and where his *polis* is, cf. *Od.* 1. 170.

29. Scully (1990), pp. 4 and 81-99.

30. Ibid., pp. 4-6.

31. See above all Sahlins (1972), pp. 185 ff., Gregory (1982) and Gernet (1981 b).

32. Morris (1986 a) and Millett (1984), (1991 b) have argued against Gregory (1982) who suggests that gift exchange belongs to tribal societies and is replaced by commodity exchange as soon as political institutions and laws of contract emerge. Both Morris and Millett show that forms of gift exchange continued to exist under the conditions of the early *polis* and the identification of gift exchange and tribal organisation was therefore inadequate. Morris and Millett are justified in suggesting on the basis of their material that gift exchange is not exclusive to tribal societies; it is nevertheless significant that they both find vestiges of gift exchange in areas which remained relatively uncontrolled by political institutions:

1. The Scope of Gift Exchange

funeral rituals and neigbourhoods in rural areas. Already Gernet associated gift exchange with myth and pre-legal exchange rather than exchange in the *polis*. It should also be mentioned that Seaford will argue in a forthcoming study that institutionalised political interaction replaced gift exchange in early archaic Greece.

33. For reasons of analytical clarity I start here from the traditional view according to which gift exchange and commodity exchange are strictly opposed modes of exchange; cf. Gregory (1982), Dumont (1980), Hyde (1979), and Sahlins (1972); I shall later depart from that binary model and support the view that in practice the two ideologies are dialectically related, overlap and condition each other; cf. Appadurai (1986), pp. 11 ff., and within a broader social theory Baudrillard (1975), (1981); for gift value and barter see esp. Humphrey and Hugh-Jones (1992), introduction.

34. See esp. Hyde (1979), and Strathern (1984 b).

35. *Il*. 9. 602-605, trans. Lattimore.

36. The classical description of archaic ethics in which moral status is controlled by society rather than an internal conscience is that of Dodds who applied the anthropological distinction between shame cultures and guilt cultures to ancient Greece. See Dodds (1951), esp. pp. 17 f. Adkins (1960 a) adopted Dodds's approach but carried it too far by, first, associating Dodds's opposition with the rather ill-chosen opposition of competitive and cooperative values, and, secondly, by regarding them as mutually exclusive, or at least bound up with mutually exclusive social systems; cf. Adkins (1960 b). See the critical response by Long (1970) and above all Rowe (1983). Redfield (1975) observes a distinction between *kleos*, *timê* and *kudos* which will be relevant later in this section: *kleos* is the honour which is attached to people and things by stories told about them. *Timê*, by contrast, is a valuation through exchange; the honour of a man can be determined by the value of the gifts that might be given to him or to his relatives in recompense for the loss of him. *Kudos*, finally, is absolute, a gift from the gods like strength for example. While *kleos*, although bestowed after death, remains a gift circulating between humans, *kudos* is divine. See pp. 32-34.

37. *Il*. 9. 116-120. Agamemnon himself asks for a recompense for Chryseis once he hears that Apollo wishes to take her away from him; see *Il*. 1. 116-120.

38. *Il*. 9. 632-636; see also 11. 131 ff. where Peisander and Hippolochos supplicate Agamemnon with the offer of a ransom for their lives.

39. *Il*. 9. 411-416.

40. Lynn-George (1988), p. 154. Lynn-George's analysis 'Mortal Loss and Epic Compensation' (ch. 3 in (1988)) provides the critical background for the following argument.

41. *Il*. 9. 388-409. See also Nagy (1979), esp. pp. 184 ff., Lynn-George (1988), pp. 153-177 and Goldhill (1991), pp. 72-93.

42. *Il*. 1. 210-215.

43. *Il*. 9. 266-304; cf. Lynn-George (1988), pp. 159-174; Gouldner (1960) stresses that the 'indeterminacy [of gift exchange] enables the norm of reciprocity to perform some of its most important system-stabilising functions'. It is interesting to note, furthermore, that Achilles promises Agamemnon gifts of unspecific number but specific in timing. When he asks Agamemnon to give Chryseis up to Apollo he says (*Il*. 1. 125-130):

How shall the great-hearted Achaeans give you a prize (*geras*) now?
There is no great store of things lying about I know of.

> But what we took from the cities by storm has been distributed; it is
> unbecoming for the people to call back things once given.
> No, for the present give the girl back to the god; we Achaeans
> three and four times over will repay you, if ever Zeus gives
> into our hands the strong-walled citadel of Troy to be plundered.

Yet there is a hint at the finite stock of gifts which human beings are able to distribute; if this were not the case, the Achaeans could pay Agamemnon immediately. Also, the three- and four-fold gifts will only be available when Zeus gives Troy to the Achaeans. Note that Agamemnon is as unwilling to accept this human offer as Achilles is (ll. 130-135).

44. *Il*. 9. 595-600.

45. *Il*. 12. 310-321.

46. Note that Achilles was not as foolish before he had suffered the injustice of Agamemnon; as quoted in note 43 above, he offers recompense from the Achaeans if Agamemnon pays to the god Apollo; promising recompense for Agamemnon if he pays Chryseis to the god, he links the cycle of exchange between humans with the one between humans and gods; see *Il*. 9. 122-129.

47. The withdrawal leads to the loss of all his ties of *philia* (which was equal to death, see below, ch. 2) to a complete loss of honour which he still tries to maintain by sending Patroclus into battle instead of him, and to the loss of even his closest friend, which in turn makes his own life worthless; cf. *Il*. 9. 701 f., 16. 80 ff., 18. 100 ff.

48. *Il*. 1. 352-355.

49. Lynn-George (1988), p. 161.

50. See Lynn-George (1988), pp. 170-174, against the view that the story of the quarrel between Agamemnon and Achilles told in books 9 and 19 of the *Iliad* were later insertions.

51. The way in which Achilles manipulates the meaning of his own gifts of reconciliation to Agamemnon will be discussed in the next section; for the refusal to share a meal see *Il*. 19. 146 ff. It should be noted that Donlan (1989) takes this passage as saying that Achilles continues to reject the gifts offered to him. However, as in the case of the shared meal which is first deferred and then never explicitly mentioned again, the passage is characterised by ambiguity rather than being a clear statement in either direction. The vagueness in which the scene is clouded indicates the character of the reconciliation ritual as one which remains incomplete to the very end.

52. For which see below, pp. 47 f.

53. *Il*. 18. 79-85, 101-106, 114-116. The question whether Achilles sacrifices his life for Patroclus or for his military companions is unclear in this passage. Sinos (1980), pp. 67 f. argues that as the grief that Achilles feels for Patroclus at his death is reciprocated by the grief of the Achaeans for Achilles, it is ultimately for the Achaeans that he sacrifices his life. Even if this is so, Achilles could not be persuaded by the embassy to rejoin battle (and give his life) for the sake of his *philoi* Achaeans as long as they give honour to Agamemnon who has dishonoured him. See *Il*. 9. 613-615 and Goldhill (1991), pp. 79-106.

54. *Il*. 24. 592-594.

55. Sinos (1980), p. 51.

56. *Il*. 1. 149-169, 9. 337-343, 411-416, 18. 98-104; and Goldhill (1991), pp. 80-88 for the significance of *philia* in Achilles' final choice.

57. Sinos (1980), pp. 55-75 and below.

1. The Scope of Gift Exchange

58. See esp. *Od.* 9. 615 f.
59. Redfield (1975), pp. 110-119; Scully (1990), pp. 106-109; 122-125.
60. For the contrasting priorities embodied by Achilles and Odysseus see esp. Edwards (1985). Segal (1983) argues that the *Odysseyan* version of *kleos* is an irony of the traditional epic ideal. This may be, but it does not affect my argument.
61. *Il.* 19. 146-148.
62. *Il.* 19. 171-270, esp. 171 f., 245 f.
63. Redfield (1975), p. 208.
64. *Il.* 23. 890-894.
65. Redfield (1975), p. 210.
66. The meaning of the 'pure gift' as an instrument of power and domination is discussed in anthropological perspective by Mauss (1990) [1925] and Sahlins (1972), and in the context of Greek culture by Donlan (1989).
67. *Il.* 6. 120-236.
68. Herman (1987), pp. 41-69, esp. p. 49.
69. *Il.* 6. 232-236.
70. First, it calls for explanation why Glaucus is made to accept the bronze armour at all; then it is particularly striking that the poet remarks on the precise quantitative value of the two sets of armour despite the social symbolism which clearly guides the exchange and which seems to make such a quantitative evaluation of the gifts inappropriate. (For an overview of ancient testimony and modern criticism see Calder (1984), pp. 31 ff. with full bibliography.) Among modern scholars, some have seen Homeric irony behind it; others have regarded the comment as a later addition. Yet others have discovered a deliberate stylistic twist in the juxtaposition of the two different types of evaluation (Leaf (1900), Perry (1937), Levy (1963)). More recent criticism has attempted to link the two problems together. It is argued that there is an *a priori* incongruity between the exchange partners which is simply reinforced by the unequal exchange and the comment of the poet. Finley added a new aspect in arguing that the exchange is not just meant to ridicule Glaucus in particular, but to denigrate the image of the Trojans in general (Finley (1978), esp. pp. 65 f.). Calder, finally, turned the argument round suggesting that Glaucus demonstrated symbolic dominance in out-giving his Achaean guest-friend. Similar behaviour could be observed cross-culturally, and was also represented in the rivalry between Achilles and Agamemnon; Achilles refused the offer of the outrageous number of gifts because he could not accept dominance (Calder (1984), pp. 33 f.). Against Calder one can hold that the case of Glaucus and Diomedes cannot be compared with either rituals of *potlatch* or the instance between Agamemnon and Achilles because the one represents gift exchange between members of different communities, while the others are instances of gift-giving within the same community. While in the former balanced reciprocity seems to be the rule in order not to destroy the delicate alliance, the latter is usually competitive and encourages over-spending (Donlan (1989)). Moreover, if Glaucus indeed acquired symbolic power by outdoing his exchange partner, why does the poet have his wits taken away in order that he should behave in a way which puts him at an advantage?
71. *Il.* 6. 230 f.
72. It has been argued that the ambush of the Achaeans which is planned by Odysseus and Diomedes (*Il.* 10) sets the framework for the representation of Odysseus' specific characteristics, that is his trickery aiming at survival rather than martial death (Edwards (1985)). It may be argued that it also explains Diomedes' action here in book 6. See however *Il.* 11. 369 ff., where Diomedes calls Paris' ambush cowardly and womanish.

73. Herman (1987).
74. *Od.* 18. 282-284, trans. Cook.
75. Mauss (1990) [1925], pp. 47 f. and 12; cf. Sahlins (1972), pp. 149-188.
76. Mauss observed that in gift exchange systems gifts have the function of creating social roles. Gifts being masculine or feminine, representing maternal kin or paternal kin etc., define the recipient as masculine, feminine, related to mother's kin or father's kin. Each transaction on occasions such as childbirth, marriage, funeral or feast not only creates an alliance but also attributes roles (pp. 8-10). In the *potlatch* where a considerable amount of expenditure is made in order to stabilise the power of the donor the same function applies in an extreme form: it is an act of recognition, 'military, juridical, economic, and religious in every sense of the word' (1990 [1925], p. 40).
77. *Il.* 23. 455; *Od.* 23. 73.
78. *Il.* 7. 171-189.
79. *Od.* 23. 73; 21. 217; for Laertes, however, the scar is not a sufficient token of Odysseus' identity (24. 329 ff.); Nagy (1983 a), p. 36.
80. *Il.* 6. 156 ff.
81. Murnaghan (1987), p. 102 n.17 draws a parallel between this story and Odysseus' self-disclosure to the Phaeacians. In both cases the recognition of the incoming stranger identifies the relationship between host and guest as dangerous for one party involved. Odysseus, being the hero who has earned the wrath of Poseidon, causes the destruction of the Phaeacians (13. 159 ff.) while Proitus' brother-in-law destroys Bellerophon once he has recognised who he is. 'The story of Bellerophontes ... is, in a sense, an inverse of this one [Odysseus among the Phaeacians]. There, when the guest is finally questioned and reveals more about himself through a *sêma*, a past enmity is brought to light that leads to danger to the guest from the host rather than danger to the host from the guest.' The parallel suggests that *sêmata* serve as the cause for the particular development of a relationship.
82. Nagy (1983 a), pp. 38-45.
83. *Od.* 22. 31 f.; cf. Nagy (1983), p. 38.
84. Sinos (1980), p. 48.
85. Ibid., pp. 47-53.
86. As Nagy (1983), p. 51, has pointed out, *epê* and *muthoi* are *sêmata* as tombstones and gifts; like the tombstone and gifts they serve social recognition and memory in cult.
87. *Od.* 24. 80-94.
88. *Il.* 17. 424-444.
89. *Il.* 10. 260-271.
90. *Od.* 19. 395. Whether in the *Iliad* the same genealogy is assumed is impossible to tell; see Clay (1983), pp. 54-86 for further discussion.
91. *Od.* 19. 390-406.
92. *Od.* 19. 396.
93. *Od.* 19. 406-412. Note the coincidence of naming and the offer of gifts, which suggests that the two are complementary aspects in the process of defining a person. The translation of *odussamenos* is controversial; it can either mean 'who has been enraged at many', as Cook translates, or it can be translated 'who has been a trouble to many'; for further discussion see Clay (1983), pp. 59 ff.; see also Goldhill (1991) pp. 24-26 with further comments on the link between naming, giving and recognising.
94. See Clay (1983), pp. 85 f.

1. The Scope of Gift Exchange

95. See Edwards (1985), pp. 15-42 for the multiple parallels between ambush warfare and the tactics with which Odysseus' defeats his adversaries.

96. *Il.* 23. 859 ff.

97. The mythical tradition about Meriones is confused and therefore nothing more specific can be said. See however the interesting further material by Clay (1983), pp. 85 f.

98. *Od.* 13. 257 ff.; 14. 192 ff.; 19. 172 ff.

99. Schadewaldt (1959); cf. Fenik (1974).

100. The meaning of the images of the shield has been intensely discussed by scholars; I have made particular use of the discussions of Redfield (1975), Taplin (1980), which includes an overview of the earlier literature, and Lynn-George (1988); yet its relationship to Achilles is hardly ever taken into consideration. See, however, the brief remarks of Goldhill (1991), p. 76 and Dubois (1982), p. 24 f.

101. E.g. Benaki Museum 7675; proto-Corinthian Chigi *olpê* at the Villia Giulia, Rome (Payne, *Protokorinthische Vasenmalerei*, pl. 29). See also pl. 1 b.

102. *Il.* 20. 259-268.

103. Lynn-George (1988), p. 190.

104. The extent to which the rejection of ambush warfare is one of Achilles' particular qualities becomes clear in the contrast and competition between Achilles' and Odysseus' strife for *kleos* represented esp. in their encounter in the first Nekyia of *Od.* 11. 467 ff. See Edwards (1985), *passim*.

105. Goldhill (1991), p. 76.

106. See for the following esp. Block (1985) and Murnaghan (1987), pp. 91 ff.

107. *Od.* 5. 167, 264; cf. 7. 259-265.

108. Ibid. 5. 321, 372, 458 ff.

109. Ibid. 6. 214.

110. Ibid. 10. 301, 341, 365.

111. Rose (1956), Stewart (1976).

112. *Od.* 19. 225-235; 250-256.

113. If gift-giving is parallel to naming (see above *Od.* 19. 409 ff.), then the same function which naming has in the *Odyssey* can be applied to gift-giving. 'Indeed, the *Odyssey* articulates how naming is both referential and at the same time descriptive, authorising, classifying (much as recognition is both a perceptual and a legitimating process)' (Goldhill (1991), p. 36).

114. Vidal-Naquet (1981 b).

115. See Goldhill (1991), pp. 5 ff. for the double function of 'recognition' as both an interpersonal act and a political act of authorisation and legitimisation.

116. It may not be unimportant that the problem of recognition is enacted in the context of *xenia* where gift exchange remained operative during the archaic and classical periods; cf. Herman (1987), *passim* and Murnaghan (1987), pp. 91-117 for the observation that all acts of recognition, identification and failed identification take place in the context of *xenia* or wooing.

117. Murnaghan (1987)

118. See Goldhill (1991) pp. 24-36 for the importance of giving one's name for establishing bonds of *xenia*.

119. For further discussion of the episode along these lines see Goldhill (1991), pp. 31-36.

120. *Od.* 9. 129 ff.

121. *Od.* 9. 263-269.

122. *Od.* 9. 530-535; cf. 11. 114-117; the utterances of Teiresias in the underworld are introduced with the word 'I see' (*opse*).

123. See esp. Nagy (1983), p. 38 with *Hymn to Hermes* 213 f.; for the frequent coincidence of mantic powers and blindness see Buxton (1980).
124. Vidal-Naquet (1981 b), pp. 90 ff. with Segal (1962), p. 17.
125. Murnaghan (1987), pp. 101-103.
126. *Od.* 6. 8, 200-205, 270 f., 7. 325 f.; cf. Redfield (1983), p. 242.
127. *Od.* 6. 115 ff.
128. *Od.* 8. 389-431, quote 430 f.
129. *Od.* 11. 351.
130. Murnaghan (1987), p. 103.
131. Ibid., pp. 103-117.
132. Ibid., p. 110. Murnaghan mentions in particular the instance where Eumaeus offers a mantle for one night only (*Od.* 14. 508-517): at this stage recognition cannot yet be permanent.
133. *Od.* 14. 321-325.
134. *Od.* 19. 255 ff.
135. *Od.* 21. 9-39 and 22. 1-32.
136. *Od.* 24. 341-345.
137. *Il.* 6. 145-150; cf. Dubois (1982), pp. 9 ff.
138. *Od.* 23. 187 ff.; cf. Donlan (1981) on the specific mode of production of usual gifts and items of treasure; Vidal-Naquet (1981 b) for the significance of the olive tree as a symbol of Odysseus' return and ownership of *oikos* and land.
139. Goldhill (1991), p. 21.
140. Odysseus' dog, finally, perceives Odysseus immediately without any sign. For a moment endowed with *noös* he realises that Odysseus is nearby. He recognises him in spite of his disguise, and without exchange of words, *Od.* 17. 301; see Goldhill (1991), pp. 12 f. for further discussion of this scene.
141. Vidal-Naquet (1981 b); see also Frame (1978).
142. Murnaghan (1987), pp. 107 ff., makes a similar observation about the different nature of tokens of recognition among members of the family but interprets it differently. Blood ties and sexual relationships between husband and wife fell into a different category from other social relationships as they could not be controlled by culture. 'In each case we are shown that there are aspects of the self that are not accounted for in the social position the hero is able to attain, aspects that testify to the realms, both outside and inside and within civilisation, that society cannot regulate' (p. 117).

2

Ownership and Transfer

Gifts, *philoi* and possessions

Gifts are the property of people. Such property has, however, little to do with property defined by law as a right of subjects over alienable objects. Property rights over a gift are, rather, transitory and determined by the fulfilment of social obligations arising from its acquisition. The intimate link between possession and social meaning of gifts prevents them from becoming objects in the sense the word has acquired in Western thought. As Mauss has suggested, the donor participates in the value of the gift, and it is this aspect which creates the most powerful obligation to reciprocate.[1] Moreover the fact that under certain conditions human beings can become themselves objects of exchange renders persons and things less distinct. The question arises how the boundary between statuses is determined when a metaphysical distinction between subjects (human beings) and objects (things) is absent.

The question is relevant to the epics since here, too, persons and things are not categorically distinguished. Slaves and women feature prominently as objects of exchange, as prizes, or as constituents of booty. The linguistic distinction made in our society between the possession of things and the relationship to people is not made in the epics.[2] As Adkins has pointed out, ownership in the *Iliad* and *Odyssey* is expressed in terms of emotion and reciprocal obligation. Relationships to both people and objects are recognised and expressed in terms of the attachment and obligation felt towards them.[3] This is evidenced most clearly by the adjective *philos*. The semantic field of this key term of the Greek language ranges in the epics from 'beloved' to 'one's own'. The heart, limbs, clothes, treasure, wives, husbands, compatriots, guest-friends and the fatherland all belong to the repertoire of *philos* objects, being at once beloved and owned.[4] The qualities which distinguish a warrior are not just personal qualities but objects attached to his body or belonging to his household as well as friends and kin. A good warrior is marked by *aretê* – moral superiority that can manifest itself in the use of tools, weapons, limbs, portions of land, the treatment of wife, children, servants, allies, suppliants as well as in the use of his heart (*thumos*) or mind (*noös*). All these *aretai* oppose the good (*agathos*) to the bad or the outsider.⁵ In a modern translation, there is a problem in rendering both meanings of *philos* with a single term. In the Homeric text, by contrast, the possessive affection conveyed by the term *philos* is crucial for understanding the conceptual homology of wealth, social status and moral excellence indicative of the world of heroes.

Complementary to the passive term *philos* is the active verb *philein*, meaning 'welcome' or 'treat in a friendly manner'. As Adkins argues, this again is not simply an emotive term for a relationship but an action of appropriation integrating and controlling what a warrior needs: provision of shelter, food, protection against enemies, and *timê*. In having secured his own position by means of *philos* objects and *philia*, the *agathos* relies on these possessions. And owing their possession to others, he is himself obliged to offer them to others.

There are, however, deviations from this pattern. Adkins discusses three passages where only one aspect of the term *philos* is implied. He argues that in the process of epic composition an increasing differentiation of the meaning of property was taking place. A re-examination of the instances which he cites, however, suggests that they are not examples of an increasing differentiation between emotional attachment and the concept of ownership, but of disputable claims to ownership because something is lacking. This can either be the emotional bond or the reciprocal obligation necessary for the claim of *philia*. The passages discussed by Adkins are the following: first, *Od.* 11. 326 f. where Odysseus mentions 'hateful Eriphyle who took precious gold in return for her own/beloved husband (*hê chruson philou andros edexato timêenta*)'; secondly, *Il.* 9. 146 where Achilles is offered the chance to 'lead away the one [of Agamemnon's daughters] that he loves/welcomes as his own (*hên k'etheleîsi philên*), with no brideprice (*anahednon*)'; and thirdly, *Il.* 3. 136 ff. where Iris explains to Helen

> But Menelaos the warlike (*rhêiphilos machês*) and Alexandros will fight
> with long spears against each other for your possession.
> You shall be called beloved/own (*philê*) wife of the man who wins you
> (*nikêsanti*).

In all three passages the moral claim to the property which is called *philos* or *philê* is in question. Is Eriphyle's husband really her own/dear if she exchanges him for gold (*chruson ... edexato*)? Will Achilles ever lead Agamemnon's daughter home as his own/dear wife if he has received her without giving a brideprice (*anahednon*)? Will Helen ever be a proper wife to either the one who only loves/welcomes battle (*rhêiphilos machês*) or the one who has won her in battle like a captive? In all cases the term *philos* is put next to the expression which seriously weakens the claim of ownership. In the first passage it stands between *chruson ... edexato*, 'took gold

2. Ownership and Transfer

in exchange for'; in the second it is put before *anahednon*, 'without a brideprice'; and in the last it follows *nikêsanti*, 'won with a spear'. As we shall see, the question of the value of a wife (or slave) was determined by the mode of her acquisition. It is one of the crucial questions in the epics whether a woman 'won with the spear' like other booty, or given 'without brideprice' like a gift of recompense, or exchanged for gold, could acquire the status of a legitimate wife. The reason the two meanings of *philos* become mutually exclusive in the passages quoted is therefore not necessarily an indication of an emerging separation of the concept of ownership from that of love. Rather they express the problems that emerged when the rules of exchange which defined the status of any particular thing or person were not observed.

The strongest relationship of love and ownership is that between Achilles and Patroclus. In this relationship we can see not only the power of obligations resulting from *philia* but also the extent to which a *philos* object – in this case a person – was part of the owner/lover/relative. Sinos has argued in some detail that Patroclus is part of Achilles' *psuchê*, that is, an element of that part of the body which was thought to survive after death and which was worshipped in ancestor and hero cults.[6] Patroclus is Achilles' attendant (*therapôn*) in battle, which seems to imply that he cannot survive without him. The moment he goes off into the fighting on his own he becomes vulnerable and dies. Achilles, for his part, in avenging Patroclus who died in his place (and wore his armour) restores his heroic identity by this act.[7] The fact that Patroclus participates in Achilles' identity is indicated in many ways. First, on a visual level, when the Trojans mistake Patroclus for Achilles as he enters the fighting.[8] Secondly, on a social level, when Patroclus is called Achilles' *therapôn*, which Sinos suggests can be something like a 'ritual substitute'.[9] Achilles seems to express this relationship between himself and Patroclus when praying that the gods may help Patroclus while he fights without him:

> Make brave the heart inside his breast, so that even Hector
> will find out whether our henchman (*therapôn*) knows how to fight his battles
> 						by himself,
> or whether his hands rage invincibly only
> those times when I myself go into the grind of the war god.[10]

Thirdly, Patroclus represents that part of Achilles which desires to return home, he is himself a Myrmidon and a friend of Achilles in Phthia. Patroclus' death marks the end of the option of a peaceful human life and forces Achilles to adopt his heroic identity. The death of Patroclus is thus symbolic of the death of one of Achilles' destinies, the life of a mortal. Sinos concludes: 'Patroclus and Achilles are two unreconcilable aspects of the same character. Defined in terms of Achilles (the major narrative character), Patroclus is the non-epic component. His *ethos* is non-martial, non-

Iliadic. His *ethos* is individual ... He is the Achilles who does not want to come to Troy, who does not want to win *kleos* in war. This is a fundamental aspect of Achilles' nature.'[11]

In the figure of Patroclus we may see a *philos* person participating in the identity of the person to whom he is *philos*. We can now ask whether *philos* objects assumed an equally important role, and whether gifts in particular transferred part of the donor to their recipient.

To begin with, gifts are *philos* objects. As the formulaic line states: *geras ... d' oligon te philon te* (*Il*. 1. 167; cf. *dosis d' oligê te philê te*, *Od*. 14. 58). We have seen how the relationship between a hero and his gifts was not simply emotional but essential to his character. The gift from Meriones to Odysseus was a kind of genealogy of Odysseus himself and explained his character in terms of his ancestors embodied in the gift.

A more detailed history is attached to the bow with which Odysseus kills the suitors and with which he gains *kleos* as a hero.[12] Penelope has to collect it from the remote store-room of the house and it is a typical item of heroic treasure:

> She stepped up on the high stairway of her quarters
> and in her stout hand took hold of the well-curved key;
> and she went on with her serving women into a chamber,
> the last room, where the treasures of her lord were lying,
> bronze and gold and iron that was highly wrought.
> There a springy bow was lying, and also a quiver
> for arrows, and in it were many arrows that bring grief.[13]

Its extraordinary qualities come to the fore only when Odysseus uses it, and only he can use it. Moreover a bow is a rather unusual weapon for Achaeans who were more typically spearmen or swordsmen. Odysseus in the *Iliad* is also a spearman and not known for any achievements in archery. The change from being an *Iliadic* spearman to becoming the *Odysseyan* bowman is part of the reorientation of heroism represented in the story of Odysseus' return. It can be illuminating, therefore, to follow the story of how this change is brought about.

Odysseus obtained bow and arrows from Iphitus the son of Eurytus who was a famous bowman and like the immortals.[14] They were gifts (emphatically put at the beginning of the line, 21. 13) which he received in Messene when collecting a debt owed him by the Lacedaemonians. A relationship of *xenia*, which crossed the boundary between communities, seems to be a highly appropriate context for signifying an exchange which had metaphysical implications.[15] Eckart has argued that the episode at Messene also bears some significant marks of being an initiation ritual. Odysseus, when setting off to Messene, is still a youth; the place where the two young men meet is some way removed from both their homes; and it turns out to be a dangerous area, typical of the liminal spaces in which initiations take place, since on his way back Iphitus is slain by Heracles.[16] In return for the bow, Odysseus gives a sword and a spear, the typical weapons of an Achaean warrior. In receiving the new identity of the *Odysseyan* warrior, he gives up the typical weapons of *Iliadic* warfare. Furthermore, the death of Iphitus on his way back has further implications for the gift exchange between him and Odysseus. Iphitus not only gives his bow and arrows to Odysseus but loses his life at the hand of the ultimate bowman, Heracles. The bow becomes part of Odysseus while its donor ceases to exist.

The exchange between Iphitus and Odysseus not only exemplifies the status of gifts as aspects of character but also shows that some kind of 'inalienability' was attached to the concept of ownership. Mauss' observation that 'in giving the gift a donor gives part of himself' is expressed in an extreme sense by the fate of Iphitus, the donor, who loses his life the moment his bow becomes part of Odysseus.

Women and property

In all gift-exchange systems described in modern ethnographies gift exchange and marriage are closely related. In the epics, too, marriage is described as an extended ceremony of gift-giving, gift-receiving and feasting. Consider, for example, the marriage ceremony which takes place at Menelaus' palace when Telemachus arrives there:

> They found him holding a wedding feast with his many clansmen
> for a son and an excellent daughter in his own house.
> He was sending the girl to the son of rank-breaking Achilles;
> he had betrothed her first in Troy and had nodded
> for her to be given; the gods were fulfilling the marriage.
> He was then sending her off with horses and chariots
> to the famous city of the Myrmidons, whom the man ruled ...[17]

Lévi-Strauss has argued that exogamy and gift exchange are complementary as both are rituals of crossing boundaries by invoking the obligation of reciprocity and recompense. Marriage rituals and gift exchange are part of a network of exchanges in which material values and women are given in exchange for, and together with, each other.[18] From an economic point of view, Lévi-Strauss' assumptions imply that women must be of a value comparable to that of material objects, thus being part of the property (in the modern sense) of their husbands. Yet, as gift value is different from the economic concept of value, so the value of women in gift-exchange systems cannot be viewed in these terms.[19] Thus Strathern writes about the relationship of women and property in two Melanesian tribes:

> Both Hageners and Danbo make certain equations between women and wealth. But I would argue that these have little to do with property in the sense of rights over objects. They are related instead to the way in which wealth items signify aspects of the person. I have suggested that if Hagen

wealth and women have the character of things, this is derived from the manner of symbolisation. The referent remains the 'person'. Such 'things' are not to be understood as objects alienable from the subjective actor: they are aspects of the person with that further quality of detachability which makes them powerful instruments in gift exchange.[20]

The question is, then, first of all whether women are exchanged for, and measured against, gifts in the *Iliad* and the *Odyssey*. Unfortunately the epics do not describe any single system of marriage transfer consistent with ethnographical data. Indeed the representation of marriage in the epics is so 'inconsistent' that it has been an important argument in the debate on the Homeric Question.[21] Of the 28 references which need to be considered in this context three simply describe a woman as *poludôros*, which explains nothing on its own. The epithet may mean that the woman has cost many gifts, or that she has come into the house with many gifts, or simply that she is full of gifts.[22] There are three examples where the father of the woman offers gifts to the groom together with his daughter.[23] In the passage quoted above, moreover, the groom receives gifts at the moment when the daughter moves from her father's household to that of her husband.[24] Two more cases can be added to this category: namely, where Penelope is said to be accompanied by many gifts (*hedna*) when given in marriage to one of the suitors.[25] In three further cases gold, silver and slaves are used by a married woman and are said to have come from her father. These may refer to a trousseau which the woman received personally (*pherna*), rather than a dowry.[26]

Thirteen passages refer to *hedna* in the sense of 'brideprice': that is, gifts from the groom to the father in exchange for the bride. Ten of these examples occur in either formulae or formulaic line-endings.[27] The fact that most of the references to *hedna* paid to the bride's family occur in formulaic lines and epithets suggests that they originate from older stages of epic composition. Three instances where this explanation does not hold have to be discussed in more detail, however. In book 13 of the *Iliad* Idomeneus kills Othryones of Cabesus who was not an inhabitant of Troy but one

> who was newly come in the wake of the rumour of war, and had asked
> Priam for the hand of the loveliest of his daughters,
> Cassandra, without bride price, but had promised a great work for her,
> to drive back the unwilling sons of the Achaeans from Troy land,
> and aged Priam had bent his head in assent, and promised to give her ...[28]

The episode describes a most unusual situation: first, the groom asks to win a wife as a prize for bravery in battle, and secondly, the courted woman does not belong to his own country. The story seems to allude to the fact that Agamemnon offers his daughter to Achilles without a brideprice while Achilles wishes to have Briseis as a wife although she is a captive of war.

2. Ownership and Transfer

Both would be wives not taken from the homeland like, for example, Andromache or Clytemnestra; and both would be won by military achievement rather than in a marriage ritual. Given that Achilles' crucial problem is that possessions (and potential wives) from home on the one hand and prizes won in battle on the other are mutually exclusive, the story of Othryones can only be read as a comment on the story of Achilles. It stands out as the inversion of norms discussed in the *Iliad*; we should therefore be careful not to take it at face value.

The other two exceptions are similarly problematic. In *Od.* 8. 266 Demodocus sings the story of Ares and Aphrodite who make love in Hephaistus' house. The crippled god, being most enraged by the adulterous act, swears that the two shall be stuck together until Aphrodite's father has paid back his *hedna*. This 'crafty scheme' causes nothing but unquenchable laughter among the gods.[29] The final example comes from the description of how the suitors woo Penelope. Eurymachus, it is said, was the most successful of the Achaeans, not only because he gave numerous gifts but also because he increased his *hedna*.[30] This passage, however, cannot be read in isolation from the fact that the entire wooing of Penelope is part of the corrupt and immoral behaviour of the suitors. It is thus difficult to tell whether the suitors follow the proper rules of courtship, or whether their behaviour is as corrupt in this respect as in all others.[31]

To summarise, the *Iliad* and the *Odyssey* contain the following representations of marriage arrangements. First, a system of brideprice which appears largely in formulae and in the narrative of abnormal behaviour. Secondly, gifts from the father of the bride to the groom.[32] Thirdly, gifts from the father to the daughter as part of her *pherna*. And fourthly, gifts given by the groom to the bride before marriage. This rather schematic survey suggests that at the time of the final stage of composition of the epics women were given in marriage together with, not in exchange for, gifts. Yet the conceptual link between gifts and women, as well as their distinction, becomes apparent not so much in an analysis of marriage transfers as in the description of the relationships of specific heroes and their wives or concubines. Since wives, captives, prizes and gifts of recompense are constantly compared and evaluated against one another, the epics seem to play with the idea that their value was, though not the same, at least comparable. Moreover, Helen, Clytemnestra, Chryseis, Briseis, Andromache and Penelope are parallel to the thematic configuration of Agamemnon, Achilles, Hector and Odysseus and participate in the epic description of these heroes. In this particular role they have the same function as heroic treasures and gifts.

In book 9 of the *Iliad* Achilles explains his anger at his prize Briseis being taken away. What reason, he asks, is there for him to fight for the recovery of Menelaus' wife when his beloved prize Briseis is taken away at the will of the king for whom he fights. The comparison of what the loss of Briseis means to Achilles with what the loss of Helen means to the house of Atreus immediately raises the question of the distinction between a woman won as a prize in battle and a wife married at home:

> And why was it that the son of Atreus assembled and led here
> these people? Was it not for the sake of lovely-haired Helen?
> Are the sons of Atreus alone among mortal men the ones
> who love (*phileousi*) their wives? Since any one who is a man, and careful,
> loves her (*phileei*) who is his own and cares for her, even as I now
> loved (*phileon*) this one from my heart, though it was my spear that won her.
> Now that he has deceived me and taken from my hands my prize of honour,
> let him try me no more. I know him well. He will not persuade me.[33]

Lattimore translates *philein*, which occurs three times within four lines in the same metrical position, 'to love', but it is crucial for this passage that the word also implies ownership and obligation. Achilles here questions whether anything *philos* can rightfully be taken away by a king. Not only is the relationship between Achilles and the king at stake but the status of his prize/bride and the meaning of *philia* as a relationship between man and woman. He compares the status of Helen with that of Briseis, which seems at first absurd. Yet the moral status of Helen, who has broken the reciprocal bond of *philia* to her husband, is more questionable than that of Briseis. The latter mourns over the dead body of Patroclus and thanks him for his promise to make her Achilles' wife:

> The husband on whom my father and honoured mother bestowed me
> I saw before my city lying torn with the sharp bronze,
> and my three brothers, whom a single mother bore with me
> and who were close to me, all went on one day to destruction.
> And yet you would not let me sorrow, when swift Achilles had cut down
> my husband, and sacked the city of godlike Mynes,
> but said you would make me godlike Achilles'
> lawful wedded wife, take me back in the ships
> to Phthia, and formalise my marriage among the Myrmidons.[34]

In her grief over Patroclus Briseis fulfils two obligations at once. First, by mourning the death of the warrior, she fulfils the proper female duty towards a dead warrior, and secondly, by agreeing to become Achilles' wife, she helps to strengthen the bond between the two friends. By the same token, her own status shifts from being a captive or prize to being a wife given in marriage legitimately. Finally, her speech tacitly contrasts Achilles' relationship to Agamemnon with his relationship to Patroclus, as the one gave her as a prize in the camp, while the other would have given her as a wife at home. The status (or value) of Briseis oscillates between wife and prize, subject and object, according to the relationship between the exchanging partners and the context in which she is given.

In his speech to Achilles Ajax reduces the value of Briseis to a level that is below that of any kin or friend. Why, he asks, does Achilles reject the

2. Ownership and Transfer

friendship of his companions, reject the recompense which people accept for the murder of kin, and reject seven slave girls in favour of a single one:

> He is hard, and does not remember that friends' affection
> wherein we honoured him by the ships, far beyond all others.
> Pitiless. And yet a man takes from his brother's slayer
> the blood price, or the price of a child who was killed, and the guilty
> one, when he has largely repaid, stays still in the country,
> and the injured man's heart is curbed, and his pride, and his anger
> when he has taken the price; but the gods put in your breast a spirit
> not to be placated, bad, for the sake of one single
> girl. Yet now we offer you seven, surpassingly lovely, and much beside
> these.[35]

Phoenix invokes the story of a long-dead hero in order to provide a model for Achilles' behaviour. Meleager having withdrawn from the defence of his city was, like Achilles, approached by his friends to change his mind. Yet neither the obligation towards his companions nor the value of the gifts they offered could move him. Only his love of, or obligation to, his wife Cleopatra was strong enough to persuade him to re-enter the battle.[36] The story of Meleager parallels that of Achilles just as the role of Meleager's friends is similar to the role of the embassy, and Cleopatra's to that of both Briseis and Patroclus. The link between Cleopatra and Patroclus is created by the similarity of their names and the fact that it is only they who can change the mind of a stubborn man.[37] In Phoenix's speech, however, it is Briseis who takes the place of Cleopatra: just as she is more *philê* to Meleager than all his other companions, so Briseis is more *philê* to Achilles than the Achaeans.[38] The comparison of the relationships between Achilles and Patroclus, Achilles and Briseis, and Meleager and Cleopatra creates confusion over the conceptual distinctions between a wife, a beloved possession and a personal friend. The comparison of the love towards women with obligations to companions and the value of recompense in the form of gifts (including concubines) suggests that the embassy scene negotiates a hierarchy of values across the boundary of persons and things.

If Hector's priorities can be taken as the model of heroic ties of affection and obligation, then the love of a wife is to be more highly valued than that of kin, elders and finally warrior companions.[39] Achilles, by contrast, suggests that the status of a wife should be compared with that of a concubine won as a prize, and each to that of a *philos* who is, as has been argued above, part of oneself. In this construction the real social difference between wife and slave-girl is diminished and they both become objects of affection and possession. Insofar as Cleopatra and Patroclus occupy the same space in the story of Meleager and that of Achilles, the value of a wife is compared with that of a male friend who, in the case of Patroclus, is part of his friend's *psychê*. This meaning attached to marriage is particularly evident in Penelope's role in the *Odyssey*, to which I will turn in conclusion.

Penelope contrasts with both Andromache and Cleopatra in living away from the site of warfare. She contrasts also with Clytemnestra in staying faithful until her husband returns home. And she contrasts with Briseis in being married in a proper marriage ritual. Odysseus contrasts with Achilles in achieving *kleos* by returning to his wife, and he contrasts with Agamemnon by not being killed on his return. The faith of Penelope thus stands for the characteristics of Odysseus which make him triumph over both Achilles and Agamemnon, and which distinguish him from Hector or Meleager. Her faith is thus not a quality which defines her but one which supports the heroism associated with Odysseus. At the centre of the *Odyssey* stands the meaning of marriage and the *oikos*, not the character of Penelope. Just as Patroclus does not gain *kleos* himself but acts as a key to Achilles' *kleos*, so Penelope is only the key to Odysseus' *kleos* without gaining it herself. In the Nekyia of book 24 the soul of Agamemnon says to Odysseus:

> Truly, you have won a wife of great excellence.
> How good was the mind of blameless Penelope,
> daughter of Icarius, who remembered Odysseus well,
> her wedded husband! And so the fame (*kleos*) of her excellence
> shall never die. The immortals shall make for men on the earth
> a delightful song about constant Penelope.[40]

Penelope is identified with Odysseus' *kleos* on another occasion. When Odysseus enters her house as a stranger he addresses her:

> My good woman, no one among mortals on the boundless earth
> would find fault with you. Your renown reaches broad heaven,
> as though of some blameless king who in a god-fearing way
> holds sway over numerous and valiant men
> who upholds good laws, and his black earth produces
> wheat and barley, and his trees are laden with fruit.
> His sheep bear young without fail, and the sea provides fish
> from his good leadership, and the people excel under him.[41]

The comparison of Penelope's *kleos* with that of a king qualifies it as an example of what Foley has called a reverse simile.[42] In such situations the simile gains priority over the description which it should only support. The reverse simile at this moment is in fact a textual strategy to describe the qualities of Odysseus within a simile on Penelope's qualities.[43]

Similarly, Penelope stands proxy for the qualities of Odysseus when she addresses Odysseus in disguise. Offering him hospitality, she states that he who offers hospitality to strangers will be blameless and his fame will spread in turn. Yet a few lines earlier she had proclaimed that Odysseus alone would be able to provide proper hospitality.[44] Thus once again, by associating fame with Penelope, the text spreads the fame of Odysseus.

Women, and wives in particular, symbolise the qualities of the heroes in epic. This makes their meaning similar to that of gifts. But they were not as directly associated with a cycle of exchange as they are in many working gift-exchange systems. We are after all dealing with a text full of images, not with a social reality. The particular status of women between subject and object is best explained by the semantic range of *philos/philê*. The double meaning of *philia* made equations between the possession of things and the love/obligation felt towards people possible, but it also required love/obligation and ownership to be in harmony. Thus the bad wife who felt no obligation towards her husband, or towards whom no obligation was felt, was a thing which could be more or less totally alienated, given away without further consequences. While the truly loved, the truly owned and the truly obliged was, although not independent, equal to the person of the hero.[45] The status of women between subject and object was thus a matter of moral evaluation, which, as I hope has become clear, emerged in a differentiated set of exchange situations.

Notes

1. Mauss (1990) [1925], pp. 47-48, 12.
2. Even in later Greek history, a precise definition of different types of rights which a person can acquire either over a person or a thing is conspicuously absent; Todd (1993); cf. Harrison (1968), pp. 228-243.
3. Adkins (1963). Although I am following Adkins' analysis, it should be pointed out that the conclusions which he draws from his material are problematic. First, he relates Homeric *philia* to his concept of 'cooperative values' and then suggests an opposition between *philia* and 'competitive values'. *Philia* seems to be not only desirable in those aspects of heroic life where cooperation is necessary and where cooperative values replace egotistic competition. As Long (1970) and Rowe (1983) have shown in more detail, the strict dichotomy of cooperative and competitive values is ill-conceived. Secondly, in relating the emotional concern with property to a general concern for 'self-preservation and survival', Adkins links the values of epic too directly with the reality of an historical social world. Given that heroic poetry is concerned only with a specific class of humans, and was relevant only for a small elite, the meaning of heroic property must be considered within this context. The epics discuss not simply physical survival, but social survival, which meant the justification of the power of an elite audience. On *philos* being an emotive rather than a possessive adjective, see also Benveniste (1969) vol. I, pp. 335-353.
4. Adkins (1963), pp. 31-34 and *Il.* 11. 407; 13. 85 (limbs and heart); *Il.* 2. 261; *Od.* 8. 277 (clothes and marriage bed); *Il.* 1. 167; *Od.* 14. 58 (prizes and gifts); *Od.* 17. 417; 14. 388 (friends and *xenoi*); *Il.* 2. 178 (fatherland); wives and husbands are *philos* regularly.
5. Adkins (1963), p. 33; cf. (1960 a), pp. 34 ff.
6. Sinos (1980), p. 74 and *Threni* VII. 1-5 fr. 133 (Snell-Maehler).
7. Sinos (1980), pp. 33-37, 67 f., 75-77, and *Il.* 18. 98-129 where Achilles explains to his mother Thetis why he has to abandon his return home and seek *kleos* in battle.
8. *Il.* 16. 282.
9. Sinos draws a link between Greek *therapôn* and Hittite *tarpassa-/tarp(an)alli-* meaning ritual substitute. Whether this linguistic relation is valid

depends on whether common roots of the two languages can be assumed or not. The question must be left open here; see Sinos (1980), p. 30 referring to N. van Broch, 'Substitution rituelle', *Revue Hittite et Asianique* 65/1959, pp. 117-146.

10. *Il.* 16. 241-245.

11. Sinos (1980), p. 75.

12. The Mnestophoria is the most *Iliadic* act of heroism of the *Odysseyan* hero; cf. Edwards (1985). The weapon with which this act is fulfilled is therefore an essential symbol of heroic action as defined by epic.

13. *Od.* 21. 8-12.

14. *Od.* 21. 13-40.

15. So Murray in Coldstream (1983), p. 207.

16. Eckart (1963); cf. Vidal-Naquet (1981 a). Similar links to ephebic rituals can be seen in Telemachus' trip to Sparta.

17. *Od.* 4. 3-9.

18. Lévi-Strauss (1969) [1949], esp. pp. 69-85 and 269-309.

19. This was the common mistake implied in the very term 'Kaufehe' against which Finley rightly argued in (1981 b).

20. Strathern (1984 b), p. 172.

21. See esp. Snodgrass (1974). For a discussion of marriage arrangements in ancient Greece see Lacey (1968), Vernant (1980), pp. 45-70, Finley (1981 b), Just (1989), pp. 70-75 and 76-104; see also Goody (1975), (1990) and Rowlands (1980). Against Snodgrass Morris (1986 b) argues that there is a clear pattern of marriage arrangements in the two epics. The customary institution at the time of Homer was brideprice. He re-interprets 14 passages which tell of a flow of gifts from the bride's family to the groom. Although Morris' contention that Homer does not describe any instance where a dowry is paid is worth considering, his conclusion that only a brideprice system was known to Homer is quite unconvincing. The strongest evidence against Morris seems to me *Od.* 2. 53 (discussed further below) which he quotes in a misleadingly abbreviated way.

22. *Il.* 8. 251, 394; *Od.* 24. 294.

23. Agamemnon to Achilles, Alcinous to Odysseus and the Lycian king to Bellephoron. *Il.* 9. 146-148; *Od.* 7. 134; *Il.* 6. 192-195.

24. *Od.* 4. 3-9.

25. *Od.* 1. 277 f., 2. 53; Morris argues that the first three cases describe nothing but further gift-giving between the men involved which is not directly concerned with the property transfer necessary for marriage; *Od.* 2. 53 may be ambivalent, but in 1. 277 f. the text says explicitly *heedna polla mal' hossa eoike philês epi paidos hepesthai*. Morris fails to quote the second half of the line.

26. Morris (1986 b), pp. 108 f. and *Il.* 22. 51 (Laothoe ransoming her sons with the wealth her father has left), *Od.* 4. 736; 23. 228 (both Penelope's slave attendants). The case of *Il.* 22. 51 can hardly be taken as a faithful description of the human social world.

27. *Il.* 11. 243 (*polla d' edôke*, 16. 178 (*porôn hedna*); *Od.* 11. 282; *Il.* 16. 190; *Il.* 20. 472 (*epei pore muria hedna*), *Od.* 19. 529 (*porôn apereisia hedna*), *Od.* 15. 367 (*muri' helonto*); formulaic repetition in *Od.* 21. 161 f. = 16. 391 f.

28. *Il.* 13. 364-369.

29. *Od.* 8. 318-327.

30. *Od.* 15. 16; cf. 18. 278.

31. Note also that Penelope does not accept the gifts with the respect that would be expected but treats them as mere booty; see *Od.* 18. 272-284.

32. Which may, however, not be the same ritual as the transfer of a dowry (*proix*) in classical times; cf. Morris (1986 b), pp. 108 f.

33. *Il.* 9. 338-345.
34. *Il.* 19. 291-299.
35. *Il.* 9. 630-639.
36. *Il.* 9. 530-601.
37. See Sinos (1980) pp. 67-70 for the parallel status of Patroclus and Cleopatra, and the association of both their names (*Patro-kleês; Kleo(s)-patra*) with ancestor worship.
38. Nagy (1979), p. 108.
39. *Il.* 6. 450 ff.; cf. Sinos (1980), p. 41.
40. *Od.* 24. 193-198.
41. *Od.* 19. 106-114.
42. Foley (1978), pp. 11 ff.
43. It must be mentioned in this context that Odysseus is compared to a virtuous woman in *Od.* 8. 522-530.

> This did the renowned singer sing. And Odysseus
> melted, and a tear from under his eylids wet his cheeks,
> as a woman weeps embracing her beloved husband
> who has fallen before his own city and his own people,
> warding off from city and children the pitiless day,
> as she sees the man dying and breathing heavily,
> And falls down upon him and piercingly shrieks.

Yet this is not a direct reference to Penelope. It is rather part of a generalising rhetoric on the relationship between husbands and wives.
44. *Od.* 19. 329-334; 314-316.
45. Felson-Rubin (1993), pp. 165 ff., stresses the equality between husband and wife in the epics. She argues that not only is Penelope defined through Odysseus but he too gains identity only through her. Although the argument is convincing, we should remember that the epics ultimately aim at the definition of the male hero thus giving priority to the representation of the male through the female.

3

Kleos and Commerce in the *Odyssey*

Commerce and commodities

There is no discussion of trade and commerce in the *Odyssey*. Yet, as tropes for Odysseus *polutropos*, they are part of the imagery of the text. On his journey and back at Ithaca Odysseus, the man of many turns, is compared to a trader and wandering stranger who has to tell stories for a reward. In the ambivalence of Odysseus' appearance lies a story which is normative. It singles out the conditions of life in an *oikos* as the norm that triumphs over its perversions.[1]

The language of the poem endorses the polytropy. *Prêtêr*, *prêxis* and *pernêmi* may refer to traders, trade and purchase, especially of slaves and booty; *ônon* is used twice for transactions which take place outside a social context; *phortos* is used for the cargo of a *prêtêr* who seeks gain (*kerdos*), and *hodaia* for his return cargo; yet all these terms for specialised transactions rely on further assumptions about the moral context in which they are used. The vagueness of terms is exploited for the rhetoric of the text. It opens up the question of the interdependence of action and its context, of how the status and intentions of the transacting partners, and the objects they exchange, validate each other.[2]

The archaeological material of the 9th and 8th centuries suggests that there was an extensive network of exchange in the Mediterranean, and a visible orientation of communities towards the sea from the beginning of the 8th century onwards. Yet there is no evidence of special trading posts or harbours on the Greek mainland, or signs of a special type of trading vessel.[3] The lack of a clear articulation of trade and commerce in the early Iron Age has led to various interpretations. Mele has argued that there were two kinds of trade, and a conflict between a class of non-professional aristocratic traders and a rising commercial class. Trade was not by definition a negative pursuit in the eyes of the agrarian elite; the exchanges over distance which aristocrats undertook could be distinguished from commercial trade as aiming at the increase of an *oikos*. The typical *prêtêres*, by contrast, were regarded as motivated by gain for its own sake, which then flowed back into trade.[4] Morris argued that there were two kinds of exchange distinguished by their social context and rules. Trade proper accounted only for a fraction of exchange, while a considerable amount of material goods was transferred in the form of gift exchange. The ideological difference between the expeditions of aristocrats and trade proper was by no means negligible; in fact the two pursuits, despite being similar in effect, were constructed entirely differently.[5]

Both arguments are based on the assumption that trade is a clearly defined activity which was distinguished at all times socially (Mele) or ideologically (Morris) from other forms of exchange. The imagery of the *Odyssey* suggests, however, that such distinctions were by no means certain. If Odysseus protests against being taken for a trader, this can hardly be taken literally as a social *faux pas* on the part of a Phaeacian who does not recognise who he is. The text draws attention rather to the confusion which arises when the context in which a person exchanges is uncertain. If there was a network of gift trade in archaic Greece, which there may well have been, the epics are not the place to look for evidence. There was a gap between the epic description of heroic society and the condition of human beings who had to provide for themselves in order to survive. The *Odyssey* dramatises that difference. One of the heroic ideals was to dispense with human food as the immortals did. Being above all concerned with bridging life and death, the traditional hero of epic had other needs than those of people whose life ended with death. In the *Odyssey* the audience was confronted with a new type of value which took into consideration the conditions of mortal life and the desire to survive.[6] Inasmuch as this type of value expressed the desire to escape death, the *Iliadic* meaning of gifts as the recompense for the loss of life was inappropriate to the concerns of the *Odyssey*.

The *Odyssey* does not break entirely with the symbolic system of heroic poetry. Odysseus gathers his means of survival in contexts which were typically associated with gift exchange: guest-friendship and feasts. The means of survival that he seeks are usually not food but clothes, which re-invest him with human status. This seems to be a strategy related to the genre of epic. Since Odysseus acts both as a hero and as a ordinary mortal he is expected to gather the gifts which identify him as a hero on the one hand, but he uses them for the purposes of mortal life on the other. The gift in the *Odyssey* is thus a rather hybrid notion. The *Odyssey* represents Odysseus' search for the means of survival as an aspect of cunning: he survives because he is *kerdaleos*, meaning both 'wily' and 'eager for gain'.

Odysseus' sense of *kerdos* makes him look like a trader, and his emphasis on the needs of life makes him look like a beggar. The *Odyssey* suggests these comparisons by the motif of disguise. Odysseus not only appears to act like a beggar but even looks like a beggar. Yet the text at once makes clear that such comparisons are mistaken, as the disguise is nothing but a cover for the real Odysseus. It thus seems to establish a distinction between deprivation in anthropological terms and deprivation in social terms. Whereas all human beings have to acquire possessions to have a place in the social order, only traders do so for the sake of their own physical survival. The *Odyssey* ends with the conclusion that Odysseus is not motivated by physical needs but by his desire to restore his position in his household. The values he acquires do not satisfy the needs of an individual but the continuity of the social order.

Just as trade does not emerge in a cultural vacuum, so objects of trade (commodities) should be considered as cultural constructs. The anthropologist Igor Kopytoff has emphasised that historians and anthropologists should ask how and why some objects or services come to be defined as commodities while others remain excluded from economic discourse. In a cross-cultural analysis he singles out two aspects of 'commodification' which can help to explain certain distinctions which are made in the *Odyssey*. First, a thing becomes a commodity when it is no longer regarded as singular or unique but becomes commonly available. This is tantamount to the dissolution of the distinction between spheres of exchange which are typical of gift-exchange systems and which usually keep the exchange of particular objects exclusive to certain social classes.[7] Secondly, a thing becomes a commodity when its biography, or history, ceases to be relevant. Slaves, for example, become commodities the moment they are withdrawn from the social context where they were regarded as individuals with a family history. Their capture or sale may later be followed by an increasing integration into the new setting which immediately results in a decrease of their commodity status. They might afterwards become commodities again, by being once more stripped of their social bonds or social context. The same seems to apply to gifts when they become commodities: it is the question of whether the biography or social description of the object contributes to its value that distinguishes a gift from an object of trade.[8]

In the epics there are three items which appear as 'singular' at some stage and as objects of trade at another: people, treasure, and song. All these items shift their status/value according to the context in which they are exchanged and evaluated. If exchanged between friends, they are endowed with all the attributes which gifts usually have. Yet if exchanged between foreigners, they are meaningless objects in the hands of their recipient. This status/value is maintained until they are exchanged and re-evaluated in a new context. The epics can contribute evidence to the anthropological discussion of 'commodification' insofar as they show how the relationship of the exchanging partners, the status/value of the objects of exchange and the meaning of the valuable to the recipient condition each other. Commerce and commodification in the *Odyssey* are part of the debate in which the status of humans, and the value of the objects they need, are defined in opposition to other humans and to the gods.

Kerdos and *kleos*

Odysseyan ideals centre around life in the *oikos* rather than around death and glory in the community of warriors. This is borne out by the different epithets standing out in each poem. While the *Iliad* emphasises the physical appearance and 'holy nature' of the community, the *Odyssey* focuses on the natural conditions of the fatherland for human use and the riches of the *oikos*.[9] But it is indicated above all by the theme of the *Odyssey*, which tells the story of Odysseus' return home and his desire to recover his marriage and *oikos*. The *Odyssey* breaks with the ethics of the *Iliad* which favour, though not unequivocally, the martial life of the warrior and the sacrifice of life for the community as a whole.

Odysseus contrasts with both Achilles and Agamemnon in the heroic qualities he represents. While Agamemnon represents political superiority and Achilles strength in open combat, Odysseus represents cunning (*mêtis*), rational deliberation and planning.[10] As Edwards points out, most of Odysseus' distinctive epithets refer to these qualities: *polumêtis*, *polumêchanos*, *poluphrôn*, *poikilomêtês*.[11] In those episodes in which he plays an important part – the embassy scene, the spying on the Trojan camp, the wrestling contest at Patroclus' funeral games – his distinct characteristics are deployed against his opponents. In the embassy scene he uses a rhetoric which in Achilles' view is typical of a man who 'says one thing but thinks another' (*Il.* 9. 312 f.). In the Doloneia he prepares an ambush which, unlike open combat, demands planning, concealment and cunning (cf. *Il.* 19. 510 ff.) And in a wrestling contest he uses skills and tricks, like an architect in a peaceful society who fits the roof of a house to keep off the force of the wind.[12]

In the *Odyssey* Odysseus achieves his return because of his sense of *kerdos*. This sense subsumes all the skills which he needs to apply in order to be successful: disguise, the construction of fraudulent stories and extracting gifts in the course of his wanderings.[13] His *Odysseyan* sense of *kerdos* is an extension of his *Iliadic mêtis*, which strongly suggests that the changing concept of value must be related to the development of an epic theme, rather than to a changing social world in which the epics were performed. In the earliest occurrences of *kerdos*, Cozzo has argued, its meaning is closely related to *mêtis*. Both refer to the skill of gaining advantage. Like the term *mêtis*, *kerdos* does not necessarily have negative connotations in the epics.[14] There seems nevertheless to be a slight but important distinction between *mêtis* and *kerdos*. While *mêtis* implies the manipulation of, and gaining power over, nature by means of technical tools, *kerdos* denotes the manipulation of, and gaining power over, people by means of trickery. In the famous passages where *mêtis* is contrasted with *biê* (might) it refers to the use of technical tools with which humans win against the power of nature.[15] The woodcutter cuts through the wood with the help of *mêtis* rather than *biê*, with the help of *mêtis* a captain keeps his ship on course, and with *mêtis* one charioteer passes another.[16] The last image, which seems at first ambiguous, in fact points forward to an episode which brings out the contrast between *mêtis* and *kerdos*. In the chariot race during the funeral games Antilochus pulls recklessly into a narrow path which makes Menelaus' horses clash with his, so that Antilochus wins the race. Not by speed but by cunning (*kerdos*) he won the race, comments the poet.[17] Antilochus did not win over nature by the speed of his chariot but tricked Menelaus into disadvantage.

Odysseus has both skills in the *Iliad*, but he also controls their distinction. Entering the wrestling contest of the games against Ajax he is characterised by both epithets – *polumêtis* and *kerdea eidôs* – in the same line.[18] Ajax and Odysseus apply all their technical skills[19] but, in the competition with his military companion, Odysseus is reluctant to win by *kerdos*. So the fight ends in a draw and they share the prize.[20]

Already in the *Iliad* cunning and the desire to gain possessions for home are related aspects of Odysseus' character. Odysseus does not feel the same moral obligation as Agamemnon to take revenge on the Trojans; nor is he torn like Achilles between return and fame. He expresses sympathy for the troops' desire to return but advises them to hold out for the sake of the exploits to be achieved:

> In truth, it is a hard thing to be grieved with the desire for going.
> Any man who stays away one month from his own wife
> with his intricate ship is impatient, one whom the storm winds
> of winter and the sea rising keep back. And for us now
> this is the ninth of the circling years that we wait here. Therefore
> I cannot find fault with the Achaeans for their impatience
> beside the curved ships; yet always it is disgraceful
> to wait long and at the end go home empty-handed.[21]

Redfield probably goes a step too far in calling Odysseus' considerations a 'kind of cost-benefit analysis, weighing present expenditure against hoped for utilities',[22] but the general meaning of Odysseus' speech to the Achaeans is indeed striking. He places the benefits gained by battle for home above the social benefits of glorious fight.

Such priorities are fully expressed in the *Odyssey*. Disguised as a stranger Odysseus reports about himself:

> ... Long ago would Odysseus have been here.
> But this course seemed to him in his heart to be better (*kerdion*):
> to get together goods (*chrêmata*) while going to many lands,
> because Odysseus knows beyond all mortal men
> about great gains (*kerdea*), and no other person might contend with him.[23]

If, as Pucci has argued, the so-called Cretan lies are disguised stories of Odysseus about aspects of himself, then a further passage articulates *Odysseyan* values in contrast to the *Iliad*.[24] In the second story he tells to

3. Kleos and Commerce in the Odyssey

Eumaeus Odysseus describes himself as the illegitimate son of a wealthy Cretan ruler. On the death of his father he inherited only a small *klêros*, but married a wife with a large dowry (*poluklêros*). His lack of property and status was compensated by unsurpassed prowess as a warrior by which he gained respect among the people. Yet neither in battle nor in his house did he seek immortal fame; he resented death in battle, and in the house he did not care about future generations. Instead his mind was on the sea – if not as a merchant, as a warrior:

> ... Work on the field (*erga*) was not dear to me
> or household-tending that raises glorious children.
> No, ships with good oars were always dear to me,
> and battles, and well-made javelins and arrows
> ...
> Nine times I had been a leader of men on swift-faring ships
> Against alien men, and many things fell in my hands.
> Of them, some satisfying things I chose, but got many
> afterwards by lot. At once my house increased, and then
> I became respected and feared among the Cretans.[25]

The emphasis on glorious exploits in warfare as a means of increasing the house contrasts conspicuously with Sarpedon's speech to Glaucus in the *Iliad*. There too a link is made between warfare and prosperity but the link is less direct:

> Glaucus, why is it that you and I are honoured before others
> with pride of place, choice meats and filled wine cups
> in Lycia, and all men look on us as if we were immortals,
> and we are appointed a great piece of land by the banks of Xanthus,
> good land, orchard and vineyard, and ploughland for the planting of wheat?
> Therefore it is our duty in the forefront of the Lycians
> to take our stand, and bear our part in the blazing of battle
> so that a man of these close-armoured Lycians may say of us:
> 'Indeed these are not ignoble men (*ou man akleees*) who are lords of Lycia,
> these kings of ours who feed upon the fat sheep appointed and drink excellent
> sweet wine since indeed there is strength of valour in them ...'[26]

For Sarpedon, being excellent in battle justifies the prosperity of the *oikos* in the eyes of those who supply it with choice meat and wine. In the *Odysseyan* version of prosperity the spoils and prizes of war provide wealth directly without the interference of glory. Inasmuch as they function as an alternative to the *erga* of the *oikos* they lose their function as symbols of *kleos*. In fact there is no mention of fame in Odysseus' Cretan story. The heroes of Troy had fought for *kleos*, which then justified their prosperity, not in order to compensate for insufficient means.

The change of the meaning of prizes and spoils in relation to the *oikos* has direct consequences for the interpretation of gift value in the *Odyssey*. When Telemachus visits Menelaus in Sparta he is offered splendid gifts by the king: three horses, a chariot and a libation cup. But Telemachus refuses the horses:

> As for the gift you would give me, let it be a keepsake.
> I will not bring horses to Ithaca, but I shall rather leave them here
> as an adornment for yourself. You rule a broad plain
> and in it there is much clover and galingale
> wheat in it, and emmer grain, and broad-growing white barley.
> In Ithaca there are no broad courses or any meadow;
> it has pasture for goats and is pleasanter than a horse pasture.
> But none of the islands that lie by the sea has good meadows
> or a place for driving horses, and Ithaca surpasses them all.[27]

In the context of gift exchange the rejection of the gift is an offence against the host and would lead to the termination of the relationship. In the *Odyssey*, by contrast, Menelaus quite willingly changes the offer into something else. Telemachus' reluctance to take the gift offered is accepted, if not approved of. While the social implications of refusing a gift, so important in the *Iliad*, are secondary, the value of the gift for the household comes into focus. Although value remains associated with gifts as works of art (*keimêlia*), the utility of a gift becomes an aspect of its value.

Odysseus' own interest in gifts makes him look like a beggar and trader before he returns to his *oikos*. In disguise, he prophesies to Penelope that Odysseus will be back soon, bringing with him glorious treasure (*keimêlia esthla*) which he begged from the people (*aitizôn ana dêmon*). The same phrase is used when Telemachus recommends to the stranger in Eumaeus' hut that he should go and beg for food from anyone who might give to him.[28] In the peacetime society of the Phaeacians Odysseus, the warrior, is taunted by Euryalus that he does not look like an athlete but a trader:

> No, stranger, I would not say that you were like a man skilled
> in contests of the many sorts that exist among men,
> but like a man who is used to a ship with many oarlocks,
> a leader of sailors who are also merchantmen
> with his mind on a load, an overseer of cargoes
> and of gain got by greed. You do not resemble an athlete.[29]

Odysseus is deeply offended by these remarks. Yet in his retort to Euryalus he reduces the possibility of distinguishing between merchant and hero even further:

> You have not spoken well, stranger; you are like a fool.
> And so the gods do not grant delightful gifts
> to all men, in shape or in mind or in speaking.
> One man is rather insignificant in looks;
> but a god crowns his speech with grace, and men behold him
> and are pleased. And he speaks without faltering,
> with soothing deference, and he stands out in the gathering.

And they look upon him as a god as he goes through the city.
And another man will be like the immortals in looks,
but there is no gracefulness to crown his speech.[30]

In the *Iliad* physical appearance is a sign of moral and social status. Achilles' status is matched by his divine beauty (3. 162-169), Odysseus' by his broad shoulders (3. 192-194) and Agamemnon's by his height (ibid.). Thersites, by contrast, gives a disgraceful speech matched by his ugly looks (2. 216-224).[31] Odysseus, by questioning whether looks are a sign of status, questions a criterion by which he himself is distinguished from a trader. And indeed Euryalus' comparison is not entirely ill-chosen. Disguised as a Cretan, Odysseus himself describes his pursuits in the terminology of trade.[32]

There are further strategies of the text which suggest that Odysseus' and a trader's pursuits are similar, without allowing an entire elision between the two. Characters who model, and are modelled on, Odysseus assume temporarily the image of traders or pirates. So, for example, when Athene first arrives at Ithaca in the disguise of Mentes she gives ambivalent credentials:

> I declare I am Mentes, son of skilful Anchialos,
> and I rule over the Taphians, who are fond of rowing.
> Just now I have come this way by ship, with companions,
> sailing on the wine-faced sea to men of alien tongue,
> to Temesa for bronze, and I carry glittering iron.
> ...
> We declare we are guest friends of one another through our fathers
> originally; if you will go and ask Laertes.[33]

The Taphians, the Greek equivalent of the Phoenicians in the epics, embody trade and commerce. Nevertheless Athene/Mentes is their ruler and above all a guest-friend of Laertes. Her disguise thus invokes and immediately refutes the comparison with traders. Similarly, Telemachus when arriving at Pylos is asked his origins and the purpose of his journey: whether he was travelling on business (*kata prêxin*) or roaming idly (*alalêsthe mapsidiôs*) like pirates who cause evil among people. Telemachus shifts the question towards a different alternative. He says he has come on private business (*prêxis idiê*), not public (*ou dêmios*), thereby distinguishing two kinds of *prêxis* and recovering one as meaningful in the heroic world: he is searching for the *kleos* of his father. However, *idios* puns on *mapsidiôs*, the pursuit of pirates; and the word *alalêmenos* is the same as Eumaeus uses when he talks about wandering beggars who tell false stories, snatching up the rewards for true information.[34] Telemachus' voyage to Nestor and Menelaus has little to do with piracy; nevertheless, being the son of the *polutropos* and receiving gifts which he will never return he suggests a link – if only to dismiss it eventually.

The concern with values which satisfy the needs of the recipient is part of a wider debate on the human condition in the *Odyssey*. As Pucci phrases it, the *Odyssey* 'opens up a series of uncanny connections': the *gastêr* (belly) as a reason for warfare, the returning hero and his need for food, or the Trojan War and its similarities to piratical expeditions.[35] During his voyage home Odysseus is driven by hunger. Hospitality and gift exchange become necessary for satisfying the demands of the *gastêr* rather than for honour alone. Necessity and need (*anankê, chreiô*) drive him from one heroic adventure to the other. Among the Cyclopes, Odysseus demands food, drink and gifts simply because he needs supplies; he approaches Nausicaa to get some clothes like a lion needing food.[36] In the palace of Alcinous he first demands food, and he clearly contrasts this desire with the desires of the heart, the *thumos* which in the *Iliad* drives heroes into battle to seek *kleos*:

> I am not like the immortals who possess broad heaven,
> either in body or form, but I am like mortal men.
> ...
> Permit me to eat dinner, burdened as I am with cares,
> for there is nothing more shameless than the hateful belly
> which bids a man to remember it by compulsion,
> even one which is much worn down and has much sorrow in his mind,
> as I now have sorrow in my mind. It perpetually
> bids me to eat and drink and makes me forget
> all I have undergone and commands me to fill up.[37]

Grief makes Achilles forget food, indeed makes it impossible for him to have any meal among humans, while Odysseus desires food in order to forget. Achilles and Agamemnon had fought for fame and revenge, while Odysseus in the *Odyssey* says that it is the *gastêr* that makes people fight enemies.[38] There is nothing positive in Odysseus' stress on the needs of the belly, which is consistently labelled with epithets of blame.[39] It has nothing to do with the image of heroism which Odysseus enacts, or in fact with the hero Odysseus himself. It is a disguise which, once he is re-established in his *oikos*, is put aside, revealing his true heroic nature. Yet on his journey, he enacts a series of social exchanges which express the constraints of the mortal condition. Marriage and return become the triumph over the adverse conditions which humans suffer as they are humans; implicitly, it is also a social triumph over all those people who travel, never returning and never gaining *kleos*. In the passage in which Athene defines Odysseus there is an interesting blend of *kleos* and *kerdos*. Odysseus' interest in goods useful for the household is driven by his desire for *kleos*. This locates him somewhere between the *Iliadic* hero fighting far away and the *Odysseyan* merchant concerned only with the cargo on his ship:

> Cunning (*kerdaleos*) would he be and deceitful who would over-reach you

in various wiles, and even if a god should confront you.
Versatile-minded wretch, insatiate in wiles, you would not
cease from deceits though you are in your own land,
or from fraudulent stories (*muthôn te klopiôn*) that
from the ground up are dear (*philoi*) to you.
Come let us say no more of this, as both of us are skilled
in shrewdness (*kerdea*), since you are the best of mortals
in plans and in stories, and I among all gods
am famed for planning and shrewdness (*mêti te kleomai kai kerdesin*) ...[40]

From gifts to commodities: captives, treasure and song

In epic, sale is by definition an exchange between strangers. As Finley observed, not once is there a sale transaction which involves either two Greeks or two Trojans.[41] This is supported by the semantic field of the word *pernêmi* and its derivatives *pratêr* and *prasis*. In all its occurrences *pernêmi* denotes transactions abroad; and it always describes the purchase or ransom of a captive. It is probably related to the word *peraô* and *poros*, which never assumed clearly commercial meanings but retained more precisely the connotations of voyage and provisioning.[42] The terminology of buying and selling is the terminology of travelling and exchanging with other people than friends and guest-friends. In the rights which the captor had over the captive, and the transfer of them, the notions of purchase and sale emerged.[43] Once a thing or a person was acquired outside a social context it declined from being a subject, or a personalised item, to being an object. Once human beings were taken as captives their value as persons was extinguished and their biography destroyed. All those things which in sum defined the status of a hero – his property, his armour (or clothes), his ties of *philia*, and his honour – were at once stripped from him. The way captives were treated and objects of sale constituted went hand in hand.

The shifting status of a person from being a subject tied by social bonds to society to being a gift endowed with affective value and finally to being a slave comparable to the value of other objects is well illustrated by the example of Briseis. As a captive she is nothing but a concubine and of less value than seven concubines; as a prize she is an object of love and affection; and the moment the text gives her a speech and reveals that she was meant to re-marry, she also tells about her Trojan past.[44]

A similar shifting status can be observed for items of treasure. In the council of the Trojans Hector describes the decline of Troy to Polydamas:

There was a time when mortal men would speak of the city
of Priam as a place with much gold and much bronze. But now
the lovely treasures (*keimêlia kala*) that lay away in our houses have
                                                                    vanished
and many possessions have been sold (*ktêmata pernamena*) and gone into
                                                                    Phrygia

and into Maionia the lovely when great Zeus was angry.[45]

The praise of the Trojan *keimêlia* as expressions of glory contrasts radically with their value as *ktêmata pernamena*. It shows the interdependence of things and a place of origin; *keimêlia* cannot be sold without ceasing to be *keimêlia*. None of the gifts we hear of in the epics is ever bought. It seems that the crucial prerequisite for the distinction between gifts and objects of sale was whether they had an identity or story attached to them and whether this identity was preserved after they changed hands.

It can hardly be accidental that Eumaeus, a slave, functions as a model of social identity lost and restored. The description of the swineherd is not an accurate social description of a slave but must be interpreted as a literary construction.[46] He is Odysseus' *philos* and his status improves as Odysseus proceeds to recover his position in Ithaca. Their relationship is strictly reciprocal. As Eumaeus treats Odysseus as a *xenos*, offering him hospitality and clothes, so Odysseus eventually re-invests Eumaeus with the status he has lost.[47] When Odysseus is welcomed in the hut he asks Eumaeus who he is. At first the slave calls himself no more than 'someone who wandered far from parents and fatherland' (15. 382). But then he gets the chance to tell that he is the son of a king who ruled an island. Phoenicians had captured and sold him to Laertes. In the household of Laertes his status had improved:

> [Laertes' wife] clothed me in a mantle and a tunic, clothes
> that were very lovely, gave me sandals for my feet
> and sent me off to the fields. And she loved (*philei*) me much in her heart.
> As it is I am now deprived of these things. Yet for me
> the blessed gods foster the work (*ergon*) at which I abide.
> From them have I eaten and drunk and given to respected men (*aidoioisin edoka*).[48]

The fact that he pursues *erga* and gives hospitality to *aidoioi* marks him as a man of social status. Engaging in agriculture, giving hospitality, being *philos* to others and being blessed by the gods were fundamental elements of the self-definition of the archaic elite.[49] Only a wife whom he could marry is notably absent. Having finished his story, his biography is complete and his status restored. And it is from then that Odysseus calls him by name.[50]

Odysseus' return too begins with the request and receipt of clothes and stories. But since his return is fraught with danger he does not simply have no clothes and no story, but arrives in disguise and tells lies, 'disguised stories'.[51] The first Cretan lie he tells to Eumaeus is far removed from his story as a hero of Troy. He describes how he was threatened with being sold and becoming a slave. A Phoenician dealer took him to his home country. But, instead of taking him as a friend, he seized him with the intention of selling him as a slave. On the way, however, their ship was struck by Zeus, and all the passengers fell overboard. A wave carried

3. Kleos and Commerce in the Odyssey

Odysseus to the island of the Thesprotian king who, rather than making him a slave, gave him back his status as a human being by presenting him with a cloak and a tunic. Nevertheless, Odysseus had not yet escaped the danger of slavery. When sent to a guest-friend by the Thesprotian king, again he became the prey of deceitful traders who took his clothes and put him in rags.[52] Yet again he was rescued. The gods removed his bonds and let him swim away from the ship to the coast of Ithaca. This time the recovery of status is decribed as a condition of life: 'The gods concealed me easily. They brought me to the homestead of a man with knowledge. For it is still my fortune to live.'[53]

It is striking that Odysseus is never reduced entirely to the status of a slave. Instead of becoming an object of sale, he becomes a gift between guest-friends: among the Phaeacians, he reports that many of his comrades were killed and sold into slavery by the Egyptians while he alone was given as a gift to a *xenos*.[54] Such stories contain important information about the relative status of gifts and items of sale. Gifts had histories and created obligations, thus being somewhat closer to persons than objects of sale. Human beings could be reduced to that status when captured and sold into slavery. An intermediate stage was to be given away as a gift or prize. Just as Briseis was accorded a high value by being the prize of Achilles, so Odysseus remained a person by being a gift to a guest-friend. In the scale that may theoretically be constructed between people and things (or subjects and objects) gifts ranged somewhere in the middle. The interface of people and things represented by gifts and prizes becomes even more apparent if the status of women is considered once more. As we saw in the last chapter, women for marriage were part of the hero, but they participated in his status to such an extent that they were ranked above other 'properties'. In the literary world of the epics, a woman like Helen for whom a war was fought, a girl like Briseis who was won in a war, and other captives taken as spoil were set in a hierarchy of value. As the story of Briseis suggests, a woman without a biography, without a story about ancestors and kin, could not become a wife, and the attachment that was felt towards her was similar to that towards other prizes or gifts. To return to Kopytoff's model, the distinction between subjects, objects, gifts and commodities has something to do with what a culture decides is 'singular'.[55] Within that model, the different status of objects of sale, slaves, treasure, women and heroes in the epics illustrate 'commodification' as a cultural process. The process is here understood as one of different degrees of 'exchangeability' which were set by the presence of social relationships and the memory of lines of descent. The highest status, attributed only to some heroes, was that of association with divine ancestry. The male hero controlled a network of reciprocal relationships with the gods, friends, kin and property and was not exchangeable. He was the subject rather than an object of exchange, and he was honoured or evaluated by, rather than within, exchange.

We can now turn to the more complicated problem of the commodification of song. The argument is based on the preceding discussion but also aims to support it. Both the *Odyssey* and Odysseus were a song. Song made mortal men immortal heroes whose story was kept alive among future generations. While the content of song immortalised heroes, the poet immortalised himself in the creation and recital of immortal deeds.[56] There was an inseparable link between the poet's fame and the fame of the hero. The role of the bard in the construction of heroic pasts probably gained importance at a time when heroic deeds became more consciously regarded as the inventions of song. As Segal has argued, 'aware of the increasing discrepancies between the heroic world of the epic cycle and the contemporary world of his audience, the poet of the *Odyssey* calls attention to the fact that the glory of heroic deeds exists only through song: it is truly *kleos* in the sense of the tales that men know by hearsay.'[57] The redefinition of the relationship of poet, poetry and the heroes of his songs influenced the value of song and the reciprocities its performance implied.

In a number of scenes in the *Odyssey* bards perform songs about Troy and the fame of the heroes. These songs resemble and contrast with the stories which Odysseus himself tells about his own heroic past and those which he tells in disguise about Odysseus. The text explores different functions of song and the different meanings it has for its author, the heroes of song and the audience. Songs represent different kinds of value inasmuch as their content stands in a different relation to the author, the hero of whom they tell, and the audience. The difference is marked by the different kind of benefit each gains from the songs. Bards give songs to their audience at a feast in exchange for *xenia*. The hero gains *kleos*, while the audience gains pleasure. Odysseus tells his own story in return for reintegration into the society of his guest-friends or into Ithaca. The *Odyssey* draws attention to the similarity between different kinds of narratives by likening Odysseus among the Phaeacians, and at home in disguise, to a bard.[58] At the same time it distinguishes them by distinguishing the reciprocities that take place in the exchange. Demodocus receives *xenia* from the Phaeacians, but from Odysseus he receives the prime piece of meat.[59] As a wandering bard, Odysseus receives mantle and tunic from the slave of the household, but being mistaken for a beggar he receives nothing but alms and abusive language.[60] As Odysseus, finally, he receives the restoration of his status as head of the *oikos* and as a hero.[61] The relationship between singer and audience, the meaning of the song and the kind of reward that it called for were mutually dependent.

The reciprocities of tale-telling take place in the wider context of Odysseus' journey. Throughout the *Odyssey* the offer of gifts and hospitality to those who tell about Troy and the return of Odysseus in either song or narrative functions not only as an obligatory reward but as an offer to receive the author into bonds of *philia* and *xenia*. Odysseus begins his reintegration into Ithaca as a nameless stranger who gradually attaches

3. Kleos and Commerce in the Odyssey

himself to the society of which he is king. The meaning of the ensuing exchanges is defined by Athene who describes Odysseus as *kerdaleos* because of his ability to tell false stories by which he will regain his position in Ithaca and *kleos*.[62] The rewards for his stories will have different meanings, each being related to the degree to which his reintegration has proceeded: first he will receive mantle and tunic, then he will be re-invested with his own clothes and power in Ithaca, and finally he will be invested with the attributes of a hero worthy of *kleos*. Just as the rewards vary depending on what his performances mean to his audience, Odysseus' own status varies according to how and in what context his performances are received. First he is *xenos*, then athlete, warrior and king, and finally hero of epic.

In a series of exchanges following his arrival in Ithaca the shifting status of Odysseus and his stories is dramatised. In Eumaeus' hut he is first nothing but a stranger and his stories are not regarded as true:

> Old man, no wanderer who came here bringing news
> could ever convince his wife and his dear son.
> Yet anyway, wanderers who need sustenance
> tell lies, and they are not willing to speak the truth.
> Whoever in wandering reaches the land of Ithaca
> comes to my mistress and utters deceptive stories.
> She receives them, offers them friendship and asks them for details,
> ...
> And you too, old man, would quickly fashion a story
> If someone gave you a mantle and a tunic and clothes.[63]

The reproach that a singer, seer or wandering story-teller bent the truth in order to gain a reward occurs also at another place in the *Odyssey*. Eurymachus taunts Halithersis that he would not babble false augury if he did not expect a gift (*dôron*) for his *oikos*.[64] Eurymachus' reproach is a parody of the reciprocities between a seer and his public in so far as Halithersis has a different status from that of a wandering seer, which is indicated by the fact that he desires a gift for his treasure rather than food or clothes. It symbolises, rather than reflects directly, the reciprocities which were assumed between author/seer and public in which the content of the story/augury and the status of its donor were together evaluated by the return. Yet the reciprocity can be perverted so that the story becomes a means of earning a living and the reward nothing but the personal gain of the recipient. This pattern goes some way towards the model of commodity exchange (or commerce) where the return is theoretically construed as the motivation for exchange. Yet while in economic theory the demand for an immediate return is constituted as the origin of exchange, in the epics it is morally condemned. 'Commodification' here conceptually implies the condemnation of the one who exchanged commodities.

The episode in Eumaeus' hut continues with Odysseus repeating his claim that Odysseus will return. This time he tells a story which curiously resembles the present situation in Eumaeus' hut. He relates how he once lay in an ambush which he had planned with Odysseus. Everybody had a mantle, only he himself had none. So Odysseus cheated his comrades by a false alarm which made one of them leave his mantle behind as he hurried to the ships.[65] As in the story, Odysseus now lies in an ambush (planned for the suitors); as then, he is in need of a mantle; and, as then, he tells a false story. Eumaeus recognises the story as that of Odysseus, and acknowledges its content by rewarding the stranger with a gift. Outwardly the reciprocities are still those between host and stranger, but implicitly they begin to symbolise the relationship between Odysseus and his friend:

> Old man, the story is excellent that you have told.
> Not a word was unrighteous (*para moiran*) or unprofitable (*nêkerdes*).
> So you shall not want for clothes or for anything else
> of the things that befit a long-suffering suppliant one meets –
> for now. But at dawn you shall bundle your own rags on,
> as there are not many mantles and changes of tunic
> to put on here, just a single one for each mortal man.
> But when the beloved son of Odysseus comes
> he himself will give you clothes, a mantle and tunic
> and will send you wherever your heart and spirit bid.[66]

It is the personal link created between Odysseus and the swineherd which serves to indicate the truth of the story, and, conversely, the evaluation of the story creates that relationship. It is 'profitable' for its recipient both in being true and in creating a relationship. Both aspects are implied in the return. In this exchange the value of the story does not lie in its material return, but in its power to stabilise the personal relationship between narrator and recipient. The gesture of the reward prompted by the story has strengthened Odysseus' social bonds to the household, his recognition as king and fame as a hero. The story of Odysseus in the hut also suggests that wandering poets received gifts and hospitality as tangible signs of their social recognition and fame.

The shifting meaning of different modes of exchange also underlies the encounter between Odysseus and Penelope. As in the hut of the swineherd, the value of the story, the relationship between Odysseus and Penelope and the symbolic value of the reward increase together. While Odysseus proceeds to recover the status he once held in Ithaca, in his tales fiction and truth approach each other.[67] At the same time, the meaning of the reward offered for his stories shifts from being a fee to a wandering story-teller towards being a prize for a hero and a token of recognition. When Odysseus, disguised as a vagrant, tells Penelope that her husband will return, she replies:

3. Kleos and Commerce in the Odyssey

> Would that this saying, stranger, might be brought to pass,
> and then you would soon know friendship and many gifts
> from me, so that a man who met you would call you blessed.
> And yet it seems to me in my heart it will be this way:
> Odysseus will not come home again, nor shall you be granted
> an escort, since there are no masters in the house of the sort
> that Odysseus was among men, if he ever existed,
> to send respectable strangers off and receive them.[68]

Here the gifts would acknowledge only that the stories of the vagrant were true. Then, in the hall, she gives the stranger an opportunity to compete with the bow against the Achaeans; however, not as a rival suitor, but as a competitor in games:

> The stranger here is very large and of a well-knit frame.
> He declares he is by descent a good father's son.
> Come now, give him the well-polished bow, so we may see.
> For this I proclaim and it shall be brought to pass.
> If he does string it and Apollo gives him the praise,
> I shall give him a sharp javelin, a defence against dogs and men,
> and a two-edged sword. I shall give him sandals for his feet
> and send him wherever his heart and spirit bid.[69]

Now the gifts have become an acknowledgment of the noble status of the archer. However, the offer of a javelin and a sword go far beyond the acknowlegment of mere social status. By her offer Penelope restores Odysseus' status as a hero. The most typical carrier of a javelin and two-edged sword was Athene. Given now to Odysseus, they acknowledge his affinity with the goddess and his place in the society of gods.[70] The meaning of gifts shifts within one episode from signifying a true story to signifying social status and heroism.

The world of epic is a world of open boundaries. The different status of people, living and dead, the different status of stories of the past and fiction, and the different status of prizes, gifts and fees are clearly understated. Yet this unreal world seems to introduce a contrast which was real and of great consequence for the history of poetry and its public.[71] It distinguished between stories which were told for the sake of a reward to the author, and stories told for the sake of rewarding their recipient. In the anthropological models of exchange, this is one of the fundamental distinctions between gifts and commodities. The debates in Homeric epic about the value of poetry show that it was not the kind of reward that determined this difference, but the relationship between author and recipient, and the status ascribed to the author in particular.

The moral distinction between gift and commodity is somewhat parallel to the distinction between true stories on the one hand and lies and fiction on the other. The transmission of knowledge was a gift of the past but invented stories were traded as commodities. From an economic point of view this shows how the emergence of commodity exchange in Western culture implied its immediate moral dismissal. From the point of view of literary history it explains why poetry came to be regarded as a commodity when prose writing became the preferred mode in which knowledge was produced and transmitted. The context of the exchange between author and audience, the 'status' of the text exchanged and the reward given once more determined one another.

Notes

1. The normative aspect of the epithet *polutropos* has been emphasised by many recent critics. See among others Clay (1983), Pucci (1987), Goldhill (1991) and Bergren (1983). As Bergren remarks, there is a constant 'effort of the text to direct this "manyness" toward a fulfilment in conclusive victory' (p. 60, n. 4).

2. See Chantraine (1940) for a discussion of *pernêmi* and its derivatives; *hodaia, phortos, kerdos* occur together in *Od.* 8. 159-164; *ônon* and *phortos* in *Od.* 14. 296 f. in relation to slave sale; and *ônon* for the sale of a gold necklace from the Phoenicians to the slave attendants of an aristocratic household in 15. 460.

3. Snodgrass (1980), pp. 136 ff.; Coldstream (1977) pp. 70 ff.

4. Mele (1979); for discussion and criticism of the debate on archaic trade, see Cartledge (1983), esp. pp. 8-10.

5. Morris (1986 a), p. 6 f. against Humphreys (1978), pp. 166 f. Morris' interpretation of the archaeological material is not entirely convincing. In the articles in which he discusses gifts to the dead ((1986 a) and (1989)) he does not reveal his method of identifying a grave deposit as a 'gift'. For example, it remains unclear why the custom of dedicating precious objects to the dead meant a 'deliberate destruction of wealth' practised with the same intentions as those described as the ritual of *potlatch*. It is also arguable whether one can conclude from the fact that metal objects had 'a very limited distribution in the Early Iron Age' that they were 'top rank gifts' ((1986 a), pp. 8-11). Morris seems to interpret his material in the light of an anthropological theory and then use it to support that theory.

6. Redfield (1983), pp. 224-227.

7. Kopytoff (1986), pp. 68-80. The concept of spheres of exchange, or spheres of value, goes back to Raymond Firth who used the term to describe the Polynesian economy (Firth (1939)). It has become popular through Bohannan's very influential description of the Tiv economy (Bohannan (1955 a); cf. Bohannan and Bohannan (1962)). The model suggests that different groups of items (for example luxuries, necessities or ritual objects) circulate each in their own sphere and cannot be compared in value, and thus cannot be exchanged for one another. A useful discussion can be found in Bohannan and Dalton (1962), pp. 1-16. Donlan (1981) has, quite successfully, applied the model to exchange in Homeric epic; yet the analysis suffers from an anachronistic economic approach as it fails to consider values such as life or glory as objects of exchange.

8. Kopytoff (1986), pp. 64 ff.; cf. Appadurai (1986), pp. 3-16 for the argument that the distinction between gift and commodity does not lie in a distinction of modes of production but in one of modes of exchange. This model makes it possible to argue that the same thing can be both gift and commodity and shifts its meaning with the ideology attached to the situation of exchange.

9. Scully (1990), pp. 4 f. and Appendix 1.

10. Nagy (1979), esp. pp. 42-58.

3. Kleos and Commerce in the Odyssey

11. Edwards (1985), p. 16; another group of epithets frequently attached to Odysseus points to his endurance of hardship.
12. For Odysseus' rhetoric see Edwards (1985), pp. 43 ff., and for his speech during the embassy scene Goldhill (1991), pp. 80 ff.; for the spying expedition and Odysseus' skill in ambush warfare Edwards (1985), pp. 15-42; for the wrestling match Cozzo (1988), pp. 15 ff.
13. See esp. *Od*. 13. 291-299, quoted below; for *kerdos* as the shrewdness to gain gifts 2. 114-121 and 18. 283 f.
14. Cozzo (1988), pp. 13 ff. and Chantraine (1968), s.v. *kerdos*.
15. See in detail Nagy (1979), pp. 47 f.
16. *Il*. 23. 316-319.
17. *Il*. 23. 422 ff. and 515; cf. Cozzo (1988), p. 15.
18. *Il*. 23. 709.
19. See esp. the technical image in ll. 712 ff.: 'The two men ... grappled each other in the hook of their heavy arms, as when rafters lock, when a renowned architect has fitted them in the roof of a high house to keep out the force (*biê*) of the winds' spite.'
20. Ibid. 710-739.
21. *Il*. 2. 291-298.
22. Redfield (1983), p. 228.
23. *Od*. 19. 282-286.
24. Pucci (1987), p. 98.
25. *Od*. 14. 222-234.
26. *Il*. 12. 310-321; see esp. Lynn-George (1988), pp. 155 ff.
27. *Od*. 4. 600-609.
28. *Od*. 19. 272 and 17. 558; cf. Redfield (1983), p. 238 who suggests that Odysseus' unreciprocated reception of gifts is represented as 'beggary on a heroic scale'.
29. *Od*. 8. 159-164.
30. *Od*. 8. 166-175; with slight emendations of Cook's trans.
31. For the role of appearance in Homeric ethics, see Bunsdorff (1992).
32. *Od*. 19. 282-286, quoted above.
33. *Od*. 1. 179-184.
34. *Od*. 3. 70-82 compare with 14. 122; cf. Goldhill (1991), pp. 38 f.
35. Pucci (1987), pp. 176 ff.
36. *Od*. 9. 259 ff.; 6. 130, see also 9. 45 ff.; 10. 273; and Pucci (1987), pp. 178 f.
37. *Od*. 7. 209-221.
38. *Od*. 17. 286-289.
39. *Kakoergos* (evildoer), *oulomenê* (accursed), *analtos* (insatiable), *lugrê* (wretched), *margê* (greedy); see Pucci (1987), p. 179; cf. Vernant (1989 b), p. 59, Svenbro (1976), pp. 50-60, who argues that only people who depend on others for their subsistence, like poets for example, are reduced to a state of a *gastêr* in archaic poetry.
40. *Od*. 13. 291-299.
41. Finley (1981 b), p. 235.
42. Chantraine (1940), pp. 11-16.
43. Benveniste (1969), pp. 129-137.
44. *Il*. 19. 291-299; quoted above.
45. *Il*. 18. 288-292.
46. Eumaeus owns a servant whom he has bought from his own resources (*Od*. 14. 451 ff.). And his house has a court which he built without the knowledge of his master (*Od*. 14. 5 f.).

47. See esp. *Od.* 14. 61-67 where he says that when Odysseus will return he will have a *kleros*, a house and a wife; Goldhill (1991), pp. 7 ff.; see by contrast Redfield (1986), pp. 34-36.
48. *Od.* 15. 368-372.
49. See above all Hesiod *W&D, passim*, with Detienne (1963).
50. He had done so once before (cf. 15. 308) but Eumaeus had never given his name formally.
51. Pucci (1987), pp. 98 ff. and Goldhill (1991), pp. 40 ff.
52. *Od.* 14. 340-342.
53. *Od.* 14. 290 ff.; quote 357-359. Return home as a metaphor for return to life has wider meaning in the discussion of life and death; see Frame (1978).
54. *Od.* 17. 419-444.
55. Kopytoff (1986), pp. 74 f.
56. For the interdependence of heroism and the poet of heroic poetry see esp. Goldhill (1991), pp. 93-103; cf. Marg (1957); Maehler (1964), Detienne (1967), Adkins (1972 c), and Scully (1981) on the reflexivity of Homer's poems.
57. Segal (1983), p. 27.
58. *Od.* 11. 363-368; 17. 337-344.
59. *Od.* 8. 477-481; 488-495.
60. Cf. *Od.* 14. 121-132.
61. Cf. *Od.* 17. 507-520.
62. *Od.* 13. 291-299; quoted above p. 52.
63. *Od.* 14. 122-132.
64. *Od.* 2. 184 f. See also Alcinous' remarks to Odysseus in 11. 363-368 which show the inverse connection and give one of various explanations why the Phaeacians offer gifts to Odysseus.
65. *Od.* 14. 462-506.
66. *Od.* 14. 508-517.
67. Goldhill (1991), p. 45.
68. *Od.* 19. 309-316.
69. *Od.* 21. 334-342.
70. For the function of Athene in Odysseus' identity see Podlecki (1961).
71. See Gentili (1988) for a different argument. Gentili relates the changing evaluation of poetry to changing socio-economic conditions of poetic production in the course of the archaic and classical periods. I have discussed the problem in greater detail in von Reden (1995).

Part II

EXCHANGE IN THE ATHENIAN *POLIS*

4

The Politics of Exchange

The ideology of spending

In many societies gift exchange is a way of conducting politics. Marshal Sahlins proposed in his influential article on 'The sociology of primitive exchange' that particular forms of reciprocity are related to particular forms of pre-political social organisation. Reciprocal exchange of goods and services is a mechanism by which people 'come to terms' with each other. Depending on pre-existing, or initiated, social relationships, the terms of exchange vary. While balanced reciprocity underwrites relationships of equality, generalised reciprocity creates, maintains and reinforces ranked relationships. In relationships of generalised reciprocity the flow of goods tends to be controlled by one of the parties involved. Usually this party spends more than the recipient party can repay in material goods which, together with the time delay of the repayment, creates a permanent debt-relationship between donors and recipients.[1]

While Sahlins' concept of generalised reciprocity provides a model of how gift-giving and expenditure link up to an entire system, Mauss' theory of the gift concentrates on the meaning of individual transactions. Mauss discussed the politics of the gift in connection with the more fundamental question of how giver and recipient become dependent on each other by the obligations arising from the 'spirit' of the gift.[2] He observed that not only were the gifts exchanged in different ratios but the exchange of unequal quantities of value could itself have different political and religious functions. First, there are rituals like the *potlatch*, practised among the Kwakiutl in Northwest America, where large quantities of valuables and hospitality are offered in order to prove that the chief is favoured by the spirits and by good fortune. Spending and sharing preserve his authority, 'humiliating others by placing them in the shadow of his name'.[3] There is a degree of violence implied in this form of giving since it puts the recipient under threat; failure to reciprocate results in the loss of freedom.[4]

Secondly, there are gifts that are given with the clear intention of receiving something greater in return. This return may take the form of more wealth and prosperity, or of something different, such as peace and averting disaster. This may also be achieved by rituals of *potlatch*, but it is associated in particular with the fact that the destruction of goods is witnessed by the gods and nature. Especially among some societies in Siberia and West Alaska, conspicuous destruction serves to incite the spirits of the gods and ancestors to make an even more generous return. Gift exchange is thought to 'produce' an abundance of riches. Here Mauss saw the origins of sacrifice: the spirits of the dead and gods were the first with whom men tried to come to terms by making a kind of 'contract'. The gods were the true owners of things, and with them it was most necessary to exchange and most dangerous not to exchange. Although the gods and spirits are here, too, associated with power, this gift-giving is not so much a way of asserting hierarchy as of offering worship.[5]

Thirdly, there are gifts which tie a group together by their continuous circulation. Mutual obligation and rank are created among a chain of donors and recipients. Gifts are never given away completely but thought to return to their original donor. Overspending is not as great and conspicuous as in rituals of *potlatch* but advantage is nevertheless implied in generosity insofar as a creditor is in the stronger position. Describing the laws of exchange among the Maori, Mauss concentrates on the *hau*, that is, the spirit of the gift which forces the recipient to make a gift himself. 'The *taonga* or its *hau* ... is attached to [a] chain of users until these give back from their own property, their *taonga*, their goods, or from their labour or trading by way of feasts, festivals and presents, the equivalent of something of even greater value. This in turn will give the donors authority and power over the first donor, who has become the last recipient.'[6]

Mauss suggested that these rather different symbolic statements were not mutually exclusive but could be regarded as complementary aspects of gift exchange. Jonathan Parry argued, however, that specific meanings and functions of gift exchange could not be generalised for all cultures of the world. Re-examining Mauss' field work, he notices a subtle difference between the 'spirit' of the gift in Hindu and Maori societies. Mauss had described the 'spirit' of a gift among the Maori as both a force which makes a gift return to its donor and a danger which compels the recipient to get rid of it.[7] Parry observed, by contrast, that in Hindu society the gift was thought to bring destruction to the one who failed to pass it on. The 'spirit' of the gift was a dangerous force which caused it to be handed on continuously. Gifts among the Hindu were alienated absolutely; their evil spirit made it necessary that they never come back.[8] Among the Maori the 'spirit' of the gift was a productive force. It urged the recipient to give something back, preferably something greater, in return for what he had received. Gift-giving is here a source of productive increase, as it normally attracts an increment while it circulates.[9]

With the help of Sahlins' model of generalised reciprocity and the distinctions made by Mauss and Parry, it is possible to identify different

4. The Politics of Exchange

functions and meanings of exchange in Greek culture. We observed that in the world of epic poetry one of the main functions of a gift was to act as a recompense. Homer was concerned with the question of what a warrior gained in exchange for the loss of his life. The exchange was not conceived of in specific exchange ratios but, rather as in Mauss' model of gifts to gods, as a sacrifice for the sake of an unspecified return. Sacrificing their lives, the warriors of epic became heroes worshipped with gifts by their human descendants. Heroes were recipients rather than givers of gifts when they were envisaged as figures of cult. In the social context of the camp, by contrast, the ideology was different. Already the *Iliad* expresses the idea that giving is a means of stabilising a position of power in a political community. Achilles feels anger not just at being stripped of his prize of honour but also at having to accept a recompense from a king to whom he does not want to subordinate himself. While he is eager for prizes of excellence which attribute to him a place of honour in the heroic order, he rejects the gifts from a political ruler.[10] The story of Odysseus implies more radically that receiving a gift has ambivalent connotations in the world of mortals. Outside the context of heroic achievement, receiving something valuable could be interpreted as ill-gained profit. Although the epics do not make a clear moral distinction between giving and receiving gifts, they suggest that gifts embody different symbolic statements in different contexts of exchange.

In the texts more directly related to life in the archaic *polis* a strong emphasis on debt avoidance can be noted. The moral advice which Hesiod gives in the *Works and Days* is based on the assumption that being at the receiving end of an exchange is both bad and disadvantageous:

> Have watchful neigbours. Measure carefully
> when you must borrow from your neighbour, then,
> pay back the same, or more, if possible,
> and you will have a friend in time of need.
> Shun evil profit, for dishonest gain
> is just the same as failure. Love your friends;
> Approach the men who come to you, and give
> to him who gives, but not, if he does not.
> We give to generous men, but no one gives
> to stingy ones. Give is a good girl,
> but grab is bad, and she gives only death.
> The man who gives ungrudgingly is glad
> at heart rejoicing in his gift, but if
> a man forgets his shame and takes something,
> however small, his heart grows stiff and cold.[11]

In this passage, giving and lending have first of all moral and economic significance. Yet in the context of the poem as a whole the same principle emerges as a justification of political power. This becomes clear when we hear that the *basileis* of Hesiod's community have forfeited their rights to power by inverting the principle of overspending. They 'devour gifts' and give nothing but 'crooked judgment' in return (248-265). Their greed for unreciprocated gifts is symbolic of their political weakness and inability to represent justice. In Hesiod we thus find a clear indication that spending is needed as a sign of strength and justice. First, it creates ties of obligation, which both facilitates survival and avoids dependence; and, secondly, it signifies moral and political superiority in that it is a sign of good fortune, which is given to the virtuous alone.[12] For Hesiod gifts create a return and an increase in prosperity. They have a positive, or 'productive', value and therein resemble the meaning of gifts among the Maori.[13]

In myth, by contrast, we find examples of dangerous gifts. In his seminal article on value in Greek myth, Gernet discussed a number of mythical tales which belong to a period later than the 7th century. All these tales express the idea that a gift must be passed on, and that it is dangerous to regard wealth and treasure as personal property. For example, in the myth of the Seven Sages a tripod offered as a prize for the wisest man is continuously passed between the participants of the contest. Thales receives it first and then hands it on to the next participant. Finally, it returns to him, but he then dedicates it to Apollo. We may assume that only the god was allowed, or able, to keep it. Similarly, in a mythical story about the tyrant Polycrates of Samos a ring, which is the emblem of his power, features as a dangerous possession. Asked to get rid of what he values most highly, he throws it into the sea. Yet it returns. The doom of Polycrates is sealed the moment he realises that he is unable to dispose of the object he regards as his most precious possession. Finally, in Aeschylus' *Agamemnon* Agamemnon expresses the fear of tyranny by his fear of using the purple tapestry that adorns the path into his palace. He hesitates to trample the cloth which he deems too precious a thing for a human to possess. And when he is finally persuaded to step on it, it leads him to his death.[14] The danger of possessions, symbolised by a gift with an evil spirit or dangerous meaning, seems to have been associated specifically with the fear of tyranny and *hubris* (violence, arrogance). *Hubris* evoked the envy of both gods and men as it was an attempt to ignore the constraints of the mortal condition.[15] In this context the obligation to give expressed the willingness to abdicate from a kind of power which was lethal in the long term. By giving away a share of his possessions, the tyrant ritually purified himself from the suspicion of *hubris*.

We have thus evidence for two ideologies of spending in Greek culture which need to be carefully distinguished. On the one hand, gift-giving and hospitality were motivated by the desire to create and maintain a superior place in the social hierarchy. On the other hand, spending was necessary in order to step down from a position of power which it was too dangerous to occupy. In the one case the gift was a symbol of increase and well-being, creating for the donor an income of material returns and power. In the

4. The Politics of Exchange

other, it was a symbolic sacrifice in exchange for a position of power which was to be regarded as a temporary gift.

Both meanings of gift-giving and expenditure feature in choral lyric. Kurke quite rightly distinguishes between odes which are written in praise of members of civic communities and those for tyrants.[16] In the case of tyrannical rulers the poet never fails to mention the lavish expenditure of the victor on men and gods. The best example of this is a victory ode by Bacchylides written for Hieron of Syracuse:

> Ah, the thrice-blessed man, who has been allotted from Zeus the honour of ruling the most people of the Greeks – he knows not to hide his towered wealth in black-cloaked darkness. The temples teem with bull-sacrificing festivals, the streets teem with acts of hospitality, and gold shines with flashing.[17]

Here the emphasis on expenditure serves to protect the victor against the dangers of *hubris*. Expenditure is a form of self-adornment; yet, being directed towards temples and feasts, it could be regarded as a form of conspicuous destruction of wealth for the sake of averting disaster. The way the strength of civic victors is praised is more subtle. Generosity and magnificence are encouraged, but the praise is transferred to the city. Just like the tyrant, the civic victor spent his wealth on others, however this did not increase his individual status but the status of the entire city. For example, when Megacles the Alkmeonid is praised in *Pythian* 7, his generous gifts to the temple of Apollo are mentioned as a collective gift of the Athenians to the god:

> Athens the mighty city!
> For the strong house of the Alkmeonids
> this is the finest prelude
> to lay as foundation-stone
> of my chariot song.
> For in what country, what clan, would you dwell
> and have more magnificent renown
> for Hellas to hear?
>
> For in every city the story runs
> of the citizens of Erechtheus,
> who build in shining Pytho
> thy porch, Apollo, marvellous to behold.[18]

The careful strategy of the poet who praises the civic athlete on the one hand, but represents him and his wealth as part of the city on the other, shows two things at once. It suggests that expenditure in the form of hospitality and public gifts was an important aspect of aristocratic public politics. The donor gained a position of respect and power in his *polis*, a return which was euphemistically called *charis*, gratitude. But it also shows that such an aristocratic position of power had to be suppressed in public praise of victors belonging to the democratic *polis* of Athens. Here the return of *charis* was diverted from the donor towards his city.[19] Ostentatious expenditure at sacrifices, funerals, weddings, festivals and other forms of hospitality were forms of aristocratic politics which aimed at a return. The emphasis on the return distinguishes the ideology of spending in *poleis* governed by a constitution from the expenditure of tyrants who spent ritually in order to escape the danger of being overthrown. The sumptuary laws attributed to Solon, which prescribed among other things the reduction of splendour at private funerals and weddings, aimed at controlling expenditure made for personal political reasons.[20] Instead, conspicuous acts of generosity were directed towards the community as a whole. They became the mark of a good citizen. The duty of the wealthy to make public contributions in the form of so-called *eisphora* (property tax) and liturgies were an invention under the *polis* which aimed to direct the politics of largess towards the community as a whole.[21] It would be wrong, however, to assume that 'the Athenians believed that part of the surplus wealth enjoyed by the members of the upper classes should be used to ensure the security of the state and the general benefit of the citizenry'.[22] The benefit lay on both sides. As Davies has pointed out, the motivation for the performance of liturgies, besides being a civic duty, was the recognised power of ostentatious generosity. Public spending was fired by *philotimia* (love of honour), and the reward was a steady income of *charis* from the other citizens.[23]

Despite being thus integrated into the democratic political process, explicit statements about the power of spending can be found only in anti-democratic thought. Aristotle regarded *megaloprepeia* (magnificence) as a political virtue. As in Hesiod and Pindar, spending was at the same time a moral and political programme. The *megaloprepês* was obliged to spend, but by doing so he also enhanced his political status. Adhering firmly to the principles of the *polis*, Aristotle advocated that money should only be spent on liturgies, and at occasions which benefit the community:[24]

> This sort of excellence [i.e. *megaloprepeia*] is found in the sorts of expenses called honourable, e.g. in expenses for the gods – dedications, temples, sacrifices and so on for everything divine – and in expenses that provoke a good competition for honour, for the benefit of the community – if for example some city thinks a splendid chorus or a warship or a feast for the city must be provided ... Large spending befits those who have the means, acquired through their own efforts or their ancestors or connections, or are well-born and reputable, and so on; for each of these conditions includes greatness and reputation for worth ... [Magnificence] is also found in those private expenses that arise only once, e.g. a wedding and the like, and in those that concern the whole city, or the people in it with a reputation for worth – the receiving of foreign guests and sending them off, gifts and exchanges of gifts; for the magnificent person spends money for the common good, not on himself, and the gifts are similar to dedications (*anathêmasin*).[25]

4. The Politics of Exchange

Aristotle clearly tries to distinguish his programme from that of private ostentation, which was unsuitable for the good life in the *polis*. The man of true political virtue knows the measure of self-adornment:

> It is also proper to the magnificent person to build a house befitting his riches, since this is also a suitable adornment; and to spend more readily on long-lasting achievements, since these are the finest, and in each case what is fitting. For what suits gods does not suit human beings, and what suits a temple does not suit a tomb.[26]

Aristotle does not, however, associate excessive spending with tyranny. The power of the *megaloprepês* was threatened by democratic modes of government which were marked by 'low birth (*ageneia*), poverty (*penia*) and mean employment (*banausia*)'.[27] Confronted with the problem that there were people who had enough money to pay liturgies, but did not belong to the traditional aristocracy, Aristotle had to ensure that the winners of the competition in public spending were not simply those who had the most money. The sign of the *banausos* was that he either spent too much or in the wrong way:

> The *banausos* who exceeds the mean exceeds by spending more than is right. ... For in small expenses he spends a lot, and puts on an inappropriate display. He gives his club a dinner party in the style of a wedding banquet and when he supplies a chorus for a comedy, he brings them on stage dressed in purple, as they do at Megara. In all this he aims not at what is fine (*poiêsei ou tou kalou heneka*) but at the display of his wealth (*alla ton plouton epideiknumenos*) and at the admiration he thinks he wins in this way (*kai dia tauta oiomenos thaumazesthai*).[28]

For Aristotle spending was a political virtue. It created reciprocal ties of obligation between unequals from which the wealthier party derived political power and status. But power and status were not the direct return made by those on whom money was spent. They were the rewards of the competition of spending among peers. By competitive spending they proved their mutual material independence which was the condition of the ideal political relationship: the friendship between '*agathoi*'.[29]

Generosity is more directly associated with gift-giving in Xenophon's *Cyropaideia*, one of the major moralising treatises of the 4th century. It is interesting to note that the story is placed in Persia where gift exchange continued to operate as a working social system in the 4th century. But the general aim of the text is not to describe Persia but to advocate values which were generated in oligarchic Greek *poleis*. It is likely that the literary figure of Cyrus ought to be identified with the Spartan king Agesilaus whom Xenophon admired, and to whom he ascribed qualities similar to those he ascribed to Cyrus in the *Cyropaideia*. In the *Agesilaus* he reports:

As men were from time to time made members of the senate (*ephoroi*) [Agesilaus] would send each one a cloak and an ox as mark of honour. Consequently, while he was thought to be honouring and exalting the dignity of their office, he was unawares increasing his own influence and adding to the power of the king a greatness which was conceded out of goodwill towards him.[30]

In the *Cyropaideia*, Cyrus is educated as a perfect Greek *anêr*. His virtues are a rehearsal of standard Greek aristocratic values which can be found throughout Greek texts. Cyrus' dress is frugal, he eats for company not to satisfy his belly, he offers drinks as a libation to his relatives and ancestors; he rears horses, and spends his leisure in hunting, games and competitions.[31] His wealth allows him to pursue his military training rather than work for a living; but, of course, wealth is less important than public praise, and the possession of money is good only if it is spent on friends.[32] Agriculture, finally, is the basis of a free life. This emerges, for example, from the negative image in which the Chaldaeans are represented. They are poor and have to fight as mercenaries (*misthou strateuontai*) since their country is mountainous and only a small part cultivable.[33]

For Xenophon, excellence among Cyrus' subjects is encouraged by gifts of honour. He takes every opportunity to describe how armies and soldiers are rewarded. *Dôra* are given to generals and stewards, while the common soldiers receive generous *misthoi* (pay).[34] Cyrus himself has no personal need for gifts. Gifts from other kings on campaign flow directly into the channels of his system of reward. In fact the only reason Cyrus accepts gifts on campaign is their utility for further generous gestures. The strategy of generosity and gift-giving is applied not only to the army and subjects in general, but also to the people engaged in commerce. Those *kapêloi* (marketeers) who supply the army most efficiently receive gifts and money for buying up more stocks.[35]

Xenophon gives a number of examples of how gift-giving creates power; conversely, accepting more than one can return is humiliating. When Gadates brings gifts to Cyrus 'as might be expected from a wealthy house', Cyrus accepts only the horses – to give to his generals; the rest he refuses. 'For if, as we part, you should give me larger gifts than you receive from me, by the gods, I do not see how I could help being ashamed (*aischunesthai*).'[36] Again, when the king of Armenia offers to Cyrus guest-gifts and money 'double the sum that he had named [as tribute] Cyrus accepted only the amount he had specified and returned the rest'.[37] And later when he had restored peace in the country,

... not one of the Armenians remained indoors, but all, both men and women, in their joy at the restoration of the peace, came forth to meet him, each one carrying or bringing whatever he had of value. And their king did not disapprove, for he thought that Cyrus would thus be all the better pleased by receiving honour from all. And finally also the queen with her daughters and her younger son came up to him bringing not only the money which before Cyrus had refused to take, but other gifts as well. And when he saw it Cyrus said: 'You shall not make me go about doing good for pay (*misthou euergetein*)!'[38]

To be at the receiving end of an exchange was a sign of weakness. In order to shake off such suspicion of weakness without ever having to refuse a gift from a friend, Cyrus passes on the gifts he receives, and specifies the amount of gifts which is acceptable.[39] At the end of the *Cyropaideia* Cynaxares gives his daughter to Cyrus together with a golden crown, bracelets, a necklace and a Median robe. The presents are the return for gifts which Cynaxares had received from Cyrus. Cyrus accepts them all, but avoids making himself a recipient by 'still [making] the young woman presents of everything he thought would please Cynaxares as much as herself'.[40] The series of exchanges was obviously a competition of power between Cynaxares and Cyrus – a competition which Cyrus was anxious not to lose.

Gift-giving was, finally, a source of lasting, rather than short-lived, wealth. Xenophon makes Cyrus outdo Croesus – the embodiment of wealth – with an experiment which proved the effect of gift-giving. When Croesus arrogantly claims to have more wealth than Cyrus because the latter is too generous in giving, Cyrus sends round a dispatch asking all his friends to contribute money. After the collection 'Croesus is said to have added it up and to have found that there was as much subscribed as he had told Cyrus he should have in his treasury by this time if he had been amassing it'.[41] The rewards of spending were thus safe sources of income, but they were not a means of making money.

Both Aristotle's and Xenophon's explicit recommendation of spending in order to affirm status within the *polis* were irreconcilable with the ideology of the democratic *polis* in which asymmetrical political relationships were suppressed in public. We shall see below that *chrêmata* could under certain circumstances become dangerous valuables in the symbolic economy of Athens as they marked unequal relationships between members of the *polis*. Nevertheless an ideological preference for spending can also be discovered in a text which in many ways reflects the public ideology of democratic Athens.

One of the few ethnographical details which Thucydides mentions in his *Histories* is the fact that in Thrace politics were conducted with gifts.[42] He observed that the Thracians, just like the Persians, gave presents to their rulers, failing which it was impossible 'to get anything done'. Yet he also distinguishes between the Persians and the Thracians. While in Persia gifts were given by the rulers to their subjects, in Thrace the rulers preferred to receive rather than to give.[43] Thucydides adds, however, that it was most shameful for a Thracian inferior not to be able to give when asked for a gift. This is indeed striking given that gift exchange is a ritual in which normally the honour of the superior party is at stake. It can only be understood as a rhetorical strategy employed by Thucydides for political purposes. To regard it as shameful not be able to give was the Greek ideology of exchange. Yet in the political practice of democracy gifts to politicians were regarded as bribes. It seems that Thucydides tried to describe Thrace, which was an ally of the Athenians, as having similar attitudes to giving as the Athenians without intimating that he accepted the practice of gift-giving in politics. Gifts were associated with corruption in Athens; yet here, too, it was an indication of weakness not to give. As Pericles is made to say in the Funeral Speech:

> When it comes to acting for others, we are different from most people, for we acquire friends not in consequence of what others do for us, but by doing it for them. He who confers the benefit (*charin*) is in a firmer position in order by his kindness to keep it owed by the party to whom it was given. Whereas he who owes it is slower to act, since he knows he returns the favour (*aretê*) not as a favour (*charin*), but as a debt (*hôs opheilêma*).[44]

The extent to which the politics of *charis* were in practice bound up with material payments becomes clear in the speech of the Corcyran envoys asking the Athenians for an alliance. This speech shows also how the interdependence of expenditure and power was masked by the ambivalent meaning of *charis*.[45] The Corcyrans begin by saying that a city which seeks alliance with another has to demonstrate the advantages that will arise for the other city from their alliance. They also have to indicate that their *charis* will remain steady. So far, *charis* can be read as meaning either gratitude or benefaction and refers to either a symbolic or a material transaction. In the next sentence, however, they ask the Athenians to consider the prospect of acquiring power that would otherwise cost them money and favours (*chrêmata kai charis*). And then 'you Athenians will win a reputation for generosity (*aretê*) among the majority of states, gratitude (*charis*) from those you protect, strength for yourself' (33.2). In the conditional the connection of *charis* with *chrêmata* could be brought into play. Yet it was inappropriate directly to associate it with the politics of Athens. The asymmetry of power implied in the Athenian exchanges with their allies required a rhetorical guise but Thucydides nevertheless alludes to it by his usage of the term *charis*, meaning benefaction at one time and gratitude at another. It suggests that there was considerable symbolic gain for the benefactor and symbolic loss for the one who had to be grateful.

Spending and receiving had a symbolic and a material aspect. Therefore Xenophon and Aristotle could compare the value of *chrêmata* with the value of honour and praise, and make them exchangeable objects in reciprocal transactions. Yet they caused opposite results in a material and a symbolic economy and these results were evaluated differently in a private and a public context of exchange. While the democratic city was anxious not to allow individuals to receive power symbolically by material transactions, material gain was socially disqualified as private commerce. For two different reasons therefore it was not acceptable either to spend or to receive material rewards as an individual.

Symbolic loss: gaining a *misthos*

Complementary to the ideology of spending was a bias against receiving. There were two apparently contradictory reasons for this, which are explained by the complex symbolism of gift exchange: receiving a gift may create honour and initiate obligation. The tension caused by this symbolic double bind is expressed in the conflict of Achilles: as a hero he has to strive for gifts and fame, but within the community of warriors these cause dependency and submission. Within the communal life of the *polis* it was on the one hand the latter that made the receipt of material values problematic; the personal obligation they created was incompatible with the freedom expected from citizens and politicians. On the other hand, in contexts which remained typical arenas of public competition, receiving material rewards was incompatible with the definition of citizenship and its rejection of heroism. Since these are two different developments of gift exchange I shall deal with them in turn.

Misthos could never be transacted between equals. The term could refer either to an honourable 'reward' or to a commercial 'payment', but it always marked an asymmetrical relationship. In most texts of the 5th and 4th centuries the term is used in a context where the translation 'wage' is most appropriate. Beneveniste argued therefore that the meaning 'reward' or 'prize' was earlier than 'wage' and already in recession by the time of Homer.[46] Will, by contrast, argued that even in the texts of the classical period 'recompense' (material or symbolic return for an honourable act) was the basic meaning of *misthos* while 'wage' (material remuneration for labour in a contractual relationship) was a specialised usage.[47]

Both Benveniste and Will construct two mutually exclusive meanings of *misthos*, because they distinguish unduly between social and economic exchange. If the entire repertoire of ancient exchange is approached from a symbolic point of view the usage appears more homogeneous. What is more, the logic of the semantic field of *misthos* suggests that it was above all their negative social symbolism which characterised commercial relationships.

As in most cases the occurrence of *misthos* is unproblematic, it will be sufficient to focus on those passages discussed by Benveniste and Will as being unusual.[48] Of the three occurrences of the term in Homer two clearly refer to a payment to an inferior who works as a *thês* (servant, dependant). In *Il.* 21. 445 Ares reminds Apollo of the time when they, alone of all gods, had to serve (*thêteusamen*) Laomedon for a *misthos*; and in *Od.* 18. 358 Eurymachus asks Odysseus in disguise whether he would like to be his servant (*thêteuemen*), promising that the wage would be sufficient (*misthos de hoi arkios estai*). The same formula is used in the third passage, which seems to contradict the pattern that can be assumed to lie behind the first two examples. At *Il.* 10. 304 Hector promises anyone who will spy in the Achaean camp 'a great gift (*dôron*); the reward will be one that suffices (*misthos de hoi arkios estai*)'. Yet the discrepancy is more apparent than real. No one but the ugly runner Dolon feels attracted by Hector's offer, and he himself fulfils the service in the most unheroic way. When discovered by Diomedes and Odysseus, he runs away like a hunted animal. The use of *misthos* in this context seems deliberately pejorative. A warrior seduced by a *misthos* is not a hero. This reading is confirmed by *Od.* 18. 358 where Eurymachus abuses Odysseus in disguise by repeating the formula of *Il.* 10. 304. The textual allusion endorses the motif of misrecognition as it intimates that Eurymachus confuses Odysseus not only with a beggar but also with the *Iliadic* Dolon.[49] If the phrase rendered in the formula is meant to be abusive, which it clearly is, it disqualifies Dolon as much as it offends Odysseus. Thus *misthos* denotes here, as in its other occurrences in Homer, a payment to an inferior person.

Another problem is posed by Plato's use of *misthos*. In the *Republic* Plato argues that in existing constitutions offices are taken over for the sake of a *misthos* rather than out of honour, which makes politicians live at the beck and call of others and not for the sake of a virtuous life.[50] He compares the *misthos* of magistrates to the *misthos* with which skilled work is rewarded,[51] thus making it indicative of the unsatisfactory state of politics in contemporary constitutions. In other dialogues too the term is used to denote relationships of dependence and inferiority.[52] It comes as a surprise, therefore, that at the end of the *Republic* Plato mentions '*athla* (prizes), *misthoi* and *dôra* which the Just man receives from gods and from men during his lifetime'.[53] Previously, he mentions some honours the Just man receives in life that he had dismissed as irrelevant earlier in the dialogue.[54] Then he proceeds to the rewards the Just man can expect after death. The fact that they are promised only after death is crucial for understanding the use of the term *misthos* in this passage. It changes the transactional order in which prizes and gifts circulate. The *misthoi* to be expected after death are not received from any other human but are gifts from the gods. Moreover they are not *athla* and *misthoi* to the Just man directly but symbolic of the benefits of the *polis* as a whole. The Just man receives the gift of being reborn into a life that he has chosen himself – which amounts to the gift of continuous life of the just *polis*. As Annas comments, 'the myth [in which the rewards are explained] puts the human race in a wider setting. Justice is guaranteed by the cosmic order; the universe is such that overall justice is rewarded and evil punished. The myth is not denying the importance of justice in an individual life, but it ignores this to stress that it is also part of the much grander working of the entire cosmos.'[55] Plato used the term *misthos* in this context because

4. The Politics of Exchange

a hierarchy between donor and recipient was accepted, and indeed natural. It was essential to the supra-individual order, and to the relationship between the *polis* and the soul of the Just man. Within the span of an individual lifetime, by contrast, accepting a *misthos* was an act of humiliation and a sign of inferiority.

The boundary between orders of exchange was not a matter of common agreement. This led to different opinions as to whether receiving a *misthos* was socially degrading or rewarding. Plato's view that there was a metaphysical order beyond the *polis* to which the leading politicians were more obligated than to the existing laws of the *polis* was by no means typical. The political community itself was normally construed as a supra-individual order to which every citizen was subject. The consequences which the different assessment of the relationship between the *polis* and its members had on the meaning of *misthos* is borne out by a 5th-century bronze tablet from Crete discussed by Will. The inscription specifies the rewards to the scribe Spensithius as follows: *trophê* (food), *ateleia* (exemption from taxes), and *misthos* of 50 jars of new wine plus something else, together worth 20 *drachmas*.[56] The *misthos* is mentioned separately from the other aspects of the payment, which would be unnecessary if *misthos* meant wage or fee. In the context of payments to the army, the *misthos* was identical with, or part of, the *trophê* given to soldiers.[57] The 50 jars of wine and the other item seem to have been something extra: a bonus or prize. As Will points out, Spensithius was not a humble wage-labourer but, a skilful artisan who was able to write Phoenician letters which made him worthy of public memory.[58] The mere fact that he was honoured with a public inscription puts him above the status of a wage-labourer. The explanation must be that in the ritual of public recognition the collective citizen body regarded itself as a supra-individual order. *Misthos*, although a payment from a superior collective to one who was inferior to that collective, was an honourable payment, as it acknowledged an individual as worthy of collective recognition.

The example from Crete has a parallel in Athens. In the speech *Against Ctesiphon* Aeschines praises past times when military leaders asked for no personal gratification in exchange for their achievement. The generals who had won the victory over the Persians had received from the people of Athens the reward (*dôreia*) of the setting up of three stone Hermae. Yet their names had not been inscribed on them. Aeschines quotes the inscriptions in full:

This reward (*misthos*) for their labour have the Athenians given (*edôkan*) to their leaders in return for their benefaction and valour. Who in years yet to come will read these lines will gladly join them in toiling for the state.[59]

Again the *polis* acted as a higher order which could distribute *misthoi* as an honourable reward. While for Plato only in the afterlife could one gain a *misthos* as a reward, for the Athenians the *polis* itself was a higher order which bestowed *misthos* as a sign of honour. It may be noted in passing that the *misthos* the Athenians paid to their generals was nothing which could be put to private use. It praised individuals only as members of a political community.

Misthos, then, unequivocally signified unequal relationships, and a lack of self-sufficiency or autarky in the recipient. Yet it was used in a negative, and by implication contractual, sense only in contexts where inequality was objectionable. Herodotus uses the term in various contexts, and it is morally negative only in those cases where an asymmetrical exchange is incompatible with the status of the exchanging partners.[60] The Mytilenians, for example, were prepared to surrender a suppliant to his pursuers for a *misthos*, and the same suppliant was finally given up, again for a *misthos*, to the Persians. Herodotus, obviously disapproving of the fact that the sacred rights of a suppliant were disregarded, found the Mytilenians guilty of receiving payment.[61] He also uses the term *misthos* for the payment the Pisistratids made in order to recover their children, which was the promise to leave Attica within five days.[62] Herodotus clearly regarded exile as an unacceptable humiliation, which he highlights by the language he uses in the story.

Enemies of Athenian democracy sought all possible opportunities of representing paid jurors and members of the assembly as inferior people. Within the political rhetoric of the assembly and lawcourts they called them hirelings of those who guaranteed them a *misthos*. This was of course a misrepresentation, as the payment to jurors came from public funds. They did not make their recipients dependent on individuals nor were they dishonourable, coming from a supra-individual order paid out of the public purse. Yet Aristophanes represented the Athenians as olive-pickers who were willing to work for whoever paid them the best *misthos*.[63] Aristotle, opposing democracy on more fundamental grounds, suggested that in democracies the public fund replaced the funds of a private *oikos* by becoming a source from which citizens earn a living. He therefore tried to prove that the political service of citizens under a democracy created an income sufficient for making a living.[64] Even if this was in fact true, Aristotle's intention was not to make some kind of economic calculation but to argue that public pay had certain political consequences. He recommended instead that the liturgy-paying class should be suspended from their duties and that poorer citizens should be paid for political services directly.[65] Both Aristophanes' and Aristotle's criticism was rooted in the same metaphysical model as Plato's. Not accepting the *polis* and its wealth as a supra-individual order of exchange, they regarded payments out of its funds to individual citizens as a *misthos* which made its recipients dependent on a paymaster.

Dôra

Dôra had their origins in heroic society and the sacred discourse of religion. Their symbolism was therefore very different from that of *misthoi*. Yet since every *dôron* tied the recipient to its donor, the effects of receiving a *dôron* could be tantamount to receiving a *misthos*. In many texts of the 5th and 4th centuries receiving *dôra* was interchangeable with receiving a *misthos*. A statement which Xenophon attributes to Socrates may be taken as a prime example. In the *Apology* Socrates calls himself freer (*eleutheriôteros*) than other people since he had never accepted from anyone either *dôra* or *misthoi*.[66]

In order to distinguish between gifts which diminished the freedom of a citizen and gifts which were given as prizes of the *polis*, a certain distinction seems to have been made between the terms *dôron* and *dôreia*. On inscriptions rewards to magistrates and benefactors are regularly called *dôreiai*, and the surviving speeches of the Attic orators confirm this usage. Only one extant speech employs the two terms interchangeably, and it serves as a useful introduction to the following discussion.

In the speech *Against Neaera* Apollodorus accuses the wife of Stephanus of having worked as a prostitute although she had received the right of citizenship from the Athenians. In §§90 f. the speaker poignantly juxtaposes the *misthos* which Neaera accepted as a prostitute, despite being an Athenian citizen, with the *dôreia* of citizenship rights which she had been given by the Athenians. The gift and the wage are represented as two mutually exclusive kinds of transaction which Neaera none the less aimed to combine. Yet in §§88 f., *dôron*, not the usual term *dôreia*, is used for the 'gift' of citizenship rights:

> For the civic body of Athens, although it has supreme authority over all things in the state, and has the power to do whatsoever it pleases, yet regarded the *dôron* of citizenship as so honourable and sacred that it enacted in its own restraint laws to which it must conform, when it wishes to create a citizen – laws which have now been dragged through the mire by Stephanus and those who contract marriages of this sort. However, you will be the better for hearing them, and you will know that these people have debased the most honourable and sacred *dôra* which are granted to the benefactors of the state.[67]

The emphatic repetition of *semnos*, sacred, provides the explanation for the change of terminology. If the *dôron* of citizenship was conceived of as sacred it suggested that the collective donor of this gift too was sacred. As the boundary of sacred and profane is particularly articulated in this passage, the term *dôron* assumes a special rhetorical function. Normally used in a positive sense only when referring to gifts from or to gods, it is applied here to a gift from the *polis* to a foreigner. It seems to emphasise that the endowment with citizen rights was a sacred transaction. *Dôra*, we may conclude, maintained a sacred meaning, putting their recipients under the strongest moral obligation.

A *dôron* became a bribe when it was transacted between individuals in a political context. According to current sociological approaches to corruption, bribery presupposes the disjunction, but not the complete separation, of two transactional orders. These orders may be distinguished as public or private, sacred or profane, tribal or governmental, ritual or juridical. The idea of corrupted exchange arises at the moment when individuals have to fill roles in both these orders but mix their respective ties of obligation.[68] Individuals begin to have the power of transacting values as representatives of different exchange networks: family, clan or personal friends may constitute the one, while the state, or any other collective order, constitutes the other. Bribery is frequently not a clearly defined crime, since it is often difficult to determine where to draw the line between the two orders of exchange. Some people may feel they have to accept gifts from a friend, while others interpret these gifts as bribes. The moral dismissal of gifts as bribes is thus a phenomenon emerging from fundamental changes in the construction of orders of exchange.

Studies on *dôrodokia* in the Greek *polis* confirm the proposition that bribery is a threat to the symbolic system of any particular society rather than a clearly defined crime. There were strict laws against bribery, but the problem lay above all in deciding when a gift fell into the category of a bribe.[69] Thus Harvey argues that *dôrodokia* was punished only when the recipient was persuaded by a gift to act against the interests of the *dêmos*.[70] Wankel also points out that many gifts changed hands unnoticed and that there was a considerable grey area in which cases could be decided rightfully in either direction.[71] Perlman, regarding bribery mainly as a problem of foreign diplomacy, draws attention to the uncertainties arising from different political norms. Athenians acting as ambassadors in foreign kingdoms were expected to submit to the local custom of gift exchange, which at home could be interpreted as bribery.[72] Put in the language of symbolic exchange, receiving a *dôron* was an offence against the *polis* as a sacred order which alone, next to the gods, was justified in creating ties of dependence and obligation resulting from gift exchange.

The most complex explanation of *dôrodokia* in the *polis* has been given by Herman. He argues that the shifting meaning of *dôra* was related to a shift of power from *basileis* with quasi-divine power to the constitutional government of the *polis*.[73] A gift merged into a bribe when it came into conflict with the idea that the community, rather than a monarch, held supreme power. The communal interest as the *raison d'être* of political organisation was the only background against which gift-giving could appear as bad. Outside the communal sphere, as for example in the exchange with gods, or with foreigners, a gift was implicitly good and bribery unknown. Conversely, being praised as one who never accepted a gift (*adôrodokos* or *adôrodokêtos*) was a civic virtue specifically invented

4. The Politics of Exchange

for the ideology of the *polis*. Gifts had created ties of obligation between heroes, as well as kings and their subjects, while abstaining from them was an explicit acceptance of the city as the only heir to heroes and kings. To quote Herman:

> In the process of remodelling the hero to the standards of communal life, the *polis* had to replace the ideal of personal fidelity, of which the gift was the closest mark, with the counter-ideal of obedience to communal rules. *Adôrodokêtos* thus came to denote a feature of the ideal citizen – virtue manifesting itself in the willingness to show more regard to communal rules than to personal obligations.[74]

Herman's model is supported by archaic poetry which expresses the dangers of *hubris* associated with an excessive desire for honour and wealth.[75] During that period, a person who ignored the limits of wealth and power was likely to be associated with heroism in the most negative way: that is, transgression of the boundary of the mortal condition. Yet Herman's propositions are challenged by the rhetoric of the 5th and 4th centuries. There are few indications that the recipients of gifts, when accused of taking bribes, were associated with a desire for excessive power.[76] Much more frequently they were accused of making themselves dependent on other people. Accepting a *misthos* they forfeited their freedom. To 5th- and 4th-century politicians *dôra* were bad not because they symbolised heroism but because they asked for a return.

A normative statement along these lines can be found in Euripides' *Supplices*, produced in the Peloponnesian war period. Here a number of *epitaphioi* are read out as paradigmatic praises of civic virtues:

> Second I name Eteocles. He practised
> Another kind of virtue. Lacking means (*tôi biôi endeês*),
> This youth held many offices (*timas*) in Argos.
> Often his friends would make him gifts of gold,
> But he never took it in his house. He wanted
> No slavish way of life haltered by money.[77]

Eteocles held office because, or although, he was poor. But though he was in need of funds, which made his personal friends offer him gold, he did not accept it, shying away from the dependence it created. Dependence on wealthy citizens, here literally identified with dependence on their money, was the threat to civic virtue associated with *dôrodokia*.[78] *Dôrodokia* was the subversion of the democratic strategy of replacing private dependence with public control. The ideal defence against charges of bribery was therefore to prove either that the defendant was personally not in need of the wealth of others, or that public prosperity was more important to him than his private income.

Conversions

The public economy of the *polis* relied to a considerable extent on gifts, or bribes, privately received by individuals from guest-friends who were outsiders of the *polis*.[79] It was not simply the 'gentle and humane nature' of the Athenians[80] that made them turn a blind eye to the large personal profits generals and politicians made in public offices, but the unspoken understanding that these profits, though gained by individuals, were vital resources for the community. Because societies realise the importance of incorporating into the public economy things of value gained by individuals, while at the same time disqualifying private acquisitiveness, rituals are invented which transform them into valuables which benefit society as a whole.[81] Bohannan and Dalton have applied the term 'conversions' to the transformation of the meaning of valuables. They observe that such conversions become more frequent the more a community feels itself under economic pressure. For example, states melt down sacred temple treasure in order to purchase weapons or food in times of scarcity. In this case valuables which have meaning in a divine order of exchange are converted into commodities. Parry and Bloch have looked specifically at the conversion of money associated with commodity exchange into valuables which are sacred. They discuss a number of rituals, such as 'drinking' or 'cooking' money, by which money gained in commerce is physically transformed into public and temple treasure. Thus money can be moved from one transactional order to another, even if these are kept separate by their rules of exchange and symbolism.

No such rituals of transforming morally disqualified *chrêmata*, or money, into a sacred value of public or religious treasure are known from the Greek world. This does not mean that the value of things was easily convertible from one transactional order to the other – that is, that it could be used interchangeably in a private, public or sacred economy. Rather it implies that the ideology of the ancient city stood in the way of making use of valuables which were gained in morally disqualified contexts, such as usury, bribery or commerce. Parry and Bloch take this as the origin of the Western tradition of condemning money and wealth in any supra-individual order of exchange.[82] However, a closer look at the function of liturgies and *eisphora* in the symbolic economy of the *polis* suggests that these can be regarded as ritual 'conversions' by which valuables gained privately, and perhaps immorally, were turned into valuables of the *polis*. The fact that citizens were not taxed, but made individual payments for specific projects in the form of liturgies, shows that private and public expenditure were carefully separated. Especially in the case of money gained as a bribe, 'conversions' seem to have been made.

In the second half of a speech against the charge of *dôrodokia*, fragmentarily preserved in the *Corpus Lysiacum*, the speaker makes the following statement:

4. The Politics of Exchange

> I must ask your attention also for what has yet to be added, so that you may understand what kind of person I am before you give your verdict. I was certified of age in the archonship of Theopompus. Appointed to produce tragic drama, I spent thirty minae, and two months later, at the *Thargêlia*, two thousand drachmas, when I won a victory with a male chorus; and in the archonship of Glaucippus at the Great Panathenaea, eight hundred drachmas on Pyrrhic dancers ...[83]

The enumeration of expenditure on *chorêgiai* extends over a number of paragraphs until the defendant turns to demonstrating that his opponents had done exactly the opposite. This type of self-praise is common stock in Attic oratory.[84] Yet the fact that it is recurrent should not reduce its significance as a mode of persuasion. Most speeches deal with suspicious forms of personal enrichment in public or private exchange. The reference to public spending as an argument in favour of the innocence of the defendant may have been a *topos*, but it had its origin in a society that gave absolute priority to public over private interests rather than in one that condemned money in general.[85] By paying liturgies a citizen converted private gain into public wealth and conspicuously re-integrated himself into the public domain.[86] Whether the money under consideration was gained originally in fair or unfair dealings was then no longer relevant.

The possibility of shifting the value of *dôra* from bribes to individuals towards gifts to the community, or *vice versa*, also lies behind the rhetoric of a speech connected with the Harpalus affair. Accusing Demosthenes of corruption when acting on behalf of the Athenians as a politician, the speaker poses this rhetorical question to the jury:

> Really, gentleman, tell me: do you think that he got nothing for proposing that Diphilus should have meals at the Prytaneum or for that statue to be put up in the market? Nothing for conferring Athenian citizenship on Chaerephilus, Pamphilus and Phidippus, or again on Epigenes and Conon the bankers? Nothing for putting up in the market bronze statues of Brasidas, Satyrus and Gorgippus the tyrants from the Pontus from whom he receives a thousand *medimnoi* of wheat a year ...?[87]

Yet in another speech it is said that such grain imports from the Pontus were not gifts from the king of Bosporus to Demosthenes or any other individual but to the Athenian people as a whole.[88] Whether one version is more accurate than the other is not relevant for the present argument, but it is important to realise that the distinction between bribery and gift-giving was made according to whether the recipient was regarded as the addressee or mediator of a gift.

Dôreia

Benefactors of the *polis*, whether citizens or members of other *poleis*, were honoured in public inscriptions erected in the *agora*. It was a public display of excellence commemorated on an immortal monument and bestowed by the collective citizen body. The tradition of aristocratic competitions over excellence being here more alive than in any other civic exchange, it implied certain problems in a democracy. The decrees of the 5th and 4th centuries, both as monuments and as texts, are evidence of the transformation of gift-giving and glory in the democratic *polis*.

The inscriptions commemorating *dôreia* show a clear pattern.[89] Citizens and foreigners were honoured with objects which had little or no value as *chrêmata*. Citizens were honoured with *prohedria* (sitting in the front seats of the theatre), *sitêsis* (public maintenance in the Prytaneum), olive crowns, gold crowns and eulogies.[90] In exceptional cases citizens were honoured with the so-called *megistai timai* (greatest honours) which meant receiving in addition to the ordinary rewards a golden statue in the *agora*.[91] Magistrates frequently, or perhaps regularly, received a golden crown as a reward (*dôreia*) if they had performed their office according to the laws and had not accepted bribes.[92] Foreigners received the honour of *proxenia* (the right to represent their city in Athens), the title *euergetês* (benefactor) and in exceptional cases the right of *isoteleia* (being taxed like an Athenian) and *enktêsis* (the right to own Athenian land).[93] Demes and tribes as well as cult associations such as the *orgeônes* and *thiasioi* followed the same principle: olive crowns, gold crowns, exemption from tribal liturgies, grants of money for sacrifice and dedication, statues.[94] Money was given only on condition that it was spent on sacrifices or for dedications to the gods. Other monetary rewards had a particular purpose, such as the payment of maintenance to the orphans of a deceased benefactor.[95]

The literary material provides evidence for the intentions lying behind the system. Non-material prizes should be the only rewards appropriate for individuals, the reward should not be associated with the name of an individual and the donor should be the collective *dêmos*. It was the collective *dêmos* that praised itself by praising its benefactors. The ideology becomes explicit in the praise of the past. In a 4th-century oration Pericles is taken as a model of correct behaviour. He had been content with an olive crown in return for having collected thousands of talents for the *polis*. Themistocles and Miltiades, after their victories at Salamis and Marathon, received a bronze statue each, but their names were not appended to them.[96] The donors had been 'the *dêmos*', not individual demarchs, while the cost of the crowns and the money for dedication were supplied from public funds, which was explicitly stated on the stele.

The ideology surfaces also in the contrast between Greece and other cultures. Herodotus frequently discusses Athenian attitudes to honour,

4. The Politics of Exchange

virtue, *chrêmata* and *aretê* in contrast to Persian attitudes. The crucial difference was that in Persia, which was a monarchy, a desire for *chrêmata* was expected, while in Athens it marked either the greed of the needy or the excess of the tyrant. One episode highlights this difference clearly. Herodotus tells of Arcadian deserters who reported to the Persian general Mardonius that the Greeks were just celebrating the Olympic festival. They also reported that olive leaves were given as prizes to the victors. Whereupon the Persian Tritantaechmes cried: 'Good heavens, Mardonius, what kind of men are these that you have brought us to fight against – men who compete with one another for no *chrêmata* but only for *aretê*.'[97] While in Persia *chrêmata* served to indicate achievement, in Greece the symbolism of *chrêmata* was incompatible with the virtue of an individual.

The Greeks, and the Athenians in particular, avoided honouring excellence with *chrêmata* because it was incompatible with equality. In an enduring awareness of the symbolic statements made by valuable objects their use in politics was restricted to exchanges between a collective donor and recipients. Outside the political context of the *polis, chrêmata*, including money, remained the most appropriate symbols of honour and status. In dedications to the gods the costs involved played an important part. A famous inscription of the Samian *Heraion*, dated to the early 6th century, illustrates this point well:

> Meniskos (?), son of Xenodokos, Demis, son of Pythokles and the Perinthians dedicate to Hera as a tithe a goldon Gorgo, a silver Siren, a silver cup and a bronze lamp – all worth twelve Samian staters – together with a stone.[98]

Notes

1. Sahlins (1972), pp. 185-275, esp. 204 ff.; cf. Donlan (1981-2), pp. 172 f. who applies Sahlins' scheme to an analysis of the Homeric epics. Similar ideas have been expressed by Bourdieu (1990) [1980] who envisages generalised reciprocity as a mode of exchange which 'covers asymmetrical power relationships' by its false assumption of circulation and delayed return. With reference to Sahlins and Finley (1981 f) he notes that pre-capitalist societies lack the institutional framework for indirect, impersonal domination such as the labour or capital market provide. Instead, personalised forms of credit and other institutions of trust are used as a means of domination in which the inability of the debtor to return in equal terms masks the asymmetry of the exchange. This he terms 'soft' domination or symbolic violence which to some extent, if not completely, substitutes for physical violence; see esp. pp. 123-129. See Hutter (1978), pp. 1-23 for a critical discussion of models of exchange in political theory. For critical comments on the concept of reciprocity in general see MacCormack (1976).
2. Mauss (1990) [1925], pp. 10-17, 39-46.
3. Ibid., p. 39.
4. Bourdieu (1971) [repr. in (1993), pp. 112-120] stresses this last point in particular; generosity is symbolic violence as it puts the recipient under a threat to reciprocate, which he cannot do.
5. Mauss (1990) [1925], pp. 14-17.

6. Ibid., p. 12; Sahlins (1972), pp. 142-169, made an important contribution to the analysis of the *hau* by pointing out that it is not a fixed essence of the gift, as Mauss assumed, but a value that increases as it is passed around. The *hau* forces the recipient not to return it to the original donor, but to a third person, which makes it an object of generalised, rather than direct, reciprocity.

7. Mauss (1990) [1925], p. 12.

8. Parry (1986), pp. 459-463.

9. Ibid., pp. 463-465.

10. See esp. *Il.* 1. 225-244.

11. Hes. *W&D* 349-363. See also Millett (1984), pp. 101-103.

12. See esp. Detienne (1963).

13. So also Millett (1984).

14. Gernet (1981 a), pp. 115-131, with Diog. Laert. 1. 27-33 and Plut. *Sol.* 4 (myth of the seven sages); Aesch. *Ag.* 905-957 (the story of the tapestry); Hdt. III. 40-43 (Polycrates of Samos).

15. For an overview of the wide range of meanings of *hubris* see now Fischer (1992), esp. pp. 493 ff. and index s.v. wealth and *hubris*.

16. Kurke (1991), pp. 218 ff. I am unconvinced, however, by the explanation she gives for the generosity of tyrants being praised so excessively. She suggests that in the case of citizens, generosity had to be controlled by the rest of the citizen body, while in the case of tyrannical power no expenditure was ever regarded as too great. 'For those victors who are tyrants, the poet applies a rhetoric of extremes which suits the pre-eminent position and gestures of his patron' (p. 224). It seems to me, rather, that the emphasis on the generosity of tyrants served to protect them against the dangers of *hubris*; see esp. Pind. *Pyth.* 2. 54-64 and 84-92.

17. Bacch. 3. 10-17, trans. Kurke.; see also Pind. *Ol.* 2. 1-8; 93-100.

18. Pind *Pyth.* 7. 1-9, trans. Bowra.

19. Kurke (1991), pp. 99-107.

20. Ruschenbusch (1966), F 71-72 c. For a summary of the sumptuary legislation see Pleket (1969), p. 49. Similar laws are attributed to Periander of Corinth, for which see Will (1955 b), pp. 513 ff.

21. Cf. Gernet (1981 d), Humphreys (1978), p. 219, Donlan (1980), pp. 52-75 and 155-171, Kurke (1991), pp. 167 ff.

22. Ober (1989), p. 199.

23. Davies (1971), p. xvii; cf. (1981), pp. 26 and 92; see also Millett (1991 b), pp. 64 f.

24. Arist. *EN* 1122 a 18-1123 b 34, trans. Irwin.

25. Arist. *EN* 1122 b 20-1123 a 5; cf. Xen. *Oec.* 2. 5-7 for a similar view yet with a different emphasis.

26. Ibid. 1123 a 6-10.

27. Arist. *Pol.* 1317 b 41.

28. Arist. *EN* 1123 a 19-27.

29. The negative definition of 'friendship between the good' (*tôn agathôn philia*) as being not for utility and not for pleasure is crucial to Aristotle's theory of perfect friendship; see *NE* 1156 a 10-1156 b 30; cf. Price (1989), pp. 130 ff.

30. Plut. *Ages.* IV. 4.

31. Persian dress I. 3. 2; II. 4. 1-6; see however VIII. 1. 40; eating habits I. 3. 7, 11 etc.; there is no gift and honour so meaningful as the sharing of food, VIII. 2. 2; pouring libations I. 3. 9; competitive hunting I. 4. 14; V. 1. 5, 12; athletes (like soldiers and farmers) give toil in return for victory I. 5. 10; horses are of special value throughout the text; while often rejecting other gifts, Cyrus always accepts horses, see for example VI. 1. 26.

32. Leisure II. 1. 16; praise and wealth I. 5. 12, II. 1. 12; Xenophon makes the comparison of the value of discourse (*logoi, epainos*) and the value of *chrêmata* which is familiar from Homer, Theognis and Pindar; the inversion of this comparison – that is, the link between lies and *kerdosunê* – is also expressed, but Xenophon qualifies it slightly: people may tell false stories for gaining something (*ti lambanein, kerdainein*), but they may also invent stories for amusing others (II. 2. 12). Wealth for helping friends VIII. 4. 31; 2. 13; when he had not yet enough money to do favours by the gift of money 'he tried to win the love of those about him by taking forethought for them and labouring for them and showing that he rejoiced with them in their good fortune and sympathised with them in their mishaps' (VIII. 2. 2).

33. III. 2. 7; cf. I. 5. 10.

34. For the different symbolism of *dôra* and *misthoi* see below in this chapter.

35. Excellence encouraged by gifts, offices and seats of honour VIII. 1. 39; *dôra* to generals and *misthos* to soldiers III. 2. 6, VI. 2. 9, VIII. 5. 23; accepting gifts in order to pay wages and gifts to army III. 2. 28; generosity to *kapêloi* VI. 2. 38.

36. V. 4. 29-32.

37. III. 2. 28.

38. III. 3. 4-3.; see also V. 5. 27 and 33.

39. The compact which he makes with Gobryas is little different from a contract. Offering to be his suppliant rather than his subject, and promising his help for avenging the murder of Gobryas' son, he asks what service he will do him in return. And when Gobryas offers him the tribute of his provinces, soldiers and daughter in marriage, he makes it a formal agreement: 'According as what you have said is true, I give you my right hand and take yours. The gods be our witnesses (*martures*)' (IV. 6. 7-10). While shaking hands was part of ritualised gift exchange in archaic Greece (Herman (1987), pp. 47-55) the presence of *martures* (though here the gods) and the specification of the return at the moment of the offer make this agreement sound like a contract.

40. VIII. 5. 20.

41. VIII. 2. 13-19.

42. Thuc. II. 97. 3-4. The passage is discussed by Mauss (1921) who believed that Thucydides had failed to understand gift exchange since, in the light of his model of the gift, Thucydides' remarks are contradictory.

43. Thucydides' observation that the Persian kings gave rather than received gifts is not borne out by other evidence. Persian kings seem to have received gifts in large quantities. In the Achaemenid Empire the royal courts and temples were redistributive centres to which gifts were given and which symbolised the power of the king. The reliefs of the Persepolis terrace give independent evidence on the practice, while Theopompus and Herodotus provide similar descriptions from a Greek point of view; see Cahil (1985) for evidence from Persepolis; for Persian gift exchange in general Lewis (1989) and Theop. *FGrHist* 115 F 263, and for Herodotus Gould (1991). The discrepancy between Persian gift exchange and Greek descriptions of it needs further investigation.

44. Thuc. II. 40. 4.; for the translation see Millett (1991 b), p. 123 and Hooker (1974), p. 167. See also Arist. *EN* 1133 a 2-4. For *charis* and reciprocity see esp. Millett (1991 b), pp. 123-126 and bibliographical note; for *charis* in Athenian politics in general see Ober (1989), pp. 226-232; for its function in epinician poetry see Kurke (1991), index s.v. *charis*.

45. Thuc. I. 32 ff.; cf. Hooker (1974), p. 168.

46. Benveniste (1969), pp. 163-179.

47. Will (1975 b).

48. For a comprehensive survey of the linguistic evidence see de Ste. Croix (1981), pp. 181-186.

49. As the chronological relationship of the *Iliad* and *Odyssey* cannot be ascertained (Pucci (1987), p. 18) it may also be argued that the formula used for the gift to Dolon hints at the passage in the *Odyssey*. This would, however, not change the present argument.

50. Plat. *Rep.* 345 e-347 d; cf. Will (1975 b), p. 436.

51. *Technai misthôtikai, mistharnikai* or even *chrêmatismoi*, 357 a.

52. In *Apol.* 31 b f. Socrates claims that he never asked for a *misthos* in return for his teaching, and in *Hipp.* 228 c Simonides is said to have attended Hipparchus constantly as he persuaded him with great *dôra* and *misthoi* of the tyrant.

53. Plat. *Rep.* 613 e. The section has puzzled commentators to such an extent that its authenticity was questioned; see Annas (1981), p. 349.

54. Plat. *Rep.* 366 e-367 d; esp. 367 d.

55. Annas (1981), p. 350.

56. Morpurgo Davies *Kadmos* 9, pp. 118-154; the inscription is dated to the beginning of the 5th century. Will (1975 b), pp. 433 f.; see also van Effenterre (1973).

57. For the 5th-century usage see Thuc. V. 47,6; VIII. 45,6; see also Meritt, *The Athenian Tribute Lists (ATL)* II, list 34 (421/0), ll. 107 f.; list 25 (439/29) col. 1, ll. 59 f.; col. 3, ll. 42 f.; IG I^2 63 (425/4) etc.; see Will (1975 b), pp. 432 f.

58. Will (1975 b), p. 434.

59. Aesch. 3. 183; see also below pp. 117-119.

60. Hdt. IV. 9 (Heracles gives *misthos* to the viper woman); IV. 151 (*misthos* given to purple fisher); VI. 23; VIII. 4; VIII. 134 (payment/bribe in a negative sense)

61. Hdt. I. 160.

62. Hdt. V. 65.

63. Ar. *Wasps* 712.

64. Arist. *Pol.* 1293 a 3-7; 1299 b 38-1300 a 4. This led to the mistaken belief among modern scholars that the *dikastikon* and *ekklesiastikon* were indeed salaries compensating for lost income during the period of service; see, by contrast, Ober (1989), pp. 136 f., and Will (1975 b), pp. 430 f. Markle (1985) tried to estimate whether citizens were able to earn a living from public pay, without considering the ideological bias of his sources.

65. Arist. *Pol.* 1320 b 2 f.

66. Xen. *Apol.* 16. See also Dem. 19. 8, and Harvey (1985) for further examples.

67. Dem. 59. 88 f.

68. Schuller (1982), pp. 9-24 discusses current theoretical approaches, with full bibliography in n. 4. There is another approach which relates the phenomenon of bribery to a rapid increase of money and commercial exchange in an otherwise traditional environment. Goods and services drift towards being 'commodified', but the traditional culture works against it by preserving a number of things and services for the symbolic economy. The fact that in most cultures certain items are consciously excluded from being commodified has been called a 'moral economy' by scholars who argue for this approach (although E.P. Thompson, who introduced the term into the social sciences, meant something quite different by it). A typical aspect of such a 'moral economy' was that political service was prevented from being purchasable. See esp. Kopytoff (1986), pp. 64 ff., Elwert (1987), with special reference to bribery, prostitution and simony, and Colace in Lewis (1989) with reference to the ancient world. This approach, however, does not explain the problems of *dôrodokia* in ancient Athens. For a theoretical approach to bribery in capitalist societies, in which economic explanations for corruption seem more appropriate, see Ackerman (1978).

4. The Politics of Exchange

69. The legal situation of bribery in Athens is discussed and documented by MacDowell (1983).
70. Harvey (1985).
71. Wankel (1982).
72. Perlman (1976), without considering the problem of bribery within the *polis*; see also Herman (1987), pp. 79-81.
73. Herman (1987), pp. 76 ff.
74. Ibid., p. 78.
75. See above and in addition Theogn. 541-542; 1103-1104; 833-836; 183-192; 47-48; cf. Nagy (1985), pp. 51-60; and Kurke (1991), pp. 195-225.
76. In Harvey's comprehensive survey of the language and rhetoric of bribery not a single reference to *hubris* is noted. The only term whose meaning goes some way towards excess, and which is occasionally given as a motivation for bribery, is *pleonexia*; yet any association of the word with transgression of the boundary between citizenship and heroism is, as far as I can see, absent. See Harvey (1985), pp. 82-89, 102.
77. Eur. *Suppl.* 871-877, trans. F. W. Jones.
78. So also Ober (1989), pp. 236-238.
79. Herman (1987), pp. 84-88 discusses the nature and extent of presents from foreign guest-friends to Athenian citizens.
80. Hyp. 5. 24-25; cf. Harvey (1985), pp. 108-113.
81. Bohannan and Dalton (1962), pp. 10 ff.; cf. Parry and Bloch (1989), pp. 26 f.
82. Parry and Bloch (1989), pp. 2 ff.
83. Lys. 21. 1.
84. See also Ant. 2.2 12; Is. 5. 41 f.; and Dover (1974), pp. 175-181, for further examples.
85. Ober (1989), pp. 230-239.
86. As Wilson pointed out, the *chorêgia* and other liturgies were institutionalised competitive events, a public display of the elite and their fight for *timê*. Wilson (1991), p. 171.
87. Din. I. 43.
88. Dem. 20. 31; cf. Garnsey (1988), pp. 138 f.
89. The epigraphical evidence appears in bulk only after 320 B.C. while literary evidence is more frequent before that date. The present argument must be based mainly on the few inscriptions dated to the 5th and 4th centuries; yet some later examples are taken as further illustration.
90. In Athens: IG II^2 169, 223 A and B; 338; in demes: IG II^2 1186, 1187 (from 319/8 B.C.), 1189, 1173, 1202, 1193; SEG XXV, 141; cf. Gauthier (1985), Osborne (1990), Maass (1972), pp. 75-95, M. J. Osborne (1981).
91. Syll. 3. 126; Tod, II. 106 (Conon); Aesch. III. 243, Dem. 23. 30 and 36 (Iphicrates); Aesch. III. 243, Arist. *Rhet.* 1411 b 6-7; Diod. XV. 33.4; cf. Dem. 20. 75 ff. and 146 f. (Chabrias); Din. I. 13 ff. (Timotheos); Ar. *Kn.* 573-576; cf. 280 f., 702 ff. (Cleon).
92. IG II^2 415, 223 A and B, l. 13 f., 672, l. 13-15; in demes: IG II^2 1251, 1257, 2797, SEG XXI 360 (290/89 B.C.); cf. Dem. 23. 89; Aesch. I. 111 f. Dem. XXII. 36, 38 f. See Rhodes (1985), pp. 14-16.
93. IG II^2, 269, 277, 304, 330 etc. See Gauthier (1985) and his argument against Veyne (1976), summarised on pp. 16-22.
94. Osborne (1990), pp. 274-276.
95. Cf. SEG XXV 141; *Hesp.* 40/1971 pp. 280-301 (daily allowance for the orphans of the victims in the events of the overthrow of the Thirty Tyrants).
96. Dem. 23. 197 f.; cf. 13, 21 ff.; Aesch. 3. 183 ff.; Lyc. frg. 8. 2 (Teubner).

97. Hdt. VIII. 26. 2-3. The Persian practice of rewarding good service with *chrêmata* is well documented in Herodotus and elsewhere. Hdt. VIII 10. 3 (reward of the first Persian captain to capture an Athenian ship; VII. 26. 2 (presents for the best equipped contingent); cf. VII. 106.1; 116; VIII. 120 (cities and individuals who have rendered service in general). See also Lewis (1989), p. 228 on Persian gift-giving in general.

98. SEG XII 391.

5

Market Exchange and Private Profit

The market in anthropological perspective

In many economies trade and commerce are associated with the market place.[1] Yet, while in conventional economic analysis the market stands for a certain kind of exchange which functions independently of the culture by which it is surrounded, the ancient *agora* was firmly embedded in the value-system of the *polis*.[2] Polanyi's distinction between reciprocity and redistribution, on the one hand, as being socially embedded, and market exchange as a 'disembedded' economic institution on the other, does not easily fit the ancient case. According to Polanyi, reciprocity and redistribution require a social network or political system for goods to be transferred. In market exchange, by contrast, material goods circulate outside a social network; here people can exchange who are socially and politically independent of each other.[3] Bohannan and Dalton introduced an important analytical distinction into Polanyi's model. They argued that the economic principle of market exchange had to be distinguished from the market place. The 'market principle' – that is, the supply-and-demand mechanism – could operate without a market place, while market places often do not function on the basis of the supply-and-demand mechanism. Especially in societies with so-called peripheral markets – societies where local production is not directed to market distribution – market exchange remains essentially social exchange.[4] Polanyi's concept of market exchange clearly refers to the market principle; nevertheless he sought the origins of it in market places and ports of trade (*emporia*).[5]

Neither a concept of exchange value nor the metaphors of commerce developed in connection with market exchange in ancient Greece. They emerged, first, as part of the definition of the human condition bound up with agriculture and the *oikos* and, secondly, in an attempt to find moral distinctions, such as between truth and lies, political government and corrupted power, or eros and prostitution.[6] Conversely, the development of the *agora* was related to the political development of the *polis*. Polanyi could observe only a 'curious connection between practical democracy and the rise of the market' but could not explain in what ways notions of buying and selling in the *agora* were dependent on the development of the *polis*, and of democracy in particular.

The development of the *agora* as a space for public exchange increased the possibility of acting politically and economically outside the closely knit social network of neighbourhood, friendship and kinship ties.[7] It implied that any exchange taking place in the centre of the city was no longer under the control of social networks dominated by individual *oikoi* but of 'the *dêmos*', however fictitious this collective agent may have been. The rules of reciprocity and redistribution remained important political and economic instruments in the *agora* as long as the *dêmos* as a whole could be located at the receiving end of any asymmetrical exchange. Rather than fostering a disembedded economy, the *agora* replaced one kind of embedded exchange with another. The *agora* thus remained a site of symbolic exchange in all its different areas: around the stalls, in political assemblies and in the law courts.

In this chapter I shall look first at the Athenian *agora* and the functions which were associated with that site in 5th- and 4th-century texts. I shall then argue that political, social and economic exchange were regarded as related aspects of civic exchange and made similar symbolic statements. Economic exchange proper remained an essential element of the symbolic economy of Athens despite the expansion of trade and sale.

Politics in the *agora*

Stallybrass and White have looked at market places as sites of cultural exchange, and their remarks are a useful starting point for comparison and contrast:

> How does one 'think' a marketplace? At once a bounded enclosure and a site of open commerce, it is both the imagined centre of an urban community and its structural interconnection with the world of goods, commodities, markets, sites of commerce and production which sustain it. A marketplace is the epitome of local identity ... and the unsettling of that identity by the trade and traffic of goods from elsewhere. At the market centre of the polis we discover a commingling of categories usually kept separate and opposed: centre and periphery, inside and outside, stranger and local, commerce and festivity, high and low. In the marketplace pure and simple categories of thought find themselves perplexed and onesided. Only hybrid notions are appropriate to such a hybrid place.[8]

The Athenian *agora* was more than a place of commerce. Indeed its commercial aspect was subordinate to its function as a centre of civic exchange. The local identity of the place was unsettled not so much by the trade and traffic of goods that came from elsewhere as by the different functions and meanings the site served and represented. As the political centre of the democratic *polis* the Athenian *agora* symbolised the assembly

5. Market Exchange and Private Profit

of citizens and the equality of all its members. At the same time it was the site of competition and ostentation, a showplace of differences in wealth and status.

The *agora* was a place of public displays. Here the city presented itself in monuments, performances of assembled crowds and individual people, and in the goods that were on offer for sale. Here, too, the status and prestige of its citizens became the focus of attention. It is significant, first of all, that a large proportion of the *Characters* of Theophrastus are defined by their habits in the *agora*, especially around its shops and tables. For example, the 'flatterer' (*kolax*) 'buys apples and pears, brings them in and gives them to the children when their father is watching, kisses them and says, "Well, youngsters, you've got a splendid father." If he goes with his patron to help him buy some shoes, he remarks that the foot is more shapely than the shoes' (II. 10). For 'the one who has lost all sense' (*aponenoêmenos*) it is not beneath him 'to be a little king among the barrow-boys, lend them money for the asking, and charge twenty-five per cent per day; or to make the rounds of the pie-and-pastry shops, the wet-fishmongers and the dry-fishmongers, and to collect the interest due to him straight out of the customer's hand into his mouth' (VI. 9). When the 'shameless man' (*anaischuntos*) goes shopping, 'he reminds the butcher of any little service he may have done him; and he stands near the scale and slips on to it some meat if possible, otherwise a bone to make soup; and if he gets away with it he's happy, and if not, he whips a bit of tripe off the table and chuckles as he hurries away with it' (IX. 4-6). The 'stingy man' (*mikrologos*) 'goes off to market, and comes home again without buying anything' (X. 13). The 'distrustful man' (*apistos*) is the sort 'who, after sending a slave to buy provisions, sends another whose job is to find out how much he paid for them' (XVIII. 4). The 'man of petty ambitions' (*mikrophilotimos*) 'buys for himself nothing, but all for friends abroad; ... when he has taken part in a procession of the knights, he hands all the rest of his equipment to his slave to take home, and then walks about the *agora* in spurs, constantly tossing back his cloak' (XXI. 7 f.). The 'mean man' (*aneleutheros*) 'will come home from the market carrying all his shopping of meat and vegetables in the fold of his gown' (XXII. 7). And 'the boaster' (*alazôn*) 'will go up to the horse market and pretend to the dealers that he wishes to buy a horse of quality', and he will 'go into a clothing-store, and ask to see clothing priced at anything up to two talents, and then browbeat his slave for coming without his money' (XXIII. 8 f.). The importance of the market as a display of social behaviour and political status is borne out by the number of references in this short essay.

In 4th-century oratory the *agora* appears as the space where events turn into news and where social reputations are created and confirmed. It is the place where the solidarity and tensions of the community become explicit. Lysias tries to make the audience believe that 'each of us is in the habit of frequenting some place: a perfumer's, a barber's, a cobbler's or wherever it might happen to be; and the greatest number visit those who are nearest the *agora*.'[9] And Isocrates describes how Callimachus, 'as if no one had any knowledge of the matter, himself mixed with the crowds, sat in the workshops, and related again and again his story, how he had suffered outrageous treatment at my hands and had been defrauded of his money.'[10] Aeschines goes so far as to remind the citizens that in the *agora* opinion can be manipulated and popular judgment led astray. He accuses his opponents of having 'mustered their forces' and having gone 'begging up and down the *agora* in the attempt to prevent the fair and orderly course of justice in the state'.[11] Since the *agora* was the barometer of public opinion it offered an occasion for ostentation in the form of conspicuous consumption and exchange: shopping at expensive stalls, wearing expensive clothes, mixing with certain people and not with others.[12] The private *persona* of the Athenian citizen turned public in the *agora*. The *agora* was a hybrid place because it was thought to manifest the moral status of citizens, which was normally evaluated in terms of agrarian success, attitudes to neighbours in the countryside, and to the gods on the occasion of festivals and sacrifices.

Shifting the assessment of citizens from the countryside to the *agora* was a deliberate strategy in the course of democratisation. The actual power-base of politicians probably remained mostly the rural *dêmos*, but ideologically the centre of politics shifted towards the city and its *agora*.[13] Ober has noted the frequent references to popular judgement in political and forensic oratory, regarding them as the result of the 'perceived democratic nature of common report':

> Athenian speakers often said to their audience, 'You all know the character or actions of a litigant, either that he was a good man who lived an upright life or an evil one who did evil things ...' the statement that everyone knew something was ... directly linked to egalitarian ideology. When Hyperides (1. 14) argued that a legal defence should be based on a man's whole life, as no individual in the *polis* could hope to deceive 'the mass of you' (*to plêthos to humeterôn*), he implied that arguments based upon common report were just and democratic. Hyperides bases his argument on the assumption that, although a clever speaker might fool the members of a jury, he could not fool 'all of the people all of the time'. Because the jury's decision stood for the decision of the society as a whole, it was right that society's opinion be taken into consideration.[14]

If the *agora* was the typical place where common report was created, Ober's hypothesis is confirmed by the fact that we hear in anti-democratic texts that the *agora* ought to be avoided. While Plato and Aristotle dismissed markets as places of trade and commerce, Isocrates criticised them as places of public display. In the *Areopagiticus* he praises the past when

> The young men did not waste their time in the gambling dens or with the flute girls or in the kind of company in which they now spend their days, but

remained steadfast in the pursuits to which they had been assigned, admiring and emulating those who excelled in these. And so strictly did they avoid the market-place that even if they were at times compelled to pass through it they were seen to do it with great modesty (*pollês aidous*) and sobriety of manner (*sophrosunês*).[15]

Isocrates' remarks are particularly significant in the context of his argument before and after this passage. A few paragraphs earlier he had praised the economy of wealthy landlords which 'came to the rescue of the distresses of the poor, handing over land to some at moderate rentals, sending out some to engage in trade, and furnishing means to others to enter upon various occupations'. The rich were happy to lend, and did not worry about being paid back, since 'thus they experienced the double satisfaction which should appeal to all right-minded men, of helping their fellow citizens and at the same time making their own property productive (*energa*) for themselves'.[16] These ideas have rightly been compared to patronage 'seen through an oligarchic haze'.[17] The display of wealth and status in public was indispensable for political success, but it did not happen in the same place as under the democracy. Isocrates praises the young of the past who avoided the *agora*, the infrequency of law suits and occasions where public contributions had to be collected, and then continues:

And so, because of these things, our forefathers lived in such a degree of security that the houses and establishments in the country were finer and more costly than those within the city walls, and many of the people never visited Athens even for the festivals, preferring to remain at home in the enjoyment of their own possessions rather than share in the pleasures dispensed by the state. For even the public festivals which might otherwise have drawn many to the city, were not conducted with sane moderation, since our people then measured their well-being (*eudaimonian*) not by their processions or their efforts to outdo each other in *chorêgiai*, or any such empty shows, but by the sobriety with which they managed their daily life (*sophronôs oikein*), and by the absence of want among all citizens.[18]

Isocrates scorns not only public exchange in the *agora* and the law courts but also the competitive outlay of wealth and status during festivals and in the theatre. Wealth should not be concealed, as he explicitly states in the same speech (34), but it should be associated with the *oikos* in the countryside. It was not the kind of exchange but the sites of exchange that were associated with different political models in the 4th century. Competition in spaces associated with the *polis*, rather than those dominated by individual *oikoi* and competition among citizens as citizens, rather than as members of a family, were the marks of democracy.

The conflict between democratic and aristocratic principles of government during the decades before the Peloponnesian war was associated in the 4th century with the personal rivalry between Cimon and Pericles.[19]

Pericles had made friends with the people on a public level while Cimon continued to distribute his private wealth to people more closely related to his rural household. Pericles' virtues were associated with the public space: the erection of monuments, the skill of public persuasion, the introduction of public pay for public service (*theorika, dikastika*), and buying and selling in the market.[20] Conversely, he was 'completely beyond gift-giving' (*adôrotatos*) which smacked of private exchange and private loyalties.[21] For Plutarch, Pericles' social, political and economic behaviour could be viewed as aspects of the same strategy. His programme of public pay, his emphasis on buying and selling in the market and his rejection of private gifts were interdependent parts of his monetary economy:

> During all these years he kept himself untainted by corruption (*analôton hupo chrêmatôn*), although he was not altogether indifferent to money making (*chrêmatismon*); indeed the wealth which was legally his by inheritance from his father, that it might not take to itself wings and fly away, nor yet cause him much trouble and loss of time when he was busy with higher things, he set into such orderly dispensation as he thought easiest and most exact. This was to sell his annual products all together in the lump, and then to buy in the *agora* each article as it was needed, and so provide the ways and means of daily life.[22]

Although in this passage Plutarch does not relate Pericles' use of private property to his policy of public redistribution, this emerges from the contrast he draws between him and his rival Cimon. Cimon made available to all his personal friends, clients and demesmen his private property at home, and 'made his followers carry a generous sum of money, and go up to the poor of better sort in the *agora* and thrust small change secretly (*siôpêi*) into their hands'.[23] It is significant that Cimon himself stayed away from the *agora* and let his followers give money to the poor secretly. Cimon's policy is associated with conspicuous generosity in the *oikos*, while in the *agora* he acted in secret.

The point of this comparison is not, as Polanyi suggested, that Pericles replaced 'the lordly patronage practised by Cimon' with free market exchange.[24] Rather, Pericles stands for the shift of patronage from the private space of the *oikos* to the public space of the *polis*. This meant abstention from accepting gifts, just as it meant the sale of agrarian produce in the market and the extension of public pay for political office. The different policies associated with Pericles and Cimon reflect the political conflict between aristocratic and democratic values, and the conflict between private and public generosity.

The *agora* was a place of 'hybrid notions' (Stallybrass and White) because it articulated the gap between the ideology of democracy and its practice. The gap had political, social and economic aspects. Economically and socially it meant that private exchange and credit shifted into a place controlled by public laws and officials without ceasing to be motivated by social interests and considerations. Politically it meant that the ideological primacy of the public as a source of power remained undermined by private loyalties and private relationships.

The rhetoric of values and the value of rhetoric

The *agora* was at the same time the site of politics, commerce, drama and litigation. Not only were they originally located in the same place but their performances and rhetoric merged into each other. In the 5th century the place of assembly was moved from the *agora* to the Pnyx hill nearby, and also the theatre was built on an extra site (see maps on pp. 112 and 113).[25] Yet they remained comparable sites of civic contests, competitive judgment and bargaining. Payments were made not only to salesmen in the stalls but also to jurymen, winners of *chorêgiai*, actors or poets. The distinction between market exchange and civic competition was spatially undefined. The Athenian public economy may be regarded as simple if we look at the flows of goods and services in isolation. Yet if we consider them as part of a complex symbolism of exchange we can understand their constraints. As the boundaries between the payment of liturgies and tributes, between rewards and salaries, prizes, gifts and bribes were not clearly marked by either space or language, all these transactions could be confused with one another. The proximity of politics, civic competitions and commerce, concentrated in the *agora*, made the confusion of their motivations an effective rhetorical strategy to mark corrupted exchange.

The polyvalence of material values is most apparent in a category of 'goods' which in economic theory are not construed as commodities: civic advice and theatrical performances. In Athens speeches and dramatic performance were consciously presented as valued (and priced) objects of civic exchange. The *agora*, the *bêma* (platform for public speakers) and the stage were sites of exchange where citizens gained *timê* which referred both to the status of people and the price of objects.

In the heat of the conflict between Athens and Macedon, Demosthenes opened one of his speeches with the words:

> A lot of money (*chrêmata*), men of Athens, you would give, I expect, if it could become clear to you what will prove our best policy in the matters now under discussion.[26]

The sentence plays on the double meaning of *chrêmata* as being both a means of payment (recompense or reward) in the symbolic economy of politics and a means of exchange in the concrete economy of the market. *Logoi* had a price insofar as orators were paid for their speeches in private litigation and they were symbolic values in the reciprocal exchanges between politicians and citizens. The speech also plays on the fact that in the democratic *polis*, *chrêmata* were improper rewards for political excellence. The conditional in the sentence is thus ambivalent: it might refer, on the one hand, to the fact that the Athenians did not know what was the best advice and, on the other, to the fact that they never gave *chrêmata* for excellent political service. Demosthenes' rhetoric exploits the fact that the value of both *logoi* and *chrêmata* was context-related. They had commodity (or exchange) value in non-civic exchange and hired labour, while they had symbolic (or sign) value in the context of political exchange.

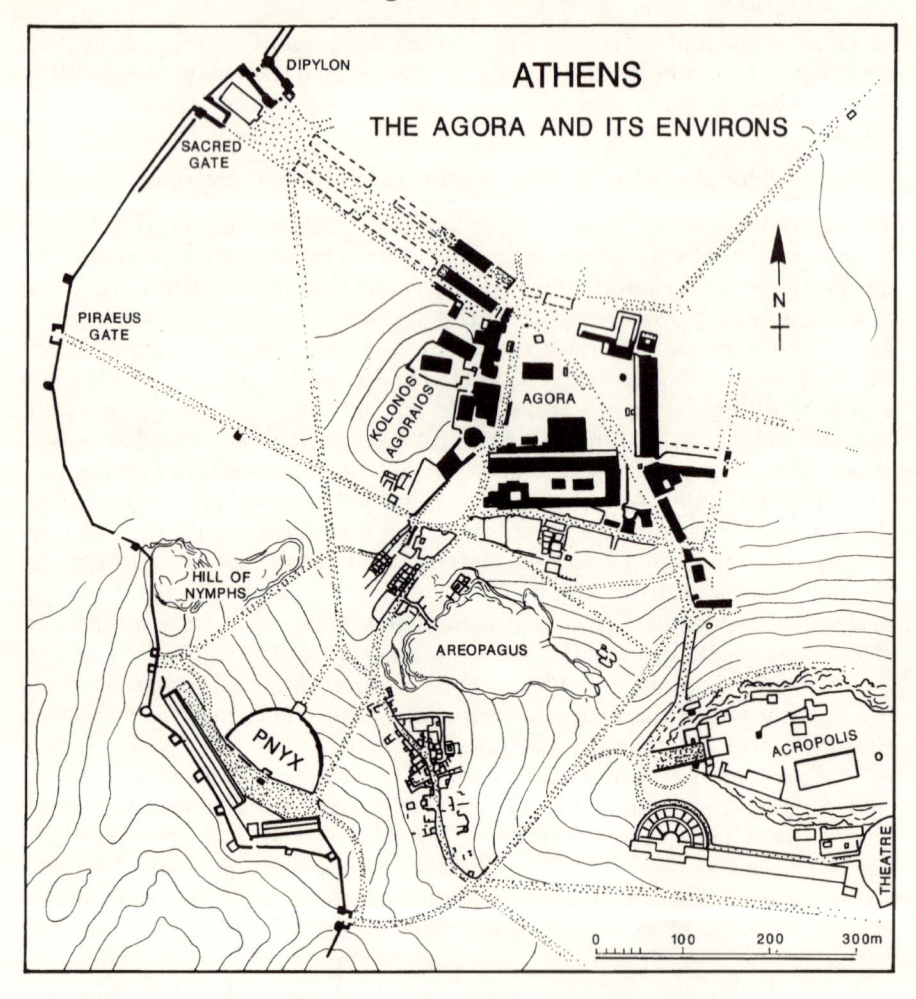

The speech continues along similar lines, shifting between the evaluation of politicians and the value of their advice in a symbolic economy and the evaluation of speeches as objects of exchange in the market economy of hired labour:

5. Market Exchange and Private Profit

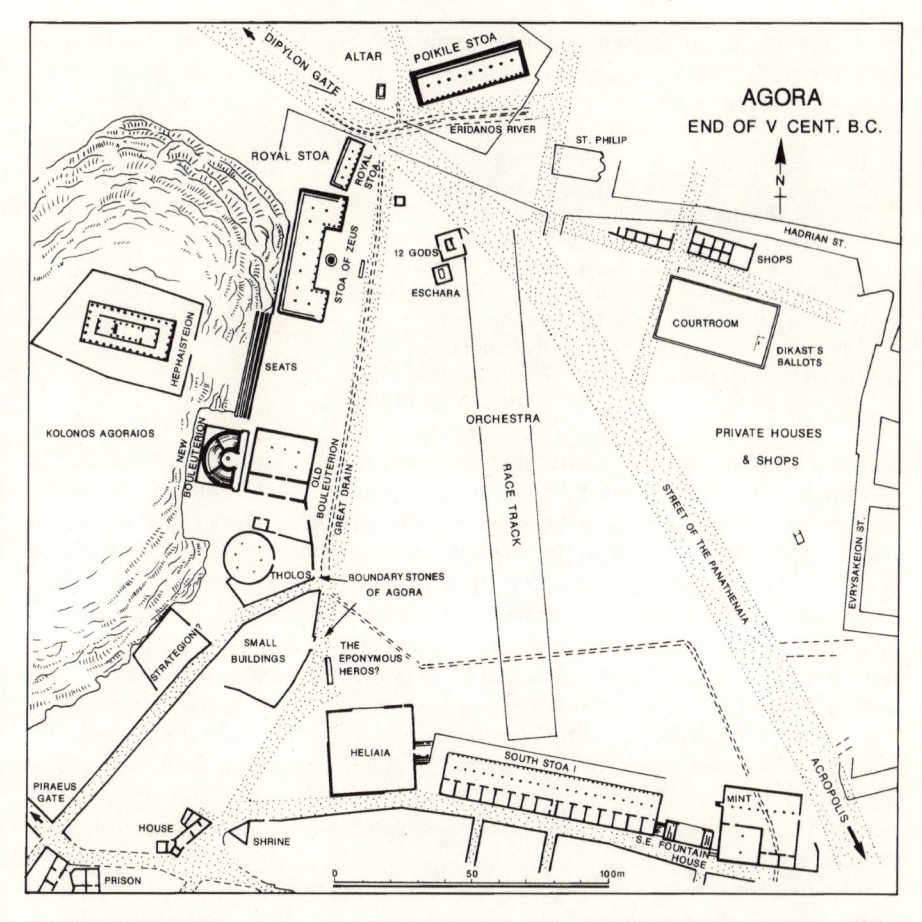

[Map: AGORA END OF V CENT. B.C.]

For not only if someone comes forward with a well-considered plan, could you hear and accept it, but also I count it part of your good fortune that more than one speaker may be inspired with suitable suggestions on the spur of the moment, so that out of the multitude of proposals the choice of the best should not be difficult.[27]

The competition of political orators and the choice which a citizen could make between objects of exchange are represented as related aspects of the same economy. That these economies had in fact to be kept strictly separate was both a condition for, and the consequence of, Demosthenes' rhetoric.

Two generations earlier Aristophanes had used a similar strategy on stage. In the *Frogs* he construed a competition of dramatic performance which addressed the problem of who could give the most valuable advice to the *polis*. The problem is represented as a competition between the two best playwrights of Athens, Aeschylus and Euripides. The scene is framed by striking monetary imagery which compares the value of citizens with the value of coinage:

> By coincidence more sad than funny
> It's very like the way we treat our money.
> The noble silver drachma, that of old
> We were so proud of, and the recent gold,
> Coins that rang true, clean stamped and worth their weight
> Throughout the world, have ceased to circulate.
> Instead, the purses of Athenian shoppers
> Are full of shoddy silver-plated coppers.
> Just so, when men are needed by the nation,
> The best have been withdrawn from circulation.[28]

In the ensuing scenario the imagery is extended by looking at the products offered by those citizens who were regarded as the most valuable citizens. Euripides and Aeschylus put their poetry to the test so as to gain the prize for being the best advisor to the city. At first there is nothing unusual about this competition as the quality of dramatic performance was always assessed in a competition between the playwrights judged by selected citizens. The irony lies rather in the way in which the quality of the performances is measured: the quality of poetry is weighed on a scale. The scale recalls two other scenes of the play. In the one it is used to weigh a sacrificial lamb (768), and in the other a cheese-seller uses it to weigh his cheese before it is sold (1369). The image of the scale thus links the value of civic advice, sacrifice and commodities, suggesting that they are comparable values in the reciprocal exchange between citizens, humans and gods, buyers and sellers.[29]

The *Frogs* plays not only on the common tradition of standards of value and standards of weight, but also on the idea that the citizen body authorised these standards. Further irony lies in confusing the meaning of prizes, which assessed the achievement of people, with the meaning of coins which assessed the value of things. The comical confusions made in the carnivalesque context of comedy suggest that different values circulating in the economy of the *polis* were exchangeable and convertible. Yet at the same time it questioned their convertibility, drawing attention to the different contexts of exchange in which they circulated.

The degree to which the authors of public *logoi* regarded their own political 'value' and that of their products as being related suggests that the economy which Bourdieu calls symbolic and the 'concrete' economy were both symbolic. This is not to say that they were not distinguished, but their distinction was not marked by an absolute distinction of types of value. Two more texts may show how the value of *logoi* could change according to the meaning attached to their exchange. Neither the means of exchange (money) nor the place of exchange (markets) distinguished the

5. Market Exchange and Private Profit

commercial value of texts from the political value of their content. Rather, the status of the donor and recipients determined whether they were part of politics or of commerce. As we have already seen in Homeric epic, the status of the giver/producer, the value of his product and the meaning of the return as either prize or fee conditioned one another.

In the *Letter to Nicocles* Isocrates compares the value of his advice to the value of gifts to a king. Conversely, he reduces the value of other gifts which the king may receive to that of commodities which are traded in order to make a bargain. Note also the ideology of spending that lies behind the following remarks:

> When men make it a habit, Nicocles, of bringing you who are kings clothes or articles of bronze or of wrought gold, or other such valuables (*ktêmata*) of which they themselves have need and you have plenty, it seems to me all too evident that they are not engaged in giving but in trading (*ou dôsin all' emporian poioumenoi*), and they are much more skilful in selling their wares than those who are professedly traders (*polu technikôteron auta pôlountes tôn homologountôn kapêleuein*). For my part, I should think that this would be the finest and the most serviceable present and the most suitable for me to give and for you to receive – if I could prescribe what pursuits you should aspire to and from what you should abstain in order to govern best your state and kingdom.[30]

The line which describes the gifts to Nicocles from other kings ('articles of bronze or of wrought gold') is a Homeric formula.[31] The allusion to heroic gift exchange is unequivocal. Yet, as soon as the comparison is made, their comparability is denied. The gifts to Nicocles are unlike the gifts which heroes exchanged among themselves because they are given by needy people who are much inferior to the recipient. They are thus much more like objects of trade, just as traders are poorer than those to whom they sell. Isocrates' own gift, by contrast, is needed by the king but given generously by the donor. It is a real gift because it creates profit for the recipient not for the donor. Again *logoi* are compared with material values, while both gift-giving and trade are interpreted in terms of their social symbolism. Isocrates doubly subverts the distinction between gift exchange and trade which Homer made: first by calling the donors of gifts traders, and secondly by constructing the value of a gift as something which is determined by the need of its recipient. Isocrates thereby succeeds in raising his own status from that of an ordinary citizen of a *polis* to that of an adequate exchange partner of the Cyprian king. At the same time he reduces the status of the other friends of the king to that of traders, if only in a metaphorical sense. Like Homer, he employs the vocabulary of trade to construct a hierarchy between people. The difference between gift exchange and trade is marked by the different motivations which lay behind them. Yet what was allegedly a distinction of motivation was in fact a distinction of pre-existing status insofar as specific motivations of exchange were ascribed to specific people. Thus the status of the exchanging partners ultimately determined the distinction of different forms of exchange.[32]

Social symbolism and economic value merge again in the remarks with which Demosthenes concludes the speech *On the Trierarchic Crown*. The issue of the speech is whether the Athenians should award the prize for the best trierarchic service to the speaker or to his opponent:

> For the wrongdoing and insolence of these men nobody is more to blame than yourselves; for you inquire what the character of every man is from the speakers who you know are doing what they do for pay (*epi misthôi prattontas*); you do not investigate for yourselves. Yet is it not absurd for you to consider these orators themselves as the basest of your citizens (*ponêrotatous*), but to regard those whom they praise as worthy men (*chrêstous*)? For they are their own masters in all that they do, and they all but sell (*pôlousi*) the public weal by the voice of the common crier (*hupo kêrukos*); and they order you to crown whomsoever they will, setting themselves up as superior to your decrees. I advise you, men of Athens, not to allow the ambitions (*philotimia*) of those who are ready to lavish their money to be dependent upon the greed (*pleonexia*) of those who serve them as pleaders – otherwise you will teach all to perform the duties imposed by you with the least possible outlay – but to hire (*misthousthai*) the largest number of people possible to utter impudent falsehoods before you in support of their claims.[33]

The rhetorical effect of this passage derives from the fact that, first, apparently contradictory statements are made within one and the same oration, and, secondly, that they are made by an orator who himself wrote speeches on commission. Demosthenes asks the question what kind of payment the citizens made when bestowing a crown on an honorand. Was a gold crown the just and equal return for expenses made? Did the payment of public liturgies have the same value as the payment to private orators who made up liturgies in their speeches? Was the value of a person better expressed by the *logoi* of dependent paid orators or by the judgment of unpaid citizens? What value lay in words which were said because the speaker needed money? If we assume that *On the Trierarchic Crown* was performed by Demosthenes on his own behalf,[34] he seems to urge the audience not to believe in speeches which were given by hired orators as their content was dependent on the payment that was given for it. Everybody knew, however, that Demosthenes himself was a professional speech writer, and in another speech he is the victim of just the same rhetoric as he uses here.[35] The conceptual confusion that lay behind the rhetoric was thus consciously made, which rendered the problems addressed even more pressing. Demosthenes compared the value of advice and the value of hired service by playing on the fact that they could both assume an economic (commercial) and a symbolic (political) value. He urged the audience to consider that only their subjective assessment of the quality of the products and of the status of their producers would create the distinction.

Sale, bribery and prostitution

The political exchange was embedded in the symbolic system of the democratic *polis* in which the receipt of money or *chrêmata* from citizens, or members of other communities, was equivalent to accepting an inferior status. The same symbolism applied to commercial exchange in the city, such as wage-labour and sale. Little is known of the commercial life of Athens itself, but the frequency with which cross-references between political and economic exchange were made suggests that their symbolism was interchangeable. The bad citizen constructed his own inferiority by selling his *logoi* as a rhetor, selling the *polis* as a politician and selling his body as a prostitute.

In the thirties of the 4th century Demosthenes gave three talents as a gift to the Athenians in order to finish repairs on their walls. In return his friend Ctesiphon proposed to the Athenians that they honour him with a golden crown. The reward was intended as a political manifesto, which would be even more effective if the crown was bestowed in the theatre. In the theatre foreigners and allies would be present, while in the assembly only citizens witnessed the ceremony. The proposal was opposed by Aeschines, Demosthenes' enemy and political rival.

Both speeches in favour of and against the proposal are preserved and dated to 330.[36] The legal debate is consciously constructed as a public competition. Aeschines compares the scenario with gymnastic contests (206), with tragic performances in the theatre (231, 238), and with the camp in battle (111). He calls civic exchange a contest of virtue where prizes are given by magistrates to the worthiest citizens (180). The rhetorical battle we witness in the two speeches is a battle over the morality of exchange between Demosthenes and the Athenians, Aeschines and the Athenians, Demosthenes and the king of Macedon, as well as between Aeschines and Macedon. Public contributions, private incomes, inheritance, bribes and prizes are represented as linked financial transactions creating the moral status of an individual citizen.

Although it is clear that Demosthenes' interest in a golden crown is politically motivated, Aeschines aims to demolish Demosthenes' political persona and represents him as an isolated privateer who only cares for himself. First of all, he argues that his interest in a golden crown is not motivated by public glory but by private greed.[37] Then, all his family had exploited the sacred links between husband and wife, father and son, citizen and country, for the sake of material profit and personal advantage. Demosthenes' maternal grandfather had betrayed Athenian land to the enemy and, being exiled, had accepted land from the enemy as a gift. He married a rich Scythian woman with an eye on her dowry and sent back one of his daughters to Athens where she married Demosthenes' father. Demosthenes himself had squandered his patrimony. In addition:

> From a trierarch he suddenly came forward as a hired writer of speeches, when he had disreputably squandered his patrimony. But when he had lost his reputation even in this profession, for he disclosed his clients' arguments to their opponents, he vaulted on to the political platform. And though he made an enormous amount of money (*argurion*) out of politics, he laid up next to nothing. It is true that just now the Persian's wealth has floated his extravagance, but even that will not suffice, for no wealth ever yet kept up with a debauched character. And to sum it all up, he supplies his wants, not from his private income, but from your perils. ... Eloquent of speech, infamous of life! For so licentious has he been in using his own body and in making children (*paidopoiia*) that I prefer not to say what he did.[38]

It is interesting to note that in this passage Demosthenes is represented as gradually extending his greed to further sources. First he squandered his patrimony; then he destroyed the opportunity of earning money as a hired speech writer; thereafter he tried to earn money in Athenian politics; and finally he resorted to Persian wealth which was famous for being unlimited. In the rhetoric of the opponent, Demosthenes' sources of income are not distinguished as either economic or political, but as increasingly greater and further away from Athens. His gradual move away from legitimate sources of wealth symbolised his gradual separation from Athens, to which he ought to be obliged as a citizen. The physical aspect of this corrupted nature is expressed at the end of the passage. Here Demosthenes is reproached for indulging in bodily perversions which, as we shall see later, were an image of ultimate excess, greed and withdrawal from public morality.[39]

Aeschines continues by contrasting Demosthenes' character with the modesty of former generals. These had wished to be honoured with anonymous statues only; others had received money only in order to dedicate it or to spend it on a sacrifice. Their crowns had been made of olive twigs rather than gold (181-187). He also contrasts Demosthenes' vices with his own civic virtue. Again, Demosthenes stands out as exploiting the public necessity of debate for his private gain:

> As to my silence, Demosthenes, it has been caused by the moderation of my life. For a little money suffices me and I have no shameful lust for more. Both my silence and my speech are therefore the result of deliberation, not of the impulse of a spendthrift nature. But you, I think, are silent when you have received, and bawl aloud after you have spent; and you speak not when your judgment approves, and not what you wish to speak, but whenever your paymasters (*misthodotai*) so order ... And the fact that a man speaks only at intervals marks him a man who takes part in politics because of the call of the hour, and for the common good; whereas to leave no day without its speech is the mark of a man who is a worker and hireling (*ergazomenou kai mistharnountos*).[40]

The largest part of the speech is concerned with charges of bribery and embezzlement of public money. For a *misthos* Demosthenes tried to enrol

5. Market Exchange and Private Profit

his private friends as citizens (85); for silver he was bought (*exôneito*) by Callias of Chalcis in order to obtain the alliance of the Athenians and to sell (*apedoto*, 92, 93) their interests, while himself stealing away the contributions of Oreus and Eretria (91-94; cf. 102-104); he used his bribes productively, paying interest on them (*tokon tou dôrodokêmatos*) to the people of Oreus at the rate of one *drachma* per month on the *mina* (105); he was bribed with dirty money which the Locrians of Amphissa had collected as port-dues from a sacred harbour, so that 'even more than before, whatever he touches, be it private citizen or ruler, or democratic state becomes entangled, every one, in irreparable misfortune' (113-114; cf. 119); finally, he is accused of taking bad gifts not only from the Greeks but also from the kings of Macedon and Persia, the ancestral enemies of the Athenians (149 ff., 156, 258 f.). Aeschines' hyperbolic diatribe climaxes in a rhetorical challenge to the judges which is again based on the idea that the law court, the *agora*, the theatre and Greece as a whole are comparable sites of competition and exchange:

> And is it not vexatious that whereas in former times the orchestra was piled with golden crowns with which the *dêmos* was honoured by the Hellenes, today in consequence of the politics of Demosthenes you go uncrowned and unproclaimed, but he is to be honoured by the voice of the herald. If any of the tragic poets who are to bring on their plays after the crowning should in a tragedy represent Thersites as crowned by the Greeks, none of you would tolerate it, for Homer says he was a coward and a slanderer; but when you yourselves crown such a man as this, think you not that you would be hissed by the voice of Hellas? ... And – strangest of all – in the same court-rooms as now do you disenfranchise those who are convicted of receiving bribes (*dôra*) and then yourselves propose to crown a man who, to your own knowledge, has always been in politics for pay (*misthou politeuomenon*)? If the judges in the Dionysiac festival are not honest in their award of the prize to the cyclic choruses, sitting as judges, not of cyclic choruses, but of the laws and the integrity in public life, do you propose to bestow your public rewards (*dôreia*) not according to the laws, and not on the rare and deserving, but upon the successful intriguer?[41]

Demosthenes defended himself successfully. Exculpating himself from the suspicion of having betrayed Athens to Macedon – which was the main charge in Aeschines' attack – he once more employs a remarkable rhetoric:

> In the matter of corruption (*diaphtharênai chrêmasin*) I have beaten Philip. Just as the purchaser has vanquished (*nenikêke*) the seller whenever he has bought something, so the man who refuses to take [bribes] and remains uncorrupted has vanquished the purchaser. Therefore Athens is undefeated in my person.[42]

The language of sale and purchase intersects with the language of politics and the battlefield. The superiority of the Athenians is symbolised by the fact that their best citizen resisted selling his services to the enemy.

Demosthenes represents the symbolic negotiation of power involved in any act of bribery not in its own context but in the context of sale. By accepting a bribe Demosthenes would have accepted that Philip should gain power over him, just as a buyer wins symbolically when he pays the seller. The comparison of bribery, sale and defeat could work only on the assumption that the entire audience shared the view that in commercial exchange there were winners and losers, just as in battles and bribery.

The ultimate loser, and at the same time the ultimate *misthôtos*, in the democratic *polis* was the prostitute. Receiving a *misthos* as a prostitute was incompatible with being a recipient of *dôreiai* from the *polis*, as we have seen above in the speech *Against Neaera*. Strictly speaking, prostitutes could not be recipients of public rewards because they needed to be slaves or foreigners in order to practise their trade in Athens.[43] Yet, as there seems to have been a large grey area between what was legally defined as prostitution of citizens and what was morally unacceptable, many cases of 'prostitution' were morally outrageous rather than illegal.[44] The speech *Against Timarchus* given by Aeschines in 345 is the best document for this. As in the case against Demosthenes, it was political enmity rather than the wish to punish a criminal offence that motivated the indictment. Both Demosthenes and Timarchus had made a formal accusation of treason against Aeschines because of their dissatisfaction with his negotiations about a peace treaty with Macedon. In retaliation, Aeschines brought an indictment against Timarchus which, if successful, would cost him his citizen rights. The charges brought by Aeschines against Timarchus are the same as those against Demosthenes in *Against Ctesiphon*. Timarchus had forfeited civic honour and freedom by squandering his patrimony, earning, and then wasting, wages, taking bribes and spending them on personal pleasures (154). Yet in Timarchus' case it is the sale of his body for buggery which is made the formal reason for the legal action. The speech has been analysed in detail by Dover and others as a source of information on Athenian homosexuality. Here I am more interested in the way sexual submission, together with the image of sale implied in prostitution, was treated as symbolic of political corruption. It may suffice therefore to concentrate on the cross-references between prostitution, bribery and sale, while for other points of interest to refer to Dover's analysis.[45]

The direction of Aeschines' indictment is well brought out at the end of his speech:

> What would he not give away (*apodoito*) who has sold (*peprakôs*) the shame of his own body? Whom would he pity who has had no pity on himself? (188)

Timarchus is accused of having prostituted himself to other citizens, but at the same of having sold his ancestral property and taken money while in political office.[46]

5. Market Exchange and Private Profit

The modern definition of prostitution as sexual intercourse bought for money does not have a direct parallel in the Greek city. One of the differences is that it could not be defined so clearly. On the one hand, prostitution denoted sexual intercourse with men or boys who were slaves or foreigners. Such relationships were available in brothels and probably usually bought for money.[47] It was a relationship that was not judged in terms of honour and shame, and was not supposed to be based on *philia*.[48] The term for that kind of prostitution was *porneia*, and although associated in classical Athens with payment it existed before the introduction of coinage. What made a *pornos* a *pornos* was his slave status rather than payment of money.[49] Sexual intercourse between male citizens, by contrast, was forbidden by law in classical Athens: to act as the passive sexual partner (*erômenos*) during childhood or as an adult, or to give one's son to another man were punished with loss of citizenship rights. We might call this prostitution also, since it was legally forbidden and from the point of view of the *erômenos* immoral. Yet the male citizen population of classical Athens had a hypocritical attitude to pederasty and prostitution. While it was a criminal offence to be an *erômenos* it was honourable for the active sexual partner (*erastês*) to be in love with a boy citizen. Even Aeschines in his speech against Timarchus was not reluctant to say:

> To be in love with (*to men eran*) those who are beautiful and chaste is the experience of a kind-hearted and generous (*kalôn kai sôphrona*) soul; but to hire for money (*arguriou tina misthoumenon*) and to indulge in licentiousness is the act of a man who is wanton and ill-bred.[50]

This double standard was the result of a changing public evaluation of male homosexuality and pederasty during the development of democracy. Pederasty was a residue of aristocratic culture, associated with patronage and confined to symposium, gymnasium and *palaestra*.[51] To act as an *erômenos* who could not but submit to the *erastês* was incompatible with political equality. Nevertheless sexual competition remained part of the competition for honour under the democracy, and the object of such competition remained the boy who was not available to everybody in the brothel.[52] If, as Halperin has argued, commercial *porneia* was consciously supported as a matter of democratic policy aiming at a shift of aristocratic culture into a public space, this policy was not successful.[53]

Against this background, it is quite obvious that the charge against Timarchus of having prostituted himself does not mean from the outset that he had sold himself or acted like a wage-labourer. The metaphor of sale is, rather, part of the general moral disqualification of his behaviour as a citizen. Homosexual relationships played an important part in the definition of the citizen, as we shall see in Chapter 9, and, like other forms of corrupt civic exchange, they were associated with commerce the moment they were censured.

Like Demosthenes, Timarchus had broken the bonds which linked a citizen with the *polis* in more than one way. He had sold the property inherited from his ancestors and had made no effort to buy anything durable instead:

> But perhaps someone may say that after selling his father's house he bought another one somewhere else in the city ... No he has nothing left, not a house, not an apartment, not a piece of ground, no slaves, no money at interest, nor anything else from which men who are not dishonest gain a living (105).

As landed property was still the most powerful symbol of citizenship, the fact that Timarchus had sold his land in order to provide cash for his physical lusts suggested that Timarchus preferred being a private 'body' to being a citizen (116). Furthermore, he had corrupted his relationship to the city in the management of public affairs. First, he had bought all public offices with private money rather than obtaining them by public vote. Secondly, he had bought them not with the cash he had in hand but with money borrowed at interest.[54] Thirdly, he developed a private economy against the public interest by taking bribes for hiding the crimes of his colleagues. Fourthly, he committed an outrage against the wealth of the *polis* by stealing public money (106 f.; 110). Cashing his inheritance on the one hand, and earning money by bribery, embezzlement and theft of public money on the other, are complementary aspects of the same civic offence. The charge of prostituting his body was yet another aspect: in the life of Timarchus, private desires, private gain and money had priority over the interests and prosperity of the city.

Bribery, prostitution and commerce are taken as mutual images in many passages of the speech. Like labour contracted out in the market, Timarchus' sexual relationships were based on contract (87 f.). Like market exchange, the sale of his body had taken place in public but served nothing but private needs. Like the business conducted in the stalls of the *agora* his prostitution should have been taxed (119-121; cf. 124; 160 f.; cf. 165). No doubt there was a market in slave prostitutes and a thriving business of brothels in which prostitutes were hired under the laws of sale. But even if Timarchus had been an *erômenos* the entertainment that he had sought as a citizen in private houses (90; 124) had nothing to do with that trade. Aeschines himself makes this clear in a passage which is a conscious reflection on his own rhetorical strategy:

> A certain speech writer who is concocting [Timarchus'] defence says that I am contradicting myself; since it seems to him impossible, he says, for the same man to have been a prostitute (*peporneusthai*) and to have consumed his patrimony. For to have sinned against one's body was the act of a boy but to have consumed one's patrimony is that of a man. And furthermore he says that those who defile themselves exact pay (*misthos*) for it. He therefore goes up and down the market place expressing his wonder and amazement that

one and the same man should have prostituted (*peporneusthai*) himself and also have consumed his patrimony (94).

It was indeed impossible to have a patrimony to spend and to be a *pornos*, because the one was exclusive to citizens and the other to foreigners and slaves. Yet by redefining the meaning of *misthos* and *porneuô* Aeschines sets out to demonstrate that Timarchus did combine the two roles. He makes *misthos* a general category of money received (including both fees and bribes) while *porneuô* becomes a general category of homosexual intercourse, including intercourse taking place in private symposia between older and younger citizens. The fact that two kinds of sex were available to an Athenian citizen in the 4th century, one in private and one in public, made possible a rhetorical link between a corrupted citizen on the one hand and a purchasable slave on the other. While Timarchus may have been corrupted as a politician and acted as an *erômenos* in private symposia, he was clearly not a slave contracting out his body, paying market tax and living in brothels. The rhetorical elision of that crucial difference suggested a link between corruption and commerce: both were an abuse of public exchange for the satisfaction of private needs.

Notes

1. Bohannan and Dalton (1962), pp. 1 ff. distinguish between marketless societies, societies with peripheral markets and market societies. Interestingly enough, only in societies where market exchange is peripheral (that is, where the market is isolated from the rest of society and where there is no direct relation between production and market distribution) is the market place the major space of sale and purchase; in market societies, where capitalist market exchange is the dominant mode of exchange and production-related to the supply-and-demand mechanism, market places tend to lose their significance as sites of exchange.

2. As Elwert (1987) and Hill (1986) have pointed out, the belief that commercial markets work independently of the cultural system that surrounds them has led to a number of social crises in African countries where markets were implanted in order to connect them to the world market. The traditional exchange system was incapable of absorbing the capitalist rules of exchange.

3. Polanyi's work has been discussed intensely among scholars; see Garlan (1973), Humphreys (1978), pp. 31-75; Godelier (1986), pp. 173-203, Nippel (1990), pp. 124-159, Jongman (1988), pp. 1-30; see also the useful summary in Austin and Vidal-Naquet (1977), pp. 7-11.

4. Bohannan and Dalton (1962), pp. 1-10; on peripheral markets see also Hodges (1987). Bohannan and Dalton's proposition led to a number of stimulating field studies in which it was argued that in many such peripheral markets market exchange was based on, and confirmed, pre-existing social relations. See esp. Davis (1973), Mintz (1967), Geertz (1979), Gell (1982); for the opposite situation see Dewey (1962) and Geertz (1963).

5. See Polanyi et al. (1957), pp. 1 ff; Polanyi (1960), and (1977), pp. 123-144.

6. For the first see above ch. 3; the other two distinctions will be discussed below, and in ch. 9.

7. For the chronological development of the *agora* see Camp (1986), esp. pp. 38

124   *Exchange in Ancient Greece*

f., Starr (1986) and Martin (1951). It is dated for Athens in the years of the early 6th century. The attempt to distinguish a commercial from a political development of the *agora*, as Wycherley (1956) and Spahn (1984) have made, is problematic; see esp. de Ste Croix (1972), pp. 267-285. Stanley's ((1976), pp. 12-33) attempt to identify a commercial market place in the epics of Homer is inconclusive; see Millett's discussion in (1991 a), n. 48. For the continuity of personalised exchange in local areas see Millett (1991 b), ch. 5; for the continuity of the local deme as a power base for politicians see Osborne (1985), pp. 88-92 and 68 f., Davies (1971), pp. i-xxxi and id. (1981).
   8. Stallybrass and White (1986), p. 27.
   9. Lys. 24. 20.
   10. Isocr. 18. 9.
   11. Aesch. 3. 1; see further Aesch. 1. 60, 90 and 125; Isocr. 7. 15; Lys. 7. 6; Dem. 18. 323 and Ober (1989), pp. 148 f.
   12. Cf. Ar. *Wasps* 493-495; Dem. 19. 225, 314.
   13. Osborne (1985), esp. pp. 68 f.; and 88-92.
   14. Ober (1989), pp. 149-150.
   15. Isocr. 7. 48; cf. Ar. *Clouds* 991; Plat. *Theat.* 173 c-d.
   16. Isocr. 7. 32-35.
   17. Millett (1989), p. 27.
   18. Isocr. 7. 53; see also 24.
   19. See esp. Arist. *Ath. Pol.* 26-28; Plut. *Per.* IX, X, XVI.
   20. Plut. *Per.* IX. 2 f.; XVI. 3 f.
   21. Thuc. II. 65. 8-9; Plutarch praises Pericles' abstinence from bribery only as far as gifts to him from others are concerned (*heauton analôton hupo chrêmatôn*). Yet he also calls Pericles' introduction of public pay a means of bribing (*sundikazein*). *Sundikazein* is a term especially used for bribing jurors (see Harvey (1985), pp. 88 f.) which intimates that paying the *dikastikon* was nothing less than bribery on a collective scale – which, theoretically speaking, is a contradiction in terms given that the rationale of bribery is a private deal between individuals for private ends.
   22. Plut. *Per.* XVI. 3 f.
   23. Plut. *Cim.* X. 2-3.
   24. Polanyi (1977), p. 165; cf. Redfield (1986).
   25. The assembly was moved to the Pnyx at the turn of the 6th century; the theatre of Dionysios was built outside the *agora* after the *ikria* (stands) located within its boundary stones had collapsed in the early 5th century. The assembly continued to meet in the theatre once a year (Dem. 21. 8-10; cf. Pickard-Cambridge (1960), pp. 67-69). For an archaeological survey see Kolb (1981). Honorary decrees for playwrights and *chorêgoi* continued to be displayed in the Royal Stoa on the north-east corner of the *agora*. See Camp (1986), pp. 46 and 100 f. See also Isocr. 8. 14. For the ideological interaction of politics, commerce and theatre see esp. the introductory scene in Ar. *Ach.*; cf. Goldhill (1991), p. 186.
   26. Dem. 1. 1.
   27. Ibid.
   28. Ar. *Frogs* 734-749, trans. Barrett.
   29. Aristotle argued that a common measurement is needed in order to make things comparable: 'All items for exchange must be comparable in some way. *Nomisma* (currency) came along to do exactly this, and in a way it becomes an intermediate, since it measures everything, and so measures excess and deficiency – how many shoes are equal to a house' (Arist. *EN* 1133a 20-23). Aristophanes' idea is based on the same idea. It should be noted in this context that one of the

5. Market Exchange and Private Profit

earliest functions of coinage was to serve as a weight standard (Grayson (1974), esp. pp. 288 ff., 324 ff., 341-2 (on Arist. *Ath. Pol.* 10)). The imagery of coinage and of the scale are therefore related. Both made different objects of exchange comparable in terms of a standard authorised by the political community of citizens.

30. Isocr. 2. 1.
31. Cf. *Od.* 16. 231.
32. See also Isocr. 9. 4 where money is involved in the exchange. See also Kurke (1991), pp. 98 ff. In Pindar money, praise and athletic achievement are given for each other in a series of exchanges between athlete, poet and audience. The point which Isocrates makes in 9. 4 is that, although being somewhat comparable, praise and money are not equal values. The former more adequately recompenses for the toils which achievement implies.
33. Dem. 51. 21-22.
34. Some scholars have attributed the speech to Apollodorus, but Blass, *Attische Beredsamkeit*, III, pp. 242 ff. attributes it to Demosthenes himself.
35. See for example Aesch. 3. 173, where Aeschines describes Demosthenes as having descended from a trierarch to a hired writer of speeches (*logographos*).
36. Aesch. 3 (*Against Ctesiphon*); Dem. 18 (*On the Crown*).
37. Aesch. 3. 171 f.
38. Ibid. 173 f.
39. In 162 Aeschines had already made an allusion to Demosthenes' sexual life, which is described there more clearly as *paiderasteia*. In the light of that passage we may regard the term *paidopoiia* in 174 as a deliberate play on *paiderasteia*, as he says in 162 the case had never been brought to the law courts and so he could only allude to it.
40. Aesch. 3. 218 and 220.
41. Ibid. 233 f.
42. Dem. 18. 247.
43. For the legal situation of prostitution and citizenship see Dover (1978).
44. For the conflicts arising from homosexual intercouse between men in the ideology of the democratic *polis* see Dover (1973 a), (1978), pp. 100-110, Halperin (1990), pp. 88-112; Winkler (1990).
45. Dover (1978) and (1964).
46. 97 ff. on the various sales of his patrimony, 106 ff. on his cases of bribery and embezzlement.
47. Dover (1978), Cohen (1987).
48. That in Lys. 3. 5 the speaker says he attempted to be good to a Plataean prostitute whom he loved sexually, and whom he wanted to make his *philos*, is not a counter-argument since, first, such a statement improved the speaker's own image in the affair (see below), and, secondly, exceptions were of course possible.
49. *Pornos, pornê* and *porneuô* are derivatives of *pernanai* (to sell); the word *pornê* for a female prostitute occurs already the 7th century, well before the introduction of money (Arch. frg. 302; cf. Dover (1978), p. 20). At this early stage the concept of sale was associated with slavery and exchange over distance, rather than with money. This ties in well with the idea that the *pornos* (first attested in an archaic inscription from Thera, IG XII. 3, 536, cf. Dover (1978), p. 20) was the term for a sexual companion who was a slave and came from abroad. *Hetairêkos*, cognate with *hetairos*, denoted a companion, comrade and, in the 6th and 5th centuries, a political partner. The female *hetaira* was opposed to the wife in that she was not a woman for marriage, and had no citizen status. Nevertheless a relationship with a *hetaira* implied more permanence than that with a *pornê* (Dover, ibid.). Dover has argued further that even in classical Athens prostitution

was not simply defined by the transaction of sex in exchange for money (although in most cases the receipt of money was made part of the disgrace attached to relationships of that kind by that time; cf. Xen. *Mem.* I. 6. 13; Ar. *Wealth* 153-159). It was the act of submission that made it a moral disgrace in the democratic city state. Whether the *erômenos* submitted himself to the *erastês* for an agreed fee or for a gift did not make much difference to the result. An aristocratic boy familiar with gymnasium and *palaestra* could hardly be regarded as a prostitute by his adult lovers, whereas a slave or a foreigner who offered his body for intercourse was always a prostitute, whether he was paid or not (Dover (1973 a)).

50. Aesch. 1. 137; cf. Cohen (1987), pp. 12 f. for further discussion of this distinction.

51. See for further discussion below, ch. 9.

52. Cohen (1987).

53. Halperin (1990), pp. 88-112.

54. For the negative political image of borrowing at interest, which could be regarded as detrimental to civic relationships, see Arist. *EN* 1121 b 34; Plat. *Rep.* 550 e; hostility against interest was naturally most widespread in antidemocratic circles, but in democratic Athens, too, lending and borrowing at interest marked relationships of social distance; cf. Millett (1991 b), pp. 40-44, 98-108.

6

Trade, Power and Tyranny in Classical Athens

Exchange and empire

There was a profusion of theories of power at the time of the Athenian empire.[1] In these theories we find a striking emphasis on trade and commercial exchange as an explanation of power and human progress. This calls for explanation, given that Athens remained an agrarian *polis* in which traders had little social prestige and often not even citizen rights.[2] In this chapter I shall argue that the emphasis on trade in descriptions of human progress had anthropological rather than economic origins. The development of human civilisation was envisaged as an advance in the way human beings conducted exchange in order to obtain the means of life.[3] The Athenians thought they had achieved a triumph over the conditions imposed on humans by the gods who had forced men to toil in agriculture, to marry and to sacrifice.[4] Inasmuch as the mythical and epic image of prosperity was associated with the gifts of the gods, the complementary image of man-made prosperity was associated with maritime trade. In that context commercial exchange had positive connotations, since it was not part of internal politics but a way in which the Athenians made use of their power over other people.

Modern economic theory describes market exchange and free trade as an autonomous sphere developing independently of a political system. Thucydides, by contrast, explains the evolution of political government as a function of exchange.[5] In the introduction to his *Histories* he explains why the Peloponnesian war was greater than both the Trojan and the Persian wars, proposing a theory of progress which relates power to maritime exchange. This interdependence did not suggest itself because Athens derived large revenue from trade. Rather, democracy was associated with a specific attitude to nature and wealth, and a specific use of it in human society.

As Edmunds pointed out, for Thucydides democracy and the navy were an episode in the humanistic revolution of the 5th century. Because of their *gnomê* (intelligence) and *technê* (technological advance) the Athenians were 'users' of *chrêmata*. Money and goods were instruments of a human strategy which made the Athenians free from the constraints of agriculture. The Spartans were weaker than the Athenians because they were *autourgoi*, people who worked for themselves. The way the Athenians used *chrêmata* was strictly parallel to the way they used the laws. The Athenians had the power to change and debate laws in assembly and law courts, while for the Spartans laws and customs were sacrosanct: given by the gods, they could not be changed by mortals.[6]

Seafaring and shipbuilding were represented as symbols of human strength from the middle of the 5th century onwards. Aeschylus and Sophocles introduced into the catalogue of achievements indicating progress the power to cross the sea. In Euripides we find a statement which extended the image to maritime trade:

> I bless the god who brought our life to order out of beastlike confusion, implanting in us first of all intelligence ... defences against the winter's cold, to ward off the chill of the sky and sea voyages to exchange with others what our own land lacks.[7]

This was the state of affairs by the middle of the 5th century, from which I shall start in this chapter. A further look at the first chapters of Thucydides' *Histories* can give a more detailed insight into how the relationship between power and trade was elaborated. His explanation of the power of the Athenians suggests that trade became part of theories of progress, not because it boosted the Athenian economy but because it stood for a particular way of controlling people and nature.

Thucydides argues that military power can be gained only if a state has *periousia* (surplus of funds). In contrast to earlier theories of power which regarded agrarian prosperity as the justification for power, he states explicitly that the surplus gained from maritime exchange (*emporia*) is important (I. 2, 7-8). Nomads who were the first inhabitants of Greece were poor because they had no cities, no exchange with other people and no *emporia*. Similarly, Agamemnon's forces, coming from tribes that did not communicate with one another, had no common wealth which they could use for the campaign in Troy (3). For Thucydides lack of political organisation, manifested in a lack of exchange, explains the relative weakness of early communities. Then the Greeks turned to the sea because communication became easier. Though they were pirates at first, they practised nevertheless the first form of maritime exchange.[8] Pirates were powerful people in their community and used their spoils, first, for their own gain (*kerdos*) and, secondly, to nourish the poor (5). Although piracy was a primitive form of maritime exchange, the political potential of such an exchange was already apparent. As Thucydides observes, it was motivated by the desire of individuals to gain power within the community and exercise patronage over the poor. It was thus the beginning of a kind of

6. Trade, Power and Tyranny in Classical Athens 129

political organisation whose hierarchy was not justified metaphysically but by human strength alone.[9] Minos, who was the first to organise a navy, acquired power in the Aegean for the same reasons as the pirates; yet his government implied a more advanced form of political organisation (4-8). He integrated the entire Aegean into an hierarchical system of communication and exchange controlled by his power. By purging the sea of piracy he made journeys safe and guaranteed that both the weak and the strong could acquire wealth:

> The weaker because of the general desire to make profits (*kerdos*), were content to put up with being governed by the stronger, and those who won superior power by acquiring capital resources (*periousia*) brought the smaller cities under their control.[10]

The political implications of the policy attributed to Minos can best be understood within Sahlins' 'scheme of reciprocity'.[11] He transformed a form of negative reciprocity (plunder and pillaging) which had been exercised by the pirates into a network of generalised reciprocity based on the idea that spending material resources creates power and patronage. According to Sahlins, this type of reciprocity is not so much motivated economically as it is a typical ranking mechanism in pre- or proto-political systems.[12] The similarities between Thucydides' description of early exchange and modern theories of patronage are striking. According to Saller, patronage is (a) an exchange of goods and/or services that is reciprocal; (b) an asymmetrical relationship inasmuch as the two parties are of unequal status, offering one another different sorts of goods and services, and (c) a personal relationship of some duration.[13] All requirements are fulfilled by the policy of Minos; while pirates exercised patronage on an intra-communal level, Minos did so between communities. Thucydides is fully aware of the political function of Minos' maritime policy. It was the application of local policies of power and patronage on a large scale.

Athenian maritime policy stood in Minos' tradition. In Thucydides' evolutionary model of Greek history the Athenians emerge as the heirs of the naval policy of Minos which was taken further by a generation of tyrants and later adopted by the main maritime powers, Corinth, Ionia and Phocaea (I. 13-18.) The connection between the government of tyrants and that of the Athenians sheds further light on Thucydides' construction of the interdependence of maritime exchange and power:

> The old form of government was hereditary monarchy (*patrikai basileiai*) with established rights and limitations (*epi rhêtois gerasi*); but as Hellas became more powerful and as the importance of acquiring money (*ktêsis chrêmatôn*) became more and more evident, tyrannies were established in nearly all the cities, revenues (*prosodoi*) increased, shipbuilding flourished and ambition turned towards the sea.[14]

Thucydides continues with the observation that the difference between tyrannies and later maritime empires was that the former used their revenues to stabilise their dominion at home while the latter used it to extend external power (I. 17). The development from tyranny to the power of maritime empires was thus parallel to that from piracy to the empire of Minos. Within that scheme, the power of Athens emerges as comparable to internal tyranny but exercised on an imperial scale. Like the past power of pirates, Minos and tyrants, the power of maritime empires was self-created; they were systems of patronage on an inter-communal scale and they were based on man-made wealth rather than agriculture.[15]

Pericles himself is made to say that like a tyrant the Athenians had to fear their subjects.[16] The moment Thucydides assesses the power of the Athenian empire within the model of internal politics, he calls it a tyranny. In the Funeral Speech, by contrast, the power of Athens had to be praised within the traditional language of aristocratic ethics.[17] In the way in which the theme of trade is rendered within this speech we see even more clearly its function in a broader anthropological theory of power:

> Because of the greatness of our city, the fruits of the whole earth flow in upon us so that we enjoy the goods of other countries as freely as our own.[18]

The prosperity of the city is modelled on the prosperity of the *oikos*. But rather than linking the wealth of the city to agriculture Pericles links it to household management (*oikonomia*). The Athenian ideology that power is based on exchange rather than agriculture remains unchallenged, yet it is here skilfully adapted to the traditional ethics according to which the power of an *oikos* rested on autarky and liberality.[19] Athens was constructed as the head of a self-sufficient *oikos*, and trade was household management on an inter-communal scale.

In the shifting rhetoric in which empire and prosperity are represented in the *Histories* themselves lies the key to understanding the meaning of trade in Thucydides' introductory chapters. Thucydides regarded neither trade nor tyranny as genuine characteristics of the Athenian empire; they were the inversions of the wealth and power associated with genealogically justified power and agriculture. The explanation of Athenian power did not lie in social and economic facts but in a superior relationship between man and nature. Agriculture remained a domain over which man had no influence well into the 4th century. It was an interaction with nature in which the farmer had to submit to the rules of soil and season. It was embedded in numerous festivals and sacrifices which celebrated the divine contribution to the agricultural process and reciprocity of divine gifts and human toil.[20] It cannot be accidental that Pericles mentions sacrifices in the Funeral Speech but explains their meaning for the Athenians in the language of human exchange: they 'provision' (*porizô*) their minds with good things.[21]

6. Trade, Power and Tyranny in Classical Athens

Thucydides' belief in the power of *gnômê* and *logos* led him to the construction of maritime trade as a means of survival that was controlled by humans themselves. Trying to demonstrate that the human *logos* was a better way of understanding human nature than religion and myth, he argued that maritime exchange was a mode of wealth creation based on the strength of the human mind. *Kerdos* was the surplus which was gained on the basis of intelligent thought. There was clearly a gap between Thucydides' anthropological evaluation of trade and his social evaluation of traders. The citizen farmer remained socially superior to the trader. We can explain this gap, however, when we remember that Thucydides' theme was not Athenian trade but history. The *Histories* were an attempt to put into practice the idea that *erga* (deeds, events, historical development) could be understood and controlled by human *logos* (thought and speech).[22] Thucydides himself realised that this was only an ideal unattainable in practice – which can be taken from his descriptions of the plague or the Sicilian expedition where the Athenians clearly lost control over events.[23] Maritime trade entered his work as one argument within his philosophical project. The power, and problems, which he associated with *emporia* were parallel to the power and problems he associated with the use of *logos*. Both *emporia* and the use of *logoi* were monuments of human progress as they replaced mythical assumptions with rational thought. Both, however, were open to serious abuse.

Comic inversions

Most texts contemporary with Thucydides give a critical account of the Athenian ideology of power. Aristophanes, in particular, makes fun of the discrepancy between the ideological self-representation of democracy and the political practice of democratic politicians. The high discourse of Athenian trade and domination is represented within the low discourse of private commerce and patronage. As we saw in the *Histories* of Thucydides, political values were context-related; the same politics were evaluated differently according to whether they were pursued in the *oikos*, the city or the empire. Aristophanes exploited this opportunity by displacing public values into the private sphere, and by confusing *oikos*, *polis* and empire.

The Athenian democracy created a sharp distinction between private and public interest which cuts across any distinction between gift exchange and commerce. Thus both gift exchange and trade could have a positive meaning when they served to maintain the power and prosperity of the public, while both had negative connotations when identified with the profit and ambition of a single person. A major conflict between democrats and their opponents arose from the problem of drawing the line between public and private loyalty.[24] While both firmly acknowledged the primacy of the *polis*, the aristocrats nevertheless regarded the *oikos* as the metaphysical and political source of power and prosperity.

The confusion between private and public exchange was the backbone of political invective. It re-presented the public ideology of maritime exchange in a private context. In the pseudo-Xenophontic *Athenian Constitution*, for example, democratic Athens is portrayed as a city where the politicians fill their bellies with the luxuries of the world.[25] As in the *Odyssey*, a desire for food and a greedy belly are negative images of the human condition which, if uncontrolled, makes people prefer bodily pleasure to public achievement.[26] The text seems to be a direct comment on Pericles' praise of Athens as the city upon which the fruits of the whole earth flow.[27] For the author of the *Athenian Constitution* the city is the stomach of its politicians, and the imported products of the world the supplies for the needs of their bellies.

A similar strategy can be observed in Aristophanes' *Knights*. The compound concept of empire, maritime exchange and prosperity is reduced to that of tyranny, market exchange, bribery and gluttony. Athenian food-trade and power are personified in the character of the 'sausage seller' who is the ideal politician for Athens. His rival, too, is presented as an addict of market products, especially fish. Eating fish seems to have had connotations of tyranny; in any case some fish were an extravagant dish whose consumption was regarded as 'undemocratic'.[28] He promises cheap sardines to the people of Athens, while he himself gobbles down greater delicacies such as tuna, squid and fish fillets. These he buys in the fish market with the money that he received as a gift or bribe (cf. 353 ff.; 928).[29] For a decision in Miletus he takes a squid and a talent; he takes Pylos after having tuna and a gallon of unmixed wine (282 f.); he receives the greatest honour of the Athenians, to dine in the Prytaneum, where again he receives fish (313); finally, he is said to be searching for cash from the allies as tunny fishers search for tunny (861). In all exchanges which satirise the behaviour of Athenian politicians the currency is money and fish. The *Knights* presents democracy as a series of personal deals where gifts, tributes and prizes land in the pockets, or stomachs, of greedy politicians. Buying, selling and eating serve as images of Athens as a 'tyrant' whose major concern is his personal safety and self-preservation.

In the *Acharnians* the entire city is staged as a market. Dicaiopolis, 'Just-City', loathes the market of Athens where everybody shouts and praises his commodities 'coal for sale, oil or vinegar' and wishes to be back home where they have never even heard the words 'for sale'.[30] The praise of rural self-sufficiency condemns not only urban dependence on market exchange but also metaphorically the commercial practices of political exchange as a whole. The meaning of the commercial imagery in the *Acharnians* has been interpreted differently by modern critics. Edmunds suggests: '[Dicaiopolis] opens a market to the Peloponnesians, Boeotians and Megarians. This is poetic, or comic, justice, since it was, in Dicaiopolis' view, the closing of the markets to the Megarians that had brought on the war ... "Just-City" has at least contrived a just city, which, with its international market, has all the advantages of Athens herself, but which for the rest is presumably identical with the rural deme to which he has returned.'[31]

Goldhill interprets the market as a typical comic inversion serving to reveal the perversions of political exchange: 'The comic inversion of the (symbolic) exchange of words, of goods, of women, of roles, performs a (carnivalised) repertoire of the city's operations. The opening scene's version of the Assembly constructs the need for a (re)solution: the narrative moves through a series of parodic and inverted transactions as Dicaeopolis realigns his position in the system of exchange (by formulating a private international treaty).'[32]

While Edmunds takes the meaning of the market for Megarians and Boeotians too literally, Goldhill seems to underestimate the extent to which market exchange was bound up with a real political programme. A combination of the literary and metaphorical reading is, I would suggest, the most appropriate: the play skilfully interweaves a parody on the metaphysics of civic exchange with that of Athenian foreign policy.

Dicaeopolis founds an alternative city which parallels Athens in being a market, but differs by its rules and morality of exchange. His market is not a public space in the centre of the city but attached to his private *oikos*. It is located in the countryside and its 'officials' (leather straps) are elected privately.[33] No money is used, taxes are paid in kind, no *kerdos* is made and the purchase of goods for personal needs is replaced by that for the communal benefit. People export peace, while importing the necessary items for the celebration of the rural festival in which the play culminates. Above all, the only people who buy in the market are the Megarians and Boeotians – foreigners, who were excluded from the Athenian *agora*. The other customers, a Spartan and an Athenian, do not receive what they want, as they only want bribes.

Before the new market is opened, peace is imported from Sparta as a commodity (175 ff.). The representation of peace as a commodity is achieved by a clever pun on *spondê* (186), which means both peace and wine for libation. This *spondê* is then 'carried' home in skins.[34] Girls for marriage are represented as sexual objects which can be obtained by purchase (cf. the comparison of Aspasia's whores and the Megarian's daughters, 520 ff.); and later the market authority Nicarchus is himself wrapped up in a parcel of merchandise (*empolê*, 930). Social metaphors (i.e. peace, sexual relationships, authority) are represented as people and turned into objects which are exchangeable and purchasable.[35] The stage is set for a series of transactions which create the just city – if only in the guise of a private market.

In the second part of the play (719 ff.) Dicaeopolis exchanges his personal peace for other 'commodities' which, although transacted in a market, serve to satisfy the needs of man in a supra-individual order. First, a Megarian enters the market in order to exchange his daughters dressed as piglets for garlic and salt. The exchange involves no money, and salt and garlic as such are nothing that a Megarian needed.[36] The daughters dressed as pigs refer to sexual pleasures as well as to the sexual rituals which were part of the Dionysia, the celebration of which is Dicaeopolis' ultimate aim. That the sale of the Megarian girls is not entirely unrelated to the idea of procreation and marriage is borne out further by an exclamation of the Megarian who only wishes to be able to sell his wife and mother that easily.[37] Secondly, a Boeotian comes along offering a variety of foods: geese, hares, foxes, moles, hedgehogs, cats, beavers, otters and eels. Again, most of the merchandise has sexual connotations, but it is also food needed for the Rural Dionysia and the Pitchers.[38] The third person, a Peloponnesian farmer, requests peace in compensation for his oxen lost at Pylos. But, mistaking Dicaeopolis' market for a site of hostile exchange, he has no success. The last client cannot exchange with Dicaeopolis either. The 'best man' of an Athenian groom offers meat in order to obtain peace. It seems that an Athenian citizen in Dicaeopolis' market can do nothing but give bribes: that is, giving a gift for a personal favour. Only when it turns out that the bride needs peace for her husband in order to achieve sexual gratification does Dicaeopolis hasten to hand it out without taking the gift in return. It seems that a bride's desire for sex was not regarded as a personal desire but referred to marriage and the continuity of human society. The play ends in the celebration of the festival which is contrasted with the pains of war. This contrast forcefully emphasises the sacred and ritual character of exchange in Dicaeopolis, Just-City, the private market.

The *Acharnians* presents a model of justice in the imagery of that ideology which the play aims to criticise. The ideology itself is not rendered in its actual form. The high discourse on Athenian power and foreign exchange is cast into the language of petty market exchange. Dicaeopolis inverts public and private, urban and rural. He concludes peace, but it is a private peace; he conducts foreign policy, but it is his own policy; he sets up a public space of exchange, but it is located in his rural *oikos*; a market is a place where everybody should be able to exchange, but he admits and excludes people at his own will; he does not use common money, but pays with his private currency (peace). In stark contrast to this privatisation of public means, his ends are ultimately directed towards the metaphysical re-orientation of the community.

Edmunds has compared Aristophanes' just city with other concepts of justice and the ideal city. Pericles in Thucydides described the best city as self-sufficient both for war and peace.[39] Self-sufficiency meant here the power to receive goods from all over the world and thus independence from local agriculture. It gave priority to the city as a political centre over rural *oikoi* and their religious and social rituals. The most sacred transactional order was the *polis* and its citizen body. For an anti-democrat like Plato, by contrast, justice and self-sufficiency meant autarky of the *oikos* and independence from foreign resources of exchange, especially markets and harbours. Home production, sacrifice and family life were the ideal for the ordinary members of his ideal city.[40] In this model the most sacred order was the *oikos* and the community between humans and gods. Dicaeopolis' just city resembles Plato's theory. Justice is founded in the *oikos* and ritually symbolised during the celebration of rural festivals. Libations, wine and sex have their place in these contexts rather than in the centre of the city. Self-sufficiency means to live without market exchange and trade, obediently accepting the reciprocities which the gods have imposed on men: marriage, sacrifice and agriculture. Aristophanes employs the images of commerce in which the Periclean ideology of power was also represented. Yet he ridiculed them by making them images of private deals and local petty trading. He unmasked the factual discrepancy between the social status of traders and the political meaning of trade, exploiting it for his own political message.

Exchange, autarky and savagery in the *Cyclops*

The Euripidean *Cyclops* draws together many themes which have been discussed in the previous sections. Satyric drama is, however, a difficult art form, so a brief introduction to the generic conditions of the play is necessary.

Satyr plays occupy a place between tragedy and comedy representing both the mythical themes and formal structure of tragedy, and the carnivalesque inversions of comedy.[41] They are closely related to Dionysiac rituals and this, together with the presence of the satyrs, imposes certain motifs on individual plays. So there is regularly a strong emphasis on wine, sex and dance; hedonism combined with wisdom represented by the chorus of satyrs (*thiasoi*); a rural setting; and a plot which evolves around the abduction, captivity, servitude and liberation of satyrs.[42] Satyr plays were probably also linked to the Dionysiac mysteries and enacted elements of the initiation ritual (*thiasos*) to that cult. This made satyric drama an ideal genre for staging liminal situations, or ambivalence of concepts and ideas. Initiation rituals place the person to be initiated into a liminal space, such as between life and death, men and women, civilisation and wilderness, animals and gods – in short, all those positions which marked the limits of the human condition.[43] The Dionysiac *thiasos* was an association outside, and antithetical to, the *polis*.[44] Thus the limits not only of human existence but also of political community were debated in satyr plays. The interdependence and contrast of civilisation and savagery were a generic feature of the plays. Savagery is part of civilisation, while any savage has the potential to become civilised.[45]

The narrative of the *Cyclops* resembles the Homeric story rather closely. Yet the presence of satyrs, including their father Silenus, adds a new element. Konstan has argued that this is not simply a formal concession to the genre of satyr play but serves to introduce a third element in between the opposition of civilised human and uncivilised Cyclops.[46] The introduction of satyrs dissolves the simple distinctions between wild and civilised, and savagery and civilised exchange, characteristic of the Homeric episode. Indeed in the renegotiation of the distinction between civilisation and savagery and their respective modes of exchange lies the actuality of the 5th-century play.

Odysseus and his companions, Silenus and the satyrs, and Polyphemus and his brothers, are three groups whose relationships to each other and to the gods become a test of their status as civilised beings. Modes of exchange and reciprocity define and express these relationships. The description of relationships in the *Cyclops* seems to rely on a repertory of exchanges that structured the life of the 5th-century *polis*. But the modes of exchange that identify civilised intercourse are not clearly concentrated on the person traditionally associated with civilisation in the story of the Cyclops. 'In the contrast ... of Polyphemus and Odysseus we have no Homeric contrast of barbarism and cool, civilised intelligence, but a juxtaposition of two related types of civilised brutality whose difference is merely that of circumstance, one being weak, the other strong.'[47] To anticipate a little, it is Odysseus' commercial attitude to *xenia* which adds to his image as a representative of civilised brutality.

Konstan has analysed a structural pattern which is encoded in the modes of exchange and culinary habits of each figure. He shows convincingly that this code is symbolic of their status and mutual relationships.[48] It is important to understand this pattern before looking at how it is confused and perverted. The status of Odysseus, Polyphemus and Silenus is distinguished by the food and drink they consume. Odysseus has a human diet of grain, meat, cheese and milk, and eats none of the other creatures of the island, i.e. cyclopes and satyrs (ll. 127, 134-136). Polyphemus eats meat, cheese and milk; like Odysseus he does not eat satyrs but, unlike Odysseus, he eats human beings (209, 216, 247-249). Since nothing is said about the diet of Silenus, it can be assumed that satyrs do not eat at all. At the level of drink, the three groups are distinguished even more sharply. While Odysseus drinks wine and eats food, Silenus does not eat but only drinks wine (which is his god) and Polyphemus is entirely unacquainted with wine. Later, however, becoming addicted to the drink, he develops the same relationship to it as Silenus (140, 545-565). Polyphemus is a paradox from a dietary point of view. If he assumes the status of a human being he must be regarded as a cannibal (which immediately excludes him from this category); but if he is not a human being he is not a cannibal. In his attitude to drink he occupies a similar position between Odysseus and Silenus. At first he does not know of it, then he likes it, and finally he becomes addicted to it, like the satyrs.

A similar mixture of identity and difference lies behind the social relationships that the three figures maintain and create. Odysseus has a

6. Trade, Power and Tyranny in Classical Athens 137

relationship of *philia* to his companions and seeks *xenia* among the creatures of the island (378, 398, 409, 478-482, 550, 695). When it comes to the discussion of the Trojan war he emphasises Paris' breach of social conventions which led to the conflict between Greeks and Trojans (283 f., 290-298). He leaves no doubt that he is well acquainted with the norms of human society, which include the moral obligation to fight for his *philoi*. Both Polyphemus and Silenus, by contrast, do not know the rules of *xenia* and *philia*; to their fellows they stand in a relationship of brotherhood (*kasignêtoi*, 445; *adelphoi* 509, 531), they break the rules of *xenia* against Odysseus and themselves receive no assistance from their brothers once in danger. Moreover they are blind to the social crime committed by Paris, and would fight instead for their own causes alone (187-197).

The degree to which each figure feels obligations towards *philoi* is symbolic of his relationship to the gods. Odysseus worships Zeus and seeks his protection. The relationship is construed as one of reciprocal obligation: if Odysseus is not protected by Zeus he will not be a god and thus not deserve worship (354 f., 606 f.). Silenus, by contrast, *is* a god: Bacchus. The play suggests an identity between wine, satyrs and their god Bacchus.[49] Polyphemus is the son of the god Poseidon, and he claims that his *gastêr* is his god (230-231, 336). Polyphemus thus also identifies himself with a god, although the identity is self-created and absurd. The construction is important, however, in order to create another opposition between the Cyclops and Silenus on the one hand and Odysseus on the other. While Odysseus knows the rules of reciprocity because he has to maintain a reciprocal relationship with the gods, Silenus and Polyphemus, identifying themselves with divinities, do not have to follow the norm of reciprocity.

Finally, exchange. Odysseus knows the rules of various civilised modes of exchange: *xenia*, sacrifice to the gods, sale and purchase (97 f., 133, 137 ff., 285 ff.); Silenus and Polyphemus are utterly ignorant of either of these exchanges. Silenus accuses Odysseus of having come to steal Polyphemus' lambs and cheese (232-235), then sells Polyphemus' property without his permission (259 f., 267 f., 270 f.), and later steals draughts of wine which he is supposed to give to the Cyclops. Polyphemus' mode of acquisition is violent appropriation; he captures the satyrs, seizes Odysseus' companions and is 'utterly indifferent to arguments about fair trade'.[50] His idea of giving is personal consumption, or giving to his own *gastêr*. Odysseus explicitly draws a parallel between the human virtue of generosity and Polyphemus' generous behaviour towards his own stomach. He asks him to forget his appetite and, instead of seeking bad gain (*ponêra kerdea*), do what is right (310-312). In summary, the relationships which Polyphemus and Silenus develop to each other and to Odysseus are characterised by theft, pillage and consumption, while the relationship typical of Odysseus is characterised by purchase.

Odysseus enters the stage as a stranger arriving at the island of Sicily. Being in want of food his first question is whether there is anything to buy.

His search for a market has the same function as the search for hospitality in the Homeric story. The Homeric image of civilisation is parodied in the *Cyclops* as that of sale and purchase. Although Odysseus does not appear to be a professional trader he is nevertheless well acquainted with the strategies of haggling. During the negotiations with Silenus he is quite keen to strike a bargain and not to be taken advantage of (133-160). The image of commerce is reinforced by terms which probably referred to the language of the market, and referred to the *Odyssey*'s images of trade. The word used when Odysseus expresses his wish to buy something on the island is *hodaô*. This word and its compound *exhodaô* occur four times in the *Cyclops* but have never been found in other extant texts.[51] In *Od*. 15. 445 *hodaia* is used for the cargo of Phoenician traders. This cargo includes the captive Eumaeus.

Furthermore, Odysseus is associated with the use of money, and with rather clever use of it at that. When he asks for sustenance Silenus inquires how much money (*chruson*) he will give in return (138). Odysseus replies that he has no gold but wine. Silenus is so delighted that he forgets about money. Odysseus, however, then offers him money (*nomisma*, 160); whereupon Silenus replies that he is no longer interested in money (*chruson*) but would give all the flocks of the island for a single cup of wine. It seems surprising that Odysseus first claims to have no money but later offers it to the satyr.[52] The answer must lie in the shift in usage from *chruson* to *nomisma* for money, and from gold to wine as the currency of satyrs. It suggests that satyrs know the value of gold and certainly of wine, whereas they do not know the value of *nomisma*. Odysseus, cunningly, offers *nomisma* which has a value for him but not for Silenus. He offers a return which has no meaning for its recipient and would, had it been accepted, have resulted in an unequal exchange. Another aspect may also be considered. Being in a position to consider *nomisma* as a value qualifies Odysseus as a civilised man. As Aristotle argued later, *nomisma* is necessary for, and the result of, life in the *polis*.[53] Conversely, the possession of *nomisma*, being a derivative of *nomos*, makes Odysseus the representative not just of civilised society but also of commerce.[54] In fact he first presents himself as possessing *nomisma* before he reveals that he is acquainted with *nomos*.[55] The pun on *nomisma* reflects the ambivalent image of the *nomoi* which Odysseus represents in the *Cyclops*. He rejects violence (258), knows the rules of civilised exchange, legal arbitration (253-260), hospitality and the laws of Zeus; but then he reminds the Cyclops that he is obliged to pay tribute since he is a subject of Hellas (289, 298), and finally resorts to an act of violence which is not at all sanctioned by divine law.[56]

As Odysseus is not free from uncivilised behaviour, so the Cyclops is not devoid of civilised qualities. Entering the stage for the first time he utters the concerns of a caring *oikonomos*:

6. Trade, Power and Tyranny in Classical Athens 139

'How are my new born lambs in the cave?
Are they at the teat, nuzzling their mothers?
Are the wicker presses filled with fresh cheese?
...
Is my dinner cooked and ready to eat?
...
And are the vats filled up, brimming with milk?
...
Cow's milk, sheep's milk or mixed?'[57]

The theoretical discussion of household management (*oikonomia*) became a topic within intellectual circles probably in the latter half of the 5th century.[58] It was concerned with the accurate arrangement of tools and utensils as well as with keeping a record of developments of stock and products. The best-known example is Xenophon's *Oeconomicus*, written in the middle of the 4th century, but the subject was new at the time of the *Cyclops*. Given that the Xenophontic *Oeconomicus* was written by a man of anti-democratic temper, and set in an extremely affluent household, we may assume that the subject was particularly popular in circles where wealth was based on agriculture. In the second part of the passage the Cyclops asks questions which seem typical of dinners and symposia. His dinner even turns into a proper symposium in the penultimate scene of the play. Here the roles are reversed and Odysseus' brutal blinding seems more uncivilised than the Bacchic enchantment of Polyphemus. Finally, Polyphemus commands slaves and owns cattle in addition to the Homeric sheep. All this gives him the air not of a wretched savage but of a man of substance.[59]

The ultimate blow to Odysseus' image as the only civilised being on stage comes in the middle of the play. The long speech of the Cyclops is preceded by a statement which reveals the injustice of Odysseus' behaviour. He reminds the Cyclops that it is not only the rules of *xenia* that should urge him to offer hospitality but also the fact that he is his subject (289-296). The remark identifies Odysseus with Athenian imperial rhetoric and, bending the truth, he represents it at its worst.[60] The Cyclops responds to Odysseus in a speech which, because of the many important allusions it contains, must be quoted in full:

Plutos is the wise men's (*sophoi*) god, little man.[61]
The rest is mere bluff and purple patches.
I don't give a damn for my father's shrines
along the coast! Why did you think I would?
And I'm not afraid of Zeus' thunder;
in fact, I don't believe Zeus is stronger
than I am. And anyway I don't care. When Zeus
pours down rain, I take shelter in this cave
and feast myself on roast lamb or venison.
Then I stretch myself and wash down the meal,

flooding my belly with a vat of milk.
Then, I rub my dress
while Zeus is thundering.[62] When the wind sweeps down
with snow from Thrace, I wrap myself in furs
and light up the fire. Then let it snow
for all I care! Whether it wants to or not,
the earth must grow the grass that feeds my flocks.
And as for sacrifice, I make mine,
not to the gods, but to the greatest god of all,
this belly of mine! To eat, to drink
from day to day, to have no worries –
that's real Zeus for your clever man!
As for those who embroider human life
with their little laws – damn the lot of them![63]

The meaning of Plutos at the opening of the speech has been discussed by Paganelli. He argues that the *plousioi/penêtes* opposition replaced the earlier contrast of *agathoi* and *kakoi* known from sympotic lyric. It was the jargon of a social class which despised democracy and the social classes which represented it, and which had succeeded in overthrowing it for a short time in 411, shortly before the production of the play.[64] Plutos was the god of the oligarchs, as Plato explicitly stated, and '*plousioi*' was the label which Thucydides and Aristotle gave to the people responsible for the coup in 411.[65] Euripides himself draws attention to the dynamics of *plutos* and the conflict between *plousioi* and *penêtes* in other plays. In the *Supplices* Theseus describes the free city (a democracy) as one where 'the people reign, and do not give power to wealth (*tôi ploutôi*), but the *penês* has an equal share in it' (404-408). In the *Aeolus* the demand is expressed that *plousioi* and *penêtes* should have absolute equality.[66] Although Paganelli links the argument of the Cyclops too directly to a specific political situation, it can be noted that the figure of Polyphemus caricatures 'certain contemporary anti-democratic ideology'.[67] The question for whom Plutos was the most important god is linked to the problem of who were the *sophoi* who are mentioned in the same line. *Sophoi* were first of all 'wise men', but by the 5th century an ironic meaning seems to have been associated with the name, giving it a connotation of 'too clever', overreaching oneself in wisdom. Euripides especially uses the title in that sense; thus in the *Bacchae*, men who set themselves against the gods are *sophoi* – they are clever but not wise.[68] As to the social origin of the *sophoi* nothing too specific can be said. We know that many sophists (*sophistai*, not *sophoi*) were born in aristocratic families, travelling and visiting their peers in other *poleis*. Their loyalty to their friends abroad was often greater than to the population of their own cities, especially when these were, like Athens and its allies, under democratic government.[69] A typical example might have been Callicles. He came from a wealthy, aristocratic family, his ideas were strongly anti-democratic and he had connections with a member of the oligarchic coup in 411.[70] Yet, as with the meaning of Plutos,

6. Trade, Power and Tyranny in Classical Athens

the matter of the *sophoi* in the Cyclopean speech should not be pressed too far; both referred loosely to anti-democratic principles and their upholders, whatever differences there might have been among them.[71]

The cosmology and morality of the Cyclops result in an extreme version of autarky: he lives for himself and from his own resources. The self-sufficiency of the Euripidean Cyclops has nothing to do with the blissful state of automatic growth which characterises the island of the Cyclopes in the Homeric version. The Euripidean Cyclops lives off the flocks which he himself breeds and rears and has no vines that grow by themselves. While in Homer the earth provides the livelihood for the Cyclops, in Euripides he is an *autourgos*: he works for himself without exchange. There is a shift from the Homeric model of savagery as being closer to the Golden Age to that of savagery as a parody of autarky. This is parallel to the shift in the image of Odysseus as the representative of civilisation to being the representative of imperialism and trade. Both the Cyclops and Odysseus represent their programme in a perverted form; while for the Cyclops autarky means self-devotion, for Odysseus maritime exchange and empire mean haggling for food and subjecting an island to the payment of tribute.

The confrontation of exchange and *autarkeia* in the encounter of Odysseus and the Cyclops is part of the debate on power which is the subtext of the play.[72] The meaning of power was inseparably linked to the debate on the relationship between *nomos* and *phusis* which dominated philosophical discussions in the second half of the 5th century. The contrast of *nomos* and *phusis* structured a wide range of ideas. For our purposes, the following distinctions may be drawn.[73] First, the *nomoi* of humans could mean civilisation: that is, the 'human condition' which made humans human and distinguished them from either animals or gods; in this meaning, *nomos* was embodied by Odysseus in the Homeric version of the story. Secondly, human *nomoi* could be opposed to divine *dikê* and then signified human laws as created after the model of the gods and their laws; this is expressed most programmatically in Aeschylus' *Oresteia*, and can be regarded as the core of Athenian definitions of justice by the middle of the 5th century. Thirdly, *nomos* could refer specifically to the constitution of the Athenians which for political purposes was identified with the natural rights of the stronger. In the Melian Dialogue Thucydides renders this idea as follows:

> Our aims and our actions are perfectly consistent with the beliefs men hold about the gods and with the principles which govern their own conduct. Our opinion of the gods and our knowledge of men lead us to conclude that it is a general and necessary law of nature (*hupo phuseôs anagkaias*) to rule whatever one can. We did not make this law (*nomos*) ourselves, nor were we the first to act upon it when it was made. We found it already in existence.[74]

This interpretation of *nomos* was politically the most controversial. 'Necessity' (*anagkê*) could be regarded as a natural principle forcing the weaker to submit to the stronger. But it could also be argued that human *nomoi* were a civilising force which controlled uncivilised necessity. The theory of the natural rights of the stronger could be used in favour of two opposed political programmes each using the *nomos/phusis* opposition in its own way. In the *Cyclops* both Odysseus and Polyphemus advocate the right of the stronger, but the one in the name of *nomos* and the other in the name of *phusis*. Revealing that both concepts could refer to the same thing, or imply their opposites, Euripides suggests that neither the contrast of *nomos* and *phusis*, nor that of civilisation and savagery, made distinctions that were absolute.

As a result, the play ends in open questions, rather than in unequivocal answers. Odysseus departs from the island triumphantly, leaving the Cyclops behind, blinded. The buyer wins over the one who worships self-sufficiency. Yet the fact that both buyer and *oikonomos* represent their ideals negatively reveals how flawed Euripides thought the ideals to be. Any strength could turn into violence and then call for expulsion. It looks as if in the *Cyclops* the stronger loses in winning and the weaker wins in losing.[75]

The dissolution of the boundary between civilisation and savagery is achieved by the departure from the Homeric opposition of *xenia*/no *xenia* to that of exchange/no exchange. While *xenia* was an unequivocal sign of civilised man, both exchange and self-sufficiency carried the potential of violence and self-destruction. The effect of the *Cyclops* rests on the polyvalent meanings of *nomos*, *phusis*, self-sufficiency and exchange. It reveals the internal tensions of Athenian thought and the indispensability of the image of exchange for its most fundamental concepts.

Notes

1. For an overview see Guthrie (1971), pp. 55-135.
2. The emphasis on trade and commercial exchange in 5th-century literature provided the material for the 'modernist' position in the long-lasting debate on the ancient economy. For a summary of the primitivist-modernist debate see Austin and Vidal-Naquet (1977) and Millett (1991 b). Ehrenberg (1951) seems to me a complete misinterpretation of the commercial imagery in Athenian comedy.
3. See esp. Schneider (1989), pp. 52-132. Schneider concentrates here on the development of *technê* in Greek thought, which is closely related to the problems discussed in this chapter.
4. The classic source for the definition of the human condition is the myth of Prometheus. See esp. Vernant (1980), pp. 168-185; cf. Vidal-Naquet (1981 b) for similar patterns of thought in epic poetry.
5. Thuc. I. 2-19; cf. Garlan (1989), pp. 198-202.
6. Edmunds (1975), pp. 40-46.
7. Eur. *Supp*. 201-213, trans. Guthrie; see also Anon. Iambl. DK II, p. 403.16-18; and in comparison Aesch. *Prom*. 442-468, 478-506; Soph. *Ant*. 332-371; all conveniently collected and discussed in Guthrie (1971), pp. 73, 79-81. See further Hdt. VII. 6. 1 where the sea is described as only potentially useful since it is so often

6. Trade, Power and Tyranny in Classical Athens 143

troubled by winds; cf. Edmunds (1975), p. 42. In the 4th century it was clearly maritime exchange, not the power to use ships, which was maintained as an image of human strength; cf. Isocr. *Paneg.* 42.

8. Sahlins (1972), defines piracy as a form of 'negative reciprocity', see esp. p. 195.

9. Garlan (1989), p. 189.

10. Thuc. I. 8. 3.

11. Sahlins (1972), pp. 191-198; cf. Millett (1991 a), Donlan (1981-2).

12. Sahlins (1972), pp. 204-210.

13. Saller (1982); cf. Millett (1989), p. 16.

14. Thuc. I. 13.

15. In I. 2 it is explicitly stated that 'because of the poverty of her soil, Athens was remarkably free from disunity', which is a prelude to the idea that Athens aimed at creating a hierarchical system among states rather than citizens, and that her power was based on differences in the amount of financial revenue each state posessed, rather than in the amount of landed property each citizen could own.

16. Thuc. II. 62. 3.

17. As Loraux has argued in detail, a funeral speech required a specific type of rhetoric. Developing out of an aristocratic type of speech, it had to adapt to that genre but transform the praise of individuals into that of the community. The language and values of a funeral speech remained thus fundamentally aristocratic and it was the rhetorical aim of a democratic speaker to praise the democracy and maritime empire of Athens in the terminology in which aristocratic values were expressed. See Loraux (1986), esp. pp. 42-56.

18. Thuc. II. 38. 2.

19. For further discussion of the politics of household management and liberality see below p. 139.

20. Vernant (1965 a), pp. 275 ff.; Brumfield (1981) gives an insight into the frequency of feasts and rituals which accompanied the agricultural cycle.

21. Thuc. II. 38. 1.

22. The theoretical and philosophical background of the *Histories* has often been underestimated by modern scholars who regard Thucydides above all as a faithful narrator of facts; see by contrast A. Parry (1980), Connor (1984) and Hussey (1985).

23. See the excellent discussion of these problems by Connor (1984), pp. 63 ff.

24. For the multiple tensions arising from the distinction of public and private friendship see esp. Connor (1971), Humphreys (1983), Goldhill (1986), pp. 79-106; Herman (1987), pp. 1-13, and Ober (1989), esp. pp. 212 ff.

25. Ps.-Xen. *Ath. Pol.* II. 4; 7-8.

26. See above, ch. 3, and Pucci (1987), pp. 165-172.

27. Thuc. II. 38. 2; quoted above.

28. In the *Wasps* we hear that 'if someone buys sea perch but refuses sprats, straightaway the sprat-seller next to him says, "This man here would appear to be buying fish with a view to tyranny" ' (Ar. *Wasps* 493-495; cf. Taillardat (1961), pp. 413-416). Davidson (1993) discusses further evidence: the myth of Polycrates, in which the tyrant is given a fish by a fisherman because it seemed 'worthy of his *archê*' (Hdt. III. 42. 1 f.); a passage in Alexis' *Pylaiai* where fishmongers are the ones who exact *basilikoi phoroi* from the people (Alexis 200 (K), 3 f.); the story of the Syrian female tyrant Artagatis who had such a desire for fish that she forbade her subjects to eat any themselves. But her life ended in disaster as a result of her *hubris*; she was drowned in a lake and devoured by fish (Ath. VIII. 346 d-e).

29. On spending bribes at the fishmongers' and on prostitutes see Aisch. I. 115; Timocl. fr. 4. 8. Harvey (1985), who takes these statements literally, seems to miss the rhetoric of such statements; see p. 94.
30. Ar. *Ach.* 28 ff.
31. Edmunds (1980), p. 16.
32. Goldhill (1991), p. 187.
33. For references see below.
34. Edmunds (1980), p. 5.
35. Newiger (1980), pp. 225 ff., Edmunds (1980), p. 5.
36. Ar. *Ach.* 729-835; garlic and salt were staples in Megara, see Sommerstein (1980) ad 813 f.
37. Edmunds (1980), pp. 16 and 25.
38. Ar. *Ach.* 860-958; cf. Sommerstein (1980), ad loc. and Edmunds (1980).
39. Thuc. II. 63. 3.
40. Edmunds (1980), pp. 28-32 and Plat. *Rep.* 372b; see also *Rep.* 327a-336b; *Leg.* 705a, 846d-852d; 915c-922a.
41. Seaford (1984), pp. 5 and 17 ff.
42. Ibid., pp. 33-45, Arrowsmith (1952), pp. 1 ff.
43. Vidal-Naquet (1981 a), Seaford (1981) who here compares the *Cyclops* with the themes of the *Bacchae*.
44. Seaford (1984), p. 58.
45. Ibid., pp. 57 ff. and Vernant and Vidal-Naquet (1981), esp. p. 110 and Eur. *Bacch.* 319-321, 988-990 which represents Pentheus as at the same time subhuman and superhuman, *pharmakos* and *turannos*, who is eventually removed from the *polis* into the Dionysiac *thiasos*.
46. Konstan (1990).
47. Arrowsmith (1952), p. 8.
48. Konstan (1990); for the relation of diet and civilisation encoded in the myth of the Cyclopes see also Shaw (1982-3), pp. 21-25, for a contrasting view Kirk (1973), pp. 162 f.
49. Wine and Bacchus were metonyms in Greek; the identity of satyrs, wine and Bacchus surfaces in the narrative pattern of satyr plays in which satyrs are normally rescued by being reunited with Bacchus and wine; cf. the first chorus (63-81), ll. 124, 622 and Polyphemus' comments (525-527); cf. Konstan (1990), pp. 223-235.
50. Konstan (1990), p. 214.
51. Apart from two occasions when Odysseus seeks to *hodaein* food (98, 133), the term is employed in the context of unjust exchange. Silenus uses the word when swearing to Polyphemus that he did not sell his flocks to the stranger (267) and, even more significantly, when describing how Dionysus had been sold by pirates as a slave abroad (12). Konstan argues with the commentaries that the term was probably regular market slang, but another association seems more appropriate. Konstan (1990), n. 5; not so, however, Seaford (1984) ad loc.
52. The passage has puzzled commentators, because of the seeming contradiction of ll. 138 and 160. It has been suggested that *nomisma* referred to the contemporary Athenian *silver* coinage alone and it was therefore correct of Odysseus to say that he had no gold (Wilamowitz, see Seaford (1984) ad 160). Seaford himself suggests that the passage is an example of Odysseyan cunning, not because he offers currency which has no meaning for the satyr, but because he offers it at a moment when he has already made the bargain.
53. Arist. *EN* 1133 b 18-20.
54. Aristophanes puns in exactly the same way on *nomisma* in the *Clouds*.

6. Trade, Power and Tyranny in Classical Athens 145

Strepsiades, knowing that in the school of Socrates knowledge is sold for money, offers any amount of *nomisma*. Yet he receives the answer that in the school of Socrates gods are no longer *nomisma* (Ar. *Cl.* 248); see further Eur. *IT* 1471; Aesch. *Sept.* 269; Pers. 858; Pind. frgm. 203 (Bowra); cf. Guthrie (1971), p. 56.

55. Odysseus invokes *nomos* the first time in ll. 299 ff.

56. Arrowsmith (1968), p. 229; the interdependence of technical knowledge (navigation!) and violence is made particularly explicit in the description of the blinding (461, 468, 484, cf. Hamilton (1979), p. 290 and note).

57. Eur. *Cycl.* 206-218.

58. See esp. Ar. *Frogs.* 975 ff.; Plat. *Prot.* 318 e.; cf. Guthrie (1971), p. 268; Singer (1959), pp. 33 f.; Spahn (1984).

59. On the 'urbanity' of the Cyclops, especially after having received wine from Odysseus, see Hamilton (1979); cf. Seaford (1984), p. 53.

60. As Seaford remarks, Odysseus' claim that the Achaeans saved Sicily from the Trojans is both false and inept: the Greeks did not save Sicily from the Trojans and the Trojans had never been a threat to the Sicilians. What gave the remark point is the fact that 'to have saved Greece from the Persians' was the rhetoric of contemporary Athenian propaganda to justify their empire; see Seaford (1984), p. 56 and ad 297, and Thuc. I. 78, V. 89, VI. 83 (where the Athenians in Sicily justify the Athenian empire).

61. Out of metre because I changed Arrowsmith's translation which does not bring out the terminology of the Greek original.

62. Again out of metre because I have adapted the translation on the basis of Seaford's critical note ad loc. Seaford leaves *peplon* (cloak) as the manuscripts and Murray's OCT have it, instead of changing it to *pedon* (earth), as Musgrave suggested, and on which Arrowsmith bases his translation. Seaford's comment (ad loc.) that the line refers to masturbation rather than to farting is corroborated by the parallel he draws with Cat. 32. 10-11 (*nam pransus iaceo et satur supinus/ pertundo tunicamque palliumque*), and fits the context better than Musgrave's emendation.

63. Eur. *Cycl.* 316-340.

64. Usually dated to 408 B.C., although nothing certain is known, Seaford (1984), p. 48.

65. Thuc. VIII. 65. 3, Arist. *Ath. Pol.* 29. 5; cf. Paganelli (1979 a), p. 219.

66. Fr. 21 N^2, cf. Paganelli (1979 a), pp. 220 f. with further references.

67. As Seaford remarks, literature and politics are never autonomous, so not every piece of literature which draws on contemporary politics turns immediately into a political tract. Seaford (1984), p. 53.

68. Guthrie (1971), p. 28.

69. Ibid., pp. 40 f.

70. Ibid., p. 102; cf. Seaford (1984), p. 52.

71. Further support for the hypothesis that the Cyclops identifies himself with a wealthy aristocratic upper class is given by the fact that he mentions his cattle in the speech (325), and that he enjoys his dinners on skins, drinking milk and masturbating afterwards (327-329) which has a parallel in the aristocratic celebration of symposia where men, reclining on pillows, enjoyed wine and sexual intercourse ; see Seaford (1984) ad loc., who compares this description with a poem by Alcaeus (fr. 338). Polyphemus' speech includes a number of further allusions to intellectual debates of the time which were in conflict with the political ideals of democratic Athens: the hostility against *nomoi* with the argument that they were man's futile attempt to overcome *anagkê* (necessity, 338 f.; cf. Guthrie (1971), pp. 102 ff.); the idea that it was 'necessity' rather than the gods that governed the world and that the phenomena of the world were the result of *phusis*, rather than divine *nomoi* (332 f.; cf. Seaford (1984) ad loc. and Guthrie (1971), p. 100 – the denial of divine interference in human affairs was, strictly speaking, not contrary to democratic ideas, but the belief in the justice of *phusis* was irreconcilable with the belief that man-made laws (*nomoi*) were just; see for further discussion below, and Guthrie (1971), ch. 4.); and, finally, the emphasis on hedonism as a philosophy of life (336 f.). Both hedonism and the idea that *phusis* in the form of *anagkê* is stronger than *nomos* are associated with the name of Callicles; cf. Plat. *Gorg.* 491 e; see again Seaford (1984) ad loc.

72. Arrowsmith (1952).

73. For the following see Guthrie (1971), pp. 55-68; cf. Heinimann (1945) and Pohlenz (1953).

74. Thuc. V. 105. 2 f.

75. Or, as Seaford ((1984), pp. 57 f.) points out, 'it is in a sense Dionysos who prevails'. The Cyclops exemplifies 'the tension between the Dionysiac and the non-Dionysiac which ... lies at the heart of satyric drama, and which is resolved by the victory of Dionysos, to whose service the departing satyrs proclaim their return (709) ... The combination of the superhuman and subhuman obliterates the upper and lower boundaries within which man is contained by his *nomoi* and thereby calls into question the polar structure inherent in Greek institutions and political theory.'

7

Violence and Corruption: Commerce in Tragedy

Civic exchange and the theatre

All aspects of civic exchange discussed in the previous three chapters crystallised in the theatre. The site of the stage, for practical reasons alone removed from the *agora* itself, embodied the intersection of, sometimes conflicting, values centred in the public space of the *polis*: religion and politics, individual and community, city and empire, money and honour, signs and symbols. Staging civic exchange and being itself the occasion of a series of civic exchanges, theatrical performance represented political exchange in a double sense. Every individual play can be read as a reflection upon the values which surrounded its own production.

Money and other *chrêmata* were involved at various levels. The actors and the playwright received prizes, the *chorus* was equipped and trained with the money of the *chorêgos*, the *chorêgos* received a prize for dedication, and from some time in the 5th century the audience was paid for tickets and attendance from public funds.[1] In the 5th century the tribute from the allied cities was displayed on stage, the names of the benefactors of the city were read out and their rewards specified, and all orphans brought up at state expense were shown to the audience.[2] The display of these payments, either literally or in the form of their results, was a manifestation of the polyvalent meaning of values in the exchanges of the *polis*. Spent and displayed conspicuously, they were statements in the symbolic economy of power, but as payments for specific needs they were an essential part of the concrete economy.[3]

The chance of interpreting any of these payments in a commercial sense was carefully avoided. Transactions which could be identified with individuals were strictly avoided: the *chorus*, the collective body of the stage, was funded by an individual, while the actors, the dramatic individuals, were paid from the funds of the city.[4] Money was not given in order to reward individual achievement. Playwrights, like benefactors and other honorands of the *polis*, were given rewards which had no monetary value: crowns, inscriptions, seats of honour. The dangers that had to be avoided in honouring victors and paying the actors were dramatised in the tragedies themselves. In turn the tragic discourse on wealth, power, corruption and *hubris* gave meaning to the rituals of exchange surrounding its performance. The display of expenses and individual achievement in the theatre was a display of power, but was at the same time controlled by the audience. Witnessing the expenses of the *chorêgoi*, and the display of tributes, of orphans, and of benefactors, judging what was the best play and paying the actors, the audience as a collective engaged in the civic meaning of the plays. Thus Demosthenes, when having to justify why he wanted to receive a crown in the theatre rather than in the assembly, gave precisely this as an explanation for the importance of theatrical performances:

> But, really now, are you so unintelligent and blind, Aeschines, that you are incapable of reflecting that a crown is equally gratifying to the person crowned wheresoever it is proclaimed, but that the proclamation is made in the theatre merely for the sake of those by whom it is conferred? For the whole vast audience is stimulated to do service to the city, and applauds the exhibition of *charis* rather than the recipient.[5]

That the function of the audience was to control what happened in front of them more in the theatre than anywhere else may be a rhetorical exaggeration. The substantive point, however, is that the audience of the theatre was expected to take part in the politics of the plays just as they did in the assembly and the law courts. As voters in politics, as judges of legal cases, and as audience in the theatre, they controlled justice whose problems were addressed in the plays.[6]

Although it is a complex genre, there are recurrent themes in tragedy. The following analysis is based on a structuralist reading of Greek drama, which has been developed by Vernant, Vidal-Naquet, Segal, Zeitlin and Goldhill.[7] Their approach draws attention to a generic pattern which runs throughout the extant plays. First, there is a general reflection upon the tension between nature and civilisation which is thought to be controlled by marriage, sacrifice and agriculture;[8] secondly, there is a vital concern about the relationship between *oikos* and *polis* and their conflicting claims to the loyalty (*philia*) of their members;[9] thirdly, there is an extended debate on the relationship between Athenian law and divine *nomos*;[10] fourthly, most plays contain a self-reflexive debate on linguistic exchange, the power of *logoi* and their manipulative force on society and its individual members;[11] and finally, they are framed in a discourse which uses Homeric imagery and mythology for the discussion of contemporary problems. All these themes are interlocked. This not only ties together scenes which seem at first unconnected, but also gives a complex meaning to every individual image.

Given the openness of the tragic text and the restricted space of this chapter, the following discussion concentrates on the *Oresteia*. I consider,

7. Violence and Corruption: Commerce in Tragedy

though, that certain generalisations can be made. Aeschylus' strategy of using a polyvalent language of exchange was reworked and extended in later tragedies.[12] The *Oresteia* is therefore not just one example, but can be taken as the inception of a tradition of using commercial imagery on stage.

Retribution and payment

The *Oresteia* enacts the redefinition of justice and its immanent images of exchange.[13] In assessing the reciprocities of society it assesses the nature of humanity and justice, and their dependence on different modes of exchange and communication. A society that destroys its own values is a society in which it is impossible to exchange. And thus this society will cause its own destruction. From this perspective the problem of just exchange is the problem of political and social continuity and survival.

Paul Millett has drawn attention to the fact that behind the striking series of financial images that pervade the *Oresteia* lies the idea of reciprocity. The same obligation could be applied both to the field of financial exchange and to justice: like must be returned for like. Vengeance could be understood as a debt owed to a relative and transmitted from generation to generation. As he summarises succinctly:

> The theme is sustained right through the *Oresteia*, where conflicting obligations owed to gods and men generate overpowering tensions. The obligation imposed on Agamemnon to exact recompense (*praktôr, prattein: Ag.* 111, 705, 812 and 823) from the Trojans for the seizure of Helen involves him in the death of his daughter, for which he has to pay (*apotinein: Ag.* 1503) with his own life. For the murder of her husband, Clytemnestra owes a debt for which she in turn faces execution (*ophelein, prattein: Cho.* 310-11; cf. *Eum.* 624). Finally, the Erinyes unsuccessfully intervene as collectors of the debt (*praktores, chreos: Eum.* 319 and 260) that Orestes incurred by killing his mother.[14]

The interdependence of moral and material debt played out along these lines can be taken a step further. Financial images were suggestive not only because they link reciprocity with credit, but because commerce was an image of corrupted exchange, as much as continuous vengeance was symptomatic of the corruption of the house of Atreus. In its negotiation of two models of justice the *Oresteia* attributes two modes of exchange and two types of value to each.

The *Oresteia* had to concern itself with (literal) value and with (symbolic) values: in the possession and bequest of the wealth of the *oikos* the chain of generational continuity as well as the continuity of power were expressed at once symbolically and materially. The distinction between the two concepts of value could be fine and negligible, or vitally important. It could either refer to the two aspects of the same order of exchange – that is, the one between humans and gods (let us call it religious) – or it could distinguish the divine from the human order in which humans exchanged among themselves without the interference of the gods (let us call this political). To the extent that these transactional orders could be regarded as being in harmony or in tension, symbolic values and literal value could converge or diverge. The poetry of previous centuries made abundantly clear that wealth was not always god-given but could be seized violently, causing illegitimate power and excess. The *Oresteia* starts from this assumption but adds complexity to the problem. The trilogy is also more difficult, since it explores the confusions which arise when the two categories of value are manipulatively confused in the speech of the characters. Here the democratic discourse on persuasion made its impact. The Homeric model suggested almost complete coincidence of material and symbolic wealth, which expressed itself in the convertibility of power, prosperity and treasure. It also expressed itself in the correlation of the value (or status) of persons and the quality of their character. Yet the homology between human power and divine wealth no longer went unchallenged in the public exchanges of the *polis*. Authority and wealth had different meanings in a supra-human order on the one hand and human society on the other. The poems of Solon and Theognis are evidence of the loss of faith in wealth as a divine signifier of power in the political order of the city state. Human *chrêmata* developed into measurable quantities of value from which certain political rights could be derived. This was incompatible with the idea of the immeasurable nature of divine blessing.[15] The *Oresteia* re-opens the question of wealth and its relation to power but integrates it into a more fundamental debate on the signifying power of signs. Just as material wealth can lead humans into excess and ruin (*hubris* and *atê*, *Ag.* 763-71.), so words can say dangerous things and bring ruin. Persuasion (*peithô*), the healing force, can become Persuasion, the daughter of ruin (*pais aphertos atas*, *Ag.* 385 f.).[16] While the *Agamemnon* and the *Choephoroi* dramatise the abuse of language and wealth in deceit and commerce, the *Eumenides* represents their healed counterparts: positive *peithô* and gift exchange based on *charis*.[17] The trilogy comes to the conclusion that justice is not a direct exchange of equal ratios paid by individuals but that it can be reached only within the public forums of the democratic *polis* where language, social exchange and the exchange of valuables are controlled by the assembled citizen body.

The formal construction of the trilogy is such that it arrives at this statement only after having engaged in a variety of images of corrupted exchange. Most notable are those of deception, theft and corrupted sacrifice. The different kinds of corruption condition each other. As Zeitlin has demonstrated, the characters of the *Oresteia* are not only unable to exchange without deceiving one another and the gods, but are also deceived about the nature of their own action.[18] Within this framework, images of commerce, money and 'sale' can be shown to have a function parallel to that of corrupted use of language and corrupted sacrifice. Throughout the play they serve to reveal the dangers of language, justice and social exchange if these are regarded as a direct exchange of equal things. Whereas (positive) *peithô*, jurisdiction in democratic lawcourts and the return of *charis* are the foundations of peace and prosperity in the *Eumenides*, deceptive language, revenge and commercial exchange are the reasons for violence and destruction in the two preceding plays.

Lattimore first drew attention to the crucial function of images in the *Oresteia*.[19] Images are used as a visualised form of ideas by employing metaphors which become literally embodied in concrete objects. Typical examples are the robe which is both a metaphor for, and an object of, entanglement, or the viper which is an image both of poisoning and of a concrete creature that poisons. This technique reduces the possibility of distinguishing between symbolic values and their concrete form embodied in material wealth, a strategy that is important for the theme of mistaken justice in exchange. *Ploutos* and *chrêmata* are signifiers in a double sense: they are metaphors of the text and symbols in the society the text aims to describe.

The *Oresteia* is saturated with the language and images of exchange, meaningful at one and the same time in social, religious, legal and economic spheres. The curse of the house of Atreus disrupted the bonds between members of the family, between generations, between *oikoi*, between *poleis* and between humans and gods. As has been suggested in a number of detailed studies, the disruption of social bonds is an image of a culture that has no chance of survival. The adultery of Helen and Paris, the death of the Argive sons at Troy, the sacrifice of Iphigenia, the murder of Agammenon and finally the murder of Clytemnestra are represented as the inversion of proper cultural bonds – that is, marriage, *philia*, sacrifice and the continuity of generations.[20] At one level this representation of disruption reflects the Hesiodic formulation of cultural survival as ensured by marriage and respect for fathers, *xenia* and sacrifice.[21] And it immediately springs to mind that all these relationships were symbolised by material transactions: *dôra*, *xenia*, *hedna* and *agalmata*.[22] If justice was observed, it was a guarantee of prosperity and continuity of the *oikos* and, by implication, the *polis*.

The *parodos* of the *Agamemnon* suggests that these different transactions interlock and that the violation of one rule of exchange brings about the collapse of the entire system. Corrupted exchange at one level is symptomatic of corruption at another. It has been demonstrated before how the themes of corruption, impiety and deception support each other throughout the trilogy.[23] Here we confine ourselves to highlighting this interaction in the example of the *parodos* which introduces the terms and images in which the problem of justice is approached. It will help us to understand the complexity of the play's commercial imagery, and how this contributes to the concepts of social exchange which are discussed in the trilogy.

The *parodos* begins with an allusion to the original crime, the seduction of Atreus' wife and the cannibalist destruction of the children by their own father:

> Ten years it is since the great contestants
> of Priam's right,
> Menelaus and Agamemnon, my lord,
> twin-throned (*dithronou*), twin-sceptred (*diskêptrou*), in twofold power
> of kings from God, the Atreidae (*zeugos Atreidan*),
> put forth from the shore
> the thousand ships of the Argives ...[24]

Agamemnon and Menelaus are called emphatically the *Atreidae* and they are said to have a 'double-throned' and 'double-sceptred' power, which is ordained so 'from the God', and which makes them literally a 'couple yoked together' (*zeugos Atreidan*). This first sentence instantly suggests that power in general is given from generation to generation, and originally from the God. It is a transaction that binds fathers and sons and humans and gods. On the other hand, the representation of Menelaus and Agamemnon as the *Atreidae* recalls the memory of the quarrel between Atreus and Thyestes, and their joint responsibility for it as members of one *oikos*. The cannibalism violated the human order in a multiple sense. Feasting, the ceremonial continuation of sacrifice, ritually expressed the difference between humans and gods by allotting to humans their portion of food. Atreus' meal, by contrast, destroyed the relationship between humans and gods by violating the constraints of the human diet. It also violated the continuity of the generations as the father consumed his own children. The exchange between humans and gods was perverted into a feast of self-destruction.

Destruction is thereafter the principle of exchange in the house of Atreus. Its members wage war against another house to avenge the original crime (*antidikos*) but also 'in retaliation' (*anti*) for a new crime. The harmony with which the two brothers used to reign and fight together in order to avenge the adultery of the wife of one of them contrasts with the disharmony of the brothers in the last generation. Yet the knowledge that the Trojan expedition led to the adultery of the wife of the other one, seduced by their common cousin, binds the two together once more as subjects of the same fate. Within a few lines the chorus give an interpretation of culture as a continuum of oppositions and exchange spanning time and distance, between generations, between *oikoi* and between humans and gods.

In the following passages the chorus expand on this theme, showing how the violation of the human order in the past leads to a series of corrupted – that is, destructive – exchanges in present and future. The war cry 'Ares'

7. Violence and Corruption: Commerce in Tragedy 153

becomes the cry of the Argives driven by Zeus Xenios against the Trojans 'for the sake of a promiscuous woman' (*amphi gunaikos poluanoros*) in retribution for their king's violation of *xenia* by adultery. The packed formulation of the sentence expresses again the complexity of the transgression which consists of, first, the breach of *xenia*, secondly, adultery committed by a man and, thirdly, the violation of the female role as the wife of one husband, rather than of many. War is fought between men, yet a woman has her part in it, and this part is sexual. The curse of the house of Atreus distinguishes and relates male and female, male and female duties, warfare and sexuality. The Trojan war is a war in which transgressors punish transgressors, as the chorus point out, and the tripartite divinity of Apollo, Pan and Zeus punish in return with delayed revenge (*husteropoinon Erinun*). Thus not only are male and female transgression related and opposed but also past and present as well as internal and external strife. So Danaans and Trojans have it alike (*thêsôn homoiôs*) and no sacrifice or libation will assuage the gods who are stern in anger. As the text puts it, sacrifice and libation are attempted but the victims do not burn (*apurôn hierôn*): that is, sacrifice is not only helpless against the wrath of the gods but literally impossible.[25] Communication and exchange between gods and humans are arrested as long as the gods persist in their anger. The breaches of *xenia*, adultery, warfare, the wrath of the gods are comparable disruptions of society which find their expression in the unburning sacrifice.

The *parodos* moves on to the separation of male and female duties and their respective roles in the generational continuum. The chorus refer to their own old age which they call childlike (*isopaida*) and lacking the strength of Ares. Thereby they first identify male adulthood with the ability to fight and secondly play out society's trigenerational structure.[26] Immediately afterwards they address Clytemnestra as 'queen' and 'daughter of Tyndareus', thereby focussing on her life in a generational perspective as a daughter for marriage, wife of the king and mother of the king's children. The two roles of Clytemnestra are not only separated in time but also associated in the present. As Goldhill puts it, 'it is precisely as "daughter of Tyndareus" that she became "queen", i.e. was married to Agamemnon, entered the system of alliances as an object of exchange.'[27] By the assimilation and division of the male and female trigenerational structure, the chorus create again a link between female adultery and male conflicts within and between households, as well as the continuity of past, present and future. Within the story of the Atreidae this meant that the Trojan war avenging a woman (*gunaikopoinôn polemôn*, 225) brought about the necessity of revenging a child (Iphigenia), and of being avenged by a child (Orestes, *dolia teknopoinos*, 155), which in turn would be avenged by divine Erinyes striking back later (*Erinun husteropoinon*, 58). The strict adherence to the vocabulary of retribution (*poinê, anti*) implies that male and female, generations, *oikoi*, cities, humans and gods engage in different transactional orders bridging and at the same time acknowledging the gap between past and present, between different social spaces and between the sexes.

The address to Clytemnestra calls forth a further sphere of exchange, already introduced by the beacon speech, but now expressed in more detail.[28] The chorus ask (85-96):

> What is there to be done? what new thing have you heard?
> In persuasion of what
> report do you order such sacrifice?
> To all the gods of the city,
> the high and the deep spirits,
> to them of the sky and the market places,
> the altars blaze with oblations.
> The staggered flame goes sky high
> one place, then another,
> drugged by simple soft
> persuasion of sacred unguents (*malakais adoloisi parêgoriais*),
> the deep stored oil of the kings.

Clytemnestra gives *dôra* to the gods because she is persuaded (*peithoi*) by the beacon light that the Trojan expedition is over.[29] In turn these visual *dôra* themselves act as persuasions (*parêgoriais*). The light of the flame is caused by the unguents which are called flattering (*malakais*) and, surprisingly, guileless (*adoloisi*). The woman is one element in a chain of communications in which signs are received and sent out. Communication between humans, and between humans and gods, is represented as the reciprocal transaction of signs and things between donors and recipients. Immediately afterwards the text draws attention to the ambivalence of signs: the chorus wonder which signs have persuaded the queen, thus implying that signs can be misinterpreted, or do not signify what they are supposed to be. After the *parodos* the chorus ask again what makes Clytemnestra order sacrifices, which prompts two speeches in reply.[30] In the first Clytemnestra describes the transmission of the message as a chain of beacon lights transmitted from one place to another like the (spoken!) message of a courier who is 'never slow or overcome by sleep' (290 f.). In the second she invents a story about what the lights might mean which is 'markedly a fictitious, imaginative weaving of words' (Goldhill). The second speech seems to hint at the arbitrary link between signs and what they signify which is the basis of rhetorical persuasion. The chorus also describe the visual signs of sacrifice, the *dôra* to the gods, as potentially, and in this case certainly, manipulative signs/items of exchange. *Malakos, parêgoria* and *pharmassein* are words which imply enchantment, poisoning, seduction, besides their more positive meanings.[31] The theme of seduction, adultery and corruption is paralleled by the mode of communication chosen by the adulteress. Most important for our context, the

7. Violence and Corruption: Commerce in Tragedy

expected persuasiveness of sacrifice introduces gifts as a persuasive power, and thereby establishes a structural identity of communication and gift exchange.

The chorus then contrast the manipulative force of persuasion represented by the (female) adulteress with their own role as *kurioi* of *peithô*. Now persuasion is associated with male authority – the greatest praise for Clytemnestra's persuasiveness will be 'Woman, you speak graciously like a sensible man' (351) – and the *dithronon kratos* of the Atreidae (109).[32] Male *peithô* is separated from female seductiveness in that it does not aim at the manipulation of the future but the replication (*throein*) of past and present. In that it is also different from the *technê* of the *mantis*. The chorus's strophe of self-description (*kurios eimi throein*) is followed by the antistrophe in which the seer's predictions are given in direct speech (*kednos de stratomantis idôn ... teraizôn*, 122-5). The introduction of the *mantis* creates a formal link between the chorus's authority of *peithô*, which lay in telling about things past or present, and Clytemnestra's version of *peithein*, which lay in the manipulation of the future. The seer represents a third form of communication – *predicting* the future, or the attempt 'to conflate the present and the future, to depict the future in the present, to remove, erase the gap'.[33] The chorus remain reluctant to accept fully the mantic reading of the future – that is, to exchange the signs of the birds into the signs of language. Instead they pray to the God in the following strophe, since it is 'only Zeus [who] cast the dead weight of ignorance finally from out my brain (165 f.)'. And later they confirm that 'what happens next I cannot speak nor see' (*out' eidon out' ennepô*, 248), although acknowledging that the *technai* of the seer are not fruitless (*ouk akrantoi*, 249). Nevertheless they remain convinced that 'justice so moves that those only learn who suffer; and the future you shall know when it has come' (250 ff.).[34] The lack of faith in mantic sign-reading came to be fully expressed in later tragedies in references to the seer's greed, especially for money.[35] The seer's inability to read signs is proved by the fact that he is addicted to a sign (money) which does not signify real value. Also he appears as subverting the reciprocity of exchange by claiming a reward in exchange for nothing. The *Oresteia* itself only lays the ground for this comparison by suggesting that the seer naively believes in the signs of the birds as being exchangeable for, or having the same value as, the signs of language (i.e. his prediction) without considering the possibility of false signification (or false value).[36]

The *parodos* ends with Agamemnon's speech to the army and their response. Agamemnon explains his dilemma: he must either sacrifice his daughter or sacrifice the army to the adverse wind (cf. the pun of *antipnoös* and *teknopoinas* in 146-155 which suggests the comparison). The sacrifice of Iphigenia collapses the distinction between sacrifice, child murder and the first part of any exchange. They appear as identical transactions viewed from a different perspective. The chorus emphasise the openness of the meaning of transactions in general as they describe the dilemma of the father. The way they refer to his daughter expresses the various aspects of her value, in the household, for men and as an object of sacrifice. In l. 209 they call her an *'agalma'*. *Agalma* is the Homeric word for a votive offering, but it could also refer to delightful objects in general, adornments of household and city, signs of glory.[37] In l. 227 she is described as the *proteleia naôn* which makes her literally the preliminary sacrifice before the departure of the fleet, but it also refers to her unmarried status; *proteleia* were especially those preliminary sacrifices performed before the marriage ceremony.[38] In l. 245 she is called *ataurôtos* which meant 'virgin' – literally, 'not taken to the bull'. In the context of the *parodos* the allusion to the bull, now as the sacrificial animal, cannot be passed over. 'This draws attention not only to the corrupted sacrifice – she is treated literally as a cow for sacrifice – but also to the corrupted nature of her relationship with her father, who, instead of giving his daughter in marriage exchange ("to the bull"), has given her (like a bull?) in sacrifice for the expedition.'[39] Iphigenia is a polyvalent value, as a treasure of the *oikos*, an object of marriage exchange and an object of sacrifice. Showing how in Agamemnon's economy valuable things or people shift their meaning according to the context in which they are exchanged, the play draws attention to the fact that the logic of Agamemnon's justice is circular and thus arbitrary. The ease with which Iphigenia's value changes demonstrates that the exact calculation of costs and rewards across contexts of exchange (i.e. marriage, family, sacrifice, warfare, personal revenge) creates dangerous confusions and therefore cannot be a standard of justice.

Agamemnon sees no way out of the moral conflict imposed on him by Artemis' wrath which caused the adverse wind. He represents it as a conflict between public and private interests (205-216). Yet the chorus draw attention to the fact that this distinction is not easily made. In 224-230 they contrast the death of the daughter with the victory of war; but by mentioning also that the war was fought in revenge for a wife (*gunaikopoinôn polemôn*, 225) they call to mind that it had its origin in the disruption of Agamemnon's own household.[40] Now it is the interdependence of domestic and political warfare that makes it impossible to contrast and compare exchange ratios. If exchange contexts are not clearly separated, their respective standards of justice become confused. Not only is the value of what is exchanged dependent on the context of exchange, but contexts of exchange need to be separated when they deal with different kinds of value.

The *parodos* has introduced us to the scope of images of exchange which lie behind the trilogy. Society is depicted as a system of exchanges which creates unity and disunity, social harmony and differences, and which bridges and exposes gaps. The impossibility of creating lasting peace, or simply of communicating, is represented as a failure to exchange and to identify different kinds of values. The fate of Atreus' *oikos* is viewed as

7. Violence and Corruption: Commerce in Tragedy

paradigmatic for society. For the audience, society is the political constitution of the *polis*, and so the mode of exchange which had corrupted the house of Atreus must be altered in the *polis*. Against that background the meaning of commerce as a metaphor for exchange that fails to create proper alliance gains in dimension, and we begin to see how commercial images, although employed for different ends, may be related to each other.

The *Oresteia* contains many terms of exchange that denote at the same time social, legal or financial retribution.[41] *Poinê, ameibein, tinein* and *anti* as either prefix or pronoun are recurrent words with which the idea of justice as an equal return is conveyed. In most cases they refer to the pertinent theme of revenge, but the fact that they also occur in more abstract contexts confirms the argument that exchange is a general image of order. In *Choe.* 965 *chronos* is made the subject of exchange: time returns everything. To add another example, later in the trilogy *charis* is given in return, rather than revenge.[42]

The terms in Greek which are most strongly associated with payment and money are *tinein* and *poinê*. But, paradoxically, while in early Greek they stand for the restoration of social peace and the termination of a cycle of revenge, in the *Oresteia* they are images of violent justice which claims death for death. One of the traditions attributed to money is that it served as a means of payment in penal law.[43] Before the introduction of coinage, the payment of any valuable object could recompense for the value of a person. As Kurke points out, '*apoina* and its synonyms ... all come from the legal or penal sphere. In that context, they express the obligation of requital and satisfaction – recompense for wrong done, wergild, or ransom. ... Especially in the case of murder, the most serious threat to a fragile society is an endless cycle of blood vengeance. *Apoina* interrupts such a cycle, replacing it with a single exchange.'[44] A passage from the *Iliad* illustrates that point. Ajax here chastises Achilles for not accepting Agamemnon's reconciliatory gifts in exchange for Briseis:

> ... And yet a man takes from his brother's slayer
> the blood price (*poinên*) or the price for a child who was killed, and the guilty
> one, when he has largely repaid (*poll' apoteisas*), stays still in the country,
> and the injured man's heart is curbed, and his pride and his anger
> when he has taken taken the price (*poinên dexamenôi*); but the gods put into your breast a spirit
> not to be placated, bad, for the sake of one single girl ...[45]

In the *Oresteia*, words like *teknopoinos* or *gynaikopoinos* are associated with blood vengeance (cf. *teknopoinos, gynaikopoinos,* or *tumma tummati teisai, Agam.* 155, 225, 1430). It is a destructive mode of exchange. The financial overtones of *poinê* and *tinein* are important for the play not because they refer to retribution in money but because they refer to exchange contexts in which 'tit for tat' was the exchange rate. Payment, *poinê*, meant direct retribution, exchange of equal ratios. Yet at the moment at which the financial aspects of *poinê* and *tinein* no longer refer to the payment of a recompense instead of revenge, but to equal exchange ratios, the bodies themselves become the return again. So in the *Eumenides* the Erinyes, demanding the body of the mother-killer Orestes, are called *praktores* (collectors of debts, fines or taxes).[46] The Argive youths fighting the war to avenge the adultery of Paris are also called *praktores*: they collect the tribute for the crime in the form of dead bodies (*Ag.* 109, 705, 812, 823). The comparison of Clytemnestra with money robbers (*argurosterê*, *Choe.* 1003) at the moment when she is accused of having caught Agamemnon in her 'foot-entangling robe' (*podistêras peplous*, *Choe.* 1000; note the pun on *stereô/stêr*) points in the same direction. In the imagery of the *Oresteia* the material value of a ransom turns into the symbolic value of a human body.[47] The inversion of the meaning of a moral concept that aimed at abandoning blood vengeance is part of the deception which characterises the condition of the house of Atreus.[48] The language of compensation becomes the language of retaliation while the value of human bodies is represented in terms of monetary value. Legal, economic and religious notions of value, if taken out of their established framework of reference, create confusion about justice in exchange and disrupt the social order. Yet their confusion in the subversive speech and action of individual characters does not aim at confusion but urges that a distinction must be made. It helped to define a distinction between law, religion and commerce, as well as their exchange rates, which transformed notions of justice in the Athenian *polis*.[49]

Agora and *Areios-pagos*

The first *stasimon* of the *Agamemnon* contains a commercial image which is meaningful within the pattern of corrupted society that pervades the *Oresteia*. Ares, the god of war, is represented here as a money-changer who weighs on the scale the 'value' of bodies fallen in battle. Zeitlin parallels the image with those of corrupted rituals in domestic life (marriage and sacrifice), on the one hand, and the distortions of agriculture as expressed, for example, in the comparison of Agamemnon's blood with a healthful and fruitful shower, on the other.[50] The image has meaning as an exchange undertaken in the wrong place as well as one that disrupts vital relationships. Ares in the *agora* is as abnormal as adultery in the household and human blood in the fields. To facilitate analysis, I quote the passage in full (438-448):

> The god of war, money-changer (*chrusamoibos*) of dead bodies,
> held the balance of his spear in the fighting,
> and from the corpse fire at Ilium
> sent to their dearest the dust
> heavy and bitter with tears shed
> packing the urns with

7. Violence and Corruption: Commerce in Tragedy

> ashes that once were men.
> They praise them through their tears, how this man
> knew well the craft of battle, how another
> went down splendid in the slaughter:
> and all for some strange woman
> (*allotrias diai gunaikos*).

In the first line Ares is called *amoibos*, someone who exchanges, avenges, returns. Yet the prefix *chrus-* relates the open term to the commercial domain. A *chrusamoibos* is defined by Hesychius as a *argurognômôn* – that is, a person who sat in the *agora* in order to exchange currencies. To compare their relative value he had to weigh them on his scale.[51] Ares conflates the symbols of money-changing, justice and warfare. As Rose comments, 'Ares holds the scales as a real dealer in gold would do, but his scale beam is a spear shaft. Like the literal gold dealer, he makes his wares pass through fire (440), but it is a funeral fire. They take the form of dust (*psêgma*, 442, commonly used as gold dust) and it is heavy (441), but in the sense that the grief is heavy. He packs it handily (444) in jars, meaning that these are pitifully light compared to living men.'[52] The ashes of dead men are, then, represented as money value and literally weighed against the grief at home which is in the other pan. The image of exchange, already familiar from the *parodos*, is here embodied in the scale used to measure exchange rates both in legal cases and in commerce. The ambivalence of the scales as both the symbol of justice and the tool of commerce throws the meaning of *amoibos* back into the legal domain, thus making it uncertain how to distinguish between the justice of different rates of exchange. Then, having just thrown open the problem of how to assess justice, or how to create equal exchange/equivalence, the chorus call to mind that the Trojan war was fought for the sake of one foreign woman (*allotrias diai gunaikos*), picking up on *gunaikopoinôn polemôn* in l. 225. Does payment, or justice, mean that the abduction of one woman must be avenged by the destruction of an entire city?

The gruesome image of the loss of dead bodies weighed on the scale of Ares contrasts sharply with the naive announcement of victory by the returning messenger (573 f.):

> For us, survivors of the Argive armament,
> the pleasure wins, pain casts no pain in the opposite scale
> (*nikai to kerdos pêma d'ouk antirrhepei*).

Nikai to kerdos, here translated as 'pleasure wins', has strong commercial overtones: in victory lies profit.[53] Together with the term *antirrhepei*, it suggests a reciprocity of suffering and success which had just been questioned by the chorus. For them, grief outweighs the joy of victory. After the statements of the chorus, and in anticipation of the further course of events, the messenger's evaluation of the Trojan war is questionable. The same victory is regarded by the chorus as being in danger of creating *hubris*.⁵⁴ And Clytemnestra's deceptively moralising statement (342) that the surviving soldiers from Troy should not be overwhelmed (*nikômenous*) by *kerdos* before they have made the journey home points in the same direction. Nevertheless the war did end in victory, and victory is undoubtedly profit. The contrast of the two interpretations of war both expressed in the image of the swinging balance introduces the problem of the relationship between Ares, Nikê and Dikê which becomes important at the end of the trilogy. This relationship is crucial for understanding fully the meaning of the image of Ares as a *chrusamoibos*.

As a political play of the 5th century the *Oresteia* dramatises the problem of justice within the *polis*. The internal relationships of the house of Atreus which are linked to the external conflict with Troy are a metaphor for political relationships within and between city states. As the city 'appropriated increasingly the vocabulary of the family'⁵⁵ the mythical conflicts of families became paradigmatic for the conflicts within the city. Ares who struck 'doubly' in the house of Atreus and between Argos and Troy⁵⁶ is thus synonymous with internal and external warfare in the classical *polis*.⁵⁷ In the course of the three tragedies it becomes increasingly clear that the concept of justice as a 'tit for tat' exchange, which guides Ares and money-changers alike, is destructive. So the victories which Ares achieves when sitting in the *agora* are anything but gain for the city.⁵⁸ What consequences did that have for the establishment of justice in the *polis*? Orestes escapes the vengeance of the Erinyes by being acquitted by the majority vote of a court. The Erinyes, the advocates of Ares, are given a place in the soil of Athens in order to be 'overseers of victory which is not bad' (*nikês mê kakês episkopa*, *Eum.* 903). Good victory is neither victory that destroys a city, nor honour achieved by successful vengeance, but victory over the adverse forces in the cultivated soil. The Erinyes are sent into the ground to fight off the danger of crop failure: 'Go then ... plunge beneath the ground. There hold off what might hurt the land; pour in the city's advantage (*to kerdaleon pempein poleôs epi nikêi*), success in the end' (*Eum.* 1007-1010). The ambivalent pleasures of gain derived from military victory are transformed into gain which is derived from agrarian fertility and which is profit for the entire *polis* (*kerdaleon ... poleôs epi nikêi*; cf. 991). When the Erinyes lament their defeat in the law court, which they can understand only in terms of military defeat and loss of honour, they are told that they are not beaten and have not lost honour; they were participants in a competition of equal votes the outcome of which came from Zeus (794-796). Zeus now reigns in the *agora* and strife becomes competition (*eris*) for good:⁵⁹

> But Zeus Agoraios ruled
> and my fight (*eris*)
> for good wins out in the whole issue.

7. Violence and Corruption: Commerce in Tragedy

A distinction is now established between external warfare and civic exchange, between Ares and *Eris*, the goddess of productive competition.[60] *Dikê* in the *polis* is achieved by peaceful exchange of *charis* rather than revengeful requital of bloodshed (980-982). Ares is banned from the political centre. Instead his place becomes the Areopagus, just outside the city. Athena calls the Areopagus the Hill of Ares, because 'here the Amazons encamped and built their shelters when they came in spite of Theseus ... and sacrificed to Ares' (685-690). The exile of Ares and the (invented) explanation of the origins of the name of the Areopagus summarises the cultural solution of the complex problem of exchange and justice which had been the problems of the trilogy. Higgins has summarised the meaning of this solution succinctly:

> Athena says that the hill of Ares is so called because the Amazons pursuing Theseus, Athens' king, encamped there, outside the city, and sacrificed there to the war god. In other words, in this trial between claims of male and female, mother and father, wife and husband, in which upheavals private and public are involved and over all of which Ares has been a presiding spirit, a settlement will come at a place where man-counselling women, in warlike hunt after a male and a king, kept vigilant watch from outside his walls. In this way Athena honours Ares and the feminine Furies at the same time as she establishes their proper sphere. Ares, that is to say, is no longer to be internal, either in family or city, but external (864), directing and defending the might of citizens against foreign aggressors.[61]

The assignment of a proper sphere for Ares outside the political centre leaves the image of the money-changer within as one of destruction and disruption. The *chrusamoibos* embodied the model of equal exchange which if applied to justice in the context of politics, led to corruption and destruction of the *polis*.

The webs of tapestry: a commodity?

The theme of *hubris* and its connection with excessive wealth runs throughout the trilogy.[62] The way it is expressed by the chorus of elders and by the Erinyes in the second *stasimon* of the *Eumenides* recalls directly the political warnings of aristocratic lyric in the 6th century.[63] By then wealth as a safe indicator of political and moral superiority was already being questioned; this found expression in the image of false coin (*kibdêla*).[64] When the chorus state (774-780) that *dikê*, in contrast to *hubris*, turns away from the power of wealth when it is *parasêmos* (stamped with a false sign), they use common imagery. Yet there is a subtle shift of emphasis which is played out fully in the carpet scene directly after the second *stasimon*.

The chorus say that the power of wealth is stamped by the false signs of praise (*ainôi*, 780). This introduces the idea that wealth is not only a sign/no sign by itself, but becomes so by the meaning/stamp given to it by language. Value, in order to have any meaning, needs to be endowed with meaning in a social act of signification. People can therefore manipulate meanings of value and corrupt relationships by false signification. In stark contrast to perceptions expressed in the 6th century, according to which wealth was simply an untrustworthy indicator of authority, 5th-century tragedy represents people as actively manipulating the signs of wealth. The art of persuasion and the deceptions caused by wealth become related problems. Not only does language (i.e. *ainos*) attribute false meanings to wealth, but wealth itself is used as a manipulative sign. In this context the variety of titles given to valuable objects becomes highly important for the meaning of the carpet scene.

Agamemnon's speech prepares the ground for the scene that follows. For the gods, he begins, justice is not dependent on what they hear. The gods 'have direct access to the signified without recourse to an intermediary of communication by a removal of the function of the exchange of signifiers: once again we see that a transcendental ... is postulated above and beyond language (and in opposition to the human world of words).'[65] Agamemnon once again draws attention to the fact that, unlike humans, the gods cannot be deceived by language or by objects which act as signs between humans – an assumption that is repeated throughout the trilogy.[66] Further on he picks up on the chorus's theme of *hubris* and envy, claiming that few men respect a friend's prosperity (most generally referred to as *philon eutuchounta*, 833). He conspicuously fails to mention the gods as those who feel envy. The statements taken together contrast the meaning of language/wealth for humans on the one hand and gods on the other. They contrast different functions of signs in the exchange between men, and between men and gods. It is important, however, that they are nothing but Agamemnon's considerations at the time, and that they are open to reconsideration by himself and by others.

Agamemnon is afraid to trample down the tapestries. Clytemnestra asks him as 'lord' (*anax*) not to let his foot touch the ground. This is open to different interpretations since the tapestry could be regarded as a symbol of sacred, not just royal, power.[67] And so Agamemnon hesitates; he is afraid to be honoured as a god rather than a mortal man. Yet the tapestry is endowed with more than one meaning, as its colourful web indicates. With conscious reference to the 'web' of words, which is often called *poikilos*, the tapestry is emphatically called *poikilos* three times (923, 926, 936).[68] The word means 'colourful', but as an attribute of language it means 'changeful', 'of diverse meaning'. Thus the textile not only is colourful but has many meanings which are both related and contradictory.

Agamemnon is afraid of stepping on the tapestry not only because it is a sacred symbol of power but also because it is the property of the house of Atreus. It is dyed purple, which marks it as an item of treasure and the possession of a king. In this meaning it is a precious item of royal exchange

7. Violence and Corruption: Commerce in Tragedy

rather than a good for subsistence. Clytemnestra makes the distinction but immediately undercuts it by her remarks (959-962):

> The sea is there, and who shall drain its yield? It breeds
> precious as silver (*isarguron*), ever of itself renewed,
> the purple (*porphuras*) ooze wherein our garments shall be dipped.
> And by God's grace this house keeps full sufficiency
> of all. Poverty is a thing beyond its thought.

Purple (*porphuras*) and silverlike (*isarguron*) are conspicuously put next to each other in the Greek, a combination which is somewhat puzzling. The equivalent colour for purple in metal is gold, as indicated by the fact that the fleece of the ram, the mythical symbol of royal power, is in some versions of the myth called purple, in others gold.[69] The substitution of silver for gold next to purple, the colour associated with mythical value, makes silver a symbol of an equal kind, despite being typically associated with Athenian coinage. The sea is thus associated not simply with the mythical value of purple but with the economic value of silver coinage.

Equally puzzling is the fact that Clytemnestra calls the abundance of purple material in the royal household a blessing that keeps off *penia* (poverty), which is a distinctly economic and political term.[70] Clytemnestra's speech consciously dissects the polyvalence of royal possessions. The economic function and the religious symbolism of royal affluence might just be regarded as two complementary aspects of wealth by the members of the royal household themselves; yet they become completely separate when looked upon by their subjects. Agamemnon expresses his anxiety that the ostentatious spoil of the tapestry would cause envy. Although he does not say at first whether he fears human jealousy or the envy of the gods, the fact that he begins to talk about the gods immediately after having expressed his fear of envy in general leaves little doubt (921). And immediately before stepping on the carpet he speaks of nothing but the envy of the gods (946 f.). Clytemnestra, by contrast, rhetorically deflects envy into the social sphere: 'Be not ashamed before the bitterness of men' (937). If we remember that Agamemnon has just mentioned before the carpet scene that the gods have a more direct approach to justice than humans, it is clear that Agamemnon assumes that the envy of the gods cannot be aroused by deceptive language, nor by man-made signs of wealth. Thus, at the moment of stepping on the ambivalent possession, Agamemnon protects himself by giving a new title to the precious tapestry (947 f.):

> Great the shame I feel to ruin such house-destroying wealth of silver-bought (*argurônêtous*) webs.

Goldhill comments that the reference to the monetary value of the material emphasises the transgression of the act. The deliberate destruction of household property was in absolute opposition to the normal ethos which aimed at continuity and stability of possessions.[71] If this is part of an explanation, it remains remarkable that the value of a symbol of power is described in monetary terms. The purple tapestry was certainly not bought with money.[72] Given that the text has just raised the question how objects change their value in different contexts of exchange, the attribute *argurônêtos* seems to withdraw the tapestry from the sphere of sacred values circulating between men and gods and to transfer it instead into a human sphere of exchange. Moreover, if there is a metaphorical relationship between the colourful carpet and Clytemnestra's crafty webs of words the redefinition of the carpet as a value in the monetary economy of humans carries over to Clytemnestra's speech.

The metaphors of the money-changer and of the money-bought webs are only two examples of how commercial images convey meanings of social disruption in a complex sense. From the material of the *Oresteia* itself one might add to these examples the fact that both Electra and Orestes accuse their mother of having 'sold' them (*pepramenoi*, *Choe*. 131-135; *eprathên*, *Choe*. 915) using this expression in order to provide an adequate term for the way in which Clytemnestra has corrupted the reciprocities between mother and children, or wife and father of offspring. More evidence can be found in later tragedies. Medea disqualifies marriage bonds by making brides buy their husbands; Hippolytus rejects the natural bonds between generations, suggesting that children be bought from temples instead; Creon discredits the craft of the seer by accusing him of money-making; more examples could be added.[73] None of these images are evidence of a society that aimed at protecting itself against a money economy. Money and commerce had their own symbolism, even if this was only negatively defined. In the tragic context monetary images served to establish a language of corruption and to describe transgressions of the reciprocities which ordered society. The fear of *hubris* was different in the 5th century than in the 6th century. It was the fear that the wealth and power of individuals was not respected as a social possession but thought of as a possession of individuals. The ritual of expressing *charis*, or, as Aeschylus puts it, of exchanging *charmata* (*Eum*. 983), symbolised the fact that wealth belonged to the *polis*. Just as the ideological artifice of social and economic equality was expressed in terms of the circulating gift, so the violation of it had a corresponding rhetoric. In a society in which the norm of reciprocity was traditionally linked with agriculture and agrarian wealth the transgression of social reciprocity was most adequately expressed in an image that was the opposite of agriculture: commerce.

7. Violence and Corruption: Commerce in Tragedy 165

Notes

1. Pickard-Cambridge (1968), discusses the often insufficiently documented procedure of payments and prizes to the participants of dramatic festivals; see pp. 94 f. for payment of the *protagonistês*, pp. 84-91 for payments made by the *chorêgoi*, pp. 77 f. for prizes to the *chorêgoi*, pp. 265-268 for dating and practical questions of the *theôrika*.
2. Goldhill (1990), pp. 104 f. with Isocr. 8. 82 and Schol. Ar. *Ach.* 504; Aesch. 3. 154. Perhaps benefactors of the city were occasionally honoured in the theatre itself, as the case of Demosthenes suggests (Dem. 19); Aesch. 3, esp. 120, however, tries to convey that Ctesiphon's request for Demosthenes to be crowned in the theatre was exceptional.
3. On the meaning and function of the *chorêgia*, partly regarded as expense, partly as an opportunity to gain prestige in the *polis*, see Wilson (unpublished).
4. Ibid.
5. Dem. 19. 120, cf. Aesch. 3. 41-56. See for discussion also Goldhill (1990), pp. 104 f.
6. To what extent a *chorêgos* could be accused of *hubris* has been discussed in detail by Wilson (1990) and Dem. 21 (*Against Medias*).
7. Vernant and Vidal-Naquet (1981), Segal (1981), Zeitlin (1982), Goldhill (1986); the list could be extended.
8. See esp. Goldhill (1986) and Segal (1981).
9. See esp. Blundell (1989) on Sophocles; also Goldhill (1986), pp. 77-106.
10. Vernant and Vidal-Naquet (1981) have argued that tragedy belonged to the development of democracy, to the advent of a legal discourse and the intensification of the administration of justice within law courts. Linking the establishment of democracy and the formalisation of legal procedures, they regard tragedy as the cultural expression of two conflicting modes of explanation. There was on the one hand the traditional Homeric model which suggested that divine intervention caused the human condition and events, and that the gods brought about success and failure. Justice was divine justice and morality was defined as human responsibility towards the gods. There was on the other hand the legal discourse where the individual alone was held responsible for his actions and where the law of the city provided the moral standard for the behaviour of its citizens and allies. Reflecting upon these conflicting world views, the authors of tragedy confronted traditional heroic values and ancient religious representations with the new modes of thought expressed in the laws of the city state.
11. See esp. Loraux (1981), Zeitlin (1982), Goldhill (1986), pp. 1-32 and (1984).
12. References will be made in the course of the discussion of the *Oresteia*.
13. The following reading of the *Oresteia* is indebted to Goldhill (1984) more than can be acknowledged by individual footnotes. Smith's (1987) analysis of economic language in *Measure for Measure* has provided important ideas and helped me formulate some problems.
14. Millett (1991 b), p. 7.
15. Gernet (1981 a).
16. See above all Buxton (1982), pp. 105-114.
17. Ibid., pp. 110-114.
18. Zeitlin (1965), pp. 493 ff.
19. Lattimore (1953), pp. 15-18; cf. Zeitlin (1965), p. 488.
20. For the representation of the alliance between Helen and Paris in terms of corrupted marriage see Seaford (1987), esp. pp. 123-128. The generational conflict

166   *Exchange in Ancient Greece*

has been analysed specifically by Freyman (1976); for the interdependence of images of murder, warfare, revenge, corrupted sacrifice and impiety see esp. Zeitlin (1965).

21. Vernant (1980), pp. 181 ff.
22. See above ch. 1.
23. Zeitlin (1965).
24. *Agam.* 40-45, trans. Lattimore.
25. Zeitlin (1965), p. 488, remarks that fireless sacrifice was made to the Erinyes (*Eum.* 107-9;). Thus the sacrifices of the cities in arms, though intended for Zeus or Ares, in fact speak the language of the sacrifices to the goddesses of revenge.
26. Goldhill (1984), p. 16.
27. Ibid., p. 17.
28. For the interrelation of light, language and other signs as signifiers see the general discussion by Goldhill (1986), pp. 1-32.
29. For the trickeries of *peithô* in the first two plays see Buxton (1982), pp. 105 ff.
30. This interpretation of Clytemnestra's speeches follows Goldhill (1986), pp. 9-11.
31. Goldhill (1984), p. 18. Buxton (1982), pp. 111 ff. regards the sexual connotations of *peitho* as positive aspects of it. Discussing the relationship of *peitho* and *thelktêria* (enchantment) he comments, '*thelk-/thelg* words are usually associated with the charms and enchantments of love. Both aspects are relevant to the final outcome of the *Eumenides*, since it celebrates the blessings in store for the *polis* as a result of the fruitfulness of union sanctioned by Peitho.' See, however, Scully (1981), p. 76 and Segal (1974), pp. 139 ff. who discuss the negative connotations of *thelgein* in archaic poetry, especially when referring to the sexual seduction of Clytemnestra by Aigisthus.
32. The authority of the chorus is compared to the *dithronon kratos* of the Atreidae (109), and called *theothen* (105), just as the latter was *Diothen* (43). The chorus is, of course, deceived of its power and its control over persuasion. Later, in the *Eumenides*, positive persuasion will come from Zeus *Agoraios*; Athena is only its mediator (826-828; 970-975; see Buxton (1982), p. 110). See further Goldhill (1984), who summarises (p. 194) '... the male is connected to the valuing of the bonds of society, extra-familial ties and relationships, ... the female is connected to the valuing of the familial bonds within the *oikos* to the rejection of the ties of society (marriage, law, regards of *xenia*). This results in the developing connection of the male with the values of the *oikos* in relation to a wider society (more than a collection of *oikoi*) and the connection of the female with the overturning of these values, through a valuing of the relations within the family itself.'
33. Goldhill (1984), p. 19.
34. In front of Cassandra they will repeat their disbelief in divination; *Or.* 1132 ff.
35. Cf. Soph. *Ant.* 1033-1047; 1055; *OT* 380-389.
36. Goldhill comments, 'The control offered by mantic prediction, sign reading, the prophetic present, slides in tension with the uncertain openness of language, particularly the language of the seer himself, where the exchange of sign for sign (in the chain of language) is not the simple economic exchange that "cashing a metaphor" metaphorically suggests' (1984), pp. 32 f.
37. Gernet (1981 a), p. 112; cf. Goldhill (1984), p. 29.
38. Zeitlin (1965), pp. 465 and 466.
39. Goldhill (1984), p. 31.
40. See also the conscious contrasting of terms related to the generational

7. Violence and Corruption: Commerce in Tragedy 167

exchange within households (*thugatros, patrôios, partheneion*) and that of warfare between enemies (*polemôn, philomachoi*) in ll. 224-230, and 231, 244, 245. The one is a private, the other a public, exchange; the one serves the community, the other the household. Agamemnon gives up his obligation as father, which is also an obligation towards the *oikos*, in exchange for his obligation as general and king. Yet this apparent alternative is violently dissolved by the interjection of *gunaikopoinôn* as the reason for the war. He sacrifices his daughter in order to complete the revenge of a wife, which will then lead to the revenge of his own wife. For a discussion of ll. 224-230 see also Goldhill (1984), pp. 30 f.

41. MacLeod (1982), p. 134, Goldhill (1984), esp. 170; Millett (1991 b), p. 7.
42. *Charin trophoisin ameibôn*, *Agam.* 729, although the grace given is here in 'blood and death'; *theoisi ... charin tinein*, *Agam.* 821; again with ironical overtones stated by Agamemnon before he is persuaded to step on the tapestry.
43. Polanyi (1977), pp. 105 ff.
44. Kurke (1991), pp. 108 ff.
45. *Il.* 9. 632-636.
46. *Eum.* 319 f. Goldhill (1986), p. 228, notes that *praktôr* was in Athens the technical term for tax-collector (cf. Dem. 7. 18; Ant. 147. 14). MacLeod (1982), p. 134 takes the term more carefully as 'collector of debt'; so also Millett (1991 b), p. 7, who concedes, however, that it had a particular field of reference in monetary exchange.
47. According to the relationship between symbols and material objects outlined by Lattimore (1953), p. 15.
48. As Zeitlin argues, corruption and destruction are represented as a result of the action of the main characters being deceived about the nature of justice; see (1965), pp. 492-499.
49. According to Zeitlin, corruption and deception are the prelude to the restoration of purity and normality. The image of corruption, in her case of corrupted sacrifice, 'helps to define ...the distortion of relationships between gods and men which results in impiety' (p. 498). In our case the deceptive conflation of distinct types of value helps define the necessary distinctions of justice in relationships of exchange. For a similar attempt, in quite a different intellectual form, however, see Aristotle's distinctions of exchange and of the different calculations of 'equal returns' in justice and sale, discussed in book 5 of the *Nicomachean Ethics*.
50. *Agam.* 1390-1392; cf. Zeitlin (1965), p. 499.
51. Hesych. s.v. *chrusamoibos*; cf. Arist. *Rhet.* 1375 b 5.
52. Rose (1957-8) ad loc.; the image is re-employed by Euripides in *Suppl.* 1127 ff.
53. Cozzo (1988), esp. pp. 73 ff.
54. See for example the 2nd *stasimôn*, 736-770.
55. Goldhill (1990), p. 112
56. For the 'doubleness' of Ares see esp. Higgins (1978).
57. For Ares as the representative of both war within the household and between cities see esp. *Agam.* 1235 and 1510.
58. As Higgins comments, 'If the *Agamemnon* has shown anything, it has revealed that Ares, not Zeus, is the real motivator of the deeds of Agamemnon, Clytemnestra and Aigisthos. It is Ares' doubleness in all its respects which has finally produced this tragedy's drama of heartrending self-destruction. The *Choephoroi* at once takes up the theme of force and Ares, as Orestes prays to Hermes, overseer of parental *kratê*, to be his ally in battle (*summachos*, 2)' (1978), p. 30.
59. 973-975; with changes in Lattimore's translation.

60. Hes. *W&D* 14 ff.
61. Higgins (1978), p. 34.
62. See *Agam.* 380-384; 470; 751; 763-771; 1002-1015; 1028; 1612; *Eum.* 326-540 etc.
63. Nagy (1985).
64. Theog. 119-128; 117-118; 966. See also Eur. *El.* 550 f. where the image of false coinage serves as an image of deceptive signification within an extended debate on signs and recognition.
65. Goldhill (1984), p. 66.
66. See for example *Agam.* 70; 152; 1170.
67. Not just his royal power, see Gernet (1981 a), p. 120 with note.
68. *Poikilos* is the word that Orestes uses when accusing Clytemnestra of having caught his father in her nets (*agreumasin*, see *Eum.* 460); cf. Jenkins (1985) for the interdependence of ambiguous language and ambiguity of textiles.
69. Gernet (1981 a), pp. 131-136.
70. See esp. the discussion of *aporia* and *penia* in Markle (1985), pp. 267-271.
71. Goldhill (1986), p. 11.
72. I have discussed this problem in more detail in relation to Menandrian Comedy in von Reden (forthcoming).
73. Eur. *Med.* 233-235; Eur. *Hipp.* 620; Soph. *Ant.* 293-303.

Part III

THE POLITICS OF MONEY

8

Embedded Money Economy

Money: a fetish of scholars and stockbrokers

Few objects have been associated more frequently with vice, lust and greed than money.[1] This is all the more surprising since it is often argued that money has brought about abstract thinking and rational calculation.[2] There is a perplexing paradox in the history of money in that it is associated both with creating and with upsetting order.[3] Both the theories that monetary exchange supports trust and state authority and that it subverts morality and power have influential adherents.[4] Even among economists, 'monetary theory reveals a state of affairs more akin to theology than to science'.[5] According to Keith Hart, there are two camps into which political and neoclassical economists are divided, and have been since the Enlightenment. One side stresses that money is a value which is independent of the context of transaction and which is measurable only against other objects. The other claims that money is a value only if guaranteed by state authority, thus presupposing moral or political conventions in order to operate as a means of exchange. In short, for the former money is a commodity itself, whereas for the latter it is a token.[6] The conflict that lies behind the argument is parallel to the conflict lying behind debates on exchange. Economic definitions of exchange imply a simultaneous exchange of equivalent values so that the individual demands of two different people create exchange and thus community. Within this model, money represents the value of the commodity received, and is thus an object of exchange itself. Conversely, those who assume that exchange includes transactions which are non-simultaneous and asymmetrical believe that the trust that is necessary to perceive these transactions as exchange creates community. In this model money symbolises the return more abstractly as a form of guarantee. The two models suggest different motivations for the use of money. In the one, people desire money because it has a value itself; in the other, people accept it for its social meaning: that is, because it can be 'cashed' socially or politically. Just as scholars have proved incapable of coming to terms with the dialectics of exchange, so they find it difficult to relate the social symbolism and the economic function of money.[7]

Parry and Bloch have argued that the moral double-bind of money is the result of its particular symbolisation in Western thought.[8] Since the Aristotelian tradition[9] money has been given an 'air of factuality'. Whether it was condemned as a commodity, or idealised as a symbol of power and trust, its meaning was intrinsic and its function absolute. In Western societies money was fetishised by scholars nearly as much as by stockbrokers.[10] If we aim to free ourselves from this tradition we have to accept that money can change its character and function according to the context in which it is used. The classic example is Baruya society where salt is given as a gift ritually exchanged and emotionally valued within the community, while it has the function of a currency in exchanges with other communities; it assesses the value of, and pays for, any imported goods. Yet, although ritually exchanged, within the community it is an all-purpose medium of exchange while in trade it adopts the function of a currency because the Baruya do not export anything else.[11] Thus Baruya salt represents money in both contexts, but it has a different meaning in each. Parry and Bloch themselves focus on changing meanings of coined money, offering a selection of field studies which describe how cash can shift from being a currency of trade to an item of social value.[12]

Money fetishism left vestiges also in works on ancient thought and history. I do not wish to refer here to the widespread assumption that money transformed the Greek economy in that it facilitated, and increased the amount of, trade.[13] More interesting are those studies which assume that money created a new concept of value which in turn transformed both thought and exchange.[14] Gernet argued that money transformed mythical notions of value into a functional concept by creating a direct relationship between value and object. 'If we distinguish between "symbol" and "sign" in such a way that the first remains charged with immediate affective meanings, whereas the significance of the "sign" is limited, or apparently limited, entirely to its *function*, it is clear that what we mean by "the origins of money" is the transition from "symbol" to "sign" ... .'[15] Gernet conceptualises money value – that is, the value of coins issued by state authority – first as culturally independent and secondly as one-dimensional. The possibility that in some contexts of exchange money represents a value as symbol, while in others it is associated directly with the value of the return, is not considered.

A similar flaw lies in the propositions of Marc Shell. Realising the extent to which philosophers and critics have used some formal similarities between economic and linguistic exchange in order to develop their ideas, he argues that developments in the economy provided the background for new forms of thought.[16] The introduction of money in Asia Minor during the 7th century gave rise to new modes of explanation not accidentally originating in the same place and at the same time. Money, which represents the abstraction of reality (i.e. of the value which it buys), brought about the distinction between 'reality' and 'idea' on a more general level.

As the most advanced form of a symbol it laid the foundations of philosophy. What is more, the ancient philosophers themselves were fully aware of their debt to economic exchange.[17] The cross-references between philosophy and monetary exchange, commerce and characters mythically associated with wealth and coinage (such as Croesus and Gyges) show that they tried 'to account for the internalisation of economic form in their own thinking'.[18] Like Gernet, Shell takes for granted, first, that money has an absolute meaning, and, secondly, that people use it for one purpose only, namely as an exchange value.

Leslie Kurke in her study of Pindar's victory odes also takes it for granted that money is an absolute force in the dynamics of history.[19] Adopting a model of formal linguistics which suggests that the two most important kinds of symbolisation (money and language) and the two most important forms of exchange (commerce and communication) are parallel and support each other, she argues that the increasing circulation of money at the time of Pindar shaped the thought models and imagery of his poetry. 'Pindar and his patrons inhabit a different world from that of Homeric gift exchange, although that system remains accessible to them. The household now operates within a money economy, as does the poet, who composes for a wage. This system too, then, necessarily shapes the poet's thinking and impinges on his work. And indeed money and wealth figure prominently in the epinikia.'[20] Money, according to Kurke, created a functional, profit-oriented, 'disembedded' economy which was in conflict with the traditional aristocratic gift economy. Yet Kurke is too sensitive to the Pindaric text itself not to see that money has a different meaning in the victory odes from its meaning in commercial exchange. She therefore turns to the idea that money had to be *appropriated* as a value for the gift economy. Money, by nature a representative of commodity value alone, was made a value in the embedded economy of symbolic exchange and generalised reciprocity. Originally hostile to money, Kurke concludes, the aristocracy redefined its meaning for the sake of symbolic exchange typically associated with gifts.[21]

The terminology of money

The Greeks had no word for money. They had the term *nomisma* which meant currency and which is identical neither with coinage nor with money.[22]

Argurion or *chrusos* are terms which were used for coined money as well as bullion. Both served as a means of exchange in commerce.[23] There are many statements in the orators which indicate that traders accepted uncoined metal in exchange for their commodities. Lysias tells his audience that in his money chest there were three talents of silver (*argurion*), 400 cyzicenes, 100 darics and 4 silver cups.[24] Xenophon, summarising the advantages of Attica for traders, mentions the silver mines in Laureion, since *argurion* could be exported instead of a return cargo.[25] If read carefully, this is a 4th-century version of past glory when Athenian coinage, not just its silver, was valid as far as the empire reached. The rhetoric worked because little distinction needed to be made between money and *argurion* in commerce, whereas the political difference was considerable.

The term *chrêmata* was the most frequent word for money. The term itself and attitudes to it are, however, much older than money in ancient Greece.[26] In the poems of Theognis and Solon the abuses of *chrêmata* are deplored as the main reason for the moral decay of the state and its members. Yet it is by no means certain that it was money proper that was made responsible for the disturbances. We should consider that an economy needs to be monetarised considerably before money has noticeable effects on the population as a whole. Numismatic evidence can hardly support the assumption that money was exchanged to any great extent before the turn of the 6th century.[27] We know little of the degree to which the silver mines in Laureion were exploited in the 6th century, and it is generally assumed that regular mining for the production of money did not begin before the time of the Persian wars. It is also important to note that the corpus of sympotic lyric covers chronologically more than a century.[28] The century of sympotic lyric was the century of the gradual introduction of coinage. Nevertheless no obvious changes in the attitude to *chrêmata* can be observed within the extant corpus.

In classical Athens the term *chrêmata* could still be used for a variety of things; these included money, but also other valuables for exchange. Thucydides, for example, arguing how much more valuable human life was than mere possessions, pregnantly uses the term *chrêmata* for possession.[29] Elsewhere Thucydides uses the term specifically for money.[30] Aristotle draws a distinction between different uses of *chrêmata* rather than between money and other kinds of valuable objects. At the beginning of his discussion of the arts of acquisition he defines *chrêmatistikê* generally as the art of acquiring things necessary for household management (*oikonomikê*); only at the end does he restrict the term to the description of the art of acquiring *chrêmata* for their own sake.[31] An interesting usage can be found in Xenophon. He employs the term ironically with reference to other debates on *chrêmata*. In the proem of the *Oeconomicus*, he defines *chrêmata* as all things that are useful (*ôphelounta*), while things that are not useful, or even harmful, are not *chrêmata* (*ta de blaptonta ou chrêmata*). Cattle, flutes, money and friends should all be called *chrêmata* if they are useful to their owner, whereas things which are more typically called *chrêmata* but in fact cannot be used adequately by their owner should not be so called.[32] Xenophon uses the distinction to differentiate between two kinds of things, those that were useful for the household and those that were not.[33] *Chrêma*, then, was not the term for any specific valuable, nor did it have precise moral connotations. Its meaning shifted

8. Embedded Money Economy 175

according to the context in which it was used and the ends to which it was applied.

The absence of a name for the phenomenon of money in Greece suggests that it gradually emerged rather than being imposed from outside. Distinct meanings and functions of coinage should therefore be analysed in relation to meanings and functions of exchange which were established before coinage appeared as a means of exchange.

The idea that money is a danger to political exchange rests on a tradition which associated the acquisition of *chrêmata* (not money!) with the violation of political order. The belief that valuable objects are objects of greed originates in a kind of exchange which was regarded as disruptive of order before coinage was used in Greece. Conversely, the idea that coinage is a medium of political exchange rests on the tradition which associated the payment of stamped tokens with political power and just recompense. The two meanings of coinage which Aristotle left to posterity, which I shall discuss below, are rooted in the politics of the 7th and 6th centuries. As far as we can judge from the elegies of Solon and Theognis, excessive wealth (*koros* and *hubris*) came to be regarded as the main threat to order (*kosmos*), while at the same time there was a desire for a political means of payment with which to reward political virtue and pay debts.

A crucial distinction between coinage and other wealth lay in the question of their origins. The recognition of coinage as a recompense meant the acknowledgment of the *polis* as an institution that controlled justice and prosperity. Agrarian wealth and ancestral treasure, by contrast, referred to a divine order of justice which could be controlled by humans, if at all, only by religious ritual. The introduction of coinage indicates a shift of authority over social justice from the gods to the *polis*. The first step towards the introduction of coinage was thus a decline of faith in the reliability of divine justice. The *polis* replaced the divine order by compensating virtue immediately and precisely rather than with what we earlier called 'indefinite certainty' (p. 21).

Little is known of the origins of coinage; but there is no doubt that it was introduced at a time when silver was scarce.[34] The use of coinage can hardly have been ubiquitous, nor the possession of monetary wealth excessive. Yet the symbolism of *chrêmata* in general was under discussion when political order was renegotiated. Herein lies the ambivalence of money in the Greek world: money had two sides because it was given by representatives the *polis* on the one hand and acquired by individuals on the other.

Money, justice and the creation of power

Hesiod defined the human condition as marked by its separation from the divine order. Having hidden the means of life (*bios*) in the ground, the gods gave to man woman, agriculture (*erga*), strife (*eris*) and justice (*dikê*) in order to survive, and to keep the human race alive.[35] It is the task of man to restore the conditions of easy survival which he had lost since Prometheus had enraged the god. The good man is distinguished from the fool by his recognition of the human condition; he ploughs the land, takes a wife, competes with his neighbour for excellence and maintains order by means of just retribution. For him the reward is prosperity and the restoration of a state of easy survival; the cities of the just flourish, they have no famine and no trouble, and their members do not have to travel to get produce from abroad.[36] The fool, by contrast, seeks wealth of his own accord. He trusts in chancy sea voyages, takes pleasure in adultery, seeks strife in court to get hold of other people's possessions, and bends justice in exchange for a bribe.[37] His life is difficult and soon will be destroyed completely.

Hesiod was convinced that the elders (*basileis*) who held power in his own community were fools.[38] They enriched themselves with gifts and gave wrong judgment. Fostering injustice, they brought evil to the city, leaving the just man to his own morality. In such a city the just man had no choice but to trust in his own work and restore the exchange with the gods by his own means.[39] Hesiod's world view is characterised by a double despair: the absence of a community between humans and gods which would bring about wealth and prosperity directly, and a lack of sense among the *basileis* which would make the gods release wealth and prosperity in exchange for toil and justice.

Solon expressed a similar double despair. There were people who had wealth righteously and others who had seized it by force, but mankind suffered from injustice collectively as the bad brought injustice to the city.[40] While for Hesiod there was still the possibility of securing prosperity by personal morality, for Solon this was no longer an option. He saw the fate of the individual as more closely bound up with his life in the community. The entire human order was in danger as the wrong people seized power and as long as Zeus punished injustice not immediately but in his own good time. The time factor which was still absent in Hesiod became crucial for Solon. Although the gods had set a clear distinction between good and bad behaviour, the power to use that distinction to create political order was limited. In the well-known fragment 13 (West) Solon first distinguishes between a desire for wealth which is given by the gods and evil wealth which is gained by violence (*hubris*) and disregard for order (*kosmos*). Yet later in the poem the distinction yields to a general despair about the indeterminacy of divine blessing or punishment.[41] The human order is in danger because of the uncertainty of divine retribution. Good and bad are alike (32), both keep their ways until they are punished; whether they farm or 'bring home gain via the fishy sea', or are craftsmen, physicians, poets or seers: all strive for wealth:

> Of wealth there lies no end visible to men. For those of us who have the most resources (*bion*) strive for twice the amount. Who can satisfy them all? The gods make mortals attain wealth, yet from them comes also destruction: Zeus sends in retribution ruin which different men have at different times.[42]

The lack of a means of retribution which was under human control seems to have been a central political problem. It has been suggested that this was the motivation for the introduction of coinage.[43] Its purpose was to create a means of retribution to (re)establish social justice within the *polis*. *Nomisma* (coinage) is linguistically related to *nemô* (to distribute, to deal out), *nemesis* (distribution of what is due, divine resentment, assignment of due anger) and *nomos* (anything allotted or assigned, convention, custom, law). As justice was conceived of as a distribution of valuables, the idea emerged that social justice could be achieved politically by the ritual distribution of pieces of metal.[44] The use of the term *nomos* increases rapidly in texts of the 7th century but first meant 'order', and especially 'military order', implying in a strong sense that something is 'arranged', 'given', 'distributed', 'measured out'. *Nomisma* was the token which materialised *nomos*. In the 5th century it could still simply mean 'measure', or 'official measure'.[45] *Nomisma* might, then, have its origins in the political necessity to express 'measure' in the construction of relationships of power and authority.[46]

The etymology of *nomisma* can only suggest where we might locate the original purpose of coinage. Yet, together with the religious and political concerns of the texts of the 7th and 6th centuries, it might be accepted as part of a tentative history. Nevertheless a direct association of the introduction of coinage with the legendary policy of Solon remains arguable. The numismatic evidence suggests that the introduction of coinage in Greece is unlikely to have taken place before the second quarter of the 6th century. The issue of coinage is also unlikely to have been a 'state initiative' from the beginning, given that the idea of the state was only in its infancy in that period. Internal politics of the 6th century seem to have been characterised, rather, by a series of more or less successful attempts by rival families to gain power with the help of a group of loyal followers. Before the 'state' issued its coinage, authorities of a more temporary kind needed a means of payment to create social peace. The iconography of coinage supports this proposition.

Coins have been defined as 'pieces of metal, stamped usually on both sides with devices which relate them to the monetary units named in verbal or written transactions so that they represent them for all purposes'.[47] The definition is useful since it makes no restrictive statement as to the nature of the transaction for which the metal pieces are used: coins can function in contexts which are political (taxes, rewards), legal (penalties and compensation) or ritual (bonus payments, prizes, gifts). It also leaves scope for the question whether the issuing authority is a central one which monopolises the mint, or whether there are a number of bodies which have either together, or in turn, the power to mint coin, such as temples, *basileis* or other para-political boards and institutions. The loose definition of coinage, now common among numismatists, leads to an equally loose explanation of the 'origins' of coinage: the beginnings of coinage must be conceived of as a development rather than an act of invention.[48]

Ancient coinage stands in more than one tradition. On the one hand, being gold and silver pieces of a standardised weight and value, it can be related to gold and silver ingots. Ingots are pre-weighed, marked pieces of metal which have been found, for example, in Sinjirli in North Syria.[49] Stamps on ingots are probably examples of standardised metal units; yet these were measures of size and relative weight rather than of value.[50] Thus before we have evidence of coins serving as standards of value there is evidence of gold and silver standards of size and weight. Balmuth observes a transition from stamped ingots to coins as currency. First, inscriptions on ingots seem to be direct imitations of inscriptions on personal seals. Secondly, one of the earliest-known coins from Asia Minor bears a similar inscription as a contemporary gem. A coin from the Ephesus hoard says 'I am the *sêma* of Phanes', while the gem of Thersis says 'I am the *sêma* of Thersis – do not open me'.[51] Thus a continuous development can be assumed from seals to ingots and early coinage. If coinage stands in the tradition of seals and ingots, the visual emblems which subsequently replaced the inscriptions on coins may be regarded as statements that marked ownership.[52] The theory of the development of Ionian coinage can be applied to the Greek use of coinage, which is usually assumed to be adopted from the Ionians.

On the other hand, coinage continues the tradition of devising simple figurative motives as personal and civic emblems.[53] Before coinage, *sêmata* were displayed on gems, rings, shields and stones. Spier has argued that there are significant iconographic links between the iconography of coinage and the *sêmata* on archaic shields, rings and gems. A ram's head, for example, which appears as a shield device on a proto-Corinthian vase and a late 6th-century gem, occurs frequently on early electrum coins.[54] A ram in a distinctive pose can be found on a 7th-century gem, on a shield depicted on a black-figure cup, on an actual bronze shield blazon, on a 7th-century electrum coin and a late 6th-century stater from Cyzikus (see pl. 1 a-c).[55] The Greek material provides similar evidence. A late geometric vase shows a series of hoplite shields, one decorated with a horse (Pegasus?), another with the old Dipylon shield, while the rest bear geometric patterns. More shield devices are shown on a proto-Corinthian Chigi *olpê* which depict a

Gorgon's head, lion's head, bull's head, boar, flying birds and eagles.[56] All are frequent coin types in late archaic Greek coinages: Gorgon's head, lion's head, bull's head and horses are known from the Athenian *Wappenmünzen* (see pl. 1 d-e); the Pegasus was the standard type of the Corinthian coinage, while the Boeotian coinage bears typically a Dipylon shield.[57] Shield devices continued to be used as coin types throughout the late archaic and classical periods. Later examples include the tetradrachm struck by the Samians at Zankle from 494 to 490 B.C., a didrachm of Camarina dated c. 460, a late 5th-century tetradrachm from Chios, an early 4th-century stater from Elis, and a number of coins from Lycia.[58]

Little is known about how the structures of power changed in the early development of the *polis*. The evidence from most places is scarce, while the early history of Athens which we know only through later texts can hardly be taken at face value. In contrast to ancient authors who represent Solon as the one who gave law and order to the Athenians, Pisistratus as the tyrant and Cleisthenes as the democratic reformer, modern scholars now argue that the 6th century was a period in which ties of personal dependence were loosened and transformed into ties of citizenship.[59] Thus Millett has suggested that in spite of the formal abolition of debt bondage at the beginning of the 6th century dependence of poor peasants on wealthy landowners continued to exist. The success of Pisistratus, who came to power after a series of short-lived *archons*, is likely to have rested on what we would call patronage. 'Pisistratus was remembered as having given practical help to peasants who were in difficulties: "He made advances of money (*proedaneize chrêmata*) to those who were without resources, in order to support their work, so that they should continue to maintain themselves by farming" (Arist. *Ath. Pol.* 16). The effect of this would presumably be to reduce peasants' dependence on local, wealthy landowners, and transfer their allegiance to the tyrant, thereby centralising patronage and buttressing the tyranny.'[60]

The centralisation of patronage was an important step in the process of state formation. 'State funds' and a public treasure were alien concepts at a time when governments changed rapidly with the temporary success of aristocratic families. Regular assemblies, council meetings and theatrical performances – areas associated most closely with public payment – did not take place in the city before the last quarter of the 6th century.

The three most important archaic Greek silver coinages reflect a similar development. They first carry a variety of emblems, but then begin to have standardised emblems towards the end of the 6th century. Typical of the earliest known series of the Aeginetan, Corinthian and Athenian coinage is a typeless reverse stamp. The Aeginetan didrachms bear at first on the obverse a turtle and on the reverse random criss-crossed lines or an indeterminate design in the shape of a 'Union Jack'.[61] After the first series (c. 570-480) a formalised skew pattern emerges. This changes again to a different symbol after the Athenian sack of the island in 457.[62] The

Corinthian Pegasus staters were first struck with a Pegasus on the obverse and a simple incuse punch on the reverse. After the first series (c. 510), the Corinthian coinage shows the helmet head of Athene as a standardised type on the reverse.[63]

The earliest Athenian coins, known as the *Wappenmünzen*, are even more distinct from subsequent issues than coins in other cities. As in Aegina and Corinth, the first series of coins bears a typeless incuse square punch on the reverse and on the obverse a changing device for each issue: an amphora, triskeles, hindquarters of a horse, forepart of a horse, bird, wheel, owl, and gorgon's head (pl. 1 d-e).[64] The standard denomination was a didrachma piece, but fractions are also known. During the period of the last two issues of the didrachm (c. 530-520), tetradrachms began to be issued which show innovations on both sides: the Gorgon's head (notably the emblem which Athene carries on her shield in myth) becomes the standard emblem on the obverse and the changing issue device (lion's head, bull's head, etc.) is relegated to the reverse (pl. 1 f). This intermediary stage of Athenian coinage resembles Corinthian Group I and Aeginetan Period I coins insofar as these too had a fixed emblem on the obverse. But instead of bearing a standard device on the reverse, the Athenian coinage continued to be made with changing issue devices. The mint underwent a final transformation when the Gorgon's head on the obverse was changed into an owl, and the reverse into the head of Athene (pl. 1 g). The civic character of the new emblem was reinforced by the ethnic *ATHE*. This type of coin appears first in hoards dated to the beginning of the 5th century. It can be found in great quantities from around 480/475.

Kraay interpreted this development as evidence of 'a deliberate attempt to popularise Athenian coinage in foreign markets, and to outbid rival currencies'.[65] This was based on the assumption that *Wappenmünzen* and *Gorgoneia* had circulated locally only. More recent analyses of the circulation patterns of archaic coinage have made this hypothesis questionable, however. It is argued that, if coins do not appear in hoards far afield, it does not necessarily follow that they were not used in foreign exchange; it may be that they were simply not deposited in hoards.[66] Therefore *Wappenmünzen* may quite possibly have played a role in exchange over distance from the beginning. The problem is still largely unsolved. As far as the meaning of the changing issue type is concerned, many interpretations have been offered. Kroll argued that the changing obverse types of the *Wappenmünzen* were the personally selected symbols of individual 'moneyers' responsible for the mint at a certain period and acting on behalf of the state.[67] Spier suggests that 'rather than as a mark of ownership, the device and inscription probably indicate the identity of the issuer of the coin, although for what reasons we can only speculate'.[68] A similar proposition was put forward by Furtwängler who suggested that the devices, rather than being chosen by the moneyers themselves, were ordered by a

Plate 1 a

Plate 1 b

Plate 1 c

Plate 1 d   Plate 1 e   Plate 1 f   Plate 1 g

Plate 2 a

Plate 2 b

Plate 2 c

Plate 3 a

Plate 3 b

Plate 3 c

Plate 3 d

Plate 3 e

Plate 4 a

Plate 4 b

Plate 4 c

Plate 4 d

Plate 5 a

Plate 5 b

Plate 5 c

Plate 6 a

Plate 6 b

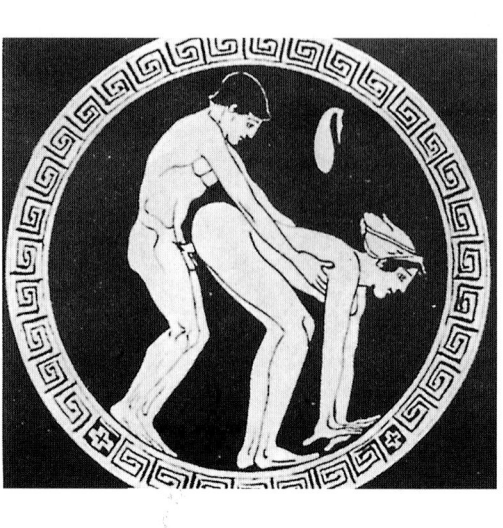

Plate 6 c

Plate 7 a

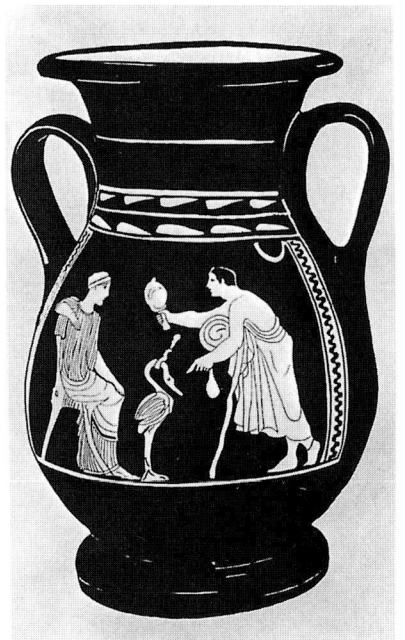

Plate 7 b

Plate 7 c

Plate 7 d

Plate 8 a

Plate 8 b

Plate 8 c

Plate 8 d

central authority.[69] Others believe that *Wappenmünzen* were issued in connection with the Great Panathenaea. In this case the iconography would represent symbols and images which belonged to the ritual context of the games. The coins would then be closer to medals than to money.[70]

If we relate the stamp of coins to the tradition of displaying *sêmata* on shields, gems and rings as symbols of ownership, personal trust and authority, the *sêma* of the coin is most likely to be meaningful in this tradition.[71] Instead of assuming that these *sêmata* were symbols of changing magistrates, which is highly unlikely in 6th-century Athens because of its almost complete lack of an administrative apparatus, we should reconsider the older view. Seltman assumed that the changing issue devices were the coats of arms of certain Athenian families.[72] This is unlikely given the ubiquity of similar emblems throughout Greece and Asia Minor over many centuries. Yet it is not unlikely that individual *archons* chose from a repertoire of emblems which served as signs of identity on shields, rings, gems and seals one that would identify their coinage as the authorised standard of value.

According to Polanyi, money is a standard of value, a means of payment, a store of wealth and a means of exchange; all these functions mutually support one other and need not be considered separately. To be a means of payment, money probably needs to be regarded as worthy to be a store of wealth; and in order to be a means of exchange and a standard of value, the issuing body must be an accepted authority. The recognition of the power of a person or institution which guarantees that the piece of metal is of precise weight and value is vital for making coin into currency. The shift from changing obverse types to a standard civic emblem would then mean the shift of ownership of coinage from individual *archons*, or tyrants, to Athens as a city. This ties in well with Millett's model. If coinage functioned first as a means of unilateral payment within the *polis* – that is, as rewards for office, as a means of redistributing common resources, as prizes, gifts and so on – then the changing issue devices on the *Wappenmünzen* reflect an unsettled stage in the question of who had the power to make such payments. The final standardisation of emblems would reflect the change in the power structure from authority identified with individual *archons* to a more abstract and stable civic government.

The history of money is bound up with the problem of who authorised coinage and thus who represented the *polis*. The winners were 'the Athenians' collectively, choosing the goddess Athene and the owl as the symbols which authorised the value of their coinage. Yet at first the new mode of payment was introduced by those changing rulers who gained and lost power over Athens during the 6th century. Members of the elite, rather than regarding coinage as the commodity of traders, took it as their token of value in civic exchange. The political struggles over whose coinage was the accepted value were a necessary step for coinage to become currency.

Chrêmatistikê before money

The negative meanings later associated with money are older than coinage. Complaints about unlimited greed, belief in false values and socially disruptive forms of exchange developed independently of money.

Hesiod complained that since *chrêmata* are the breath of life for wretched mortals (*psuchê peletai deiloisi brotoisin*) people die among the waves.[73] Yet he associates gain (*kerdos*) not simply with sea journeys but with all methods by which the unjust man acquires wealth: lying, swearing false oaths, taking bribes and neglecting the works of agriculture.[74]

At the beginning of the 6th century, sympotic lyric expressed an even stronger opposition between the evil power of *chrêmata* on the one hand and *kosmos* (order) and *dikê* on the other. In the often quoted fragment 4 (West) attributed to Solon the poet links outrage (*hubris*), excess (*koros*) and the desire for *chrêmata* to the inability to keep silence and order at a banquet:

> But our city, although she will never perish by the destiny of Zeus or the will of the blessed gods, ..., her own people swayed by *chrêmata* wish to ruin this great city by their folly. But the mind of the leaders of the community is without justice (*dikê*). What awaits them is the suffering of many pains because of a great outrage (*hubris*). For they do not know how to check insatiability (*koros*), nor can they make order (*kosmos*) for their present merriment (*euphrosunê*) in the peace of a banquet (*dais*) ... they acquire wealth, swayed by unjust deeds (*adikois ergmasi*) ... and, not caring at all about sacred or public property, they steal from one another by forcible seizure, and they do not uphold the holy institutions of *Dikê* who silently observes the present and the past, and who will in the future come to exact complete retribution (*apoteisomenê*).[75]

The imagery of the poem is firmly embedded in the context of symposium and song.[76] The same values that led to happiness and stability in the community of the *polis* were experienced in the community of the feast. The symposium was the place of education and prepared citizens for their tasks in public life. What were to become civic values – such as order, equality and equal measure (*kosmos, ison, meson* and *metron*) – have their exact parallels in the symposium. Similarly, excess (*koros*) and outrage (*hubris*), or doing something beyond measure (*huper meson*) were experienced as destructive of the peace of feasts, and became thus an image of danger to political order.[77] *Polis* and symposium are destroyed by the same forces: deception and *mêtis* (guile) are causes of *stasis* (unrest, civil war), while *charis* (grace), *terpsis* (joy), *euphrosunê* (merriness and harmony) and *hêsuchia* (peace) are the foundations of both the just community and the merry symposium.[78] The strict parallelism between *polis* and symposium is important; it shows that unjust acquisition of *chrêmata* was a cause of disorder arising outside the strictly economic context.

8. Embedded Money Economy

Similar attitudes are expressed in the poems of Theognis.[79] People have become leaders of the *agathoi* because of their injustice and gain of *chrêmata*. In ll. 667-682 he deplores his own loss of *chrêmata* to the base (*kakoi*) who are now in power:

> ... They have deposed the pilot (*kubernêtês*), the noble one (*esthlos*) who was standing guard with expertise. They seize *chrêmata* with force (*biê*) and order (*kosmos*) has been destroyed. There is no longer an equitable distribution (*dasmos isos*) directed from the middle (*es to meson*) but the carriers of merchandise (*phortêgoi*) rule, and the base (*kakoi*) are on top of the noble (*agathoi*). I am afraid that perhaps a wave will swallow the ship.[80]

It is important to note that the riches of the *kakoi* cannot be associated with any occupational background; nor are their *chrêmata* necessarily objects other than those which gave power to the traditional elite. In short, it is hardly possible to argue that an emerging commercial class, or a class of traders, destroyed with their new wealth consisting of money the secure political symbolism of wealth associated with agriculture and agrarian prosperity in Hesiod.[81] The 'carriers of merchandise' belong to the state-as-ship metaphor within which the poem is presented. *Phortêgoi* are literally the 'carriers of goods which belong to others'. The expression is based on the idea that bad possessions are those which are seized from others.[82] The distinction between the possessions of the good and those of the bad was not that between land and money but was defined by a moral distinction between their modes of acquisition.

The association of *chrêmata* with excess was created in opposition to the traditional image of wealth gained from agriculture. *Dikê* and *mesotês*, the signs of *aretê*, were concepts associated with controlled exchange, whereas *koros* and *hubris* were metaphors of uncontrolled growth.[83] *Koros* denoted excessive vegetation as opposed to cultivated land which was the result of human toil (*ponos*). In linking the wealth of the *kakoi* to the *koros* of nature Theognis intimated that the *kakoi* brought about an inversion of the positive link between virtuous *ponos* and agrarian fertility. Hesiod had represented the human condition as an exchange. The gods had hidden the fruits of the earth so that man had to plough in order to eat; he had to fuel the fire in order to cook and to forge weapons, and he had to couple with women in order to gain offspring. Automatic and speedy growth, by contrast, had marked earlier generations of mankind who had lived only for their own extinction.[84] Excessive and speedy growth was also the sign of the garden of Adonis the plants of which grew rapidly only to be burnt by the sun before their time. And as his plants died prematurely, so Adonis himself died before maturity.[85] Whereas fertility was dependent on the observation of the seasons, *koros* happened out of season, without control, and had no chance of lasting.

Theognis applied the laws of vegetation to the social world. In one of his poems he explicitly includes wealth which is acquired 'out of season' as an indication of the injustice of the bad:

> A possession that comes from Zeus, and of right and in seemly wise, abides for evermore; but if someone wins it unrighteously and out of season with a covetous heart, or by unright seizure upon an oath, at first it seems to get him gain, but in the end it becomes bad likewise, and the mind of the Gods overcomes him.[86]

Whereas those *chrêmata* which were gained with justice were permanent values, *chrêmata* which were not acquired in harmony with gods and the seasons would be lost in the long term. The speedy and excessive growth of the *kakoi* marked them as outsiders to civilisation and as subhuman. Those who were nobles now used to be those who grazed outside the *polis*, and wore goatskins.[87]

The confrontation of *ploutos* and *aretê* separated two kinds of exchange: wealth which was received from the gods in the timeless order of agrarian prosperity and human fertility on the one hand, and wealth acquired in the limited time span of a single human life outside the seasonal cycle of agriculture on the other. In effect this was often equal to the distinction of landed property and wealth gained in trade. Yet it was not the different kind of goods but their different meaning in relation to time and orders of exchange which was crucial to the distinction.

Aristotle and the two sides of the coin

Aristotle discusses the function and origin of coinage in two different works and in two different contexts.[88] The one is related to the meaning of wealth and commerce, the other to the origins of the *polis*. The distinction between the two origins and functions of coinage corresponds well with the distinction between money as a token and money as a commodity. The one was a means of unilateral payment in a system of generalised reciprocity, the other a means of binary exchange in commerce.

Aristotle evaluated the two functions completely differently. Coinage as payment was necessary in order to achieve justice in the *koinônia* (community) of the *polis*.[89] As a standard of value it made different sorts of need (*chreia*) commensurate and was thus a crucial instrument for creating just relationships in the community of people whose products or needs were of necessity different:

> The number of shoes exchanged for a house (or for a given amount of food) must correspond to the ratio of builder to shoemaker. For if this does not happen, there is no exchange and no community. ... All goods must therefore be measured by some one measure, as we said before. Now this unit is in truth *chreia* which holds all things together ... but money has become by convention some kind of representative of demand; and this is why it has the

name money (*nomisma*) – because it exists not by nature but by convention (*nomos*).[90]

Aristotle's remarks on the exchange between builder and shoemaker, or farmer and doctor, were clearly not statements on justice in the market place, but on justice in the social interaction between citizens.

Coinage used as a means of payment was not exchanged for the sake of profit (*kerdos*), nor could it ever create *kerdos*. It was a recompense for the loss of goods given to those who needed them rather than a good that was needed itself. In the discussion of coinage as payment Aristotle does not consider exchange between communities and retail trade, which suggests that he regarded exchange within and between communities as distinct concepts. One function of coinage was exclusive to exchange within the *koinônia* of citizens. Exchange between citizens, whether monetary or other, was guided by generosity and *charis* (reciprocal gratitude) which, as we saw in Chapter 4, was part of the ideology of spending. Although Aristotle says that in principle everyone wishes to receive back an equal return for what he has given, the calculation of returns remains imprecise as to its amount and timing. Paying back is being kind in return and being gracious: 'This is what is special to grace; when someone has been gracious to us, we must do a service for him in return, and also ourselves take the lead in being gracious again.'[91] Exchange within the *koinônia* is submitted to moral principles and the ideal of goodness. This was possible because in the concept of coinage attached to civic exchange coins were envisaged as having no intrinsic value (that is, they could not function as a commodity). They were introduced as a convention (*nomisma*) for the regulation of the mutual relationships of citizens in the generalised reciprocities of the *polis*.

In the *Politics* Aristotle discusses origins, function and the social consequences of coinage quite differently. He presents a cluster of ideas which can be identified with the function of money as a means of exchange. In this context coinage had its origins in exchange between communities and was thus from the outset not concerned with the cohesion of the *polis*. It was a means by which different countries conducted their imports and exports, and it was regarded as useful rather than good:

When mutual help [between the inhabitants of foreign countries] grew stronger, and people imported what they needed, and exported what they had too much of, coinage came necessarily into use. For the things that people need by nature are not easily carried about, and hence men agreed to employ in their dealings with each other something which was intrinsically useful and easily applicable to the purposes of life, for example, iron, silver and the like. Of this the value was at first measured simply by size and weight, but in the process of time they put a stamp upon it, to save the trouble of weighing and to mark the value.[92]

Aristotle builds straight into the construction of the origins of this type of coinage a moral bias. It was not invented to facilitate exchange between members of the *polis* but between members of different communities which stood in no political or morally binding relationship. Coins in commerce were exchanged not in order to bind together citizens but to receive something from foreigners. Instead of exchanging things with the help of coinage people had begun to exchange things in order to increase their coinage. Traders perverted the original chain of C-N-C (*chrêma-nomisma-chrêma*), which had been introduced to facilitate exchange between households, into one of N-C-N.[93] In usury people acted even more abnormally since they received more *nomisma* than they had given. Aristotle's argument against usury was reinforced by the fact that *tokos* meant both 'interest' and 'offspring'. The implicit allusion to natural growth highlighted the very unnaturalness of professional lending at interest and the coin by which it was symbolised. People who employed their possession of coins in order to gain interest confused the realm of *nomos* (convention) with that of *phusis* (nature). Finally, coinage used in commerce was an expression of dependence:

> When the inhabitants of one country became more dependent on those of another, and they imported what they needed ... coinage came necessarily into use.[94]

Given the natural superiority of the self-sufficient *polis*, those people who became dependent on other *poleis* forfeited their freedom and were further removed from the natural good.[95]

Because of a series of wrong assumptions a thing which was a convention between humans (*nomisma*) came to be regarded as a value by nature; commerce was motivated by the false demand for things which were not valuable to human life by nature and was thus itself against nature. In contrast to *chrêmatistikê* which was necessary for maintaining the *oikos*, it aimed at the increase of a medium of exchange, rather than at the increase of *oikos* and *polis*.[96] Aristotle concludes his remarks:

> Some persons are led to believe that getting wealth is the object of household management, and the whole idea of their lives is that they ought either to increase their money wealth (*nomismatos ousian*) without limit (*eis apeiron*), or at any rate not lose it. The origin of this disposition in men is that they are intent upon living only, and not upon living well; and, as their desires (*epithumias*) are unlimited, they also desire that the means of gratifying them should be without limit. Those who do aim at a good life seek the means of obtaining bodily pleasures; and, since the enjoyment of these appears to depend on property, they are absorbed in getting wealth; and so there arises the second species of wealth-getting. For, as their enjoyment is in excess (*en huperbolêi*), they seek an art which produces the excess of enjoyment; and if they are not able to supply their pleasures by the art of getting wealth they try other causes using in turn every faculty in a manner contrary to nature.[97]

Aristotle here links the possession of money to excess in general. But, rather than regarding money as the origin of it, he takes it only as symbolic of desires which are against nature. His analysis is modelled on the contrast of justice and *hubris* familiar from Solon and Theognis. The patterns of thought are strictly parallel. Not only are the dangers of excess represented in the imagery of nature and vegetable growth, but it is also taken for granted that natural increase is limited while unlimited increase is unnatural or dangerous. Nature controlled by, rather than endangering, human order generates justice, while the disregard of the rules of natural growth is equal to injustice and destructive natural forces. Money was symbolised within a system of metaphysical assumptions which explained how humans and nature could live in harmony.

If Aristotle distinguished two meanings of money, did he relate them in any way to each other? He himself clearly distinguished them as two kinds of value, although this distinction was ethical and not economic. In the world of ordinary people, which was characterised by a confusion of virtue and commercial exchange, the two contexts in which money changed hands had to be kept apart. In the outline of the ideal state he prescribes the physical separation of the political and the commercial *agora*, and the exclusion of commerce from the former.[98]

Notes

1. The impossible task of giving a general explanation of the mystification of money has been attempted by Desmonde (1962). The book, though unsatisfactory from an analytical point of view, serves as a good illustration of the variety of beliefs associated with money. See also Crump (1981) and Parry and Bloch (1989), who take the mystification of money as a starting point for their attempts to demystify money.

2. Marx called logic 'the money of thought', since both money and logic were abstractions of nature and reality; see Marx (1968) [1844]; money also created the distinction between use value and exchange value which was equal to the creation of a distinction between real value and value as an 'ideal', or abstraction of reality; Marx (1962) [1867], esp. pp. 104-108; for a recent philosophical analysis along these lines see Müller (1977), and in application Gernet (1981 a), Shell (1978), (1982).

3. Compare Marx's conception of money as 'logic' or 'ideal' (although with negative social implications) with St Paul's warning that 'the love of money is the root of all evil'; cf. Le Goff's essay on the extension of this warning in medieval thought (1986).

4. For the latter Bohannan (1959); for the former Gernet (1981 d), Will (1955 a), (1955 b), pp. 497 ff. MacFarlane (1985) proposes that money complicates the moral order, or 'eliminate(s) absolute moralities' (p. 72), following Simmel's observation that money is subversive of moral polarities; cf. Parry and Bloch (1989), pp. 3-5 and 17 f.; Parry (1989).

5. Hart (1986), p. 638.

6. Ibid., pp. 643-647 traces the distinction back to Locke and a school of thought later associated with the name 'metallists' on the one hand and the anti-metallist tradition represented by Barbon on the other. The 'money-as-commodity theory',

systematically put forward by Ricardo and Mill, was then followed by Marx and held sway over British liberal economics well into the 20th century. It still lies at the heart of Keynsian monetary theory. It was opposed by German idealist thought influencing the work of Knapp (1921), Weber (1972) [1922] and Simmel (1989) [1900]. While the 'money-as-commodity theory' argues that money is related to markets, and has its origins in commercial exchange, the 'money-as-token theory' insists that money rests on social institutions of trust and credit and originates in the public administration of justice. Hart himself argues that both functions are interdependent, symbolised by the fact that 'the coin has two sides' (p. 647).

7. See by contrast Crump (1981), Strathern (1992), Parry and Bloch (1989), Parry (1989), Appadurai (1986).

8. Like Hart they trace two different traditions in monetary theory which roughly correspond to the conceptual distinction of 'money-as-commodity' and 'money-as-token'. In addition they link the former to ideas which condemned money from a moral point of view and the latter to a tradition which associated with it more positive social consequences. They see the origins of the divide not in the Enlightenment but in the Renaissance, or even in Aristotle. See Parry and Bloch (1989), pp. 1-19.

9. As I shall argue below, it is not Aristotle himself but the scholastics who should be associated with these ideas.

10. Parry and Bloch (1989), pp. 2-6.

11. Godelier (1977); cf. Crump (1980), p. 5.

12. Parry (1989), Carsten (1989), Toren (1989).

13. The Greeks themselves attributed the increase of trade to the invention of money (cf. Hdt. I. 94; Arist. *EN* 1133 a 17-20.). It is, however, important that this was only one of the meanings given to money, while others were given in other contexts; see below.

14. A third direction, also left aside here, may be seen in works like that of Ure (1922) and Silver (1992). Although both contain some interesting observations in detail, their general hypothesis that money lay behind all images and thoughts which share some characteristics of it, whether shape, type of metal, iconography, or value as a symbol, remains inconclusive.

15. Gernet (1981 a), p. 112, (Gernet's italics).

16. Shell (1978), pp. 1-11. Ideologies must seek material explanations for their justification (e.g. astrology looks to the stars, physiognomy to the face, sociology to the biochemistry of the brain, sexual needs, social class etc.) and the economy provides the material basis for the explanation of thought and language themselves.

17. In his first chapter he discusses how Herodotus and Plato associated the myth of Gyges (who in ancient texts appears as the archetypal minter, was a tyrant and possessed a ring which made him invisible so that he could escape the punishment for a crime he had committed) with justice and its subversion. The myth created the foundations of abstract political thought. It also brought about concepts of reality which included the 'invisible' and the abstract 'form' as part of reality; cf. pp. 12-62. See, however, Gernet's (1981 e) discussion of the distinction between visible and invisible property, from which it emerges that it was not money that lay behind the distinction of *phanera ousia* and *ousia aphanês*.

18. Shell (1978), p. 62.

19. Kurke (1991), pp. 1-12 acknowledges her debt to Bourdieu's theory of language and symbolic power (cf. Bourdieu (1991), esp. pp. 66-89) and Barthes' theory of the exchange value of poetic performance (cf. Barthes (1970), esp. pp. 95

ff.). Her theoretical background alone thus encourages thoughts about the significance of value, and its representation in the form of money in literature.

20. Kurke (1991), p. 165.

21. Kurke also draws upon the Greek distinction between visible and invisible property (*phanera/aphanês ousia*) relating the latter to the emergence of a disembedded economy ('invisible property is the product of those who privilege pure economic considerations over the social and political embedding of property', p. 227). Whether she believes that the notion of invisible property was related to the emergence of money is left open. There are, however, good arguments against such an assumption. Kurke rightly points out that the distinction between *phanera ousia* and *ousia aphanês* was rhetorically important in forensic debates of the 4th century where the total value of the property which an individual owned became relevant in cases of property exchange. It seems that the distinction was made in order to conceal wealth invested in loans rather than to distinguish between use value and money; cf. Gernet (1981 e).

22. *Nomisma* referred most generally to anything that was sanctioned by current or established usage. This meaning became more and more associated with coinage yet never lost its wider connotations. (See for example Aesch. *Choe.* 269; Eur. *IT* 1471; Ar. *Nub.* 248; cf. Laroche (1949), pp. 14 ff.). *Nomisma* could also denote a measure, and perhaps more specifically a measure of capacity, a meaning which is still alive in Aristophanes' *Thesmophoriazusae* (348).

23. For the use of bullion alongside coined gold and silver pieces see Thuc. II. 13; cf. Howgego (1990), pp. 4-7.

24. Lys. 12. 11.

25. Xen. *Por.* III. 2.

26. Hes. *W&D* 320, 407 etc.; Hom. *Od.* 2. 78.

27. Howgego (1990), p. 3 specifically makes this point, while it is implied by Carradice and Price (1988), Kroll and Waggoner (1984), Holloway (1981), Kraay (1976), Starr (1977), Crawford (1972), who date the beginnings of coinage around the middle of the 6th century.

28. According to Figueira and Nagy (1985), Theog. 29-52 was composed before the rise of the tyrant Theagenes. Ll. 891-895 are dated to the second quarter of the 6th century, while ll. 773-782 seem to belong to a period after the Persian invasion of Megara.

29. Thuc. II. 60. One is reminded of Achilles' remark comparing the value of life with that of valuable posessions: 'Man can win tripods and bay horses by the head, but there is no raiding or winning a man's life back again, when once it has passed the guard of the teeth' (Hom. *Il.* 9. 407-409).

30. Thuc. II. 65; III. 40.

31. Arist. *Pol.* 1256 a 1 ff. Between 1256 b 28 and 1258 a 8 *chrêmatistikê* and *oikonomikê* are used as if mutually exclusive, and instead *ktêtikê* is used as the general term, until in 1258 a 8 *chrêmatistikê* becomes again the general term for both *oikonomikê* and *chrêmatistikê* in the narrower sense; cf. Koslowski (1979), p. 68, note 41.

32. Xen. *Oec.* I. 1 ff., esp. 9, 11-14. There is a tacit change of terminology in lines I. 7 and 8: while Socrates has spoken so far of *ktêmata*, Critobulus takes him as having said *chrêmata* and the ensuing remarks are made on *chrêmata*. Terminology corresponds to that in Socrates' discussion of friendship in Xen. *Mem.* II. 4-7; here Socrates begins his statement with considerations of the 'acquisition' (*ktêsis*) and 'use' (*chreia*) of friends. See further Millett (1991 b), p. 116.

33. Although Xenophon talks deceivingly about the importance of profit (*ta ôphelounta* not *kerdos*), the standard of profit is not the individual but the *oikos*.

34. An extreme view is taken by Vickers (1985 b), who dates the earliest coins from Asia Minor to 550 B.C. (p. 23), the transition from *Wappenmünzen* to *Gorgoneia* to 480 B.C. (which implies a beginning of the *Wappenmünzen* somewhere at the end of the 6th century, p. 32), and the introduction of the *owls* at a time of 'unprecedented [economic] growth' between 479 and 462 B.C. (p. 29). Extreme in the opposite direction is Silver (1992) who on the basis of mythical imagery sees evidence for coinage 'before the 7th century' (p. 48). Ancient historians begin to give more credence to numismatic than to textual evidence; so for example Starr (1977), p. 110, Crawford (1972), p. 5 and Ehrenberg (1968), pp. 24 and 71. The high chronology is still defended by Kagan (1982), pp. 346 ff. on the basis of the literary tradition, and Weidauer (1975); see also Will (1955 b), pp. 488-502 for Corinth and (1955 a) for Athens.

35. Hes. *W&D* 9 ff.; 43 f.; 175-178; 276-280; cf. Detienne (1963), Vernant (1980), pp. 168-185; see also Crotty (1982), pp. 44 ff.

36. *W&D* 225-237.

37. *W&D* 320-340.

38. *W&D* 219, 225 f., 264.

39. *W&D* 298-310; 381-412.

40. Cf. Sol. frgm. 4 (West).

41. Crotty (1982) emphasises that this is a clear inconsistency; the same inconsistency he discovers in Simonides' poem discussed by Plato (*Prot.* 344c-345e). Although there is a strict distinction between excellence and badness, the uncertainty of divine retribution in terms of time reveals men's limited powers of securing happiness for themselves (cf. pp. 33-39).

42. Sol. frgm. 13 (West), 71-76.

43. Will (1954 a); in (1955 a), p. 17 and (1955 b), pp. 497 ff. he links the introduction of coinage specifically to the reigns of Solon of Athens and Cypselus of Corinth and their politics of abolishing debt bondage. Coins handed out from the treasure of confiscated property offered the opportunity for the indebted population to purchase their freedom without putting the creditors in a position of economic disadvantage. The hypothesis must be called into question on chronological grounds as numismatic evidence now suggests that coinage was not introduced into Greece not before the second quarter of the 6th century. Despite the chronological problems, Will's attempt to relate the introduction of coinage to a crisis of social debt and credit is still worth considering on theoretical grounds.

44. Will (1954 a), pp. 227 ff.; to what extent coins symbolised portions of food is unclear. Laum (1924), pp. 114-115, argues that the distribution of coinage may have originated in the idea of symbolising handouts of food. The association of coins with *obeloi* (roasting spits), especially in connection with the Argive Heraion, suggests that the value of coins had something to do with the value of food, and served as food substitutes in a ritual and political context (offerings and rewards to magistrates). An ancient literary tradition has it that the tyrant Pheidon of Argos introduced coinage while withdrawing from circulation the iron spits (*obeloi*) which had served as currency before. As the story has it, the *obeloi* were then dedicated to the Heraion (Etym. Or. s.v. *obolos*). Some scholars believe in the story partly because a bundle of iron spits has been excavated on the site of the Heraion, partly because the similarity of the word *obelos* (spit) with the denominations *obolos* and *drachma* (a handful [of spits]) is suggestive. (See Cook (1958), p. 257 and C. Waldstein, *The Argive Heraion*, I, pp. 61 ff.) *Obeloi* are thought to have been used for roasting meat or baking cakes and were dedicated as votive offerings or given as gifts to public officials (see esp. clay models of tables filled with meat and cakes found in the Argive Heraion; Waldstein, *The Argive Heraion*, II. p. 42; cf.

8. Embedded Money Economy

Laum (1924), p. 116). Further support for the hypothesis of the link between food distributions, or dedications, and coins has been seen in the meaning of the word *pelanos* which, apart from being the name of a weight equal to the Athenian *obolos* (Nic. Epigramm., 488), could refer to a 'round cake offered to the gods' (*LSJ* s.v. *pelanos* quoting a phrase in Paus. 8.2.3); *pelanos* was the name of an (iron?) coin (the *tetrachalkos*, Hsch.); and *pelanos* occurs as the term for 'fee' in a Delphic inscription from the 5th or 4th century (see *LSJ* s.v. *pelanos*, III; cf. Silver (1992), p. 52). The evidence remains inconclusive, however. Some better evidence may be found in the mythical association of coins with loaves of bread, for which see Silver (1992), pp. 56-61.

45. Ar. *Thes.* 348; cf. above, p. 106.
46. Will (1954 a), pp. 226-229 and Laroche (1949), pp. 14 ff. and 173 ff.
47. Grierson (1977), p. 7.
48. Balmuth (1971), p. 1.
49. Ibid., p. 7. In Homer we hear of 'talents of gold' given as rewards in social and juridical rituals.
50. Balmuth (1971) for further discussion. Grayson (1974) argues that the idea of absolute weight was largely absent in antiquity and that standardisation of weight units was dependent on standardisation of coin denominations. Grayson's evidence is compelling, but it does not contradict the idea that units of metal were fixed without being currency.
51. Stater from Ephesus (c. 600) London British Museum 123544; gem belonging to Thersis: see Rossbach, 'Griechische Gemmen' *Archäologische Zeitschrift* 41/1883, pl. 16, no. 19.
52. Balmuth (1971), p. 6; see also the 5th-century staters of Gortyn, inscribed *Gortynos to paima* (this is the coin of Gortyn), cf. Shell (1978), p. 159 (pl. 8) and id. pp. 66 f. for the relationship of *sêma*, seal and *charactêr* which could refer both to the stamp on the coin and the identity of a human being.
53. Boardman (1968), id. (1970).
54. Cf. the Macmillan *aryballos* in Payne, *Protokorinthische Vasenmalerei* (1933), pl. 22; D.A. Amyx, *Corinthian Vase Painting of the Archaic Period* (1988), 31-32, no. 1; compare with Weidauer (1975), no. 48 (London), and Boardman (1968) no. 519 (London) which is a common gem type. See Spier (1990), notes 54-56.
55. Spier (1990), p. 112 with full documentation; see also Weidauer (1975), nos. 42-54; W. Wroth, *British Museum Catalogue of the Greek Coins of Mysia* (1892), 24, no. 48, pl. 5, 11; Boardman (1968), no. 517; D. von Bothmer, *The Amasis Painter and his World* (1985), pp. 217-220, no. 60; J. Thimme, *Antike Meisterwerke in Karlsruhes Schloss* (1986), pp. 170 f.
56. Spier (1990), p. 114 with further examples.
57. Cf. Kraay (1976) nos. 220-226.
58. For a broad overview of the repertoire of devices see Kraay (1976).
59. See esp. Ober (1989), Buchanan (1962), Millett (1989).
60. Millett (1989), p. 23.
61. In Holloway (1971) called 'Early Linked Series', or in Kroll and Waggoner (1984), pp. 336 ff. 'Period I-coins'. There are only 44 coins known from that period and all struck from a mere 15 obverse types; see also Kraay (1976), pp. 41 ff. and nos. 113-115.
62. Cf. Kraay (1976) nos. 123 and 126.
63. In Ravel (1936) 'Group I' and Group II'; cf. Kraay (1976), pp. 78-81; Kroll and Waggoner (1984), p. 333. cf. Kraay (1976) nos. 220-226.
64. Kraay (1976), pp. 56-60; Kroll (1981), pp. 10-23; cf. Kroll and Waggoner (1984), pp. 327.

65. Kraay (1956), p. 63.
66. Howgego (1990), p. 3.
67. Kroll (1981), pp. 2 ff.
68. Spier (1992).
69. Furtwänger (1982), pp. 19-24. Kroll and Waggoner (1984) draw attention to parallel cases of changing issue types known from Cyzicus, Mytilene-Phocaea and Abdera between the late 6th and 4th centuries. Changing issue types are also known from pre-Hellenistic coinages where it seems to be taken for granted that they refer to changing magistrates responsible for the mint (see note 41). Yet, as Kroll and Waggoner point out, it is not clear whether the same evidence can be interpreted in the same way for early Greek coinages.
70. Yalouries (1950), pp. 52-55; Hopper (1968), p. 22; Cahn (1971), p. 84. Yet it has been held against this view that although a horse or an amphora might well have had some meaning in the context of the festival, beetle, bull's head or lion's head, which are equally frequent on *Wappenmünzen*, are not known to have been symbols related to the games. Above all, a *Nikê*, the agonistic symbol *par excellence*, never appeared on *Wappenmünzen*; cf. Kroll and Waggoner (1984), note 42.
71. Price (1983); Carradice and Price (1988), p. 27. See also Ure (1922), but with the mistaken belief that this was a specific characteristic of tyrants, which is made unlikely by the more recent approaches to the chronology of early Greek coinage discussed above.
72. Seltman (1924), pp. 19-24; see already against him the reviews by Robinson (*CR* 39/1925, pp. 124 f.) and van Bucken (*CR* 40/1926), pp. 181 ff.; cf. Spier (1990), p. 119.
73. Hes. *W&D* 686; the idea of motion and restlessness seems fundamental to the idea of gain and acquisitiveness outside the divine order.
74. Hes. *W&D* 248-266; 276-285.
75. Solon fr. 4 (West), 1-17; trans. based on Nagy (1985), pp. 59 f.
76. *Euphrosunê* is both a poetic and a social signifier. It is the programmatic term for the social harmony which an audience needs in order to listen to poetry; and it is the condition for bringing about *ainos*, the ability to understand poetry, which was thought to be restricted to a socially exclusive audience. (See Nagy (1985), pp. 24 and 60.) The lack of order that marks the *adikoi* excludes them from participating both in feasts and in the meaning of poetry performed in their course.
77. Levine (1985), and Theog. 497 f.; 479-483.
78. Levine (1985), pp. 186-194, and Theog. 309, 312, 757-764, 773-788.
79. The *Theognidea* are probably not the work of a single poet, nor even of a single generation of poets. Figueira and Nagy date the entire corpus between the last quarter of the 7th century and the second quarter of the 5th century. The elegies attributed to Theognis, Solon, Mimnermus and Tyrtaeus are very similar, with some verses even containing the same lines (Figueira and Nagy (1985), pp. 1 ff.). This must be due to problems of transmission which make it difficult to relate the corpus of sympotic lyric to any time more specific than some date between the 7th and early 5th centuries. Although I shall argue further below that the problems addressed by Solon and Theognis were not the result of, but anticipate, the problems associated with coinage, some of the poems clearly use monetary imagery; see esp. the term *kibdêla/kibdêloi* (counterfeit, forgery) as a metaphor for false value of both things and friends (Theog. 117-118, 119-128 and 966).
80. Trans. based on Nagy (1985), p. 22; *dasmos* is the Homeric term for distribution of food and spoil and *es meson* is the place where the prizes set out in contests were placed (see *LSJ*, s.v. *mesos*); for Homeric usages in Theognis and their function see Knox (1989), p. 100.

8. Embedded Money Economy 193

81. Kurke has argued that behind the moral teaching about the nature of wealth and exchange lies the anxiety over *kapêleia* which began to threaten the economy and society of the late archaic *polis*. Theognis' obsession with the dangers of deception was caused by the observation of trade and retail trade, which he thought were motivated by the desire for *kerdos* and conducted on the basis of deceit. Kurke's argument is based on the similarity between the Theognidean text and the well-known passage in Herodotus where Cyrus responds to the Spartan Lacrines: 'I have never been afraid of men who have a special meeting place in the centre of their city where they swear this and that and cheat each other (*exapatôsi*; cf. Theog. 59, 1113, 254 etc.). Such people, if I have anything to do with it, will not have merely the trouble of Ionia to chatter about but their own' (Hdt. I. 153. 1). Here, and in the description of Lydian *kapêleia* (Hdt. I. 136. 2 and I. 155.4), Kurke observes an association of trade with deceit also typical of Theognidean thought (Kurke (1989) pp. 536-540. Further passages quoted by Kurke as supporting evidence are Diog. Laert. I. 105 and Plat. *Rep.* 371d). Kurke seems to confuse cause and effect in her argument. First, even if later texts commonly linked *kapêleia* with deceit, it does not imply the opposite conclusion that the Greeks, whenever they talked about deceit, thought of *kapêleia*. Secondly, Gentili observed that *apataô*, which is the key notion for Kurke's interpretation, is regularly used in erotic contexts, so that it is much more likely that in instances where Theognis uses the term in other contexts the first allusion will have been to erotic exchange rather than retail trade (Gentili in *QUCC* 26/1977, p. 115). As Lewis has shown, politics and the symposium, pederasty and political *philia*, were domains which served as models for each other, while trade and seafaring appear in the *Theognidea* not as a model for deceitful exchange, but for gaining wealth outside the seasonal cycle of agriculture.

82. Humphreys (1978), p. 166 on *phortêgoi*. Solon fr. 4. 40 ff., Theog. 1197-1202 and Hes. *W&D* 641-642 make clear that farmers did go on sea voyages.

83. Nagy (1985), pp. 55-63.

84. Hes. *W&D* 41 ff., 119-122; cf. Vernant (1980) pp. 168-185, esp. 176.

85. Nagy (1985), p. 62 and Detienne (1977), pp. 187-226. 'In opposition to the normal cycle of seasonal agriculture, which lasts for eight months, the abnormal cycle of the unseasonal gardens of Adonis lasts but eight days (cf. Plat. *Phaed.* 276b). Like his excessive and violently growing plants Adonis himself dies *proêbês*, before maturity [*hêbê*].' Nagy draws attention to the fact that in dying before maturity Adonis equals the second generation of 'silver man' in the Hesiodic myth of generations:

> But when the time of maturing and the full measure of maturity arrived
> they lived only for a very short time, suffering pains
> for their heedlessness, for they could not keep overweening
> outrage [*hubris*] away from each other ... (Hes. *W&D* 132-135.)

As appears from this passage, unseasonal and excessive growth, premature death and *hubris* were related themes.

86. Theog. 197-208. For the translation of *para kairon* see Nagy (1985), pp. 64-68.

87. Theog. 53-60.

88. *EN* 1132 b 21-1134 a 22; *Pol.* 1256 b 40-1258 a 19. There is an extensive literature on these passages. I have used esp. Will (1954 a), Koslowski (1979), Meikle (1979), (1991 a) and (forthcoming); Lowry (1969), (1974), (1987), pp. 181 ff.

without sharing the economist's approach of the latter two; see also Langhohn (1983), Bertoud (1981), Campese (1977), Gordon (1961), Soudek (1952).
   89. For the following see esp. Will (1954 a) and the succinct summary of Will's research in Austin and Vidal-Naquet (1977), pp. 56-58 and nos. 1, 2 and 44.
   90. Arist. *EN* 1133 a 21-34.
   91. Ibid. 1133 a 1-5; cf. 28.
   92. Arist. *Pol.* 1257 a 31-38 trans. Everson.
   93. Meikle (1991 a), pp. 168 f.
   94. Arist. *Pol.* 1257 a 31 f.
   95. Ibid. 1257 a 32-36.
   96. Ibid. 1257 b 32-39.
   97. Ibid. 1257 b 37-1258 a 10.
   98. Ibid. 1331 a 31-33.

9

Money in Gymnasium and Palaestra

Money and pederasty

The evidence both from texts and coin hoards suggests that there was a rapid increase and spread of coinage at the turn of the 6th century in political centres such as Aegina, Corinth, Athens and some towns in Magna Graecia. The increase coincided with the standardisation of the obverse type and the depiction of a civic emblem on the reverse. I suggested in the last chapter that this second stage in the development of Greek coins could be regarded as the establishment of state coinage in the proper sense. Only then did the *polis* as a whole authorise its value. Being thus symbolic of the power of states governed by themselves coins could be distributed for that reason alone.[1] Related to this meaning is Aristotle's theory that political *koinôniai* create social justice by the use of coinage. We gain an even more immediate insight into the political functions of money if we look at the early 5th century itself. In Pindar's victory odes the athletic victor is symbolically linked to his community by the praise of his power to spend money. Pindar both uses established notions of generosity and reinforces the idea that monetary payments are part of the reciprocal relationships of the members of a *polis*.[2]

Another context in which money appears as a symbol of power and citizenship is the representation of *paideia* (education) on vase painting. Both the mode of representation and its content are alien to us but central to the political life of the late archaic city state. The social life of citizens in gymnasium and *palaestra* was the public display of power and virtue as defined by the traditional elite. What is more, it displayed how power and virtue are transmitted from one generation to another. Gymnasium and *palaestra* were the arenas of the private education of children. In a combination of musical and literary education, athletic contest and homosexual intercourse, the next generation was prepared for its future political role. In the pictorial representation of the life of a leisured class the transaction of money played an important part – either, as some have argued, as the symbol of payment to prostitutes, or as a symbol of generalised reciprocity between teachers and pupils, lovers and beloved.[3]

Vase painting must be related to the social function of pottery in the late 6th and early 5th century. It is generally agreed that the decoration of vases was not random but had some connection with the use to which they were put. What is more, pots were not intended for use as containers alone but were objects whose possession and display were their most essential functions.[4] The possession and exchange of cups and cauldrons as precious items symbolising status and rank goes back to the Mycenaean period. Whether pottery stands in a direct tradition of such containers, usually made of gold and silver, can be left aside here.[5] What is important is that pottery was used for dedications to the gods, to the dead and to victors in athletic contests, which marks them as items of symbolic exchange like their metal predecessors. The meaning of pots in social, religious or political exchange overlapped. As Robertson has pointed out, a specific container may first have been given from friend to friend, then displayed as a family treasure and finally placed in a grave in honour of the deceased.[6] There were of course special shapes related to specific functions of the container in the first instance (e.g. *lêkuthoi* or prize-*amphorai*), but the fact that most painted pots were found in graves shows that they were polyvalent and could switch their function in the course of their history.

For the analysis of the decoration of pottery the social and religious function of the pot itself has at least two important consequences. First, if pottery circulated in socially charged exchange contexts the imagery must reflect a positive representation of the donor, dedicator and recipient.[7] This means that we are confronted with an idealised rhetoric about reality, rather than with images of reality itself.[8] Ostentation is a form of communication; it can only work within a social context in which principal assumptions are shared. These may be altered and subverted within individual representations, but subversion and alteration operates only within a culturally accepted framework. Even if it is difficult to reconstruct cultural codes it can at least be claimed that any meaning derived from an individual painting was socially recognisable and thus general. It has been argued, moreover, that Athenian red-figure pottery represents individuals as participating in achievements for which Greece, and specifically Athens, praised itself collectively. The imagery is by no means individualised but a form of 'cultural exhibitionism'.[9] Though often commissioned privately, vase painting was meaningful to a larger public.

Secondly, if painted pottery was meaningful in different contexts it can be assumed that its images were themselves polyvalent. As well as their immediate social narrative, most paintings refer to mythical and historical events. This bestows further dimensions on the action of individual figures. A warrior, for example, represents a mixed reality of individual achievement, historical events and mythical heroism.[10] The social meaning of a motif had a generalising rhetoric, suggesting an interdependence of human and heroic action across time and space. It may be argued that a frivolous scene of sexual exchange in symposium or *palaestra* can hardly have

9. Money in Gymnasium and Palaestra

carried metaphysical meanings. Yet the depiction of sexual intercourse on funerary steles must make us cautious.[11] As we shall see below, in sympotic lyric sexual relationships between symposiasts are symbolic of the harmony and tensions of the *polis*; pursuit and flight of lovers were explained metaphysically as the necessary condition of civilised order. The variety of social functions of pottery placed and displaced the narrative of its images from one context to another. The contextuality of meaning was clearly recognised; many images can be read as self-consciously and ironically questioning their immediate meaning. While most vase paintings were polyvalent, ambivalence seems to have become the very theme of some of its examples.[12]

On a number of red-figure vase paintings, dated roughly between the second half of the 6th and the first half of the 5th century,[13] money pouches are part of the pictorial representation of exchange between adult men and boys, older and younger boys, men and women, as well as between patron and client in gymnasium, *palaestra* and *agora*.[14] The question arises whether the offer of a money pouch to a figure representing a sexual partner signifies a scene of prostitution – that is, the purchase of sex as a commodity – or whether this interpretation is insufficient or even problematic.

In the light of late 5th- and 4th-century texts, answers seem straightforward. The few literary statements we have from this period suggest that taking money for sexual favours was dishonourable. Yet, although sometimes associated with the market and wage labour, it was not the idea that the body became a commodity that marked prostitution.[15] Rather, the submission implied in accepting a *misthos*, and the sexual violation of the body of a person who carried political honour, defined the act as a moral transgression.[16] To be a sexual partner of another citizen was illegal for an Athenian even before he had reached adulthood. A citizen boy giving his body for sex and accepting money in return was disfranchised, while adult citizens who used boys as lovers were prosecuted under the law of *hubris* (violence). This could result in capital punishment.[17] It is significant that the prosecution of *erômenoi* and *erastai* was not a private case between individuals but a public indictment (*graphê*). The defendant was thought to have committed an offence against the civic community by violating the honour of a citizen.[18] Slaves and foreigners, by contrast, were available on the prostitute market, and it was not illegal either for them or for their clients to have sexual intercourse. The fact that giving money to, and violating the body of, a non-citizen was not a criminal offence shows that it was civic honour that was at stake in cases of prostitution.

The symbolism involved in sexual exchange is clearly expressed by 4th-century authors.[19] Sex was regarded as an asymmetrical relationship between lover (*erastês*) and loved one (*erômenos*), and it was viewed as parallel to the relationship between givers and recipients of money. In Plato's *Symposium* the Athenian Pausanias distinguishes the good *erômenos* from the bad one in that the good *erômenos* gives in only after some time of courtship, and in order to gain *paideia*, while the bad one submits instantly and for the sake of money. Therefore, Pausanias argues, the Athenian custom has it that a lover must pursue his beloved and the beloved must flee:

> This is the motive which lies behind our general feeling that two things are discreditable [*sc.* for the *erômenos*], first, to give in quickly to a lover – time which is the best test of most things, must be allowed to elapse – and secondly, to give in on account of either his money (*chrêmata*) or his political power.[20]

In this passage it is clearly expressed that money and the political influence of the *erastês* are for some *erômenoi* more seductive than his moral qualities, although a good lover must concentrate on the latter. If we read this statement independently of its moral qualification, it suggests that ritual pursuit, money and power occupy a similar space in sexual seduction.

For the *erastês* the opposite applies. Although submitting ritually and emotionally to the *erômenos* for the time of the pursuit, his success marks him as *kalos* (good and superior). Yet again the time of his ritualised submission is compared with the submission of the one who begs for money:

> Besides this, the universal encouragement which an *erastês* receives is evidence that no stigma is attached to him; success in a love affair is glorious, and it is only failure that is disgraceful, and we do not merely tolerate, we even praise, the most extraordinary behaviour in a lover in pursuit of his beloved, behaviour which would meet with the severest condemnation if it were practised for any other end. If a man, for example, with the object of obtaining a present of money or a public post or some other position of power, brought himself to behave as a lover behaves towards his favourite, begging and praying for the fulfilment of his requests, making solemn promises, camping on doorsteps, and voluntarily submitting to slavery such as no slave ever knew, he would be restrained from such conduct by enemies and friends alike; the former would abuse him for his flattery (*kolakeias*) and lack of free spirit (*aneleutherias*), and the other would give him good advice and feel shame for him.[21]

Again, pursuing a person for the sake of his money is *kolakeia*, which goes some way towards seeking patronage, and both mean making oneself a slave.[22] Moral distinctions apart, sexual exchange could be envisaged within the same symbolism as civic exchange.

If we look at vase painting in the light of the literary evidence, the images depicting money pouches represent either exchanges between citizens and slaves or transgressive behaviour punished by law. Both these positions are inconclusive. If all boys to whom money is offered are slave prostitutes we have to ask why they are represented as if they were citizen

9. Money in Gymnasium and Palaestra 199

youths. They are usually crowned, wear a *himation* (cloak), have athletic bodies, and often carry a spear. If they are citizen boys acting illegally, the question arises why they are shown in postures and with attributes which are symbolic of *paideia*: athletic contests, hunting and musical education. *Erômenoi* often wear their cloaks closed up high to their noses and display reluctance to submit.[23] Bazant has argued that the imagery of red-figure vase painting contrasts the 'good *erômenos*' with the 'bad' one, by juxtaposing the offer of gifts with that of money pouches. Yet, as vase painting has its own generic conventions, Bazant continues, the distinction between the one and the other is not one of separate representation. Rather, the bad prostitute is contained in the image of the good lover like a part of a 'mosaic'. The money pouch may therefore be offered to a boy who otherwise represents a good *erômenos* in order to convey the idea that the bad and the good are closely related. The representation of prostitution participated in the representation of positively evaluated *eros* at the moment when the money pouch entered the image.[24] Although Bazant's general observations are suggestive, it is questionable whether money means what he assumes. The money pouch always appears as an attribute of the *erastês*. It is always the superior lover offering it to the boy rather than the boy having already received it. Take, for example, pl. 4 a. Against the background of the other paintings shown in this book, it is a an unusual representation. On the far right an adult man with all civic attributes offers money and a flower of favour to another man of equal age and status. Whatever this painting might mean, it is certainly not the representation of sexual exchange with a boy prostitute. We should conclude that money pouches are symbolic details describing the *erastês* and his attitude to the *erômenos*, not the social status of the boy.

Money in late archaic vase painting, then, does not seem to have the same semantics as in textual representations of sexual exchange in the classical period. An explanation for this difference may lie in the changing attitudes both to money and to the relationships in which it circulated. As has been discussed above, the payment of money was associated with asymmetrical relationships which came to be regarded as unworthy of a democratic citizen. Yet despite being condemned, unequal relationships were not absent in 5th- and 4th-century Athens. Millett has shown how personal dependence and patronage continued to exist in a disguised form in the democratic *polis*. Under the title of *kolakeia* (flattery) we can assume a kind of behaviour which was well known but ideologically pushed to the margins. *Kolakeia* was an issue of both comic and oligarchic political representations in Athens from the Peloponnesian war period onwards. Fragments of comedies with the title *Kolax* by Eupolis in the 5th century and Menander in the last decade of the 4th century have survived. In the latter one *kolax* blames another for having become rich more quickly than any honest man could ever dream of doing.[25] Aristotle's pupil Theophrastus defined *kolakeia* as 'an attitude or relationship which is degrading in itself, but profitable (*sumpheros*) to the one who flatters'.[26] Aristotle himself comments on flattery in a more extended philosophical context:

> Of those who try to give pleasure, he who does this with no ulterior motive aims at being pleasant and is anxious to please; but he who does so in order that some advantage may fall to him in respect of money (*chrêmata*), or anything else that money procures, is a *kolax*.[27]

It seems that *kolakeia* was clearly identified with monetary payments between unequal social partners. The democratic city tried to suppress such relationships ideologically without ever making the attempt to fight social and economic inequality. The kind of exchange which symbolised this inequality most starkly – payment of money for personal service – was cursed, without thereby reducing the problems behind it. Deeply resented within the democratic ideology, patronage was not ill-regarded by the aristocratic elite at the turn of the 6th century. Consequently, money had a different symbolism. Against this background, let us take a fresh look at the semantics of the money pouch in late archaic vase painting.

Money, power and the *agathos*

If the surviving examples of vase paintings depicting money pouches can be taken as a representative sample, two general observations may be made from the outset. First, no money is ever offered in symposiastic scenes, but only in those which refer to *palaestra* and gymnasium, or an open environment. Secondly, money pouches are exclusively found in the hand of the *erastês*, and never in the hands of divine suitors.[28] More precisely, they are found in most cases in the hands of a figure in a specific posture which can be described as standing on one leg, leaning on a stick, with the other leg held backwards.[29] The inhibition of movement, indicated by the posture itself, is enhanced by the fact that the money pouch is carried on the side where the figure rests on the stick so that movement is impossible without withdrawing the money pouch.

Pl. 3 a-b shows the two sides of a red-figure *pelikê* representing a bearded man (the *erastês*) offering money to a youth on face A and a lyre on face B. The images are almost identical, except that face B shows a sponge in the field and the lyre is passed over with the free, right hand. On face A the *erômenos* makes a gesture as if about to reach out for the money.

The pictures should be read not only as scenes of gift-giving but as a visual representation of relationships. As Bazant has pointed out, in red-figure vase painting the visual sign becomes the sign of a sign. The depiction of a column, for example, is not just the sign of a real column but

9. Money in Gymnasium and Palaestra

of a column that stands for a house.[30] Similarly, a hare is not just a picture of the gift of a hare but of what the gift stands for: courtship, hunting and sexual intercourse. Various categories of gifts can be distinguished as symbolising different meanings of the interaction. There are pedagogical gifts in the narrower sense, such as lyre, writing board or book; there are animal gifts, such as hares, cocks, leopards, game and birds; there are gifts of purely figurative meaning, such as apples, flowers, crowns and twigs; and there are money bags and pieces of meat.[31] None of these objects has just one possible meaning; they are polyvalent, cutting across the concept of object and symbol. Analyses of animal gifts on vase painting suggest, for example, that a hare was not only meaningful as a gift but also an attribute of status and a sexual symbol.[32] In addition, Lewis has demonstrated that pederasty was construed as a ritual which tamed the boy and initiated him into civilised society and politics. In accordance with the mythical image of hunting as a crossing of boundaries between civilisation and wilderness, the erotic chase of a boy was parallel to a hunt in which the *erômenos* assumed the role of the hunted wild animal.[33] If so, the gift of a hare also described the stage of the relationship in which the hunt had not yet come to an end. This is most clearly shown in the contrast between pl. 4 b and other images. A youth, close to maturity, as indicated by his growing beard and the walking stick in his left hand, embraces a younger boy who has obviously submitted to his courtship. In the background hangs a cage with a hare. The domesticated wild animal suggests that the hunt has come to an end. The older boy finds fulfilment in sexual pleasure, while the younger is initiated into the phase of *paideia* which his gift, a lyre, symbolically indicates.

Gifts of money in courtship scenes do not seem to play any role that is distinct from that of other gifts.[34] They have the double function of being the sign of money as recompense and of symbolising what money stands for. There is no indication of a tension between the money pouch, either as sign or as what it stands for, and other such signs. On a red-figure *kylix* (pl. 2), a hare is offered together with, or as an alternative to, money, while no moral distinction seems to be made between the two gifts. A moral statement may be implied in the contrast of the representation of each couple in any series of couples. On both sides of pl. 2 money is offered by a figure in a specific posture; and on face B the boy in the centre wears his mantle half open while the boy on the left is covered up to his chin. This may be significant since a closed mantle probably stands for chastity in the imagery of courtship scenes.[35] Against the second proposition representations like those on pl. 3 c are clear counter-examples; they show that the money pouch also features in exchanges involving a 'chaste' boy. The posture of the offering *erômenos*, by contrast, is the same in all exchanges involving the gift of money in vase painting. This aspect is discussed in more detail below but we can conclude for the moment that while the status of the *erômenos* may vary, that of the *erastês* does not.

If we focus on the different type of figure who gives a gift, rather than on the different type of gift that is given, the images appear in a new light. It is not the meaning of the gift as such, but the status embodied by the donor, that carries the moral and political information of the image. As a result, it is not money used in pederastic relationships as such, but the use of money by a certain type of citizen, that is evaluated. The depiction of money pouches is the depiction both of an object and of a symbol. As an object it is conspicuously placed in the hand of the donor, while as a symbol it describes his status and the meaning of his relationship to the recipient.

If this is the pattern, a number of other paintings can be interpreted. Pl. 3 c does not just depict the potential exchange of love for money, but juxtaposes the refusal of the boy to uncover his body with the withdrawal of the money pouch. The juxtaposition is clearly emphasised by the fact that the boy reaches out for the money while the *erastês* has an erection. Desire and withdrawal are combined in both figures. The desire for sex and withdrawal of money on the one hand, and the desire for money and refusal to submit on the other, are complementary. In a more positive way, the same reciprocity is depicted in pl. 3 d. Here the positive offer of money as something parallel to the offer of sexual favours is suggested visually by the juxtaposition of the offer of money with the boy's gesture indicating that he is willing to please the *erastês*. Pls 3 e, 6 c and 7 a relate in a more abstract way the reciprocity of sexual relationships. The bags suspended behind the couples may be taken both as symbols of desire and payment on the one hand and as submission and receiving payment on the other. The *erômenos* was not supposed to gain pleasure from the sexual act; gifts, money and *paideia* could therefore all be taken as the return for, and symbol of, the submission of a youth to an adult. Conversely, the pleasure of intercourse, the power to give money and the ability to offer *paideia* symbolised the status of a citizen.[36]

Excursus: constituting a visual context

Although visual texts provide valuable information about Athenian culture, research on their interpretation from a cultural distance is yet in its infancy (but see now Stewart 1997). Much progress has been made, however, by looking at the iconography of vase painting in terms of semiotics. Taken from a semiotic perspective, the image is not a realistic reproduction of reality but a series of signs that creates a new reality. Each detail, as well as empty space, gives meaning to the painting as a whole, and, in turn, the painting as a whole specifies the meaning of its details. Yet, as in the case of narrative,[37] an image is not just a combination of signs but a system in which each sign receives meaning by its variants, opposites and subversions. To render vase painting a meaningful source of concepts and thoughts, images must be considered as a series. Meaning is encoded in repetitions, contrasts and visual comments that paintings make on each other.[38]

An individual vase painting must be read, first, as a construct of syntactically related signs, and, secondly, as part of a series of other such constructs. Frontisi-Ducroux and Lissarrague have rightly pointed out that the interpretation of a painting is crucially dependent on the question of what wider group of images suggests to the viewer the meaning of any particular painting.[39]

The number of images that depict money pouches is limited and confined to a certain period. To constitute them as a series in itself is therefore not helpful. Yet the contexts to which they have been related are unsatisfactory. Paintings which depict money pouches have often been catalogued under the heading of 'scenes of everyday life'.[40] Or they have been discussed as scenes of courtship, which is more specific but no more explanatory.[41] Finally, they have been used simply as illustrations of sexual behaviour and practices, which does not lead beyond the understanding of their immediately accessible content.[42]

A certain uniformity of the formal aspects of the representations should first be noted. All images have similar spatial patterns and similar symbolic details. Their narrative is represented as an interaction mostly between two, and never more than three, figures. They depict one couple, or a series of couples, of either men and boys or men and women. The older, or male, partner offers money either on its own or together with other gifts and symbols of courtesies to the loved one (pls 2, 3 a-c). The addressee responds typically with a positive gesture reaching out to the item offered, or with a negative one such as turning the eyes or body in the opposite direction. Images depicting such scenes are almost exclusively placed on either storage containers for oil (*pelikai* and *amphorai*), wine-mixing bowls (*kratêres, oinochoai* and *stamnoi*), or cups (*kulikes* and *skuphoi*). Such 'vases' refer to a specific area of male interaction in symposium, gymnasium and *palaestra*. Since these areas were dominated by an urban leisured class, they refer to a specific social class of people identified with power, wealth and status.

Beard has suggested that the most important narrative detail of vase painting is the human figure.[43] Looking for a common figure that unites all red-figure vase paintings depicting money pouches, our attention is drawn to a cloaked person. Typical of this type of figure is a certain kind of garment and the presence of a walking stick. Because of its recurrent features some scholars have called this type of figure 'youth in *himation*' or '*Manteljüngling*'; but given that in the series under consideration the central figure is mostly a bearded adult, the label is somewhat misleading. Essential for the 'youth in *himation*' is not his age but the presence of walking stick and mantle, and his representation in a repertoire of standardised postures.[44] In a systematic analysis of red-figure vase painting of the 6th to the 4th century B.C., Hollein has taken this figure as a point of departure for establishing a bounded group of images on civic exchange. The 'youth in *himation*' displayed civic virtues as appropriate in different social contexts. Hollein argues that the different posture or movement of the central figure made different statements about the ethical status of that figure. First he sets out to define the *Manteljüngling* as a 'type'; then he analyses variations of the type. The identification of different types is made on the basis of the specific posture of the figure. Type 1 stands on one leg, the other held backwards, leaning on his stick (see for example pl. 2 b, central bearded figure). Type 2 steps forward with the arm opposite the forward leg outstretched, thus adopting *contrapposto* (not illustrated, as irrelevant in our context). Type 3 stands on both feet and holds one of his arms inactively without assuming *contrapposto* (pl. 4 d). He then identifies the various types and their stereotyped variations as representations of *scholê* (Type 1), *dunamis* (Type 2) and *aretê* (Type 3). In addition, he assumes that, whereas Type 1 and Type 3 represented aristocratic values, Type 2 was a figure which embodied a democratic ideal.[45]

There are, then, a number of aspects by which 'courtship scenes' can be related to a wider visual context. First, they are a subgroup of a bounded group of vase paintings in which the 'youth in *himation*' is the essential carrier of meaning. Secondly, this figure acts as the representation of civic values in a space of male interaction of political significance. Thirdly, the variation of the posture of the 'youth in *himation*' is part of the pictorial expression of normative behaviour for male citizens in relation to other citizens.

The limits of money

Only the *scholê* type of 'youth in *himation*' is represented with a money pouch in his hand. We may read this now as the visual expression of the idea that pederastic relationships were restricted to the morally controlled domain of male *scholê*, which implied moderation and control of excess. Yet the images of sexual exchange, if taken as a series, also reflect the conflicts and tensions on which the political and erotic life of the citizen rested. The *erastês*' sexual desire is juxtaposed with a posture suggesting self-control and measure rather than excess; the *erômenos*' desire for money is juxtaposed with a style and drapery of garment which suggests chastity and reluctance to submit (see pl. 3 c). The boy's desire for money is finally juxtaposed with the adult's control of it, so that the imagery becomes a comment on hierarchy in terms of an interdependence of virtue, masculinity and adulthood.[46] Sexual submission implied the social domination of the one who courted. As Dover has put it, there was no sex between equals. This seems to be a further connotation of the money pouch in the hand of an *erastês* and, conversely, this is why in the classical *polis* accepting money for sexual favours was incompatible with citizenship rights. Through the contrast to the classical attitude to money and to sexual relationships between citizen adult and youth, we can understand the significance of the money pouch on late archaic vase painting.

One further observation is vital for understanding the meaning of money in civic exchange. If we compare vase paintings of symposium, gymnasium and *palaestra* with sympotic and choral lyric, some important parallels and differences emerge. All combine the representation of aristocratic exchange with contest, *paideia* and pederasty, and all represent *erôs* and *philia* as a crucial element of political relationships.[47] They also articulate similar problems in a network of mutual metaphorical referencing: friendship and enmity, victory and submission, effort and recompense, sexual pursuit and flight. Finally they express the power and dangers of wealth (or money), and the necessity of controlling it by exercising moderation.[48]

Yet there are also differences. In sympotic lyric a negative, or at least ambivalent attitude to money is expressed. The recompense for *philia* and sexual satisfaction of the sympotic lover was *philia* combined with *paideia*. In the *Anacreonta* only a foreign prostitute and a painter are associated with material rewards (*drachmê*, *misthos*).[49] Choral lyric seems to have adopted a different attitude. Here money became a value which was part of the reciprocities between poet and victor. It is important, however, that the references to payment (*misthos*, *chrêmata*) in choral lyric are part of the praise of the victor aiming to present his generosity in a positive light. As Kurke has stressed, Pindar grounds wealth completely in its uses in society; thus money, together with the rest of a victor's wealth, is a powerful image of his prestige.[50]

Symposium on the one hand and public praise on the other should be regarded as ideologically different contexts of aristocratic exchange. The same distinction can be observed in vase painting: the iconographic repertoire used for the public spheres of gymnasium, *palaestra* and *agora* is different from that used for the symposium and *kômos* (revel). According to Hollein, scenes of the symposium represent the 'youth in *himation*' in the context of excess and *hedonê*, while the gymnasium and *palaestra* are the central sites of male *aretê* and *scholê*. Together with the imagery of the hoplite's farewell and Dionysiac *thiasos* they are complementary, but different, spheres where civic virtue develops.[51] The difference between the ideas associated with the symposium on the one hand and the gymnasium and *palaestra* on the other suggests that the absence of money pouches as gifts to *erômenoi* in scenes of symposia is not accidental. The symposium remained a sphere which was hostile to money as recompense.

Money as a gift to lovers in gymnasium and *palaestra*, by contrast, referred to the sphere of athletic contest and victory; here money had a positive image in the exchanges that linked victor, poet and audience, as the choral lyric of the same period suggests. Here the *erastês* represented himself as a citizen whose wealth was owed to the city. Money expressed the ability of the male citizen to control the danger of disorder by means of the symbols that the city had created for itself in order to produce and reproduce social harmony. It had a metaphysical meaning to the extent to which the city and the relationships of its members were endowed with metaphysical justification. Beyond this, it was a specifically human and political symbol. The fact that gods never court with money on vase paintings is probably not so much an expression of the idea that they avoided 'bad *erômenoi*' or prostitutes as that the coin was an exclusive symbol of man and his city.

A shifting symbol

The money pouch as pictorial detail contributed to ambivalent meaning, which, conversely, indicates that its semantic field was broader than that defined by the exchange context of *paideia*. So far we have looked only at money pouches in the exchanges between *erastai* and *erômenoi*. Yet they occur also in the imagery of *hetairika* (sexual exchange with courtesans and female prostitutes), and in images that seem to refer to the purchase of pots themselves.

Because of the ambivalence of pictorial details and the simple patterning of space, the meaning of an image could easily shift and subvert the meaning of related images. This not only made the same painting meaningful in different contexts but thematised ambivalence itself. Confusion was created and thought provoked either by the content of a single painting, or by the comparison of different ones.[52] By replacing an *erômenos* with a *hetaira*, a pederastic relationship changed into a heterosexual one. By replacing book and lyre given by the *erastês* to the *erômenos* with a hare, cock, quail or piece of meat, the intellectual aspect of a pederastic relationship changed into the sexual one. By replacing sponge and strigil in the space between the figures with wool basket or mirror, the scene rapidly moved from male to female space, or to the brothel. The exchangeability of details in a patterned imagery offered the opportunity to compare and contrast different modes of behaviour in the life of the citizen.

Between the scenes of *hetairika* and pederasty there are significant overlaps.[53] If one compares images like pls 2 and 3 e with 5 a-b and 7 a, the similarities are more striking than the differences. One might note a stronger emphasis on haggling in the images of *hetairika* than in those of pederasty, but this does not seem to be essential. Money pouches appear exclusively in the hands of men, they are offered by a 'youth in *himation*' of Type 1, the scenes may be set in *palaestra* and gymnasium (cf. the sponge and strigil in pl. 5 a-b), and gifts of money are depicted together with, or in contrast to, other gifts such as mirrors and flowers (cf. pl. 7 b). Yet the

9. Money in Gymnasium and Palaestra

parallels must be regarded as a play on reality, rather than the depiction of reality itself, given the factual differences in status between citizen *erômenoi*, slaves and foreign *hetairai*.

It has been argued that not all women receiving money on vase paintings can be regarded as prostitutes. The vase depicted in pl. 4 c-d has been a particular target of academic debate. What is striking is the juxtaposition of the offer of money to a woman in an undefined space (face A) with the offer of money to a woman standing next to a wool basket (face B). The wool basket has generally been regarded as a symbol of female virtue and a wife's role in the domestic space. Although it occurs in other scenes of *hetairika* on vase painting, it always seems to be a decontextualised symbol of married female life in all such scenes. Beazley argued that, since spinning was so clearly associated with female virtue, while prostitution was its very opposite, they could not both be part of the same image. Therefore, if on some vases money bags were given to women whose environment was symbolised by a wool basket it must have meant that money changed hands between husband and wife for purposes concerned with the administration of the household.[54] Rodenwaldt argued in the opposite direction. Since money could signify only commercial sex the wool basket should be interpreted as a characteristic of prostitutes who worked in a more respectable environment.[55]

Keuls added a new hypothesis based on examples such as pl. 7 c-d. Here a woman is shown with basket and distaff but is nevertheless offered money by a suitor. Keuls argued that money did not signify simply a relationship between a lover and a *hetaira* but should be taken more generally as a

> symbolic expression of the power of money in human relations. In the pederastic and *hetaira* scenes it represents not the actual money paid, but the fact that money controls the interaction of the participants. In the domestic scenes ... the pouch symbolises the fact that it is the man who holds the purse strings. The money pouch was in fact an economic phallus. The circumstance that the object is remarkably genital in shape is perhaps not wholly accidental.[56]

Apart from the fact that 'economic phallus' is perhaps a rather anachronistic term, Keuls' interpretation of the money pouch as a symbol of the polyvalent relationship between men and women, rather than of prostitution or the weekly budget to a wife, accords best with the modes of signification typical of red-figure vase painting in general.[57]

It seems, however, that her interpretation can be carried a step further. The juxtaposition of face A and B of pl. 4 c-d may not depict one and the same symbolic scenario. It should be noted, by contrast, that on one side the money pouch is held by a Type 1 figure, while on the other it is shown in the upright position which Hollein classifies as Type 3. If vase painting indeed dramatises ambivalence, then pl. 4 c-d is the best example of the ambivalence of money. Beard has argued convincingly that the three pictures of the *kylix* shown in pl. 5 juxtapose men's interaction with women in the outside world – that is, with *hetairai* – to their function in the domestic world (face C shows a woman sacrificing at the domestic hearth). The juxtaposition of these two types of female image with which a man was confronted in his life as a citizen subverted the strict division between women as *hetairai* and women as wives, or between the division of male domains in *palaestra*, gymnasium and symposium and the domestic domain symbolised by the wife at the hearth. In juxtaposing these spheres it questioned, and at the same time asserted, the necessity of such distinctions.

A similar kind of subversion seems to be intended on the vase shown in pl. 4 c-d. On face A a money pouch is given by a figure, signifying *scholê* by his posture, to a woman who is not further described by her environment. On face B the money is given by a man displaying *aretê* to a woman standing next to her wool basket. If the woman on face B indeed represents a wife in her domestic sphere, *hetairika* and *scholê* in the outside world (face A) are compared to marriage and *aretê* in the *oikos* (face B). The money pouch, rather than defining unequivocally a specific type of relationship between man and woman, stands for the various aspects of male life in the *polis*. In both images it defines normative behaviour, yet in a different context. In face B it is viewed together with the wool basket, the symbol of the virtue of the wife, as the clear spatial patterning of the painting into left (man), centre (wool basket/money pouch) and right (woman) suggests. And on face A it is depicted together with the controlled posture of the male suitor displaying his freedom as a purchaser of prostitutes. If this imagery aims at any kind of subversion of cultural categories it is not because it represents the payment of money to a sexual partner. Rather, it lies in the fact that the two sides of the pot represent two functions of money, distinct and yet similar. The imagery does not aim at conveying the moral difference of prostitution and marital love, but the different aspects of male virtue in either the public space of the *polis* or the private space of the *oikos*. In both spheres money had its proper function defined by the context, maintaining the kind of justice appropriate for that context.

The visual association of images of *hetairika* and pederasty can be interpreted in the same way. Within the former, the money pouch assumed a commercial meaning fostering the association of money with the market and payment of *misthoi* to foreigners and slaves. In the latter it had a political meaning defining the asymmetrical relationship between *erastai* and *erômenoi*. Yet the visual comparison between the two reduced their difference and mixed their symbolism. It consciously confused the meaning of money, the political force, with money, the disruptive force of commerce. It also confused the meaning of symposium, excess and sexual transgression with that of gymnasium, *palaestra* and *paideia*. It may be argued that this artistic strategy asserted the distinction of two meanings of money. Yet the development of the symbolism of money in civic relationships later in the century tells us that this was ultimately unsuccessful.

Money, pottery and symbolic exchange

We have seen that money could function as a social reward in relationships between *erastai* and *erômenoi*. In the imagery of *paideia* it was a symbol of power and, if used by the right person, of self-control. We have also seen how the imagery of money as a political symbol shaded into the imagery of money as a symbol of commerce when the context in which it was depicted changed. We now have to address the question to which aspect of money we have to relate those images which represent money pouches in exchanges with the potter himself. According to current interpretations, such images depict the reality of the potter's life and of the citizen going round shopping.[58]

The following interpretation is based on two assumptions. First, painted pots were prestigious possessions and served as objects for display. Secondly, they were given and received as highly valued gifts in relationships of friendship, as pl. 8 d indicates. The question then arises how the artist himself participated in the exchanges between donor and recipient, and in the social exchange for which the display of pottery was intended. The social status of potters and painters makes it unlikely that they themselves joined in on the occasions when pottery was used and displayed. Yet, if the painter's contribution to the creation of a civic image was ignored, the question arises why this happened, given that it was fully accepted, indeed important, that the poet mentioned his influence on the creation of fame. The social status of painters and poets cannot have been very different, given that there is some evidence for poets and artists having competed with each other for social recognition.[59] How can it be, then, that the poet could raise himself to the status of a friend of his patron while the vase painter depicted himself as a shopkeeper with whom the citizen had nothing other than a commercial relationship? The problem, however, is not that the Greeks regarded poets and painters differently, but that art historians have not sufficiently considered the function of self-representations of potters and painters on vase paintings. The images suggest that the importance of the artist for the creation of civic images was not entirely unrecognised.

The self-representation of the author in poetry has often been noted recently. Goldhill, for example, remarks in a broad outline:

> In the *Odyssey*, the bard receives his livelihood by singing; the (self-)representation of the lyric poet in sympotic literature replaces such recompense with an image of poetry as an object of exchange between *philoi*, while 'court poetry', such as that of Ibicus, with its (heroic) praise of contemporary figures

also makes plain the interplays of power involved in the literature of patronage. Pindar whose songs are requested and paid for by an individual in search of immortal *kleos*, substitutes for the (subordinating) gesture of praising on (financial) demand a series of different models of exchange between *philoi*. Where seventeenth- and eighteenth-century poets, to frame a perhaps misleading contrast, speak from the position of 'humble servant', Pindar's text seeks to create an (aristocratic) ideal of *philia* for which the affiliations and obligations of *xenia* provide a crucial and recurrent rhetoric.[60]

Crotty, furthermore, has emphasised the vital function of the poet for the recognition of achievement as achievement:

The symposiastic poem is not 'about' the symposium; rather, it is part of the celebration. No more is erotic poetry 'about' love; it is itself part of the lovers' relationship, a move in the lover's strategy to win the beloved. Similarly, the epinician is not a disinterested account of victory, nor is the narrative concerning the victorious athlete; the poem – addressed to the victor – is itself the recognition and acknowledgement that is vital to the completion of the victory.[61]

Kurke, finally, has drawn attention to the fact that the self-evaluation of the poet was part of the ritual of praise. She suggests that *philia* between poet and patron, rather than being a 'substitute' for the subordinating financial relationship between poet and patron was part of it. Discussing *Isthmian* 2, in which Pindar reminds his patron that his poem has a price, she proposes that 'immortality [of the victor] appears here climactically, as the result of a whole series of wise and willing expenditure culminating in the commission of celebratory song'.[62]

In the imagery of vase painting we encounter two forms of self-praise. On some vases potter, painter and metal worker are honoured by the goddess of craftsmanship.[63] The quality of the product is presented as being acknowledged by the rewarding gesture of a goddess. The divine presence in the workshop may also suggest that the artist conceived of his inspiration as being given by the goddess. As Vernant has shown, the artist was regarded as a mediator, not the creator, of forms and beauty.[64] The approval of the goddess which is depicted in these two paintings might be a visual expression of this idea.

Another way in which pottery could be evaluated visually was to depict it next to, or exchanged for, a money pouch (see pl. 8 a-d). The meaning of these representations is quite different from that of the former examples; it assesses the social value of pottery rather than its quality in relation to the divine model. Yet we should not fail to recognise that in the scenes of purchase it is also the evaluation of pottery and the potter/painter which is at stake, rather than shopping in the market. In pl. 8 a the money pouch is visually set into a relation to the pot, which is of the same shape as the one on which it is shown. Pl. 8 b depicts the reciprocity of the exchange between potter/painter and patron by combining the gesture of offering pottery with that of receipt of money.[65] There are three prominent features in the picture which stand out because no more details are given: the figure of the potter, the money pouch and the pots themselves. In the absence of any further pictorial narrative the viewer must relate them to each other – that is, the pottery to the money, the money to the potter/painter and the potter/painter to the pots. In this circle of visual relationships the three elements of the image evaluate each other. The invisible recipient of the pottery is present in the money pouch as the patron who is able to spend. Finally, the potter/painter represents himself as a youth (unbearded) and citizen (leaning on a walking stick), which marks him as a recipient who is worthy of, yet subordinate to, the invisible patron. The imagery establishes a hierarchical relationship between potter/painter and patron in the representation of potter/painter and his product, which enhances the prestige of the patron. Pl. 8 c-d associates the image of exchange between potter/painter and patron with the imagery of friendship. That the two paintings should not be understood as a sequential narrative is clear from the fact that the figures of the purchaser and donor are different. The two images compare and contrast gift-giving and purchase on an abstract level. They suggest that they are two comparable modes of exchange and two comparable ways of symbolising the status of a citizen. The patron (or owner of the pot) is praised twice by being the purchaser on the one hand and the recipient of a gift on the other. The fact that the donor is a youth leaves no doubt about the hierarchy of donor and recipient in the second image.

If the imagery of red-figure pottery is regarded as the imagery of civic power and prestige, the meaning of the money pouch in scenes of purchase appears in a new light. It must be related to the meaning of money as a means of payment in a system of generalised reciprocity rather than as a means of exchange in commerce. If the money pouch is a pictorial sign that aims to symbolise pottery as objects of commerce, it would reduce the status of its producer, which, in turn, would make the pot invalid as an object of display. It is more likely, therefore, that the money pouch as a symbol of the power to pay made the pot an object worthy of its owner. It established the relationship between painter/potter and patron as one of *philia*, if only hierarchically defined, and the pot as a value worthy of the patron's money. The financial link between purchaser and potter was socially accepted. As Aristotle argued later, money was designed to secure proportionate reciprocity, creating just relationships between citizens and making society possible.[66]

Notes

1. For the cross-references between money and medals see Laum (1951-2) and, more recently, Price (1983).
2. Kurke (1991) rightly stresses the pedagogical function of praise in this context; cf. p. 260.
3. Halperin (1990) and Bazant (1985) maintain the view that money was the reward for prostitutes only, while Dover (1978), Koch-Harnack (1983) and Reinsberg (1989) have argued that it was much closer to a gift.
4. Scheibler (1983), pp. 11 ff.; Bazant (1981), pp. 4-12, cf. (1985), p. 55; Beard (1991) raises further questions whether images and shapes symbolised the space in which they served as display.
5. Vickers (1985), cf. (1984) has argued that both the technique of vase painting and the low prices recorded for painted pottery are indications that they were imitations of containers in silver and gold. Pottery was the 'poor man's silver' substituting the precious objects of a much wealthier class, or wealthier material culture; see (1985), pp. 116 ff.; see also Bazant (1985), p. 56. Hoffmann (1988) concentrates on the latter aspect. Pottery emerged not so much because most people could not 'afford' metal-ware as because burial practices changed. 'In a stable, progressive society the tendency is for the grave goods to diminish. A diminishing proportion of the society's growing wealth is buried with the dead' (p. 152).
6. Robertson (1991), pp. 5 ff.
7. Bazant (1985) argues that the function of containers as objects of gift exchange shifted to that of objects of ostentation no longer associated with exchange (p. 57); this theory poses further questions. It must be asked, first of all, how an object of display is endowed with value. Three options are theoretically possible. First, objects have value because they have a high market value, i.e a high price because of the supply-and-demand mechanism; secondly because they have a high symbolic value, i.e. are objects which circulate in highly-valued exchange contexts (cf. Renfrew (1986)); and thirdly, because they have a family or religious tradition, i.e. are evaluated by their age or sacred meaning (cf. Geary (1986)). The first option does not apply to pots, as the prices found on individual pots show (cf. Johnston (1979), p. 33; Vickers (1985 a), p. 116). The second option is the one that Bazant contests, while the third is not applicable to Athenian pottery if used in Athens itself. Against Bazant, I would argue that pottery had a high value because it continued to be exchanged in significant contexts between aristocratic *philoi*. This is at the same time an argument against the long-drawn debate between Vickers (1984) (1985 a) and Gill (1988 a) (1988 b) (1988 c) on the one hand and Boardman (1988 a) (1988 b) on the other. The contentious question was whether trade in pottery between Athens and Etruria can be regarded as a trade in a luxury product or not, given that the prices of pottery in Athens were so low (three drachmas are recorded for a large red-figure *hydria*). Both Vickers/Gill and Boardman have discussed this problem in terms of a cost/profit calculation. Instead one should consider the cultural contexts of long-distance trade, i.e. what meanings were attached to exotic or foreign objects. Herriger (1991) rightly draws attention to the possibility that painted pottery was a luxury product in Etruria not because it was expensive to buy in Athens, but because it was associated with Athenian upper-class culture, such as symposia, wine-drinking athletic contests, etc; see Herriger (1991), pp. 119-121.
8. Bazant (1985), p. 56.

9. Money in Gymnasium and Palaestra

9. Ibid., p. 59; see also Francis (1989) and Hollein (1988).
10. Francis (1990), Bazant (1985).
11. Boardman and La Rocca (1975), p. 82; cf. Bazant (1985), p. 58.
12. Frontisi-Ducroux and Lissarrague (1990), Beard (1991), Bazant (1985).
13. Bazant (1985), p. 39.
14. The illustrations of this chapter are a representative sample which could be extended. The pattern of survival of painted pottery makes it a meaningless project to aim at a complete collection of all images depicting money pouches. As the range of variations of themes tends to be limited, I assume that the images represented in this sample are representative of the range of variations that was created around the theme. (Cf. Bazant (1985), pp. 39-45.) Further, but similar, examples are discussed by Beazley (1931), Rodenwaldt (1932), Herbig (1954), pp. 270 f., Crome (1966), pp. 245 ff., Shapiro (1981), Keuls (1985), pp. 260-264, Koch-Harnack (1983), Reinsberg (1989), pp. 181 ff.
15. See above pp. 121 f.
16. Dover (1978), pp. 19-38; Halperin (1990), Cohen (1991), pp. 172-178. Alongside terms like *hubrizein* and *hetairein* (*Tim.* I. 16 and I, 26) we find *epi misthô hetairein* (*Tim.* I. 13) or *to sôma hubrei pipraskein* (*Tim.* I. 29.). There is disagreement, however, as to the relative importance of accepting payment or committing *hubris* in the definition of the offence; see Cohen (1991), pp. 172-178.
17. Cohen argues that the prostitute himself also committed *hubris*, which meant in this case violence committed against his own body (Cohen (1991), p. 178). Dover (1978), pp. 37 ff. argues more convincingly that it was only in the special situation of the case against Timarchus that an *erômenos* was sued because of *hubris*.
18. Dover (1978), p. 35; Halperin (1990), p. 96; Cohen (1991), p. 180. The same applied to sexual assault or rape of women.
19. Cf. Dover (1978), pp. 100-109.
20. Plat. *Symp.* 184 a-b trans. Dover. In other places Plato expressed the view that a man who is sexually used as a woman – that is, submits himself to the power of the lover – acts against nature. See Plat. *Phaed.* 250 e; *Laws* 836 e; 841 d; cf. Cohen (1991), p. 178 for further discussion.
21. Plat. *Symp.* 183 b-c.
22. For *kolakeia*, usually translated as 'flattery', as a disguised form of seeking patronage see Millett (1989), p. 30 f.
23. Dover (1978), pp. 100 ff.; Koch-Harnack (1983) p. 163; for the symbolism of spears, animals and musical instruments see Koch-Harnack (1983), pp. 59 ff.
24. Bazant (1985), p. 41.
25. Men. *Kolax*, 40-55.
26. Theoph. *Characters* II. 1, quoted from Millett (1989), p. 31.
27. Arist. *EN.* 1127a7; trans. Millett (1989), p. 32. The translation of *chrêmata* as money seems justified here, given that it is distinguished from other valuables that *chrêmata* procure.
28. Kaempf-Dimitriadou (1979), Bazant (1985), p. 41.
29. An exception is pl. 4 d; for which see p. 207.
30. Bazant (1985), p. 51.
31. Bazant (1985), p. 41 calls pieces of meat the 'équivalent en nature' of money pouches. The gift of meat is difficult to interpret; it does not seem to be transacted directly from *erastês* to *erômenos*; therefore it can probably not be regarded as the equivalent of money bags.
32. Koch-Harnack (1983), pp. 97-105; Hoffmann (1974), pp. 206-212; Reinsberg (1989), p. 176; see also Bruneau (1965).

33. Lewis (1985), pp. 213-222; cf. Vidal-Naquet (1981 a) and Segal (1981) for the imagery in 5th-century literature.

34. Koch-Harnack (1983), pp. 161-172; Reinsberg (1989), pp. 185-187.

35. Cf. Koch-Harnack (1983); Neumann (1965); Keuls (1985).

36. Dover (1978), p. 103. It is important to notice that the money pouch is typically held in the hand of a male adult addressing a boy or a woman, or by an older boy addressing a younger one. For an interesting exception see pl. 4 a.

37. Barthes (1970).

38. Lissarrague and Schnapp (1981), Hoffmann (1988), Bazant (1985), Beard (1991); see also the articles in Bérard et al. (1989), Frontisi-Ducroux and Lissarrague (1990); and the conference proceedings in Christiansen and Melander (1988).

39. Frontisi-Ducroux and Lissarrague (1990).

40. See, for example, Gerhard (1842), Vol. IV; Boardman (1975).

41. Shapiro (1981), Bazant (1985).

42. Dover (1978), Koch-Harnack (1983), Keuls (1985), Reinsberg (1989).

43. Beard (1991), pp. 19-21.

44. Karozou (1962) pp. 450 ff., Stupperich (1977) and Hollein (1988). German scholars have worked intensively on this particular representation. Stupperich has described two further characteristics of the *Manteljüngling*: first, fragility of posture, and secondly, in certain subtypes, the free leg pointing outwards (cf. Hollein (1988), pp. 13-14).

45. Hollein's analysis is indebted to Fehr's (1977) study on *Bewegungsweisen und Verhaltensnormen*. Fehr argues that the Greeks associated certain values with physiognomic particularities and body movements in particular (see for example Plat. *Charm*. 159 a f.; Phocyl. frgm. 11 D; Theog. 331 and also Hom. *Od*. 17. 245 f.). *Sophrosunê* was expressed by orderly and sparse movement (*hesuchiotês, kosmiotês*). *Aretê*, which Fehr calls a competitive value, was expressed by the ability to control the distinction between 'light' and 'heavy' movements. These were appropriate each in different social contexts (dance, sport and warfare) (pp. 16-24). Both movement and control of movement were represented in sculpture of the 5th and 4th centuries. They could also be combined and juxtaposed in the same statue, and in that case they indicate visually the juxtaposition of the competitive value of *aretê* with the co-operative value of *sophrosunê* (pp. 82-83).

46. For the cross-cuttings between power and potency see also Dover (1978), p. 105 and Schauenburg, *MdAI* 90/1975, pl. 25, 1-3.

47. Plato and Aristotle constructed *philia* as a relationship between equals. Yet other texts suggest that *philia* was a much more general term for all those relationships which were positively connoted, including a variety of asymmetrical relationships (cf. Kurke (1991) for *philia* between poets and their patron; Goldhill (1986) for *philia* as a concept of both political and family ties). Most scholars have concentrated on friendship in political theory in which *philia* indeed 'tends towards equality between people' (Hutter (1978), p. 21); see also Fraisse (1974) and Price (1989). A wider social analysis of *philia* is still lacking.

48. See esp. Lewis (1985) who discusses the thematic links between the political and erotic poems in the *Corpus Theognideum*; see also Levine (1985); for lyric poetry on wealth see above, pp. 182 f.; for the cross-cutting of images of *paideia, philia* and pederasty in Pindar see Crotty (1982), pp. 76 ff., Goldhill (1991), pp. 128 ff., Kurke (1991), pp. 5, 17, 88, 252 ff.; for wealth and money in Pindar see Pavese (1966), Woodbury (1968), Gzella (1971), Colace (1978) and Kurke (1991).

49. Anacr. frgm 10, 16 (Bgk).

50. Kurke (1991), p. 249. See, by contrast, Detienne (1967), Gzella (1971), Svenbro (1976) and Gentili (1988). Gentili argues that the different attitude to

money was the result of socio-economic change in which poetry became a commodity and the relationship between poet and patron one of paid employment. Anacreon, who worked as one of the first courtier poets at the court of Polycrates of Samos, already marks a shift in the conditions of poetic production. Yet by the time of Simonides and Pindar, poetry had become completely a product at the disposal of the 'highest bidder', the relationship of poet and patron one of contract, and poetic achievement measurable in terms of financial returns. This contrasted with the old model represented by Solon and Theognis who had combined the roles of poet, symposiast and politician; cf. (1988), pp. 160-162. Gentili's model can be questioned on various grounds. Sympotic and choral lyric represent a different relationship of poetry and money, not only as a result of historic change but, first, because they had a different function, and, secondly, because individual poets started from different metaphysical assumptions which had feedback effects on their self-evaluation. Simonides, the archetypal poet associated with money, thematised the gap between truth and language, or the limited power of humans to control happiness by means of moral superiority (cf. Christ (1941), Detienne (1967), pp. 109-173, Crotty (1982), pp. 33-40). Inasmuch as money was bound up with questions of the relationship of humans and gods, divine retribution etc., the question of how praise was most adequately recompensed was affected too. While sympotic lyric was produced for a limited audience of peers, choral lyric aimed at the integration of the victor into a broader political public (Nisetich (1977), p. 141, Kurke (1991), p. 254). Both themes affected the evaluation of poetry and changed attitudes to its reward, regardless of the socio-economic conditions of its production. Cf. Pavese (1966), Woodbury (1968), Kurke (1991), von Reden (1995).

51. Hollein (1988), pp. 71-117 for the former, pp. 118 ff. for the latter.

52. Bazant (1985) for the former; Frontisi-Ducroux and Lissarrague (1990), Beard (1991) for the latter.

53. The two forms of sexual exchange had also their own imagery not found in the representation of the other. So among the images of *hetairika* the interdependence of sex and education is missing, while *erômenoi* are never depicted in a 'brothel' (or temple ?), i.e. in a building represented by columns and roof (see Keuls (1985), fig. 239), or in any explicit sexual situation; cf. Keuls (1985) and Reinsberg (1989).

54. Beazley (1931), p. 24.

55. Rodenwaldt (1932), pp. 7-21, cf. Herbig (1954), pp. 270 f., Crome (1966), pp. 245 ff.

56. Keuls (1983), p. 229; cf. (1985), pp. 260-264.

57. Keuls' second proposition that money pouches in a man's hand symbolised male dominance in the domestic environment is, like her notion of the economic phallus, modernistic. There is no evidence that at the beginning of the 5th century the division of labour in the household attributed the financial side to the man. The division of tasks was rather between outdoor and indoor occupations, leaving *oikonomia*, whether in its financial or other sides, largely to women. *Oikonomos* was in the 5th century a term applied to women and had negative connotations if used as a label for a man; cf. Spahn (1984), p. 305 with further discussion; for the range of tasks of women in the *oikos* generally, see Just (1989), pp. 116 f. and 136.

58. For example, Bazant (1985), p. 41, Thompson (1984) and Boardman (1975), p. 221, who has collected scenes of potteries under the heading 'industry and commerce'.

59. For that matter we have to assume that the producers of statues and painters of vase paintings had no significantly different status; see for this CVA

Milano 2 III.1, pl. 1, where their work is depicted in the same image, may be one piece of evidence. Svenbro (1976), pp. 176 ff. discusses the cross-references to artistic production in lyric poetry.

60. Goldhill (1991), pp. 130 f.

61. Crotty (1982), p. 81.

62. Kurke (1991), p. 248 with Pind. *I*. 2. 32 f.

63. See, for example, Boardman (1975), figs 101 (cup by the Euergides Painter, Athens National Museum Abv. 166) and 323 (kalpis by the Leningrad Painter, CVA Milano 2 III, i, pl. 1).

64. Vernant (1965).

65. Potter and painter co-operated in the same workshop and the work of both contributed equally to the result and value of the painted pot; cf. Scheibler (1983) and pl. 1, which depicts potter and painter as both working in the same workshop and earning the praise of the goddesses. I shall therefore make no distinction between the two kinds of artist.

66. Arist. *EN* 1133 a 6-1133 a 27; cf. above pp. 184 ff.

Conclusion: Rethinking Economics

> Contrairement aux autres animaux sociaux, les hommes ne se contentent pas de vivre en société, ils produisent de la société pour vivre; au cours de leur existence ils inventent des nouvelles manières de penser et d'agir sur eux-mêmes comme sur la nature qui les entoure. Ils produisent donc de la culture, fabriquent de l'histoire, l'Histoire.
>
> Godelier (1986) [1984], p. 1

We are all accustomed nowadays to thinking of exchange, markets and money in terms of economics. Technically we calculate incomes, outgoings, costs and profits in quantitative units of value, and in so doing isolate the function of exchange from the social and metaphysical statements that it entails.

It has often been argued that Western economic analysis is deeply rooted in Christian models of thought and Early Modern political philosophy; yet instead of analysing the modes of thought that lead to commerce and the change of meanings of value in societies that have different metaphysics, scholars have focused on the development of markets and monetary exchange in order to understand the development of concepts of commerce. Thus for both Polanyi and Finley economic analysis was a 'discovery' which the Greeks of the classical period were unable to make since markets and money did not yet dominate their economy.[1] The language of capitalist economics has so dominated our way of thinking about exchange that it has led to the construction of a history according to which people are necessarily driven into markets and money use. Here is a subtle example of a circular argument: economic behaviour is represented as the result of a history that economic theory presupposes in order to justify itself.

Max Weber's sociological definition of 'economic activity' shows most clearly how such definitions depend on typically Western metaphysical assumptions.[2] 'Economic activity' he called the practice which is oriented towards the fulfilment of demands or needs and in which people deal peacefully with valuables over which they have power as proprietors. 'Rational economic activity', by contrast, he called the systematic, goal-oriented activity which presupposes the understanding of the economic process and which did not exist before the emergence of Western economic theory.[3] Yet even in his definition of primary 'economic activity' Weber takes it for granted that all societies make the same categorical distinctions.

First, it presupposes the distinction between people who act economically on the one hand and things that are the objects of economic activity on the other. Secondly, it presupposes a clear concept of property in contrast to socially binding relationships towards people. Thirdly, it makes an axiomatic distinction between the use of natural resources – that is, production – and the use of other people – that is, exchange. And finally it is based on an absolute concept of utility which does not allow for changing meanings of 'demand' and 'need'.

None of our Western distinctions was completely absent in antiquity. I have aimed to show in this book, however, that they were not as unquestioned as they are in our culture. Rigid status boundaries between citizens and outsiders, free men and slaves and men and women made it impossible to think of humans as never the objects of exchange or property. The idea that agrarian produce was the gift of the gods given in exchange for toil and justice also made it unnecessary to distinguish between production and exchange. The acquisition of valuables from nature (or the gods) and from other people were not distinguished categorically as long as the question of the distinction between nature and culture was unsettled. Since the boundaries between people and things, and nature and culture were not drawn so clearly as in Western thought, the distinction between the value of objects and the value of people or personalised gifts shifted whenever the metaphysical definition of the human condition shifted.

The 'individual' is in the centre of economic analysis. Since the Enlightenment the 'individual' has been the term for a free person whose freedom is symbolised no longer by political rights but by the right to own the produce of his labour. Economic theory appropriated the idea that the 'individual' exists without society – that is, can theoretically be thought of independently of his political status. The key terms of political economy, such as production, consumption, value and self-interest, all describe relationships between people and things rather than between people. Rational economic activity is an activity in which people pay no attention to the political meaning of their behaviour but satisfy their interest in certain things ('necessities') in the most efficient way. In Greek thought, by contrast, no concept similar to the 'individual' existed. Instead, a person was either a member of a community or no person – that is simply a body. Any interest that he pursued not as a member of a community could thus only be understood as an interest of his body. Two further differences emerge from the absence of the Western concept of the individual. First, that self-interest did not refer to the interest of a 'self' independent of an 'other', but to an interest that could be satisfied only either by others or at the cost of others, and, secondly, that the distinction between use value and exchange value did not apply since the value of an object was always conceived of as having a social dimension.

In the first two chapters we looked at the metaphysics of exchange laid down in heroic poetry. The 'self' of a person was created by the gifts of other people and the gods. The main function (or 'use') of valuables was to recompense a person for the loss of life or a temporary lack of social status. 'Self-interest' was an important motivation of exchange inasmuch as a person's life and glory after death were dependent on gifts; yet the pursuit of this self-interest meant at the same time that a person was willing to accept the social obligations arising from the gifts. Self-interest and gift-giving were not conflicting principles but two stages of one moral and social strategy. In the context of such metaphysics objects were never totally alienable from people. Since the value of possessions was that of a sign of the relationship between the donor and recipient, the epics convey a concept of ownership that is closer to our concept of relationship and suggest that there was an open boundary between the status of subjects and objects of exchange.

In chapter three we focused on the representation of commerce in the epics. We observed that a distinction between gift exchange and commerce was made but that it was ideologically rather than empirically founded. Every object was potentially an object of commerce, while every person who received something could 'look like' a trader. The distinction between gift exchange and commerce was dependent on the social context from which the object was taken, the status of the exchanging partners and the kind of 'need' the object was meant to satisfy. The epic concept of value cuts across the distinction of use value and exchange value inasmuch as the use value of gifts lay in their meaning as objects of exchange necessary for the symbolisation of social roles, while commodities had a value only for traders who needed an immediate return for the sustenance of their bodies. Yet a new concept of utility emerged when the life in the *oikos* became a more important value than death in battle. The epics suggest that the value of objects had to be realised in life rather than after death as a recompense for a life lost in battle.

In Part II we discussed the semantics of exchange in the context of the archaic and classical *polis*. I argued that Greek texts do not distingush between socially meaningful and economically functional forms of exchange but that the entire repertoire of exchanges taking place within a *polis* symbolised the political status of its members. Both the ability to give gifts and to pay money in a political or economic context were signs of power, freedom and absence of debt. Conversely, receiving money or gifts signified inferiority, dependence and, if not legal, metaphorical slavery. A person who needed to make a profit – that is, aimed at receiving more than he had given – thus forfeited his autarky, preferred slavery to freedom and reduced his status of a political being to that of a mere 'body', like a prostitute.

The symbolism of exchange was more important than the empirical distinction between trade and agriculture. In chapter six we looked at various texts influenced by the ideology of the Athenian empire. Although trade and traders continued to have a lower status than agriculture and farmers in democratic Athens, maritime exchange – that is, the ability to pay for foreign products with surplus money – came to be represented as a symbol of Athenian power. At the same time the import of foreign products marked perfect autarky – originally a value associated with the self-sufficiency of an agrarian *oikos* – since it meant independence from the gods who controlled the fertility of the local soil.

Yet the images of trade and monetary exchange that could carry positive connotations in the context of relationships between *poleis* were images of injustice, violence and war within the *polis*. In chapter seven we saw that in Athenian tragedy the model of justice that required equal exchange ratios and was typical of both commerce and blood vengeance was exposed as a destructive model of justice between citizens. In the *Oresteia* it was banned from the *agora* to a place outside the city, which indicated metaphorically that citizens should never exchange with each other in this way whether in politics or in the food market. Alternatively the trilogy suggests that political stability and peace rest on gift exchange.

In Part III we turned to the introduction of coinage in the Greek *polis* since money is often regarded as the origin of market exchange and a 'disembedded' economy. Although the Greeks themselves associated it in the late 5th and 4th centuries with trade and apolitical behaviour, I argued that at the turn of the 6th century money was part of the embedded economy of civic exchange. There are some indications that the introduction of coinage was motivated by the desire to create a political means of payment controlled by humans so that they would not have to rely on the uncertain rewards of the gods. Monetary payments were at first meaningful within the political symbolism of exchange rather than introducing a new economic or 'disembedded' mode of exchange. A moral double-bind emerged parallel to the ideology of spending in which the ability to pay was regarded as good and a sign of power and patronage, while receiving money was bad and a sign of submission to others and to the desires of one's body.

Since direct textual evidence of the early meanings of money is lacking, we looked in the last chapter at vase painting. Here the iconographic detail of the money pouch given by a lover to his beloved boy seems to carry positive meanings. In the context of gymnasium and *palaestra*, the places of education for the political elite, unequal relationships and patronage were accepted and indeed necessary for initiating the young into the role of leading citizens. The money pouch in the imagery of civic exchange confirms that paying money symbolised patronage and was morally good where the inequality of the exchanging partners was taken for granted. Vase painting depicts money also in a more commercial context. Paying a female prostitute or the potter himself appears as a display of the power of a citizen. Through the visual comparison of different money relationships vase painting seems to arrive at a distinction between the two functions of money as a means of payment and as a means of exchange.

The meanings of ancient exchange are complex and not easily represented in a coherent model. The preceding studies aimed at highlighting only those aspects where ancient exchange defies the categories of Western ethics and economics. Preoccupied with the political symbolism of exchange, the Greeks may have been unable to 'discover' economic analysis as Polanyi argued; yet in looking at meanings of exchange in antiquity we might rediscover the symbolic statements made in a market economy.

Notes

1. Polanyi (1957) and (1960); Finley (1970); Meikle (1979) against Polanyi and Finley but also using modern economic theory as the model against which ancient thought is tested.

2. Humphreys (1978), p. 158 argues convincingly that Polanyi's distinction between the substantive and formal definition of 'economy' is based on Weber. Weber's influence on Finley was frequently acknowledged by Finley himself, but see also Austin and Vidal-Naquet (1977), Introduction.

3. Weber (1972) [1922], p. 32.

Bibliography

Abbreviations of journals are those used in *L'Année philologique*.

S.R. Ackerman (1978) *Corruption: A Study in Political Economy*. New York.
A.W.H. Adkins (1960a) *Merit and Responsibility: A Study in Greek Values*. Oxford.
—— (1960b) 'Honour and Punishment in the Homeric Poems.' *BICS* 7, pp. 23ff.
—— (1963) 'Friendship and Self-Sufficiency in Homer and Aristotle.' *CQ* 13, pp. 30-45.
—— (1971) 'Homeric Values and Homeric Society.' *JHS* 91, pp. 1-19.
—— (1972a) *Moral Values and Political Behaviour in Ancient Greece*. London.
—— (1972b) 'Homeric Gods and the Values of Homeric Society.' *JHS* 92, pp. 1-19.
—— (1972c) 'Truth, *Kosmos* and *Aretê* in the Homeric Poems.' *CQ* 22, pp. 5-18.
—— (1982) 'Values, Goals and Emotions in the *Iliad*.' *CPh* 77, pp. 292-326.
J. Annas (1981) *An Introduction to Plato's Republic*. Oxford.
A. Appadurai (ed.) (1986) *The Social Life of Things*. Cambridge.
G. Arnott (1972) 'Parody and Ambiguity in Euripides' *Cyclops*.' In *Antidosis. Festschrift für W. Krauss*. Wien, pp. 21-30.
W. Arrowsmith (1952) Introduction to 'The Cyclops'. In D. Grene & R. Lattimore (eds.), *The Complete Greek Tragedies*. Vol. III. *Euripides*, pp. 224-30.
—— (1968) 'Euripides' Theatre of Ideas.' In E. Segal (ed.), *Euripides: A Collection of Critical Articles*. New York, pp. 13-33.
M. Athorp (1980) 'The Obstacle to Telemachus' Return.' *CQ* 30, pp. 1-20.
M.M. Austin & P. Vidal-Naquet (1977) *Economic and Social History of Ancient Greece: An Introduction*. London.
N. Austin (1969) 'Telemachus Polymechanos.' *CSCA* 2, pp. 45-63.
M.S. Balmuth (1971), 'Remarks on the Appearance of the Earliest Coins.' In D.G. Mitten, J.G. Pedley & J.A. Scott (eds.), *Studies Presented to Georg M.A. Hanfmann*. Mainz, pp. 1-7.
A. Bammer (1985) *Architektur und Gesellschaft in der Antike*. Wien.
—— (1990) 'A Peristercos of the Geometric Period in the Artemisium of Ephesus.' *AS* 40, pp. 1-26.
F. Barth (1967) 'Economic Spheres in Dafur.' In Firth (1967), pp. 149-74.
R. Barthes (1970) *S/Z*. Paris.
J. Baudrillard (1975) *The Mirror of Production* (trans. M. Poster; French orig. 1975). St. Louis.
—— (1981) *For a Critique of the Political Economy of the Sign* (trans. C. Levin; French orig. 1972). St Louis.
J. Bazant (1981) *Studies on the Use and Decoration of Athenian Vases*. Prague.
—— (1985) *Les citoyens sur les vases athéniens*. Prague.
M. Beard (1991) 'Adopting an Approach II.' In Rasmussen & Spivey (1991), pp. 12-35.
J.D. Beazley (1931) *Der Pan Maler*. Berlin.
—— (1956) *Attic Black Figure Vase Painters*. Oxford.

—— (1963) *Attic Red Figure Vase Painters*. Oxford.
C.S. Belshaw (1965) *Traditional Exchange and Modern Markets*. New York.
E. Benveniste (1969) *Le vocabulaire des institutions indo-européenes*. Vol. 1, *Économie, parenté, société*. Paris.
C. Bérard, J.-L. Durand, A. Schnapp, P. Schmitt et al. (1989) *A City of Images*. Princeton.
J. Bergman (1987) 'Religio-phenomenological Reflections on the Multilevel Process of Giving to the Gods.' In Linders & Nordquist (1987), pp. 31-42.
A.L.T. Bergren (1983) 'Odyssean Temporality: Many (Re)Turns.' In Rubino & Shelmerdine (1983), pp. 38-73.
A. Bertoud (1981) *Aristote et l'argent*. Paris.
M. Bettali (1985) 'Case, bottegha, ergasteria: note sui luoghi di produzione e di vendita nell' Atene classica.' *Opus* 4, pp. 29-42.
P.M. Blau (1964) *Exchange and Power in Social Life*. Wiley.
M. Bloch (1989) 'The Symbolism of Money in Imirina.' In Parry & Bloch (1989), pp. 142-64.
E. Block (1985) 'Clothing Makes the Man: A Pattern in the *Odyssey*.' *TAPhA* 115, pp. 1-11.
M.W. Blundell (1989) *Helping Friends and Harming Enemies*. Cambridge.
J. Boardman (1968) *Archaic Greek Gems*. London.
—— (1970) *Greek Gems and Finger Rings*. London.
—— (1974) *Athenian Black Figure Vases*. London.
—— (1975) *Athenian Red Figure Vases*. London.
—— (1980) 'Art in Seals.' In E. Porada (ed.), *Ancient Art in Seals*. Princeton, pp. 101-19.
—— (1988) 'Trade in Greek Decorated Pottery.' *OJA* 7, pp. 27-33.
—— (1991) 'The Sixth Century Potters and Painters of Athens and their Public.' In Rasmussen & Spivey (1991), pp. 79-102.
J. Boardman & E. La Rocca (1975) *Eros in Griechenland*. Munich.
P. Bohannan (1955) 'Some Principles of Exchange among the Tiv.' *American Anthropologist* 57, pp. 60-9.
—— (1959) 'The Impact of Money on an African Subsistence Economy.' *Journal of Economic History* 19, pp. 491-503.
P. Bohannan & G. Dalton (eds.) (1962) *Markets in Africa*. Northwestern University Press.
P. & L. Bohannan (1968) *Tiv Economy*. Evanston.
E. Boisacque (1916) *Dictionnaire éthymologique de la langue grecque*. Heidelberg.
H. Bolkestein (1939) *Wohltätigkeit und Armenpflege im vorchristlichen Altertum*. Utrecht.
P. Bourdieu (1971) 'Le marché des biens symboliques.' *L'Année sociologique* 22, pp. 49-126.
—— (1977a) 'The Economics of Linguistic Exchanges.' *Social Science Information* 16, pp. 645-68.
—— (1977b) *Outline of a Theory of Practice* (trans. R. Nice; French orig. 1972). Cambridge.
—— (1990) *The Logic of Practice* (trans. R. Nice; French orig. 1980). Cambridge.
—— (1991) *Language and Symbolic Power* (ed. J.B. Thompson). Cambridge.
—— (1993) *The Field of Cultural Production* (ed. R. Johnson). Cambridge.
C.M. Bowra (1964) *Pindar*. Oxford.
E.F. Bruck (1926) *Totenteil und Seelgerät im Griechischen Recht*. Munich.
A.C. Brumfield (1981) *The Attic Festivals of Demeter and their Relation to the Agricultural Year*. New York.

P. Bruneau (1965) 'Le motif des coqs affrontés dans l'imagérie antique.' *BCH* 89, pp. 90-121.
J.J. Buchanan (1962) *Theorika: A Study of Monetary Distribution to the Athenian Citizenry during the 5th and 4th Centuries BC*. New York.
H. Bunsdorff (1992) *Zur Rolle des Aussehens im homerischen Menschenbild*. Göttingen.
W. Burkert (1987) 'Offerings in Perspective: Surrender, Distribution, Exchange.' In Linders & Nordquist (1987), pp. 43-56.
R.G.A. Buxton (1982), *Persuasion in Greek Tragedy*. Cambridge.
N. Cahil (1985) 'The Treasury at Persepolis: Gift Giving at the City of the Persians.' *AJA* 89, pp. 373-89.
H.A. Cahn (1971) 'Dating the Early Coinages of Athens.' In *Kleine Schriften zur Münzkunde und Archaeologie*. Basel, pp. 81-97.
W.M. Calder III (1984) 'Gold for Bronze: *Iliad* 6.232-6.' In K. Rigsby (ed.), *Studies Presented to Sterling Dow on his 80th Birthday*. Durham/NY, pp. 31-4.
J.M. Camp (1986) *The Athenian Agora*. London.
D. Campagner (1988) 'Reciprocità economica in Pindaro.' *QUCC* 29, pp. 78-93.
S. Campese (1977) 'Polis ed economia in Aristotele.' In S. Campese, F. Calabi, A.A. Bertrametti et al. (eds.), *Aristotele e la crisi della politica*. Naples, pp. 13-60.
I. Carradice (1987) 'The Regal Coinage of the Persian Empire.' In id. (ed.), *Coinage and Administration in the Athenian and Persian Empires*. *BAR* 343, pp. 73-108.
I. Carradice & M. Price (1988) *Coinage in the Greek World*. London.
J. Carsten (1989) 'Cooking Money: Gender and the Symbolic Transformation of Means of Exchange in a Malay Fishing Community.' In Parry & Bloch (1989), pp. 117-41.
P. Cartledge (1982) 'Sparta and Samos: A Special Relationship?' *CQ* 32, pp. 243-65.
—— (1983) ' "Trade and Politics" Revisited: Archaic Greece.' In P.D.A. Garnsey, K. Hopkins & C.R. Whittaker (eds.), *Trade in the Ancient Economy*. London, pp. 1-15.
—— (1993) *The Greeks*. Oxford
P. Cartledge & D. Harvey (eds.) (1985) *Crux: Studies Presented to G.E.M. de Ste Croix on his 75th Birthday*. Exeter.
P. Chantraine (1940) 'Conjugation et histoire des verbes signifiant vendre.' *RPh* 14, pp. 11-24.
—— (1968) *Dictionnaire étymologique de la langue grecque. Histoire des mots*. Vol. II. Paris.
D. Cheal (1988) *The Gift Economy*. London.
G. Christ (1941) *Simonidesstudien*. Freiburg.
J. Christiansen & T. Melander (eds.)(1988) *Proceedings of the 3rd Symposium on Greek and Related Pottery*. Copenhagen.
J. Clay (1983) *The Wrath of Athena. Gods and Men in the 'Odyssey'*. Princeton.
D. Cohen (1987) 'Law, Society and Homosexuality in Classical Athens.' *P&P* 117, pp. 3-21.
—— (1991) 'Sexuality, Violence and the Athenian Law of Hubris.' *G&R* 38, pp. 171-88.
P.R. Colace (1978) 'Considerazioni sul concetto di *Plutos* in Pindaro.' In E. Livrea & G.A. Privitera (eds.) *Studi in Onore di Anthos Ardizzoni*. Roma, pp. 737-45.
J.N. Coldstream (1977) *Geometric Greece*. London.
—— (1983) 'Gift Exchange in the Eighth Century BC.' In R. Hägg (ed.), *The Greek Renaissance of the Eighth Century*. Stockholm, pp. 201-6.
W.R. Connor (1971) *The New Politicians of Fifth-Century Athens*. Princeton.

—— (1977) 'Tyrannis Polis.' In J.H. D'Arms & J.W. Eadie (eds.) *Ancient and Modern. Essays in Honour of Gerald F. Else.* Ann Arbor, pp. 95-109.
—— (1984) *Thucydides*. Princeton.
R.M. Cook (1958) 'Speculations on the Origins of Coinage.' *Historia* 7, pp. 257-62.
A. Cozzo (1988) *Kerdos: Semantica, ideologia e società nella Grecia antica*. Rome.
J.D. Craig (1967) '*Chrusea chalkeiôn.*' *CR* 17, pp. 243-5.
M.H. Crawford (1972) 'Solon's Alleged Reform of Weights and Measures.' *Eirene* 10, pp. 1ff.
J.F. Crome (1966) 'Spinnende Hetairen?' *Gymnasium* 73, pp. 245-7.
K. Crotty (1982) *Song and Action: The Victory Odes of Pindar*. Baltimore and London.
T. Crump (1981) *The Phenomenon of Money*. London.
—— (1985) 'Money, Primitive.' In A. & J. Kuper (eds.), *The Social Science Encyclopedia*. London.
F. Damon, C. Gregory & M. Strathern (1981) 'Alienating the Inalienable.' *Man* 16, Correspondence.
J. Davidson (1993) 'Fish, Sex and Revolution in Athens'. *CQ* 43, pp. 53-66.
J.K. Davies (1971) *Athenian Propertied Families, 600-300 BC*. Oxford.
—— (1981) *Wealth and the Power of Wealth in Classical Athens*. New York.
J. Davis (1992) *Exchange*. Buckingham.
W.G. Davis (1973) *Social Relations in a Philippine Market*. Berkeley, Los Angeles and London.
W.H. Desmonde (1962) *Magic, Myth and Money: The Origins of Money in Religious Ritual*. New York.
G.E.M. de Ste. Croix (1954) 'Greek and Roman Accounting.' In A.C. Littleton & B.C. Yamey (eds.), *Studies in the History of Accounting*. London, pp. 14-74.
—— (1972) *The Origins of the Peloponnesian War*. London.
—— (1981) *The Class Struggle in the Ancient Greek World*. London.
M. Detienne (1963) *Crise agraire et attitude religieuse chez Hésiode*. Paris.
—— (1967) *Maîtres de vérité dans la Grèce archaïque*. Paris.
—— (1977) *The Gardens of Adonis*. The Harvester Press.
M. Detienne & J.-P. Vernant (1978), *Cunning Intelligence in Greek Culture and Society*. Brighton.
M. Detienne & J.-P. Vernant (eds.) (1989) *The Cuisine of Sacrifice*. Chicago.
A. Dewey (1962) *Peasant Marketing in Java*. Glencoe.
E.R. Dodds (1951) *The Greeks and the Irrational*. Berkeley, Los Angeles.
W. Donlan (1980) *The Aristocratic Ideal in Ancient Greece*. Lawrence, KA.
—— (1981) 'Scale, Value and Function in the Homeric Economy.' *AJAH* 6, pp. 101-7.
—— (1981-2) 'Reciprocities in Homer.' *CW* 75, pp. 137-75.
—— (1982) 'The Politics of Generosity in Homer.' *Helios* 9, pp. 1-5.
—— (1989) 'The Unequal Exchange between Glaucus and Diomedes in the Light of the Homeric Gift-Economy.' *Phoenix* 43, pp. 1-15.
M. Douglas (1990) Foreword in Mauss (1990), pp. vii-xviii.
K.J. Dover (1964) 'Eros and Nomos.' *BICS* 11, pp. 31-42.
—— (1973a) 'Classical Greek Attitudes to Sexual Behaviour.' *Arethusa* 6, pp. 59-73.
—— (1973b) 'Thucydides.' *G&R New Surveys* 7. Oxford.
—— (1974) *Greek Popular Morality in the Time of Plato and Aristotle*. Oxford.
—— (1978) *Greek Homosexuality*. London.
R. Drews (1983) *'Basileus': The Evidence for Kingship in Geometric Greece*. New Haven.

P. Dubois (1982) *History, Rhetorical Description and the Epic: From Homer to Spenser.* Totowa, N.J.
G. Dupré & P.P. Rey (1973) 'Reflections on the Pertinence of a Theory of the History of Exchange.' *Economy and Society* 2, pp. 131-63.
J.-L. Durand & F. Lissarrague (1980) 'Un lieu d'image? L'espace du louterion.' *Hesperia* 49, pp. 89ff.
W. Eckart (1963) 'Initiatory Motives in the Story of Telemachus.' *CJ* 59, pp. 49-57.
L. Edmunds (1975) *Chance and Intelligence in Thucydides.* Cambridge, Mass.
—— (1980) 'Aristophanes' Acharnians.' *YCS* 26, pp. 1-41.
A. Edwards (1985) *Achilles in the Odyssey: Ideologies of Heroism in the Epic.* Königstein.
M. Edwards (1990) 'Neoanalysis and Beyond.' *CA* 9, pp. 311-25.
V. Ehrenberg (1951) *The People of Aristophanes: A Sociology of Attic Old Comedy.* Oxford.
—— (1968) *From Solon to Socrates.* London
G. Elwert (1987) 'Ausdehnung der Käuflichkeit und Einbettung der Wirtschaft: Markt und Moralökonomie.' In K. Heinemann (ed.), *Soziologie wirtschaftlichen Handelns.* Opladen, pp. 300-21.
B. Fehr (1977) *Bewegungsweisen und Verhaltensideale.* Bad Bramstedt.
N. Felson-Rubin (1993) 'Bakhtinian Alterity, Homeric Raport.' *Arethusa* 26, pp. 159-71.
B. Fenik (1974) *Studies in the Odyssey.* Hermes Einzelschriften 30. Stuttgart
J. Ferguson (1958) *Moral Values in the Ancient World.* London.
T.J. Figueira (1984) 'Karl Polanyi and Ancient Greek Trade: The Port of Trade'. *AW* 10, pp. 15-30.
T.J. Figueira & G. Nagy (eds.) (1985) *Theognis of Megara.* Baltimore.
M.I. Finley (1951) 'Some Problems of Greek Law: A Consideration of Pringsheim on Sale.' *Seminar* 9, pp. 72-91.
—— (1952) *Studies in Land and Credit in Ancient Athens. 500-200 BC: The Horos Inscriptions.* New Brunswick.
—— (1962) 'Classical Greece.' In *Proceedings of the International Conference of Economic History.* Vol. I. Aix-en-Provence, pp. 597-607.
—— (1968) 'Slavery.' *International Encyclopedia of the Social Sciences* 14, pp. 307-13.
—— (1970) 'Aristotle and Economic Analysis.' *P&P* 47, pp. 3-25.
—— (1975) 'The Alienability of Land in Ancient Greece.' In id., *The Use and Abuse of History.* London, pp. 153-60.
—— (1978) *The World of Odysseus* [1954]. Harmondsworth.
—— (1981) *Economy and Society in Ancient Greece.* London 1981.
—— (1981a) 'Land, Debt and the Man of Property in Classical Athens.' In id., (1981), pp. 62-76.
—— (1981b) 'Marriage, Sale and Gift in the Homeric World.' In id., (1981), pp. 233-45.
—— (1981c) 'Was Greek Civilization Based on Slave Labour?' In id., (1981), pp. 97-115.
—— (1981d) 'The Ancient City.' In id., (1981), pp. 3-21.
—— (1981e) 'The Servile Statuses of Ancient Greece.' In id., (1981), pp. 133-49.
—— (1981f) 'Debt Bondage and the Problem of Slavery.' In id., (1981), pp. 150-66.
—— (1985) *The Ancient Economy* [1973]. London.
R. Firth (1939) *Primitive Polynesian Economy.* New York.
—— (ed.) (1967) *Economic Anthropology.* London.
N.R.F. Fisher (1976) *Social Values in Classical Athens.* Dent.

—— (1992) *Hubris*. Warminster.
H.P. Foley (1978) 'Reverse Similes and Sex Roles in the Odyssey.' *Arethusa* 11, pp. 7-26.
M. Foucault (1970) *The Order of Things* (trans. from French orig. 1966). London.
J.L. Fraisse (1974) *Philia: La notion d'amitié dans la philosophie antique*. Paris.
D. Frame (1978) *The Myth of Return in Early Greek Epic*. New Haven.
E.D. Francis (1990) *Image and Idea in Fifth-Century Athens: Art and Literature* (ed. M. Vickers). London.
J.M. Freyman (1976) 'The Generation Gap in the *Agamemnon*.' In S. Bertman (ed.), *The Conflict of Generations in Ancient Greece and Rome*. Amsterdam, pp. 65-74.
F. Frontisi-Ducroux & F. Lissarrague (1990) 'From Ambiguity to Ambivalence: A Dionysiac Excursion through the Anakreontic Vases.' In Halperin et al. (1990), pp. 211-56.
A.E. Furtwängler (1982) 'Griechische Vieltypenprägung und Münzbeamte.' *SNR* 61, pp. 19-24.
Y. Garlan (1973) 'La place de l'économie dans les sociétés anciennes.' *La Pensée* 171, pp. 118-27.
—— (1979) 'Signification historique de la piraterie grecque.' *DHA* 4, pp. 1-16.
—— (1988) *Slavery in Ancient Greece*. Ithaca and London.
—— (1989) *Guerre et économie en Grèce ancienne*. Paris.
N. Garnham & R. Williams (1980) 'Pierre Bourdieu and the Sociology of Culture: An Introduction.' *Media, Culture and Society* 2, pp. 207-33.
P.D.A. Garnsey (1988) *Famine and Food Supply in the Graeco-Roman World*. Cambridge.
P. Gauthier (1985) *Les cités grecques et leurs bienfaiteurs (IVe-Ie siècle avant J.-C.)*. BCH Suppl. XII. Paris
P. Geary (1986) 'Sacred Commodities: The Circulation of Medieval Relics.' In Appadurai (1986), pp. 169-91.
C. Geertz (1963) *Peddlers and Princes*. Berkeley.
—— (1979) 'Suq: the Bazaar Economy in Sefrou.' In C. Geertz, H. Geertz & L. Rosen, *Meaning and Order in Moroccan Society*. Cambridge, pp. 123-244.
A. Gell (1982) 'The Market Wheel: Symbolic Aspects of an Indian Tribal Market.' *Man* 17, pp. 470-91.
B. Gentili (1981) 'Verità e accordo contrattuale (*sunthesis*) in Pindaro fr. 205 (Sn.).' *ICS* 6, pp. 215-20.
—— (1988) *Poetry and its Public in Ancient Greece*. Baltimore and London.
E. Gerhard (1858) *Auserlesene Vasenbilder*. Vol. IV. Berlin.
L. Gernet (1933) 'Comment charactériser l'économie de la Grèce antique?' *Annales d'histoire économique et sociale* 2, pp. 561-6.
—— (1955) 'Le droit de la vente et la notion du contrat en Grèce après M. Pringsheim.' In id., *Droit et société en Grèce ancienne*. Paris, pp. 201-24.
—— (1981) *The Anthropology of Ancient Greece* (trans. from French orig. 1968). Baltimore and London.
—— (1981a) 'Value in Greek Myth' [1948]. In Gordon (1981), pp. 111-46.
—— (1981b) 'Law and Pre-law in Ancient Greece' [1948/9]. In id., (1981), pp. 143-215.
—— (1981c) 'Religion and Society in Ancient Greece.' In id. (1981), pp. 3-12.
—— (1981d) 'The Nobility.' In id. (1981), pp. 279-88.
—— (1981e) 'Things Visible and Things Invisible.' In id., (1981), pp. 343-51.
G.-F. Gianotti (1975) *Per una poetica Pindarica*. Turin.

D.W.J. Gill (1988a) 'The Distribution of Greek Vases and Long Distance Trade.' In Christiansen & Melander (1988), pp. 175-85.
—— (1988b) 'Expressions of Wealth: Greek Art and Society.' *Antiquity* 62, pp. 735-43.
—— (1988c) 'The Trade in Greek Decorated Pottery: Some Corrections.' *OJA* 7, pp. 369-70.
—— (1991) 'Pots and Trade: Spacefillers or Objets d'art?' *JHS* 111, pp. 29-47.
M. Godelier (1977) 'Salt Money and the Circulation of Commodities among the Baruya of New Guinea.' In id., *Perspectives in Marxist Anthropology*. Cambridge, pp. 127-51.
—— (1978) 'Politics as Infrastructure: An Anthropologist's Thoughts on the Example of Classical Greece and the Notions of Relations of Production and Economic Determinism.' In J. Friedman, M.J. Rowlands (eds.), *The Evolution of Social Systems*. London, pp. 13-28.
—— (1986) *The Mental and the Material* (trans. M. Thom; French orig. 1984). London.
R.F. Goheen (1951) *The Imagery of Sophocles' Antigone*. Princeton.
M. Golden (1984) 'Slavery and Homosexuality at Athens.' *Phoenix* 38, pp. 308-24.
S. Goldhill (1984) *Language, Sexuality, Narrative: the 'Oresteia'*. Cambridge.
—— (1986) *Reading Greek Tragedy*. Cambridge.
—— (1990) 'The Great Dionysia and Civic Ideology.' In Winkler & Zeitlin (1990), pp. 98-129.
—— (1991) *The Poet's Voice*. Cambridge.
J.R. Goody (1975) 'Bridewealth and Dowry in Africa and Eurasia.' In J. Goody & S.J. Tambiah (eds.), *Bridewealth and Dowry. Cambridge Papers of Social Anthropology* 7, pp. 1-58.
—— (1990) *The Oriental, the Ancient and the Primitive*. Cambridge.
B.L. Gordon (1961) 'Aristotle, Schumpeter and the Metallist Tradition.' *Quarterly Journal of Economics* 75, pp. 608-14.
—— (1963) 'Aristotle and the Economic Problem in Greek Thought.' *Rev. Soc. Econ.*, pp. 147-156.
—— (1975) *Economic Analysis before Adam Smith*. New York.
R.L. Gordon (ed.)(1981) *Myth, Religion and Society*. Cambridge.
J.P. Gould (1991) *Give and Take in Herodotus*. Myres Memorial Lecture. Oxford.
A.W. Gouldner (1960) 'The Norm of Reciprocity.' *American Sociological Review* 25, pp. 165-78.
M. Granovetter (1985) 'Economic Action and Social Structure: The Problem of Embeddedness.' *Am. Journ. Soc.* 91, pp. 481-510.
C.H. Grayson (1974) *Greek Weighing*. Unpublished D.Phil. thesis. Oxford.
C.A. Gregory (1980) 'Gifts to Men and Gifts to Gods: Capital Accumulation in Contemporary Papua.' *Man* 15, pp. 626-52.
—— (1982) *Gifts and Commodities*. London.
P. Grierson (1977) *The Origins of Money*. London.
J. Griffin (1980) *Homer on Life and Death*. Oxford.
F. Gschnitzer (1965) 'Basileus: Ein terminologischer Beitrag zur Frühgeschichte des Königtums bei den Griechen'. In *Festschrift für L.C. Franz.*, pp. 99ff.
S. Gudeman (1985) 'Economic Anthropology.' In A. & J. Kuper, *The Social Science Encyclopedia*. London, pp. 222-3.
—— (1986) *Economics as Culture*. London.
H. Gundert (1933) *Pindar und sein Dichterberuf*. Frankfurt.
W.K.C. Guthrie (1971) *The Sophists*. Cambridge.
S. Gzella (1971) 'The Fee in Ancient Greek Literature.' *Eos* 59, pp. 189-202.

R. Hägg (1987) 'Gifts to the Heroes in Geometric and Archaic Greece.' In Linders & Nordquist (1987), pp. 93-9.
D.M. Halperin (1990) *One Hundred Years of Homosexuality*. London.
D.M. Halperin, J.J. Winkler & F. Zeitlin (eds.) (1990) *Before Sexuality*. Princeton.
R. Hamilton (1979) 'Euripides' Cyclopean Symposium.' *Phoenix* 33, pp. 287-92.
A.R. Hands (1968) *Charities and Social Aid in Greece and Rome*. London.
L. Hannestad (1988) 'The Athenian Potter and the Home Market.' In Christiansen & Melander (1988), pp. 223-30.
A.R.W. Harrison (1968) *The Law of Athens*. Vol. I. Oxford.
K. Hart (1982) 'On Commoditisation.' In E. Goody (ed.), *From Craft to Industry*. Cambridge, pp. 38-49.
—— (1986) 'Heads or Tails? Two Sides of the Coin.' *Man* 21, pp. 637-56.
D. Harvey (1985) 'Dona Ferentes. Some Aspects of Bribery in Greek Politics.' In Cartledge & Harvey (1985), pp. 76-117.
F. Heinimann (1945) *'Nomos' und 'Physis'*. Darmstadt.
R. Herbig (1954) 'Verkannte Paare.' In *Neue Beiträge zur klassischen Altertumswissenschaft. Festschrift für B. Schweitzer*. Stuttgart, pp. 270-1.
G. Herman (1987) *Ritualised Friendship in the Greek City*. Cambridge.
E. Herring (1991) 'Power Relations in Iron Age Southeast Etruria.' In E. Herring, R. Whitehouse J. Wilkins (eds.) *The Archaeology of Power*. London, pp. 117-33.
W.E. Higgins (1978) 'Double-Dealing Ares in the *Oresteia*.' *CP* 73, pp. 24-35.
P. Hill (1986) *Development Economics on Trial*. Cambridge.
R. Hodges (1987) *Primitive and Peasant Markets*. Oxford.
H. Hoffmann (1974) 'Hahnenkampf in Athen.' *RA*, pp. 195-220.
—— (1977) *Sexual and Asexual Pursuits*. Occasional Paper of the Royal Anthropological Institute of Great Britain and Ireland 34. Dublin.
—— (1980) 'Knotenpunkte. Zur Bedeutungsstruktur griechischer Vasenbilder.' *Hephaistos* 2, pp. 127-53.
—— (1988) 'Why Did the Greeks Need Imagery?' *Hephaistos* 9, pp. 143-62.
D.G. Hogarth (1908) *The Archaic Artemisium*. London.
H.G. Hollein (1988) *Bürgerbild und Bildwelt der attischen Demokratie auf den rotfigurigen Vasen des 6.-4. Jh. v. Chr.* Frankfurt.
R.R. Holloway (1971) 'An Archaic Hoard from Crete and the Early Aeginetan Coinage.' *ANSMusN* 17, pp. 1-21.
—— (1981) 'The Date of the First Greek Coins: Some Arguments from Style and Hoards.' *RBN* 130, pp. 5-18.
G.C. Homans (1968) 'Social Behaviour as Exchange.' In E.E. LeClair & H. Schneider (eds.), *Economic Anthropology*. Toronto and London, pp. 109-21.
J.T. Hooker (1974) '*Charis* and *Aretê* in Thucydides.' *Hermes* 102, pp. 164-9.
—— (1987) 'Homeric *Philos*.' *Glotta* 65, pp. 44-65.
—— (1989) 'Gifts in Homer.' *BICS* 36, pp. 79-90.
R.J. Hopper (1968) 'Observations on the Wappenmünzen.' In C.M. Kraay & G.K. Jenkins (eds.), *Essays in Greek Coinage Presented to Stanley Robinson*. Oxford, pp. 26-38.
S. Hornblower (1987) *Thucydides*. London.
S. Howell (1989) 'Of Persons and Things. Exchange and Valuables Among the Lio of Eastern Indonesia.' *Man* 24, pp. 419-38.
C.J. Howgego (1990) 'Why did Ancient States Strike Coins ?' *NC* 50, pp. 1-26.
C. Humphrey (1985) 'Barter and Economic Disintegration.' *Man* 20, pp. 48-72
C. Humphrey & S. Hugh-Jones (1992) (eds.) *Barter, Exchange and Value: An Anthropological Approach*. Cambridge.
S.C. Humphreys (1978) *Anthropology and the Greeks*. London.

—— (1983) 'Public and Private Interests in Classical Athens.' In id., *The Family, Women and Death: Comparative Studies*. London, pp. 22-32.
E.L. Hussey (1985) 'Thucydidean History and Democritean Theory.' In Cartledge & Harvey (1985), pp. 118-38.
H. Hutter (1978) *Politics as Friendship: The Origins of Classical Notions of Politics in the Theory and Practice of Friendship*. Waterloo, Ontario.
L. Hyde (1979) 'Some Food We Do Not Eat: Gift Exchange and the Imagination.' *Kenyon Review* n.s. 1, pp. 56-67.
—— (1983) *The Gift: Imagination and the Erotic Life of Property*. New York.
L.H. Jeffery & A. Mopurgo-Davies (1970) '*Poinikastas* and *poinikazein*: BM 1969 4-2,1. A New Archaic Inscription from Crete.' *Kadmos* 9, pp. 118-54.
I. Jenkins (1985) 'The Ambiguity of Greek Textiles.' *Arethusa* 18, pp. 109-32.
D. Johnson (1981) 'The Wool Basket and the Money Pouch: Textile Working as a Home Industry in Ancient Greece.' *Equity*, pp. 26-33.
A.W. Johnston (1979) *Trademarks on Greek Vases*. Warminster.
W. Jongman (1988) *The Economy and Society of Pompeii*. Amsterdam.
R. Just (1989) *Women in Athenian Law and Life*. London.
S. Kaempf-Dimitriadou (1979) *Die Liebe der Götter in der attischen Kunst*. Bern.
D. Kagan (1982) 'The Dates of the Earliest Coins.' *AJA* 86, pp. 343-60.
S. Karozou (1962) 'Scènes de Palestre.' *BCH* 86, pp. 430-66.
E.C. Keuls (1983) 'Attic Vase-Painting and the Home Textile Industry.' In W.G. Moon (ed.), *Ancient Greek Art and Iconography*. Wisconsin, pp. 209-30.
—— (1985) *The Reign of the Phallus*. New York.
G.S. Kirk (1962) *The Songs of Homer*. Cambridge.
—— (1973) *Myth: Its Meaning and Function in Ancient and Other Cultures*. Cambridge.
—— (1976) *Homer and the Oral Tradition*. Cambridge.
—— (1985) *The 'Iliad': A Commentary*. Vol. I. Cambridge.
—— (1989) 'Homer'. In P.E. Easterling & B.M.W. Knox, *The Cambridge History of Classical Literature* [1985] Vol. I, Part 1 (pb. ed. Cambridge, pp. 1-50.
G.F. Knapp (1921) *Staatliche Theorie des Geldes*. Munich.
B.M.W. Knox (1989) 'Theognis.' In P.E. Easterling & B.M.W Knox (eds.), *The Cambridge History of Classical Literature*. Vol. I, Part 1 (pb. ed.). Cambridge, pp. 95-105.
G. Koch-Harnack (1983) *Knabenliebe und Tiergeschenke. Ihre Bedeutung im paederastischen Erziehungssystem*. Hamburg.
F. Kolb (1981) *Agora und Theater, Volks- und Festversammlung*. Berlin.
D. Konstan (1990) 'The Anthropology of Euripides' *Kyklôps*.' In Winkler & Zeitlin (1990), pp. 207-27.
I. Kopytoff (1986) 'The Cultural Biography of Things: Commoditisation as Process.' In Appadurai (1986), pp. 64-91.
J. Korver (1942) *De terminologie von het credit-wezen in het Greksch*. Amsterdam.
P. Koslowski (1979) 'Haus und Geld. Zur Aristotelischen Unterscheidung von Politik, Ökonomik und Chrematistik.' *Philosophisches Jahrbuch* 86, pp. 60-83.
C.M. Kraay (1956) 'The Archaic Owls of Athens: Classification and Chronology.' *NC* 16, pp. 43-67.
—— (1964) 'Hoards, Small Change and the Origins of Coinage.' *JHS* 84, pp. 76-91.
—— (1976) *Archaic and Classical Greek Coins*. Berkeley, Los Angeles.
J.H. Kroll (1981), 'From Wappenmünzen to Gorgoneion to Owls.' *ANSMusN* 26, pp. 1-32, pls. 1-2.
J.H. Kroll & N.M. Waggoner (1984) 'Dating the Earliest Coins of Athens, Corinth and Aegina.' *AJA* 88, pp. 325-40.

L. Kurke (1989) '*Kapêleia* and Deceit.' *AJPh* 110, pp. 535-44.
—— (1991) *The Traffic in Praise*. Ithaca and London.
W.K. Lacey (1968) *The Family in Classical Greece*. Ithaca.
S. Langdon (1987) 'Gift Exchange in the Geometric Sanctuaries.' In Linders & Nordquist (1987), pp. 105-13.
O. Langhohn (1983) *Wealth and Money in the Aristotelian Tradition*. Oslo.
E. Laroche (1949) 'Histoire de la racine 'nem-' en grec ancien.' *Études et commentaires* IV. Paris.
R. Lattimore (1953) *Aeschylus, 'Oresteia'*. Chicago.
B. Laum (1924) *Heiliges Geld*. Munich.
—— (1930) *Über das Wesen des Münzgeldes*. Halle.
—— (1951-2) Über die soziale Funktion der Münze. Ein Beitrag zur Soziologie des Geldes.' *Finanzarchiv* 13, pp. 120 ff.
J.R. Leach & E.R. Leach (eds.) (1983) *The Kula: New Perspectives in Massim Exchange*. Cambridge.
W. Leaf (1900) *The Iliad*. London.
M. Lefkowitz (1980) 'Autobiographical Fiction in Pindar.' *HSPh* 84, pp. 29-49.
J. Le Goff (1986) *La bourse et la vie*. Paris.
D.B. Levine (1985) 'Symposium and the Polis.' In Figueira & Nagy (1985), pp. 176-96.
C. Lévi-Strauss (1969) *The Elementary Structures of Kinship* (trans. J.H. Bell, J.R. von Sturmer, R. Needham; French orig. 1949). Boston.
E. Lévy (1976) *Athènes devant la défaite de 404 av. J.-C.* Athens.
H.L. Levy (1963) 'The Odyssean Suitors and the Host-Guest Relationship.' *TAPhA* 94, pp. 145-53.
D.M. Lewis (1989) 'Persian Gold in Greek International Relations.' *REA* 91, pp. 227-34.
J.M. Lewis (1985) 'Eros and the Polis in Theognis Book II.' In Figueira & Nagy (1985), pp. 197-222.
T.J. Lewis (1978) 'Acquisition and Anxiety: Aristotle's Case Against the Market.' *Cambridge Journal of Economics* 11, pp. 69-90.
T. Linders (1987) 'Gods, Gifts, Societies.' In Linders & Nordquist (1987), pp. 115-22.
T. Linders & G. Nordquist (eds.) (1987) *Gifts to the Gods*. Uppsala
F. Lissarrague & A. Schnapp (1981) 'Imagerie des Grecs ou Grèce des images.' *Les temps de la réflexion* 2.
G.E.R. Lloyd (1979) *Magic, Reason and Experience*. Cambridge.
A.A. Long (1970) 'Morals and Values in Homer.' *JHS* 90, pp. 121-39.
E. Löwy (1932) 'Zur Chronologie der frühgriechischen Kunst.' *Sitzungsberichte der Akad. Wiss. Wien phil.-hist. Klasse*. 213.4, pp. 3-41.
N. Loraux (1981) *Les enfants d'Athena*. Paris.
—— (1982) '*Ponos*. Sur quelques difficultés de la peine comme nom de travail.' *Annali del Istituto Universitario Orientale di Napoli. Archeologia et Storia Antica* 4, pp. 171-92.
—— (1986) *The Invention of Athens*. Cambridge, Mass.
A.B. Lord (1991) *Epic Singers and Oral Tradition*. Ithaca and London.
S.T. Lowry (1969) 'Aristotle's Mathematical Analysis of Exchange.' *History of Political Economy* 1, pp. 44-66.
—— (1974) 'Aristotle's Natural Limit and the Economics of Price Regulation.' *GRBS* 15, pp. 57-63.
—— (1979) 'Recent Literature on Ancient Greek Economic Thought.' *Journal of Economic Literature*. 17, pp. 65-86.

—— (1987) *The Archaeology of Economic Ideas*. Durham, N.Y.
J.V. Luce (1978) 'The Polis in Homer and Hesiod.' *PRIA* 78, pp. 1-15.
M. Lynn-George (1988) *Epos: Word, Narrative and the 'Iliad'*. Basingstoke.
M. Maass (1972) *Die Prohedrie des Dionysostheaters in Athen*. Munich.
J. MacCormack (1976) 'Reciprocity'. *Man* 11, pp. 89-104.
D.M. MacDowell (1978) *Law in Classical Athens*. London.
—— (1983) 'Athenian Laws about Bribing.' *RIDA* 30, pp. 57-78.
A. Macfarlane (1985) 'The Root of All Evil.' In D. Parkin (ed.), *The Anthropology of Evil*. Oxford, pp. 65-85.
C. MacLeod (1982) 'Politics and the *Oresteia*.' *JHS* 102, pp. 124-44.
A.L. Macrabis (1984) 'Comparative Economic Value: The Oxen-Worth.' In K. Rigsby (ed.), *Studies Presented to Sterling Dow on his 80th Birthday*. Durham, N.Y., pp. 211-15.
H. Maehler (1963) *Die Auffassung des Dichterberufs im frühen Griechentum bis zur Zeit Pindars*. Göttingen.
G. Majorana (1936) 'Le teorie della moneta e del valore in Aristotele.' *Giornali delle Economisti* 31, pp. 51ff.
S.W. Manning (1992) 'Archaeology and the World of Homer: Introduction to a Past and Present Discipline.' In C. Emlyn-Jones, L. Hardwick & J. Purkis (eds.) *Homer: Readings and Images*. London, pp. 117-42.
W. Marg (1957) *Homer über die Dichtung*. Münster.
M.M. Markle (1985) 'Jury Pay and Assembly Pay at Athens.' In Cartledge & Harvey (1985), pp. 289-326.
R. Martin (1951) *Recherches sur l'agora grecque*. Paris.
K. Marx (1962) *Das Kapital*. Vol. I [1867]. Berlin.
—— (1968) *Ökonomisch-philosophische Manuskripte* [1844]. Berlin.
—— (1974) *Grundrisse der Kritik der politischen Ökonomie* [1857-8]. Berlin.
M. Mauss (1914) 'Les origines de la notion de monnaie.' *Anthropologie* 25, Suppl. Paris.
—— (1921) 'Une forme ancienne de contrat chez les Thraces.' *REG* 34, pp. 388-97.
—— (1990) *The Gift* [1925]. (trans. H.D. Hall). London.
S. Meikle (1979) 'Aristotle and the Political Economy of the Polis.' *JHS* 99, pp. 57-73.
—— (1991a) 'Aristotle and Exchange Value.' In D. Keyt and F.D. Miller (eds.) *A Companion to Aristotle's Politics*. Oxford, pp. 156-81.
—— (1991b) 'Aristotle on Equality and Market Exchange.' *JHS* 111, pp. 193-5.
—— (forthcoming) *Aristotle's Economic Thought*. Cambridge.
A. Mele (1979) *Il commercio greco arcaico. Prêxis ed emporie*. Naples.
P.C. Millett (1984) 'Hesiod and His World.' *PCPhS* 30, pp. 84-115.
—— (1989) 'Patronage and Its Avoidance.' In A. Wallace-Hadrill (ed.), *Patronage in Ancient Society*. London, pp. 15-47.
—— (1991a) 'Sale, Credit and Exchange in Athenian Law and Society.' In P. Cartledge, P.C. Millett & S.C. Todd (eds.), *Nomos*. Cambridge, pp. 167-94.
—— (1991b) *Lending and Borrowing in Ancient Athens*. Cambridge.
S.W. Mintz (1959) 'Internal Market Systems as Mechanisms of Social Articulation.' *Proceedings of the American Ethnographical Society*. Seattle, pp. 20-30.
—— (1967) 'Pratik: Haitian Personal Economic Relationships.' In M.D. Diaz & G.M. Foster (eds.), *Peasant Society: A Reader*. Boston, pp. 98-110.
F.W. Mitchel (1964) 'Derkylos of Hagnous and the Date of IG II^2 1187.' *Hesperia* 33, pp. 337-53.
I. Morris (1986a) 'Gift and Commodity in Archaic Greece.' *Man* 21, pp. 1-17.
—— (1986b) 'The Use and Abuse of Homer.' *CA* 5, pp. 81-129.

—— (1989) 'Circulation, Deposition and the Formation of the Greek Iron Age.' *Man* 24, pp. 502-19.
G. Most (1985) *The Measures of Praise: Structure and Function in Pindar's Second Pythian and Seventh Nemean Odes*. Göttingen.
S. Murnaghan (1987) *Disguise and Recognition in the Odyssey*. Princeton.
M. Müller (1966) *Athene als göttliche Helferin in der Odyssee*. Heidelberg.
R.W. Müller (1977) *Geld und Geist*. Frankfurt.
G. Nagy (1979) *The Best of the Achaeans*. Baltimore and London.
—— (1981) 'The Deceptive Gift in Greek Mythology.' *Arethusa* 14, pp. 191-204.
—— (1983a) '*Sêma* and *Noêsis:* Some Illustrations.' *Arethusa* 16, pp. 35-55.
—— (1983b) 'On the Death of Sarpedon.' In Rubino & Shermaldine (1983), pp. 189-217.
—— (1985) 'A Poet's Vision of His City.' In Figueira & Nagy (1985), pp. 28-73.
H.-J. Newiger (1957) *Metapher und Allegorie. Studien zu Aristophanes*. Munich.
—— (1980) 'War and Peace in the Comedy of Aristophanes.' *YCS* 26, pp. 219-317.
M.P. Nilsson (1951) *Cults, Myths, Oracles and Politics in Ancient Greece*. Lund.
W. Nippel (1982) 'Die Heimkehr der Argonauten von der Südsee.' *Chiron* 12, pp. 1-39.
—— (1990) *Griechen, Barbaren und 'Wilde'. Alte Geschichte und Sozialanthropologie*. Frankfurt.
F.J. Nisetich (1977) 'Convention and Occasion in *Isthmian* 2.' *CSCA* 10, pp. 133-56.
N.J. Oates (1963) *Aristotle and the Problem of Value*. Princeton.
J. Ober (1989) *Mass and Elite in Democratic Athens*. Princeton.
M.J. Osborne (1981) 'Entertainment in the Prytaneion.' *ZPE* 41, pp. 153-70.
R.G. Osborne (1985) *Demos: The Discovery of Classical Attika*. Cambridge.
—— (1990) 'The Demos and its Divisions in Classical Athens.' In O. Murray & S. Price (eds.), *The Greek City. From Homer to Alexander*. Oxford, pp. 265-93.
—— (1991) 'Pride and Prejudice, Sense and Subsistence: Exchange and Society in the Greek City'. In J. Rich and A. Wallace-Hadrill (eds.) *City and Country in the Ancient World*. London, pp. 119-46.
L. Paganelli (1979a) '*Ploutos* in Eur. *Cycl.* 316.' *Siculorum Gymnasium* 32, pp. 217-22.
—— (1979b) *Echi storico politici nel Cyclope euripideo*. Padova.
A.M. Parry (1971) (ed.). *The Making of Homeric Verse: The Collected Papers of Milman Parry*. Oxford.
—— (1980) *'Logos' and 'Ergon' in Thucydides* [1957]. Hildesheim.
J. Parry (1986) 'The Gift, the Indian Gift, and the "Indian Gift".' *Man* 21, pp. 453-73.
—— (1989) 'On the Moral Perils of Exchange.' In Parry & Bloch (1989), pp. 64-93.
J. Parry & M. Bloch (eds.) (1989) *Money and the Morality of Exchange*. Cambridge.
C. Pavese (1966) '*Chrêmata, chrêmat' anêr* ed il motivo della liberalità nella secondo Isthmia di Pindaro.' *QUCC* 2, pp. 103-12.
S. Perlman (1976) 'On Bribing Greek Ambassadors.' *GRBS* 17, pp. 223-33.
B.E. Perry (1937) 'The Early Greek Capacity for Viewing Things Separately.' *TAPhA* 68, pp. 403-27.
A. Pickard-Cambridge (1968) *The Dramatic Festivals of Athens* (rev. ed. by J. Gould and D.M. Lewis). Oxford.
A.J. Podlecki (1961) 'Guest-Gifts and Nobodies in *Odyssey* 9.' *Phoenix* 15, pp. 125-33.
M. Pohlenz (1953) '*Nomos* and *Phusis*.' *Hermes* 81, pp. 418-35.
K. Polanyi (1944) *The Great Transformation*. New York.

—— (1957a) 'Aristotle Discovers Economic Analysis.' In Polanyi, Arensberg & Pearson (1957), pp. 65-94.
—— (1957b) 'The Economy as Instituted Process.' In Polanyi, Arensberg & Pearson (1957), pp. 243-70.
—— (1960) 'On the Comparative Treatment of Economic Institutions in Antiquity, with Illustrations from Athens, Mycene and Alalakh.' In C.H. Adams & R.M. Kraeling (eds.), *City Invincible*. Chicago, pp. 329-50.
—— (1977) *The Livelihood of Man*. New York.
K. Polanyi, C. Arensberg & H.W. Pearson (1957) *Trade and Market in the Early Empires*. Glencoe, Ill.
M. Poster (1988) *Jean Baudrillard: Selected Writings*. Cambridge.
A.W. Price (1989) *Love and Friendship in Plato and Aristotle*. Oxford.
M. Price (1983) 'Thoughts on the Beginnings of Coinage.' In C. Brooke et al. (eds.), *Studies in Numismatic Method Presented to Philip Grierson*. Cambridge, pp. 1-10.
F. Pringsheim (1950) *The Greek Law of Sale*. Oxford.
P. Pucci (1987) *Odysseus 'Polutropos'. Intertextual Readings in the 'Odyssey' and the 'Iliad'*. Ithaca and London.
A.H. Quiggin (1949) *A Survey of Primitive Money*. London.
B. Qviller (1981) 'The Dynamics of the Homeric Society.' *Symbolae Osloenses* 56, pp. 109-55.
T. Rasmussen & N. Spivey (eds.) (1991) *Looking at Greek Vases*. Cambridge.
O. Ravel (1936) *Les 'Poulins' de Corinthe*. Vol. 1. Basel.
G. Redard (1953) *Recherches sur 'chrê', 'chrêstai': étude semantique*. Paris.
J.R. Redfield (1975) *Nature and Culture in the 'Iliad'*. Chicago.
—— (1983) 'The Economic Man.' In Rubino & Shermeldine (1983), pp. 218-47.
—— (1986) 'The Development of the Market in Ancient Greece.' In B.L. Anderson & A.J. Latham (eds.), *Market in History*. London, pp. 29-58.
C. Reinsberg (1989) *Ehe, Hetärentum und Knabenliebe im antiken Griechenland*. Munich.
C. Renfrew (1986) 'Varna and the Emergence of Wealth in Prehistoric Europe.' In Appadurai (1986), pp. 141-68.
P.J. Rhodes (1985) *The Athenian Boule*. Oxford.
—— (1988) *Thucydides. History II*. Warminster.
W. Ridgeway (1892) *The Origins of Metallic Currency and Weight Standards*. Cambridge.
M. Robertson (1991) 'Adopting an Approach I.' In Rasmussen & Spivey (1991), pp. 1-12.
G. Rodenwaldt (1932) 'Spinnende Hetären.' *AA* 47, pp. 7-21.
J. Röpke (1969) 'Nationalönomie und Ethnologie.' *Sociologus* 19, pp. 101-34.
C.J. Rowe (1983) 'The Nature of Homeric Morality.' In Rubino & Shermaldine (1983), pp. 248-75.
M.J. Rowlands (1980) 'Kinship, Alliance and Exchange in the European Bronze Age.' In J. Barrett & R. Bradley (eds.), *Settlement and Society in the Later Bronze Age. BAR* 83, Oxford, pp. 15-55.
H.J. Rose (1956) 'Divine Disguises.' *HThR* 49, pp. 63-72.
—— (1957-8) *A Commentary on the Surviving Plays of Aeschylus*. Amsterdam.
C.A. Rubino & C.W. Shermaldine (eds.) (1983) *Approaches to Homer*. Austin.
L. Ruggin (ed.) (1982) *Genesi dello spazio economica*. Naples.
—— (1982a) 'Aristotele e la genesi dello spazio economica.' In id. (1982), pp. 49-117.
E. Ruschenbusch (1966) *'Solônos Nomoi': Die Fragmente des Solonischen Gesetzeswerkes mit einer Text-und Überlieferungsgeschichte*. Wiesbaden.

K. Rutter (1981) 'Early Greek Coinage and the Influence of the Athenian State.' In B. Cunliffe (ed.) *Coinage and Society in Britain and Gaul: Some Current Problems.* London, pp. 1-9.
M. Sahlins (1972) *Stone Age Economics.* London.
R.P. Saller (1982) *Personal Patronage under the Early Empire.* Cambridge.
W. Schadewaldt (1959) 'Kleiderdinge: Zur Analyse der *Odyssee.*' *Hermes* 87, pp. 13-26.
I. Scheibler (1983) *Griechische Töpferkunst.* Munich.
E.L. Schieffelin (1980) 'Reciprocity and the Construction of Reality.' *Man* 15, pp. pp. 503ff.
A. Schnapp (1988) 'Why Did the Greeks Need Images?' In Christiansen & Melander (1988), pp. 568-87.
H. Schneider (1989) *Das griechische Technikverständnis.* Darmstadt.
W. Schuller (ed.) (1982) *Korruption im Altertum.* Munich.
A.N. Schulski (1974) *Economic Doctrine in Aristotle's Politics.* Presented at the Conference for the Study of Political Thought. Toronto.
E. Schwimmer (1979) 'Reciprocity and Structure: A Semiotic Analysis of Some Orokaiva Exchange Data.' *Man* 14, pp. 271-85.
S. Scully (1981), 'The Bard as the Custodian of Homeric Society.' *QUCC* 8, pp. 67-83.
—— (1990) *Homer and the Sacred City.* Ithaca and London.
R.A.S. Seaford (1981), 'Dionysiac Drama and the Dionysiac Mysteries.' *CQ* 31, pp. 252-75.
—— (1984) *The 'Cyclops'.* Oxford.
—— (1987) 'The Tragic Wedding.' *JHS* 107, pp. 106-30.
—— (1994) *Reciprocity and Ritual: Homer and Tragedy in the Developing City State.* Oxford.
C.P. Segal (1962) 'The Phaeacians and the Symbolism of Odysseus' Return.' *Arion* 1.4, pp. 17-63.
—— (1974) 'Eros and Incantation: Sappho and Oral Poetry.' *Arethusa* 7, pp. 139-60.
—— (1981) *Tragedy and Civilisation: An Interpretation of Sophocles.* Baltimore.
—— (1983) '*Kleos* and its Ironies in the *Odyssey.*' *AC* 52, pp. 22-47.
B. Seidensticker (ed.) (1989) *Das Satyrspiel.* Darmstadt.
E. Seitz (1950) *Die Stellung der Telemachie im Aufbau der 'Odyssee'.* Marburg.
C.T. Seltman (1924) *Athens: Its History and Coinage Before the Persian Invasion.* Cambridge.
—— (1954) *Greek Coins.* London.
H.A. Shapiro (1981) 'Courtship Scenes in Attic Vase Painting.' *AJA* 85, pp. 131-43.
R.A. Sharp (1986) 'Gift Exchange and the Economy of Spirit in the Merchant of Venice.' *Modern Philology* 83, pp. 250-65.
B.D. Shaw (1982/83) 'Eaters of Flesh, Drinkers of Milk: The Ancient Mediterranean Ideology of the Pastoral Nomad.' *Anc. Soc.* 13/14, pp. 5-31.
M. Shell (1978) *The Economy of Literature.* Baltimore.
—— (1982) *Money, Language and Thought.* Berkeley, L.A.
E.S. Sherratt (1990) 'Reading the Texts: Archaeology and the Homeric Question.' *Antiquity* 64, pp. 807-24.
A. Shewan (1926-7) 'Telemachus at Sparta.' *CJ* 22, pp. 31-7.
M. Silver (1992) *Taking Myth Economically.* Leiden.
G. Simmel (1989) *Philosophie des Geldes* [1900]. Frankfurt.
K. Singer (1959) 'An Inquiry into the Beginning of Economic Thought and Language.' *Kyklos* 11, pp. 29-55.
D. Sinos (1980) *Achilles, Patroklos and the Meaning of 'Philos'.* Innsbruck.

N. Smith (1987) 'The Two Economies of *Measure for Measure.*' *English* 36, pp. 197-222.
A.M. Snodgrass (1971) *The Dark Age of Greece.* Edinburgh.
—— (1974) 'An Historical Homeric Society?' *JHS* 94, pp. 114-25.
—— (1980) *Archaic Greece.* London.
J.M. Snyder (1981) 'The Web of Song: Weaving Imagery in Homer and the Lyric Poets.' *CJ* 76, pp. 193-8.
A. Sommerstein (1980) *Aristophanes, 'Acharnians'.* Warminster.
P. Soudek (1952) 'Aristotle's Theory of Exchange: An Inquiry into the Origin of Economic Analysis.' *PAPhS* 96, pp. 45-75.
P. Spahn (1984) 'Die Anfänge der antiken Ökonomik.' *Chiron* 14, pp. 301-23.
J. Spier (1990) 'Emblems in Archaic Greece.' *BICS* 37, pp. 107-29.
P. Stallybrass & A. White (1986), *The Politics and Poetics of Transgression.* London.
P.V. Stanley (1976) *Ancient Greek Market Regulations and Controls.* Diss. Berkeley, L.A.
C.G. Starr (1977) *The Economic and Social Growth of Early Greece 800-500 BC.* New York.
—— (1986) *Individual and Community: The Rise of the Polis.* Oxford.
D. Stewart (1976) *The Disguised Guest: Rank, Role and Identity in the Odyssey.* Lewisburg.
M. Strathern (1984a) 'Marriage Exchanges: a Melanesian Comment.' *American Review of Anthropology* 13, pp. 41-73.
—— (1984b) 'Subject or Object: Women and the Circulation of Valuables in Highlands New Guinea.' In R. Hirschon (ed.), *Women and Property. Women as Property.* London and Canberra, pp. 158-75.
—— (1988) *The Gender of the Gift.* California.
—— (1992) 'Qualified Value: The Perspective of Gift Exchange.' In Humphrey & Hugh-Jones (1992), pp. 169-91.
R. Stupperich (1977) *Staatsbegräbnis und Privatgrabmal.* Münster.
J. Svenbro (1976) *La parole et le marbre.* Lund.
J. Taillardat (1961) *Les images d'Aristophane: Études de langue et de style.* Paris.
O.P. Taplin (1980) 'The Shield of Achilles within the *Iliad.*' *G&R* 27, pp. 1-21.
C.G. Thomas (1966a) 'The Roots of Homeric Kingship.' *Historia* 15, pp. 387-407.
—— (1966b) 'Homer and the Polis.' *P&P* 21, pp. 5ff.
H.A. Thompson (1984) The Athenian Vase-Painters and their Neighbours. In P.M. Rice (ed.), *Pots and Potters.* California, pp. 7-20.
G. Thomson (1966) *The 'Oresteia' of Aeschylus.* Prague and Amsterdam.
S.C. Todd (1993) *The Shape of Athenian Law.* Oxford.
C. Toren (1989) 'Drinking Cash: The Purification of Money through Ceremonial Exchange in Fiji.' In Parry & Bloch (1989), pp. 142-64.
P.N. Ure (1922) *The Origins of Tyranny.* Cambridge.
V. Vanberg (1987) 'Markt, Organisation und Reziprozität.' In K. Heinemann (ed.), *Soziologie wirtschaftlichen Handelns.* Opladen, pp. 263-79.
H. van Effenterre (1973) 'Le contrat de travail du scribe Spensithios.' *BCH* 97, pp. 31-46.
J.-P. Vernant (1956) 'Aspects psychologiques du travail dans la Grèce ancienne.' *La Pensée* 66, pp. 80-4.
—— (1965) *Mythe et pensée chez les Grecs.* Paris.
—— (1965a) 'Travail et nature dans la Grèce ancienne.' In id. (1965), pp. 274-94.
—— (1965b) 'Hestia-Hermes. Sur l'expression religieuse de l'espace et du mouvement chez les grecs.' In id. (1965), pp. 155-201.

—— (1965c) 'La formation de la pensée positive dans la Grèce archaïque.' In id. (1965), pp. 373-402.
—— (1976) 'Some Comments on Class Struggle in Ancient Greece.' *Critique of Anthropology* 7, pp. 67-81.
—— (1977) 'A propos du Promethée d'Hésiode.' *ASNP* 46, pp. 904-44.
—— (1980) *Myth and Society in Ancient Greece.* Bristol.
—— (1989a) 'Food in the Countries of the Sun.' In Detienne & Vernant (1989), pp. 164-9.
—— (1989b) 'At Man's Table.' In Detienne & Vernant (1989), pp. 21-86.
J.-P. Vernant & P. Vidal-Naquet (1981) *Myth and Tragedy in Ancient Greece.* Brighton.
P. Veyne (1976) *Le pain et le cirque.* Paris.
M. Vickers (1984) 'The Influence of Exotic Metals on Attic White Ground Pottery.' In H.A.G. Brijdr (ed.), *Ancient Greek and Related Pottery.* Amsterdam.
—— (1985a) 'Artful Crafts: The Influence of Metalwork on Athenian Pottery.' *JHS* 105, pp. 108-28.
—— (1985b) 'Early Greek Coinage, a Reassessment.' *NC* 145, pp. 1-44.
P. Vidal-Naquet (1963) 'Homère et le monde mycénien.' *Annales ESC* 18, pp. 111-48.
—— (1981a) 'The Black Hunter and the Origins of the Athenian Ephebeia.' In Gordon (1981), pp. 147-62.
—— (1981b) 'Land and Sacrifice in the *Odyssey.* In Gordon (1981), pp. 80-94.
J. Vondeling (1961) 'Eranos.' *Historische Studien* 17. Groningen.
S. von Reden (1995), 'Poetry and its Value – Reconsidered'. *CQ* 45, pp. 1ff.
—— (forthcoming), 'The Commodification of Symbols: Representations of Exchange in Menander.' In C. Gill, N. Postlethwaite, R. Seaford (eds.) *Reciprocity in Ancient Greece.* Oxford.
H. von Steuben (1989) 'Die Agora des Kleisthenes – Zeugnis eines radikalen Wandels?' In W. Schuller et al. (eds.), *Demokratie und Architektur.* Munich, pp. 81-91.
F.T. von Straten (1981) 'Gifts for the Gods.' In H.S. Versnel (ed.), *Faith, Hope and Worship.* Leiden, pp. 65-151 and 285-311.
P. Walcot (1969) '*Chrusea chalkeiôn*: A Further Comment.' *CR* 19, pp. 12ff.
G.R. Walsh (1984) *The Varieties of Enchantment: Early Greek Views of the Nature and Function of Poetry.* Chapel Hill.
H. Wankel (1982) 'Die Korruption im klassischen Athen.' In Schuller (1982), pp. 29-53.
M. Weber (1972) *Wirtschaft und Gesellschaft* [1922]. Tübingen.
T.B.L. Webster (1972) *Potter and Patron in Classical Athens.* London.
L. Weidauer (1975) *Probleme der frühen Elektron Prägung.* Freiburg.
D. Whitehead (1983) 'Competitive Outlay and Community Profit. *Philotimia* in Democratic Athens.' *C & M* 34, pp. 55-74.
E. Will (1954a) 'De l'aspect éthique des origines grecques de la monnaie.' *RH* 212, pp. 209-31.
—— (1954b) 'Trois quarts de siècle des recherches sur l'économie grecque antique.' *Annales ESC* 9, pp. 7-22.
—— (1955a) 'Réflexions et hypothèses sur les origines du monnayage.' *RN* 17, pp. 5-23.
—— (1955b) *Korinthiaka: recherches sur l'histoire et la civilisation de Corinthe des origines aux guerres mediques.* Paris.
—— (1972) *Le monde grec et l'Orient.* Vol. I: *Le Ve siècle.* Paris.
—— (1975a) 'Fonctions de la monnaie dans les cités grecques de l'époque classique.'

In M. Dentzer, Ph. Gauthier & T. Hackens (eds.), *Numismatique Antique: problèmes et méthodes*. Nancy, pp. 233-46.

—— (1975b) 'Notes sur *misthos*.' In J. Bingen, G. Cambier & G. Nachtergael (eds.), *Le monde grec: hommages à Claire Préaux*. Brussels, pp. 426-38.

P.J. Wilson (1991) 'Demosthenes 21 (*Against Medias*): Democratic Abuse.' *PCPhS* 37, pp. 164-95

—— (unpublished) *The Athenian 'Choregia': Power, Wealth and Prestige*. Paper to the Annual Meeting of the Classical Association 1992.

J.J. Winkler (1990) 'Laying Down the Law. The Oversight of Men's Sexual Behaviour in Classical Athens.' In Halperin, Winkler & Zeitlin (1990), pp. 171-209.

J.J. Winkler & F. Zeitlin (eds.) (1990) *Nothing to Do With Dionysos?* Princeton.

L. Woodbury (1968) 'Pindar and the Mercenary Muse: *Isthm*. 2. 1-13.' *TAPhA* 99, pp. 527-42.

R.E. Wycherley (1956) 'The Market of Athens: Topography and Monuments.' *G&R* 3, pp. 2-23.

N. Yalouris (1950) 'Athena als Herrin der Pferde.' *MH* 7, pp. 52-5.

F. Zeitlin (1965) 'The Motif of Corrupted Sacrifice in Aeschylus' *Oresteia*.' *TAPhA* 96, pp. 463-505.

—— (1982) *Under the Sign of the Shield: Semiotics and Aeschylus' 'Seven against Thebes'*. Rome.

T. Zielinski (1924) '*Charis* und *Charites*.' *CQ* 18, pp. 158-62.

Additional Bibliography, 2002

T.O. Beidelman (1989) 'Agonistic Exchange: Homeric Reciprocity and the Heritage of Simmel and Mauss'. *Cultural Anthropology* 4, pp. 227-250.

H. Berking (1996) *Schenken. Zur Anthropologie des Gebens*. Frankfurt.

P. Cartledge (2002) 'The Economy (Economies) of Ancient Greece.' In Scheidel & von Reden (2002) pp. 11-32 (abr. repr. from *Dialogus* 5 [1998], pp. 4-24).

J. Davidson (1997) *Courtesans and Fishcakes: The Consuming Passions of Classical Athens*. London.

J. Davies (1998) 'Ancient Economies: Models and Muddles.' In H. Parkins & C. Smith, *Trade, Traders and the Ancient City*. London, pp. 225-256.

G. Elwert (1991) 'Gabe, Reziprozität, Warentausch. Überlegungen zu einigen Ausdrücken und Begriffen.' In E. Berg, J. Lauth & A. Wimmer (eds) *Ethnologie im Widerstreit. Kontroversen über Macht, Geschäft, Geschlecht in fremden Kulturen*. Festschrift. H. Löffler. München, 159-177.

T. Figueira (1998) *The Power of Money. Coinage and Politics in the Athenian Empire*. Pennsylvania.

A. Gadi, V. Groebner & B. Jussen (2001) (eds) *Negocier le don – Negotiating the Gift*. Göttingen.

C. Gill, N. Postlethwaite & R. Seaford (1998) *Reciprocity in Ancient Greece*. Oxford.

R.W. Hefner (1998) (ed.) *Market Cultures: Society and Morality in New Asian Capitalism*. West View Press.

C. Howgego (1995) *Ancient History from Coins*. London.

L. Kallet-Marx (1993) *Money, Expense and Naval Power in Thucydides' History 1-5.24*. Oxford.

—— (1994) 'Money Talks: Rhetor, Demos and the Resources of the Athenian Empire.' In R. Osborne & S. Hornblower (eds) *Ritual, Finance, Politics: Athenian Democratic Accounts Presented to D.M. Lewis*. Oxford, pp. 217-251.

—— (1998) 'Accounting for Culture in Fifth-Century Athens.' In D. Boedecker

& K. Raaflaub (eds) *Democracy, Empire and the Arts in Fifth-Century Athens.* Cambridge, MA, pp. 43-58.
H.S. Kim (2001) 'Archaic Coinage as Evidence for the Use of Money.' In Meadows & Shipton (2001), pp. 7-22.
J.H. Kroll (1998) 'Silver in Solon's Laws.' In R. Ashton & S. Hurter (eds) *Studies in Greek Numismatics in Memory of M.J. Price.* London, pp. 225-232.
L. Kurke (1993) 'The Economy of *Kudos*.' In C. Dougherty & L. Kurke (eds) *Cultural Poetics in Archaic Greece.* Cambridge.
——— (1995) 'Herodotus and the Language of Metals.' *Helios* 22, pp. 36-64.
——— (1999) *Coins, Money, Games and Gold.* Princeton.
——— (2002) 'Money and Mythic History: The Contestation of Transactional Orders in the Fifth Century BC.' In Scheidel & von Reden (2002), pp. 87-113.
A. Meadows & K. Shipton (2001) *Money and its Uses in the Ancient Greek World.* Oxford.
L. Mitchell (1997) *Greeks Bearing Gifts: The Public Use of Private Relationships in the Greek World.* Oxford.
A. Möller (2000) *Naucratis: Trade in Archaic Greece.* Oxford
——— (forthcoming) 'Classical Greece: Distribution.' In I. Morris, W. Scheidel & R. Saller, *The Cambridge Economic History of the Graeco-Roman World.*
I. Morris (1994) 'The Athenian Economy 20 years after *The Ancient Economy.*' *CPh* 89, pp. 351-366.
R. Osborne (1996 a) *Greece in the Making: 1200- 479 BC.* London.
——— (1996 b) 'Pots, Trade and the Archaic Greek Economy.' *Antiquity* 70, pp. 31-44.
L. Ray & A. Sayer (1998) (eds) *Culture and Economy after the Cultural Turn.* London.
W. Scheidel & S. von Reden (2002) (eds) *The Ancient Economy.* Edinburgh.
M. Schofield (1998) 'Political Friendship and the Ideology of Reciprocity.' In P. Cartledge, P. Millett & S. von Reden (eds) *Kosmos: Essays in Order, Conflict and Community in Classical Athens.* Cambridge, pp. 37-51.
R. Seaford (1998) 'Tragic Money.' *JHS* 118, pp. 119-139.
——— (2002) 'Reading Money: Leslie Kurke on the Politics of Meaning in Archaic Greece.' *Arion* 9, pp. 145-165.
——— (forthcoming) *Money, Metaphysics and Tragedy.* Oxford.
A.F. Stewart (1997) *Art, Desire and the Body in Ancient Greece.* Cambridge.
H. van Wees (1998) 'The Law of Gratitude: Reciprocity in Anthropological Theory.' In Gill, Postlethwaite & Seaford (1998), pp. 13-49.
S. von Reden (1995) 'Deceptive Readings: Poetry and its Value Reconsidered' *CQ* 89, pp. 30-50.
——— (1997) 'Money, Law and Exchange: Coinage in the Greek Polis.' *JHS* 117, pp. 154-176.
——— (1998) 'The Commodification of Symbols: Reciprocity and its Perversion in Menander.' In Gill, Postlethwaite & Seaford (1998), pp. 256-278.
——— (2001) 'Demos' *Phialê* and the Rhetoric of Money in Fourth-Century Athens.' In P. Cartledge, E.E. Cohen & L. Foxhall (eds) *Money, Labour and Land: Approaches to the Economics of Ancient Greece.* London, pp. 52-65.
——— (2002) 'Money in the Ancient Economy: A Survey of Recent Research.' *Klio* 84, pp. 141-174.
B. Wagner-Hasel (2000) *Der Stoff der Gaben. Kultur und Politik des Schenkens und Tauschens im archaischen Griechenland.* Frankfurt.
U. Wartenberg (1995) *After Marathon: War, Society and Money in Fifth-Century Greece.* London.

Index

Achilles 16, 18-26 *passim*, 29, 31, 46-8, 51-4, 61-2, 66, 69, 157
Adkins, A. 39 n.36, 45-6, 55 n.3
Aeschines 108, 148
   Against Ctesiphon 91, 117-19
   Against Timarchus 120-3
Aeschylus 114, 128, 141, 220
   Agamemnon 82, 149-64 *passim*
   Choephoroi 150, 157-8, 164
   Eumenides 150, 151, 158, 161, 164
agalma 82, 151, 156
Agamemnon 16, 19, 18-26 *passim*, 50-2, 54, 61-2, 128, 155-8, 156, 161-4
agora 16, 98, 105-13 *passim*, 119, 123 n.7, 124 n.25, 147, 158-61, 187, 197, 220; *see also* market
agriculture 86, 105, 127, 130, 134-5, 183-4, 219-20
   and power 6, 130
   vs commercial exchange 128, 130, 141-2, 164, 176-7, 184
   see also erga
alienability of possessions 45, 49, 80, 219
Andromache 51
Anacreon 205
ancestors
   gifts to 13-14, 16, 152
   gifts from 30-1, 48, 69
apoina, poinê 8, 19, 23, 153-4, 157
Ares 158-61
argurion, see money
aretê 5, 45-6, 88, 99, 118, 186-7, 205, 208
aristocracy 6-8, 9, 58-9, 81-5, 98, 140-1, 173, 200, 204, 205; *see also* Cimon
Aristophanes 92, 131
   Acharnians 132-5
   Frogs 113-14
   Knights 132
Aristotle 84-5, 92, 108, 138, 140, 174, 211
   Nicomachean Ethics 84-5, 184-5, 200
   Politics 85, 185-7
Athene 20, 65, 73
autarky 92, 134-5, 141-2, 186

Bacchylides 83
bards *see* Demodocus
barter 3
basileia, basileis 16, 81-2, 176, 178
Bazant, J. 199, 212 n.7
Beard, M. 203, 208
benefactor, benefaction 86, 88, 93, 98-9, 147
Benveniste, É. 89-90
Bloch, M. 3, 96, 172
Bohannan, P. 96, 105
Bourdieu, P. 99 n.1, 114
bribery, bribes 46, 88, 94-7, 98, 102 n.68, 110, 111, 117-20, 132-4, 182; *see also misthos*
brideprice 8, 46-7, 50-1
Briseis 19, 51-3, 67, 69
burial *see* funerary rites

Cartledge, P. 6
charis 83-4, 88, 148, 150-1, 161, 164, 182, 185; *see also* benefaction
chorêgia 97, 109, 111, 147-8; *see also* liturgies
choral lyric, *see* Pindar, Bacchylides
chraô, chreia, see need, demand, utility
chrêmata 62, 87-8, 98-9, 111-12, 128, 174-5, 182-6, 198, 205; *see also* money, property, wealth
chrêmatistikê, chrêmatismos 5, 110, 174, 182-7
Cimon 110-11
classification and exchange 27
clothes 67, 107
   as gifts 31-2, 35-6, 69, 70-2
Clytemnestra 51, 153-5, 158, 161-4
coinage 7, 9, 111-14, 163, 172
   and order 175, 179, 184-5
   as a civic symbol 181, 185, 200-10
   definition 177-8
   origins 173-5, 177-81, 184-6
   nomisma 138, 177, 184-6
   see also money, *chrêmata*
commerce, *see* commodity exchange
commodification 7, 60, 67-74
commodity exchange 1, 71-2
   vs gift exchange 1, 73-4, 96
   see also market exchange

Index

community 17, 81-2, 84, 89, 94-5, 105-6, 135, 171
   koinônia 184-5,
   as order of exchange 3, 91-2, 182-4
   see also individual vs community, justice
conspicuous consumption, *see* spending
conspicuous destruction 74 n.5, 80, 82, 83, 163-4
consumption 4, 218
   as exchange 4, 22, 25, 86
   see also food, hospitality, *xenia*
contract 122
corruption, *see* bribery
counterfeit, *see kibdêla*
Cozzo, A. 61-2
credit *see* debt
Cyclops 33-4, 66, 135-42

dead, gifts to, *see* funerary rites
debt 18, 79-82, 88, 149, 219
dedication 82, 84, 98-9, 196
demand 18, 71, 218; *see also* need, utility
Demodocus 70
Demosthenes 97, 111-13, 117-22,
   Against Neaera 93, 120
   On the Crown 117, 148
   On the Trierarchic Crown 116
dikê, *see* justice
Dinarchus 97
Diomedes 26, 41 n.70
disguise, *see* clothes as gifts
distribution 2, 177
Donlan, W. 13, 14, 40 n.51
dôreia, dôron, dosis, dôtinê 8, 18, 21, 22, 25, 27, 33, 35, 48, 64, 71, 86-7, 88, 90, 93-9, 119, 120, 151, 154
dôrodokia, *see* bribery
dowry 8, 35, 50-1, 63, 117, 151, 164

economic theory 1-3, 71, 105, 127, 171-2, 217-19
economics, *see* economic theory
economy
   ancient 1-9 *passim*, 105-6, 109, 111, 113-14, 147, 172-3, 217-21
   disembedded 8, 173, 220
   embedded 8, 171-5 *passim*, 220
   see also symbolic economy
education, *see paideia*
egotism, *see* self-interest
eisphora, *see* spending, tax
emporia, see *trade*
Enlightenment 1, 171, 217-18
erastês, erômenos, *see paideia*, prostitution, sexual exchange
erga, ergazein 63, 68, 118, 131, 176-7; *see also* labour

euergetês, *see* benefactor
Eupolis
   Kolax 199
Euripides 114
   Bacchae 140
   Cyclops 135-42
   Hippolytus 164
   Medea 164
   Supplices 95, 128, 140
exchange
   between generations 14, 29-30, 31, 36, 63, 117, 149, 151-8, 161
   linguistic 26, 70-4 148, 155, 162-3
   symbolism of 18, 26-7, 80, 81, 89-93 *passim*, 96, 115-17, 197, 211, 220
   with the gods 4, 8-9, 19, 80, 94, 134-5, 149-50, 153-4
   see also market exchange, gift exchange, sexual exchange, spheres of exchange, sacrifice, trade
exchange value 18-24, 105, 112, 218-19
expenditure, *see* spending

fame 16, 17, 24, 54-5, 70, 72, 209
   kleos 18, 21, 24, 29-30, 39 n.36, 54-5, 61-7, 70-1
family, *see oikos*
fee, *see misthos*
feasting, *see* hospitality
Finley, M. 4-5, 13-14, 67, 217
food 22, 25, 59, 64, 66, 70, 86, 132-4, 136, 152, 201
   as payment 91, 132, 134, 201, 213 n.31
funeral rites 7, 14, 25, 28-9, 85, 196

generosity 27, 79-80, 83-9, 110, 115-16, 137, 185, 205
Gentili, B. 214-15 n.50
geras 22-3, 48
Gernet, L. 82, 172, 188 n.17
gift exchange
   as image of order 14, 21-2, 26, 150, 210-11
   decline of 17, 27, 33
   functions in epic 13, 18
   in Persia 85, 88-9, 99, 101 n.43
   in Thrace 88-9
   rules of 14, 18, 26
   symbolism of 18, 26, 27
   see also brideprice, dowry, *geras*, hierarchy and exchange, trade, *xenia*
Glaucus 21, 26, 41 n.70, 63
glory, *see kleos*
gods
   gifts to 8, 37 n.6. 85, 154
   gifts from 19-22, 130, 152
Godelier, M. 172, 217

Index

Goldhill, S. 6, 36, 133, 148, 153, 154, 163-4, 209-10
Gouldner, A. 39 n.43
greed *see* self-interest

Hart, K. 171, 187-8 n.6
Hasebroek, J. 4
Hector 17, 23-4, 53, 90
hedna, see brideprice, dowry
Helen 46-7, 51-2, 149, 151
Herman, G. 13, 94-5
Herodotus 92, 99-8, 188 n.17, 193 n.81
hero cult 14, 23-4, 29-31, 36-7, 81
heroic poetry 13-16
Hesiod 14, 81-2, 151, 176, 182-3
hetaira/hetairika 93, 125-6 n.49, 206-9; *see also* prostitutes
hierarchy and exchange 14, 18, 25-6, 33, 36-7, 79-92 *passim*, 116-17, 129, 197-200, 205, 210-11
  see also exchange, gift exchange
Homer 8, 115, 119, 148, 150, 173
  Iliad 13-57 *passim*, 81, 89-90, 157
  Odyssey 8, 13-76 *passim*, 81, 89-90, 132, 135-6, 141, 209
Hollein, H-G. 204, 207
honour, *timê* 17, 18-22, 27, 39 n.36, 46, 67, 95, 98, 147, 198-9, 209; *see also* fame, value
Hooker, J.T. 13-14
hospitality 7, 8, 13, 26-7, 33-7, 54, 64, 69, 70, 79, 82, 84, 137; *see also* food, *xenia*
household, *see oikos*
hubris 82, 95, 148, 150, 160, 161-4, 175-6, 182-4, 187, 197
Hyperides 108

individual
  vs community 25, 60, 89, 91, 94, 96-7, 106, 117, 121, 147, 164, 174, 197, 218-19
  vs things 45, 218
  in economic theory 218-19
inheritance 3, 24, 30, 63, 117-18, 183-4
Isocrates 108
  Areopagiticus 108-9
  Letter to Nicocles 115

justice, *dikê* 16, 18, 134-5, 141, 182-4, 208
  and divine gifts 21, 91-2
  and human gifts 18, 21, 82, 91-2, 195
  and revenge 23, 149, 158-9, 220
  as exchange 148-9, 151, 156, 158-62, 176-83

kapêleia, kapêloi 86, 115, 193 n.81
keimêlia, treasure 64, 67-8, 71, 150, 163, 196

kerdos, profit 18, 58-67 *passim*, 72, 81, 96, 117, 128, 131, 137, 159-60, 182, 219
Keuls, E. 207-8, 215 n.57
kibdêla 161, 192 n.79
kinship, *see philia*
kleos, see fame
koinônia, see community
Konstan, D. 135-7
Kopytoff, I. 60, 69
koros 175, 182-3
Kraay, C. 180
Kroll, J.H. 180
Kurke, L. 7-8, 83, 100 n.16, 157, 173, 189 n.21, 193 n.81, 205, 210, 214-15 n.50
Kwakiutl 79

labour 6, 176, 183; *see also erga*, production
Laum, B. 190 n.44
lending 81, 107, 186; *see also* debt
Lévi-Strauss, C. 49
Lissarrague, F. 203
liturgies 84, 96-7, 116
Lloyd, G. 6
Locke, J. 187 n.6
Lynn-George, M. 20, 21, 25, 31
Lysias 97-8, 107-8

marriage 7, 20, 32, 34-5, 36-7, 61, 66-7, 87, 117, 134, 135, 207-9
  as exchange 49-51, 151-8, 161, 164
  wedding 49, 84
  see also brideprice, dowry, women
market 114, 132-4, 138, 209-11, 211
  principle vs place 105
  symbolism of 106-7, 133
  sociability of 105-8
  see also agora, market exchange
market exchange 1-9 *passim*, 105-6, 111
maritime exchange, *see* trade
Marx, K. 187 nn.2, 3
Mauss, M. 14, 27, 45, 49, 79-80
megaloprepeia, see generosity
Meleager 21, 53
Menander
  Kolax 199
Millett, P. 149, 179, 199
misthos 5, 73, 86, 89-92, 116, 197
  bribe 117-23
  for public service 92
  to prostitutes 120-3, 205
money 1-9 *passim*, 84, 97-8, 107, 114, 118, 121, 127-30, 132, 138, 147, 159, 163-4, 173-5, 220-1
  as a commodity 171-3, 187, 187 n.6
  as a gift 9, 201-2, 206
  as a means of payment 111, 157, 177-8, 181, 184, 211, 220

as a token 171-3, 184-5, 187 n.6, 138
in non-Western societies 96, 172
see also chrêmata, coinage
Morris, I. 13-16 *passim*, 58-9, 74 n.5
motivation of exchange 1, 64, 71-2, 79, 82, 86, 97, 110-11, 116
Murnaghan, S. 36, 44 n.142

Nagy, G. 28
name as gift 30, 33, 35
nature (as order of exchange) 90-1, 127, 133-4, 141-2, 176, 218
need, *chreia* 18, 60, 66, 86, 115, 116, 122, 133-4, 184, 219; *see also* demand
nomos, nomoi 138, 141-2, 148, 177, 185-6
nostos 20, 61, 66

Ober, J. 108
obligation: arising from gifts 18, 22, 25, 27, 45, 79, 89, 95, 219
Odysseus 24, 27, 28, 30, 32, 48-9, 54, 56-74 *passim*, 90, 136-9
oikos
   as condition of life 33, 36, 61
   unit of power 16, 70-1, 109-10, 131, 133-5
   unit of production 4, 63, 105, 174, 186, 207-8, 219
   unit of reproduction/family 4, 24, 63, 148-9, 151, 157-8, 207-8
   vs *polis* 6-7, 133-5, 137-9, 148, 208
oikonomia, oikonomos 4, 138-9, 142, 164, 174, 215 n.57

Paganelli, L. 140
Parry, J. 3, 80, 96, 172
paideia 195-6, 198-202, 205, 208
Patroclus 22-4, 47-8, 52-4
patronage 109-10, 128-9, 179, 197-200, 220
Penelope 27, 32, 36, 51, 54, 64, 72-3
Pericles 88, 98, 109-10, 130
pernêmi, prasis 67, 125 n.49; *see also* purchase
Phaeacians 32, 34, 59, 70
philia, philos 23, 45-8, 52-3, 67-70, 85, 136-7, 148, 151-8, 185, 205, 209-12, 214 n.47
Phoenicians, *see* trade
Pindar 7-8, 173, 195, 205, 210
   Pythian 7 83
   Isthmian 2 8, 210
piracy 65-6, 128-9
Pisistratus 179
Plato 90-2, 108, 134-5, 140
   Republic 90
   Symposium 197-8
ploutos, see wealth
Plutarch

Life of Cimon 110
Life of Pericles 110, 124 n.21
Polanyi, K. 2-3, 8, 105-6, 181, 217, 221
Polycrates of Samos 82
ponos, toil 25, 130, 183
potlatch 74 n.5, 79-80
prater, prêter 58, 64-5
praxis, prêxis 58, 65, 67
price 111, 210-11; *see also* value
prize 25, 29, 45, 52, 63, 69, 72-3, 82, 89-90, 111, 114, 147-8, 181; *see also* geras
production 2, 6, 80, 135, 218; *see also* erga, labour
profit, *see* kerdos
property 18, 45-6, 59-60, 63, 69, 82, 122, 163-4, 219
prostitution, prostitutes 7, 93, 105, 120-3, 195, 197-200, 219-20; *see also* sexual exchange
Pucci, P. 62, 66
purchase 58, 67, 119-20, 133, 137-8, 163-4, 209-11

ransom, *see* apoina
Redfield, J. 25, 62, 79
reciprocity 2-3, 26, 79, 105, 134-6, 136, 164, 202, 211
   balanced 3, 79
   generalised 3, 79, 129, 173, 184, 195, 211
   negative 3; *see also* piracy, spoil, theft
recognition, tokens of 27, 32-7
redistribution 2, 105
retail trade, *see* kapêleia
revenge and exchange 23, 149, 152-8, 220; *see also* apoina
rings 82, 178, 181

sacrifice 80, 84, 98, 114, 130, 134-5, 151, 153-6
Sarpedon 63
Sahlins, M. 3, 79-80, 129
sale 60, 68, 117-20 *passim*, 132, 137-8, 150, 164
Seaford, R. 10 n.24, 17, 146 n.75
self-interest 2, 63-7, 117-18, 218-19; *see also kerdos*
self-sufficiency, *see* autarky
sêma, sign 27-32, 34, 36, 65, 150, 154-5
   and coinage 161, 178-9, 181
sexual exchange 120-3, 133, 197-209 *passim*; *see also* prostitution
Shell, M. 172-3, 188 n.17
sign, *see sêma*
Sinos, D. 47-8
slavery, slaves 6, 45, 58, 60, 67-9, 107, 197, 208-9, 218
   and exchange 95, 123, 198, 219

social relations as exchange 18, 33-4, 133,
    136-8, 152-8, 185, 201-2, 210-11
  see also philia, hospitality, xenia
Solon 84, 176-7, 179, 182, 187
Sophocles 128
  Antigone 164
spheres of exchange 3-4, 60
spending 81-7, 185, 210, 219-20
  public 5, 84-7, 96-7, 109, 116, 117
  see also generosity, tax
spoil 23, 26-7, 63-4
Strathern, M. 49-50
supply-and-demand mechanism 105
surplus, periousia 128-9, 131, 220
symbolic economy 87, 89, 96, 106, 111, 114, 147
symbolic exchange 106, 209-11
symposium 123, 139, 182, 197, 200, 203, 205-6

Taphians, see trade
tax, eisphora 84, 96, 122, 158, 178
Theognis 150, 175, 183-4, 187, 205
Theophrastus
  Characters 107, 199-200
Thucydides 87-8, 127-31, 140, 141-2, 174
theft 3, 119, 122, 137, 150, 158, 176
timê, see honour
timing of return 21-2, 157, 176-7, 185, 198
toil, see ponos, labour
trade, traders 1-9 passim, 58-9, 64-6, 115, 127-8, 131, 137-8, 176, 182-7 passim, 220
treasure, see keimêlia
tribute 63, 86, 132, 139, 141, 147-8
trust 107, 171-2

use value 218-19; see also value, exchange value
usury 96-7, 186
utility 64, 174, 219

value 26, 105, 149, 157-8, 172, 185, 211, 218-19
  and honour 88-9, 111-14, 116
  and language 161-2
  of gifts 18, 63-4
  of life 18-24 passim, 59, 219
  of poetry/logoi 60, 70-3, 114-16, 214-15 n.50
  of pottery 196, 209-11, 212 n.7
  of women 47, 49-55, 63, 69
  see also honour
Vernant, J.-P. 4-6, 148, 165 n.10, 210
Vidal-Naquet, P. 4, 36, 148, 165 n.10
virtue, see aretê

wage, see misthos
Wappenmünzen 179-81
wealth 1, 5, 8, 20, 63, 79, 83, 85, 87, 118, 127, 131-40, 150, 161-4, 175, 182-4;
  see also chrêmata, money, property
Weber, M. 4-5, 217-18
wergild, see apoina
Will, É. 4-6, 89-90, 91, 190 nn. 43-4
women 68, 206-9
  as gifts 20
  as objects of exchange 52-3, 153, 156
  as property 45-7, 49-55
  see also bridewealth, Briseis, dowry, Penelope, value
Woodbury, L. 7
work, see labour

Xenophon
  Apology 93
  Agesilaus 85-6
  Cyropaideia 85-7
  Oikonomicus 139, 174
[Xenophon]
  Athenian Constitution 132
xenos, xenia 8, 26, 33-5, 48, 65, 68-9, 70-1, 136-8, 151-3, 210; see also hospitality, philia